THE CITY IS OURS

THE CITY IS OURS

SQUATTING AND AUTONOMOUS MOVEMENTS IN EUROPE FROM THE 1970S TO THE PRESENT

Bart van der Steen, Ask Katzeff, and Leendert van Hoogenhuijze

PM
PM PRESS

WHY CALL IT
TOURIST SEASON
IF WE CAN'T
SHOOT THEM?

RESISTE

NO JUSTICE
NO PEACE   5/03/12

VALFRIHET FÖR ALLA –
INTE BARA FÖR DE RIKA

UTAN HUS BLIR DET BUS!

NU FÅR DET VARA NOG MED NEDSKÄRNINGARNA –

UNGDOMSHUS NU!

Initial page: Squatting graffiti in Amsterdam, 2007. Photo: Josh MacPhee.
Following page spread: Squat action at the Eerste Oosterparkstraat in Amsterdam. Photo: Hans Bouton.
Next page spread: Graffiti on the roof of Blokes Fantasma, Barcelona, 2009. Photo: Josh MacPhee
This page: Ungdomshuset poster, Copenhagen. Courtesy of Interference Archive.

*The City Is Ours: Squatting and Autonomous Movements in Europe
from the 1970s to the Present*
© 2014 Bart van der Steen, Ask Katzeff, and Leendert van Hoogenhuijze
This edition © 2014 PM Press

ISBN: 978-1-60486-683-4
LCCN: 2013956924

Cover and interior design: Josh MacPhee/Antumbradesign.org

10 9 8 7 6 5 4 3 2 1

PM Press, PO Box 23912, Oakland, CA 94623
www.pmpress.org

Printed in the USA.

Contents

Preface

George Katsiaficas

RECENT INSURGENCIES SUCH AS the Occupy movement of 2011 seem to arise from nowhere. The book you are holding in your hands provides evidence to the contrary. Strikingly similar European movements emerged decades ago in more than a dozen countries. Long before anyone talked about 'the 99%,' squatters in Europe were taking over what belongs to all of us—our homes. Despite political, linguistic, and cultural differences, these grassroots upsurges ran on parallel paths. All were self-directed and simply refused to remain observant of the 1%'s monopoly on housing.

These instances of revolt may be largely unknown, but they are empirical proof of movements' continuity. The mainstream media have portrayed the New Left of 1968 as larger than life, thereby turning subsequent waves of protest into parodies, if not entirely ignoring them. Simultaneously, the mythologised events of 1968 have been used to legitimate the integration internationally of protesters into the Establishment after the high point of protests.

Outside the realm of media spectacles, however, the everyday experiences of tens of thousands of people in many parts of the world in the 1970s were of struggles for world peace, for equality of men and women, for justice for racial minorities, and for decent places for human beings to live. As radical clusters of activists emerged within European peace and feminist movements, counter-cultural squatters galvanised a multifaceted formation independent of political parties that eventually became known as the *Autonomen*. By creatively synthesizing direct-democratic forms of decision-making and militant popular resistance, the autonomous activists embodied a new kind of politics—a 'conscious spontaneity'—or merger of theory and practice that did not rely on professional politicians.

Beginning in the 1970s, European squatters fought for and won control of hundreds of group houses, where they lived collective forms of life that negated the atomisation of contemporary society; their egalitarian and leaderless structures stood outside normal hierarchical relationships rather than re-producing them; and autonomously determined campaigns and productions avoided the alienation of heteronomously determined work. In their everyday lives, squatters lived differently and proved that life can be fun, that relation-ships can be heartfelt, that domination is unnecessary, and that life can be more than consuming endless gadgets and gimmicks. Squatters' occupation of public space transformed individual survival into communal ecstasy and collective au-tonomy. As we become familiar with them, we can understand how squatters freed their everyday lives and brought depth and continuity to more narrowly focused movements.

Although such 'marginal' groups appear to exist on the edge of society, they are often central to social change. From those excluded by the 'two-thirds society,' social movements emerged which ushered in new values (feminism, sexual liberation, equality for foreigners) and new forms of social organisation (group living, self-directed programs of work and study, cooperative working relationships). Within the autonomous women's movement and the upsurge against nuclear power after Chernobyl, youthful squatters led generalised re-sistance to the system as a whole. As citizens' initiatives and new social move-ments followed their own internal logic, the radical autonomous activists ex-pressed fundamental opposition to the capitalist world system. From Italy via Zurich, the ideas of generalised resistance appeared in Hamburg and Berlin, where, merged with the practice of Dutch squatters, the German Autonomen were consolidated. In addition European squatters played a critical role in forging the 'black bloc,' a militant tactic for protests that spread internationally from Europe.

By the mid-1980s, as activists consolidated their groups, they went be-yond ritualised marches around single-issue campaigns and local issues. They built urban bases that served as focal points for autonomous dual power. The proliferation of movement tactics, and ideas, which I have termed the 'eros ef-fect,' grows from the capacity of human beings to grasp instinctually the need to be free—and to find ways to do so. The subversive potential of largely unknown actions is revealed in this book. Step by step, movements build upon each other. As Bart van der Steen notes, 'From "1968" to the present, there has been a con-tinuity of radical left movements in Western Europe, and in the evolution of these movements, history has played an important role. In fact, the history of the radical left from 1968 to the present can be seen as a continuous attempt to overcome the failures and weaknesses of predecessor movements.'[1]

For their part, the authorities also learned from history. After 1968, po-lice carefully drew European radicals into increasingly violent confrontations. At the same time, German authorities led an international propaganda offen-sive against squatters, attempting to isolate and criminalise them by linking them with urban guerrilla groups. Internationally coordinated police assaults

---

Previous page spread: The squat symbol marks Miles de Viviendas, a former squat in the Barceloneta neighbor-hood in Barcelona, 2009. Photo: Josh MacPhee.

were not far behind. The new police tactic can be traced to Roman Herzog, then minister of the interior in Baden-Württemberg (and, from 1994 to 1999, president of Germany), who publicly charged that the Red Army Faction was infiltrating and recruiting from the squatters' movement. Authorities claimed to be able to link 70 of 1,300 known squatters to armed groups. The mass media ran stories pointing out that Knut Folkers, serving a life sentence for terrorism, had been arrested in 1974 in a squatted house, and Susanne Albrecht (then 'Wanted for Terrorism') had been part of a group that had occupied a vacant house in Hamburg in 1973. Connecting squats and guerrilla fighters was one of the government's chief means of trying to isolate the movement, which, for its part, refused to ignore the plight of the imprisoned 'terrorists.'

As RAF members died from prison hunger strikes and assassinations, riots broke out as a result of people's frustration and rage. With activists isolated and embittered, secretive militant actions replaced public protests as many people's choice tactic. Many people envisioned a military breakthrough, yet most failed to appreciate that such a rupture would have to involve millions of ordinary citizens. Individuals may be compelled by circumstances beyond their control to resort to desperate measures to survive, but to determine the movement's overall strategy mainly from externally imposed circumstances is to foreclose the insurgency's self-determination. As the tactics of underground individuals overdetermined the popular movement's articulation of its own vision and direction, one immediate effect was the stifling of popular participation.

There are two critical aspects of every movement: one is building up the base, the counter-institutions, and safe areas where our everyday lives, culture, and art can break through the system's hegemony; the other involves organizing confrontations with elite domination. Does premature armed struggle contract public space for building our counter-institutions (including squats)? Do armed actions undertaken in the name of the movement provide more public space for demonstrations and assemblies? Or does premature radicalisation of the movement's confrontations with the state undermine base building and outreach to new constituencies?

In retrospect, it appears that the very political conditions for a genuine revolution were undermined by premature armed struggle. 'Vanguards' created by the 'iron fist' of the state have been little better than corporations thrown up by the 'invisible hand' of the market. Both are products of domination and violence. Genuine revolutionary leadership develops through contact with each other as human beings, not solely through confrontations with the state.

Unlike the black/white lines drawn by armed struggle, popular movements embody erotic, life-affirming dimensions. During the 1980 riot at the Dutch queen's coronation, protesters' compassionate care for an injured policeman revealed their humanity. Similar kindness was shown to 'enemy' soldiers a few weeks later during the Gwangju Uprising in South Korea, when armed insurgents safeguarded captured soldiers and released them unharmed—in one case, even with his rifle (but not his ammunition). The necessity to activate the entire citizenry is why the Gwangju Uprising (and in Europe, the 1871 Paris Commune) is so important. In such rare moments of history, insurgencies re-create the participation of the Athenian polis and reveal the potential for all of us to unite for genuine change.

To transcend the multiple crises faced by humanity in the twenty-first century, the participation of millions of people is required. As new insurgencies develop and find ways to counteract the ravages of the capitalist world system, the experiences of European squatters will be one of many guiding lights that help to illuminate the road ahead.

Foreword
REDISTRIBUTE THE GRAVEL! SQUATTING AND AUTONOMY: VARIATIONS ON A COMPLEX SUBJECT
Geronimo

THERE ARE MANY REASONS to squat an empty building. The most straightforward is financial. The less money one spends on rent, the more opportunities remain for other things in life—the things that make life beautiful. Another reason that is equally legitimate but makes the situation incomparably more complex is the desire to 'live differently.' What does one want to achieve with this 'different life'? Is it to escape the existing forms of repressive daily life? Or, even grander still, is it to achieve true autonomy? And what do we mean by this strange and wondrous thing: autonomy? Are we talking of those forms of individual autonomy that are a prerequisite to becoming a 'citizen'? Or does the autonomy practiced in bold actions such as squatting demonstrate yet another form of libertarian-anarchist communism?

THE SQUAT AS A DOOR TO THE 'RADICALLY DIFFERENT'

Looking at the history of squatting in the German Federal Republic after 1968, one could paraphrase an enigmatic remark by comrade Lenin ('behind every strike lurks the revolution!'), stating: 'Behind every squatter action still lurks the radically different!' A multitude of visions and ideas on autonomy are linked to this 'Great Unknown.'

      This book deals with the history of squatting in Europe after 1968 from a wide range of intellectual perspectives. The contributions show that squatting is not solely about the realisation of a certain lifestyle or philosophy that differs from the mainstream. Rather, every squatter action contains elements of militancy and dual power. In squatter collectives, women and men, intellectuals and craftsmen, militants, artists, left-wing activists, punks, junkies, and 'non-political' people have to somehow live together. It is much easier said than happily done. What should the squat become and what should everyday life in the squat look like? Should the building be renovated through basic means of craftsmanship and DIY techniques? Should it be made habitable in the long term with the goal of growing old together? Or, instead, should it serve as a brief moment in history, as a romantic island-of-retreat from the hard life out there? An island, it must be stated as well, could change into a base from which to fight the system and the state, and sometimes both.

SQUATTING AS PART OF REVOLT AND COUNTER-CULTURE

The history of squatting in the Federal Republic offers examples of all the things described above. Squats in large cities have at times transformed into major political upheavals. Several squats evolved into unparalleled threats to public order. Time and again, the police had to back down from planned evictions because of massive protest actions, local governments cracked under the pressure, and occasionally a mayor had to interrupt his holiday. The contentious form of such actions also ensured that the general societal condition was questioned. In this post-1968 terrain, left radicalism mixed with aspects of the youth revolt outside of the universities. In the late 1970s, this gave way to something that in the 1980s evolved into what we now call the Autonomen (the autonomous movement).

The formative phase of the autonomous movement was the 1980s, when the autonomous activists (who had grown up in a decade of socially desired educational advancement) managed time and again to turn around their marginality and potential redundancy, from the system's point of view, through the creation of potentially self-sufficient free spaces. This can be seen as a modest kind of counter-societies situated beyond the welfare capitalism of the West and the 'real socialism' of the East.[1] Or, as a contemporary interpretation stated: for a moment, 'an anarchist hedonism' was not willing to let itself be 'disciplined . . . through long-term strategies for social change.'[2] Militant confrontations with the state apparatus underlined the movement's stubbornness, even more so because the movement refrained from articulating either concrete or theoretical demands. The title of Michael Haller's 1981 collection of essays, *Aussteigen oder rebellieren* (Drop Out or Rebel), captures what he perceptively calls 'the ambiguous nature of the youth revolt.' The contributions from Copenhagen, Amsterdam, Zurich, and Italy survey this amalgam of attitudes, practices, ideas, and confrontations.[3] The keywords in this collection of articles range from the 'dream of paradise' exemplified by the *indiani metropolitani* (urban indians) and *autonomia* in Italy; to 'playing with fire' and the 'power of fantasy' in the course of the 'youth unrest' in Zurich; and the 'open hostilities' in the youth rebellions in Hannover, Bremen, and Göttingen. It covers the development of the squatter movement in West Berlin and the 'gilded crowbar' of the squatters in Amsterdam; the 'village in the city' exemplified by the large-scale commune Christiania in Copenhagen; along with autonomous ways of life in the context of a 'trans-bourgeois perspective,' general attitudes of refusal and the demand for a 'new sensitivity.'

From a bird's-eye view, these heterogeneous attitudes, ideas, and motivations constituted the political drive behind the left-egalitarian motivated confrontations of the early 1980s, which also entailed romantic-conservative elements. The government-oriented demand for participation, articulated by social democracy during the 1970s, was radicalised by the autonomous activists' practice of and demand for immediate self-determination. Beyond all political manifestations, the occupied, formerly empty, houses served as sites where a 'different' life could be realised. Subsequently, the autonomous movement that grew out of this dazzling revolt gained influence on the politics of the all-incorporating and consensus-enforcing society of the Federal Republic. For the movement, there was no real contradiction between 'rebelling' and 'dropping out.' Depending on the situation and their strategy, either or both applied. By defending squatted houses and social centres and by throwing a multitude of stones at armoured police forces, the autonomous movement was at times able to disrupt the institutionalisation of the Green Party within the state apparatus, while also influencing the ideas and actions of urban guerrilla groups. To put it boldly: they opted for squatting and battling the system through street fights instead of armed struggle or parliamentary politics.

AUTONOMOUS SQUATS SOMEWHERE BETWEEN WAR AND PEACE

The autonomous movements flourished until the end of the Cold War. After the fall of the Berlin Wall the 'real-socialist' states transformed into formally democratic, but in fact rather authoritarian, regimes. At the same time, the all-incorporating welfare states of the West mutated into exclusionary societies, both ideologically and in practice. Partly due to the subsiding of the anti-colonial/anti-imperialist drift in the Third World, the urban guerrilla groups, with their roots in 1960s, dissolved. The Green Party was 'integrated' into the system (*gleichgeschaltet*) while the social democratic party continues on an increasingly bellicose neoliberal path. Today, the Autonomen are confronted by dramatic political situations that seem to have no alternative.

Any political interpretation of the last forty years of squatting in the Federal Republic must take into account that these events unfolded in a period of profound social peace. The fact that squatters time and again rightly attacked this 'peace' as hypocritical, idle, and corrupt does not change the absence of overt war in those years. This is most notably illustrated by the fact that despite all the civil war scenarios invoked by the media, the police, politicians, and the squatters themselves, even the occasionally intense confrontations between police and squatters unfolded against the background of a tacit taboo on killing. Will this continue to be the case in the future?

Autonomous activists stick to their claim of wanting to break out into a different society, but are no longer the interesting grumblers that they used to be. From the perspective of state and capital, they are completely redundant and this has resulted in a decisive change of the terrain of struggle. A recently published book on the housing struggle in the 1970s and 1980s boldly illustrates this with a photo.[4] It shows two bearded men writing a slogan on the wall of an occupied house in West Berlin in 1982: 'It is better for our youth to occupy houses than foreign countries.' At the time, a militant anti-war movement was able to continuously debar public army ceremonies while the peace movement mobilised millions in protests against rearmament with U.S. missiles. It is frustrating to see the picture today, when the governing ethos seems to be the opposite: 'It is better for our youth to occupy foreign countries than empty houses.'

This is currently the unwritten state religion of the Federal Republic: the global war on terrorism, which U.S. vice president Dick Cheney declared in October 2001 would last for fifty years or more. Of these fifty years, twelve have passed so far, so we'd better brace ourselves. Whether the ever occupy-happy autonomous activists are capable of dealing with this completely new constellation remains an open question.

I would like to conclude with three anecdotal excursions. From the history of squatting in the Federal Republic, I will (with some humour, bitterness, and hope) take a few giant strides to the present.

RADICAL LEFT MILITANCY AND GENDER RELATIONS

In 1973, the collective Rote Klinke from Bonn published a so-called *Handbook for Squatters*. It is almost certain that the origins of the book lie in Frankfurt, where the book was distributed as a collection of photocopied texts. This becomes clear in the preface, where it is made clear to the 'comrades' that 'individual protests by students' are far from constituting 'true struggle.' Even more so: true struggle cannot be fought 'on the level of critical theory . . . but only on the level of revolutionary strategy.' The squatters are 'a vanguard in the housing struggle' that can only be decided 'on the streets.' Fully in line with the spirit of direct action, the text contains a fierce attack on the 'self-proclaimed theoretical Marxists (*Schreibtischmarxisten*) and professional sectarians' as well as the 'polit-bureaucrats' for whom it is 'always too early or already too late to undertake action.' These 'shirkers' are nothing more than the 'Tartuffes of communism to flatter the women.'[5]

The practical section of the handbook has clear military undertones, containing instructions on how to battle police by using crowbars and shields made of television screens, Molotov cocktails, and other materials. Additionally, there are instructions for the construction of *chevaux de frise* (portable defence barriers), well-devised barricades, and booby traps.[6]

Soon after publication, the handbook ironically played a prominent role in a police instruction film made by the Hamburg police department in May 1973. The film laid out a blueprint of how to evict squatters, illustrated by the coldly calculated and brutal eviction of a squatted house in the Hamburg Eckhofstrasse that same month. The contents of the handbook were quoted almost enthusiastically by the sonorous voice-over, which subsequently described the eviction in sober, bureaucratic diction reminiscent of reports on the combat of partisans on the Eastern front.[7]

I can still clearly remember how the contents of this handbook were studied to great detail in the mid-1980s by my comrades in the Hamburg Hafenstrasse, when they started to barricade their houses against further police raids.

A message posted on a squatter action in Freiburg in 2007 on the radical left internet portal Indymedia shows that the text is still relevant to squatter activists. The introduction of the 1973 handbook is integrally copied and digitised, supplemented by a brief introductory note stating that of course 'times have changed,' but that the text is 'still very much worth reading.'[8] There is however one interesting difference. In the last sentence, in which the 'flattered women' are clearly dismissed as political actors, the women have silently been replaced by 'flattered voters.' The sentence now states that the 'shirkers' are the 'Tartuffes of communism' who 'flatter the voters.' The triumph of feminism since the mid-1970s seems to have necessitated the militant squatters of the twenty-first century to undertake this falsification. As they said beforehand: times have changed.

ANTI-SEXISM FEARS 'TRANSGRESSIONS' AND THUS STRIKES OUT AGAINST AUTONOMY

We must contain the potential for civil war that emanates from these houses, from this group of anarchists. These squats are breeding grounds for political criminality. An atmosphere of terror is bred there and serious offenses are perpetrated. Take for example the cases of rape and the drugs scenes in the houses Bockenheimer Landstrasse 111 and 113 and the Schuhmannstrasse 67/69. Or take for example the Rote Hilfe (Red Aid) group that is housed there and which publicly proclaimed its support for the terrorist acts of the Baader-Meinhof gang.
 —Knut Müller, Frankfurt chief of police, *Frankfurter Neue Presse*, March 30, 1973

In a book published in January 2011, the 'fe*male' author Amantine places the writer of these lines next to convicted sexual offenders from the 1980s Hamburg Hafenstrasse. S*he does so in a chapter entitled 'sexism in the autonomous scene and squatted houses.'[9] This was neither the result of a misunderstanding nor a coincidence. Rather, it is the logical outcome of the current anti-sexist discourse.

According to this line of reasoning, rape (a crime) is a general manifestation of patriarchy—'a thousand forms of repression'—and thus trivialised so that less serious forms of problematic behaviour with regards to the interaction between sexes can be dramatically denounced as 'sexism!'[10] Through this shrewd political mix-up, people who openly diverge within the complex and contentious field of sexuality versus sexism are marked. More precisely: the one who deviates stops being a comrade, is nothing more than a criminal, and should therefore be excluded from the autonomous groups and networks. To do this, however, Amantine needs to describe the squatter scene to some extent as a breeding ground for sexual offenses and thus falls—as chance would have it—in the trap of the police discourse articulated by the chief of police from 1970s Frankfurt: squatters are 'anarchists' who prepare for 'civil war,' leading to 'terrorism, RAF, rape, drug trade and Red Aid.'

It is not that easy to preserve one's sense of humour in the face of such a critique. This calls into mind the history of the left in the twentieth century, when deviation, opposition, and critique, at least in the era of Stalinism, were branded criminal offenses. For now, it suffices to note that the 'autonomous collectives' that form the starting point of Amantine's politics constitute a sort of 'free space,' which is just another way of saying that everyday human conflicts should be eliminated through repressive disciplinary measures. This, however, does not lead to pluralism, liberation, or autonomy. It solely stimulates a fear of sanctions, subordination, and conformism. In short, the 'free spaces' in squatted houses are transformed into socialisation agencies aimed at producing conformist and authoritarian behaviour.

Just as it is correct to assume that there still exists a social democratic party even though it has nothing to do with social democratic politics, there are 'autonomous collectives' that—under the influence of a treacherous anti-sexist discourse and in the name of cold, calculated victim stewardship—denounce every perceived 'transgression' as 'criminal,' which is to say sexist. In this way, a clear and hostile message is sent to any form of autonomy, which does not originate from a repressively produced consensus but from the potential for conflict between people. It is clear that the future of autonomy cannot be written through the anti-sexism of 'autonomous collectives.' Autonomy can only be approached by throwing off the straightjacket of victimisation and through an open stance towards all possible forms of 'transgression,' of which the squatting of houses is only one.

REDISTRIBUTE THE GRAVEL!

After the nuclear catastrophe in Fukushima in the spring of 2011, several thousand people gathered early on a Saturday morning in Hamburg for an anti-nuclear demonstration. As the demonstrators passed the squatted houses of the Gängeviertel, the squatters seemed at first surprised by the protest, but immediately joined their cause with a banner stating: 'redistribute the gravel!' In doing so, they referred to a campaign initiated a year earlier by radical leftist groups titled Castor schottern (Shake up Castor). Their aim was to avert atomic waste transports to the nearby town of Gorleben (popularly known as Castor Transports) by removing the gravel (in German: *Schotter*) from between the train rails. The word 'Schotter' is at the same time colloquial German for money, of which still little is known other than that there exists a great deal of it and ever less 'trickles down' to the lower orders of society. The possibly autonomous squatters from the Gängeviertel cannot be thanked enough for this original slogan. The message, after all, specifically catered to the intellectually smug and wed-to-catastrophe anti-nuclear movement, while at the same time pointing to an extraordinarily important issue. As a matter of fact, the slogan 'redistribute the gravel' captures the spirit of every squatter action.

Will the future see autonomous squatter actions? Most certainly, even when the Autonomen, for good reasons, have long disappeared. There have been occupations long before their existence, and they will occur after—despite international developments and complex autonomous discussions on sexuality and sexism. In the end, all people on this planet need an affordable roof over their heads and wish to spend their time, money, and energy on the other, more important things in life.

Introduction
SQUATTING AND AUTONOMOUS ACTION IN EUROPE, 1980–2012
Bart van der Steen, Ask Katzeff, and Leendert van Hoogenhuijze[1]

IN RECENT TIMES, urban revolts and radical movements have become a frequent topic of discussion.[2] Since December 2010, people have occupied spaces, made political demands, and clashed with the authorities in major cities across the globe: from Tahrir Square in Cairo to Zuccotti Park in New York, and from the capitol building in Madison, Wisconsin, to the Puerta del Sol square in Madrid. Their demands have above all focused on democratic rights. For most of those involved, democracy is not solely defined as the right to vote but more fundamentally as the possibility to take control of one's own life and community and to truly participate in society and decision-making processes.

The first spectacular wave has by now passed. Its consequences are still being felt, however, not only in the Middle East, where the revolts have made way for long-drawn, arduous, and at times violent struggles for democracy and social justice that have encountered considerable setbacks, but also in the United States and Europe, where the Occupy movement has fanned out into a multitude of movements struggling against austerity politics and repression.

Even though these protests are taking place simultaneously, the protests and revolts in the United States, the Middle East, and Europe are not directly connected. Although the Occupy movement did refer explicitly to the Cairo movement as an example, and the protesters on the Tahrir Square proclaimed their solidarity with those in Madison, the contexts in which these movements are active are very different.[3] The symbolic power of a shared form of struggle is strong, but intensive political bonds between these different movements have not developed.

Europe, too, has witnessed a series of intense social conflicts the last few years. Most of these unfolded in an urban setting and involved large numbers of youths who clashed with the authorities. Examples are the riots in the Paris *banlieues* (2005), the December revolt in Athens (2008), the

London riots (2011), the 12 March Movement in Portugal (2011) and the M15 movement in Spain (2011).[4] Some of these protests in France involved mainly 'second generation immigrant' youths who responded to their under-privileged position and police brutality. Initially, this was the impression in London as well, but studies have shown the involved 'feral underclass,' as the secretary of justice called them, to be of a more 'mixed' nature. Both events were widely denounced in the mainstream press as apolitical and destructive. Other conflicts, such as the protests in Greece, Portugal, and Spain, explicitly attacked the austerity politics of their respective governments that had been forced upon them by external bodies like the EU and the IMF and triggered by the financial crisis. These protests were initiated by university students and were to some degree promoted as being unaligned to political parties or even apolitical. The student protests in London in 2010, now completely overshad-owed by the 2011 riots, can be seen in a similar light. In yet others, youths resisted commercialisation and exclusionary urban politics and demanded a 'right to the city' for all. Such movements unfolded, for example, during the struggle for the Youth House in Copenhagen and the Gängeviertel complex in Hamburg.[5]

These urban conflicts and the political issues they touch upon are remi-niscent of the wave of urban revolts of 1980. In St Pauls, Bristol, predominantly black youth clashed with the police after a police raid on a popular café. Also in 1980, youths in Zurich, Amsterdam, and Berlin occupied buildings and public spaces and clashed with the police.[6] The latter wave of occupations soon spread to others cities and countries and heralded a new cycle of protest in which the urban, youth culture and public space played a central role.[7] In 1981, riots broke out in both France and Britain, starting with the Brixton Riots, all in response to police brutality and racism.

A significant actor in these revolts was the squatter movement: a radical libertarian youth movement in which radical politics merged with underground culture. Squatters organised occupations, demonstrations, and often also clan-destine sabotage actions. In cities such as Amsterdam and Berlin, the move-ment grew rapidly. In 1981, J.W. van der Raad counted more than 206 squatted buildings in Amsterdam, housing more than 1,300 activists. Around the same time, West Berlin counted 284 squats.[8] But squatting also spread to other cities and smaller towns.

Because of the movement's focus on squatted houses and autono-mous social centres, youth culture, alternative ways of living, and radical poli-tics were from the start directly interlinked. Large squatted complexes often housed punks, runaway youths, artists, and political activists. In squatted so-cial centres, political meetings were organised next to punk shows and alter-native art exhibitions. Squatting was a political practice, a way of living, and also part of a youth subculture.

Previous page spread: Amsterdam squatting poster, 1980. Courtesy of Interference Archive.

Most political activists, however, did not limit themselves to the occupation, running, and defence of buildings. Rather, squatted houses often served as an infrastructure from which other political actions were organised. As squatter activists began participating in the struggle against nuclear weapons and power plants, large infrastructural projects, neo-Nazi groups, and government cuts, the term 'autonomous movement' came to replace the initial 'squatter movement.' 'Autonomous' also made explicit the links with radical movements of the 1970s, such as the Italian *Autonomia* movement.[9]

In Germany, for example, the terms *Hausbesetzer* (squatter) and *Instandbesetzer* (a combination of the terms *Hausbesetzer* and *Instandsetzer*, that is, renovator) were soon replaced by the term *Autonom*. This happened as early as 1982, when the massive wave of squatting in West Berlin came to an end. The term signalled the movement's broadening field of action.

In Spain, too, the term 'squatter' preceded the term 'autonomous.' In fact, the first squatter group in Barcelona used the English term: it was called Colectivo Squat de Barcelona. After that, the term *okupa* became standard, while later autonomous became more common.

In Denmark, the term *besætter* (occupier) remained dominant throughout the 1980s, with the abbreviation *BZ* referring to the movement as a whole. In the 1990s, however, it became more common to refer to the movement as autonomous, partly because opportunities and possibilities for squatting had changed drastically and squatting became less prominent in the movement's action repertoire.

In the Netherlands, the term *kraaker* (squatter) always remained dominant. The term 'autonomous' was used from 1980 onwards, but only incidentally and by a specific faction of the movement. The term 'kraaker' refers to the Second World War period, during which resistance groups used the term (previously referring to burglary) to refer to illegal sabotage actions and break-ins. Most probably because of the associations it thus triggered, it soon pushed aside the activists' previous name: 'housing pirates.'

There were also cities where the term 'squatter' or 'autonomous' never became common. In Athens, for example, the movement first referred to itself as 'wild youth' and later claimed the term 'anarchist.' Even so, in their way of organising, their action repertoire, and ideology, they remained very similar to the previously mentioned movements.

The squatter/autonomous movement of the 1980s has received some attention from journalists, social scientists, and historians. There are contemporary studies, often commissioned by governments, that try to analyse social composition and demands of these movements, often with the goal of assessing the extent to which they (will keep on) threaten(ing) public order.[10] Furthermore, there are social science studies that mainly focus on the inner dynamics of these movements, such as an examination of their interaction with the media and the authorities, or of processes of radicalisation.[11]

Pro-squatting graffiti in Barcelona, 2009. Photo: Josh MacPhee.

Authors close to the movement have also aimed to reconstruct the movement's histories.[12]

The historiography that has thus come into being is scattered and unbalanced. First, the available literature tends to focus on a specific number of cities, known for their 'spectacular' movement histories. These cities include Berlin, Amsterdam, Zurich, and Copenhagen.[13] Other cities are often ignored, especially in English-language publications. Accordingly, little information is available on squatter/autonomous movements in Vienna, Barcelona, or Poland. The problem does not seem to be based on language alone: the British city of Brighton, for example, has a vivid movement and movement history that have still not received much attention.

Additionally, the cities deemed central in movement histories are all set in Northwestern Europe. Historian George Katsiaficas, for example, wrote the only truly wide-reaching history of European autonomous movements. While starting his story in the industrialised cities of Northern Italy and devoting some time to Zurich, he focuses mainly on Amsterdam, Copenhagen, and especially Berlin.[14] This has led some scholars to view autonomous movements as mainly a Northwestern European phenomenon. Most of these link their inception and development directly to the specific political systems and welfare regimes in this region.[15]

Finally, most studies limit their time frame and focus to the 1970s and 1980s. London has been an exception, with most studies focusing on the 1960s and 1970s,[16] but these too have understood the autonomous movement as something of the past.

Limiting the focus to a period of ten years and one specific region of Europe leads to a distorted image of the movement's history, neglecting almost twenty years of more recent movement history and leaving out the experiences of activists in many other cities. The resulting image of these movements is thus distorted, important factors influencing their development are obscured, as well as the effects they can have. To get a clearer view of what these movements are, how they develop, and what influence they (can) have, it is important to see the whole movement: not only in Northwestern Europe during the 1980s, but in the whole of Europe over the last thirty years.

This collection aims to expand the historiography both geographically and with regard to the time frame. It includes studies on the squatter/autonomous movements in Vienna, Poznań (Poland), and Barcelona, cities that have so far received only little attention in English-language publications. The case studies also cover a time span of thirty years or more, from the early 1980s or earlier to the 2010s, while also discussing the movements' possible futures. By doing so, they provide not only a more complete, clearer image of these movements, but an overview of the movement's history, with an eye to the future.

EXPLAINING THE FOCUS ON 1980S NORTHWESTERN EUROPE

There is a strong current in the present historiography that focuses (1) on autonomous movements in Northwestern Europe, and (2) on the 1980s. How can this be explained and how has it affected the literature? In part, the focus on this region can be explained by the fact that the centre of the youth revolts of 1980 indeed lay in cities in Germany, Switzerland, the Netherlands, and Denmark. In Italy, the youth revolt of the 1970s had been effectively repressed by 1980, with a great number of activists either imprisoned or exiled, leading to the 'Italian winter' of the 1980s after the 'hot autumn' of the 1970s.[17] In other Southern European countries, such as Spain and Greece, social movements were only just recovering from the dictatorial regimes and the democratisation struggles of the 1970s. This was the case in cities such as Barcelona and Athens. These movements were not yet connected to movements in the Northern and Eastern Europe, still in the grip of communist dictatorship.

The protest wave of 1980 in Northwestern Europe has also been explained by structural sociopolitical factors. Social scientist Hans Peter Kriesi and his colleagues have done so in their impressive research project, based on systematic newspaper analysis, through which they constructed a data set of social movement actions in Germany, France, the Netherlands, and Switzerland from 1968 to 1989.[18]

According to Kriesi et al., there were more political opportunities for new social movements such as the squatter movement in Northwestern Europe than in Southern Europe, because the conflicts between labour and capital had been pacified in the North through a corporatist economic system.[19] This diffused the conflict lines between traditional left and conservative parties, and opened up space for new social movements and movement parties such as the Greens. In Southern Europe on the other hand, the political lines of conflict between labour and capital remained much more antagonistic, thus tying the public to the traditional left and right parties. Here, the previously mentioned new social movements thus had much less influence. According to this framework, the influence and size of new social movements such as the autonomous movement are thus linked to a specific sociopolitical system and welfare regime.[20]

NEW DEVELOPMENTS AND OLD NARRATIVES

The research of Kriesi and his team encompasses the thirty years from 1968 to 1989. Though large in scope, it also leaves out a number of European countries, especially those in Southern Europe and the United Kingdom. Furthermore, it does not cover the 1990s and after. Were social movements as marginal outside of Northwestern Europe?

The case of Italy, 'the only country where the [1968 youth] rebellion turned into a workers' revolt,' seems to disprove this point.[21] Here, the 1970s saw massive radical youth and social movements, which reached the peak of their strength in 1977.[22] There were active squatting and radical action movements in Southern Europe and in Britain in the 1980s as narrated by the chapters on Barcelona, Athens, and Brighton in this collection. In his chapter on squatting in Poland, Grzegorz Piotrowski additionally speaks of squatted houses in 1980s East Berlin and Hungary.[23]

Especially in the 1990s, squatting again took a leap in Italy with the social centre movement: houses were squatted or rented with the aim of giving them a public function as a centre for both local residents and activists.[24] Not long after, Britain followed suit.[25] At the same time, squatting spread to Eastern Europe: not only to East German cities such as East Berlin and Leipzig but also to Poland and Slovenia (the Metelkova City Autonomous Cultural Centre in Ljubljana). Thus, squatting is a practice that can clearly take root and flourish in very different political settings and regional constellations.[26]

Interestingly, the new cycle of occupations in the early 1990s in Southern and Eastern Europe coincided with a deeply felt crisis among older activists in the Netherlands and former West Germany, the earlier hot spots of autonomous action. In these years, a part of their infrastructure disintegrated. In Amsterdam, for example, the important squatter weekly *Bluf!* was discontinued (1988) and an intense conflict within the movement led to the hospitalisation of a number of activists (1987).[27] The movements seemed to be losing activists, strength, and know-how. Important squats were evicted. This crisis experience was voiced in a number of, occasionally controversial, texts.[28] The German writer Geronimo, for example, who had gained fame for his first history of the autonomous movement in Germany in the 1980s, *Fire and Flames*, dubbed his second book, covering the first years of the 1990s, *Glow and Ashes*.[29]

The coinciding of squatting waves in some parts of Europe and crises in others signify that the protest cycles were not yet synchronised. This would happen later, with the rise of the alterglobalisation movement at the end of the 1990s. But most importantly, it showed that squatting and autonomous movements were not limited to a specific region or era, or to a specific sociopolitical system.[30]

The post–Cold War practices of squatting in Great Britain and Southern and Eastern Europe offer possibilities to expand the narrative of 1980s Northwestern European autonomous movements. In her work, Nazima Kadir shows that, at least for Amsterdam, this has not yet been the case. Rather, the movement there seems caught in a linear narrative, focusing on one specific protest cycle that covers the years 1979–1988, which influences not only research but also the expectations and imaginations of activists.[31] The 1980s movement is idealised and projected unto the imaginations and desires of activists who envision the perfect movement as massive, militant, and capable of spectacular occupations and street fights. The image of the movement has thus become static, blind to the movement's evolution, and the cause of many of the current activists' experience of a 'schizophrenic' world, in which the real movement and its myth continuously clash.

This mythic movement also idealises a specific vision of militancy. According to this vision, radical movements in the 1980s were able to beat police forces during street fights and ward off evictions by barricading houses and sometimes even entire streets. Major examples are the Vondelstraat barricades in Amsterdam in February–March 1980, the Ryesgade blockade in Copenhagen in September 1986, the Barrikaden-Tage in Hamburg in November 1987, and the eviction of the Mainzer Strasse houses in Berlin in November 1990.[32] In all these cases, the barricades lasted several days. The movement has often been pronounced dead because it would no longer be able to pull off such actions.[33] But this perspective both overestimates the strength of the movements of the 1980s and underestimates the subversive potential of the movements that came after. It is based on a far too limited understanding of what militant politics could be.

To extend the field of research and to broaden our vision to include movements from other regions and from more recent times, we need to move away from the classic linear grand narrative and the myths surrounding the autonomous movement of the 1980s. Instead, we need to acknowledge that this movement represented only one specific protest cycle after which many have followed and will follow in the future.

CONTINUITIES AND CHANGE

Since 1968, Europe has witnessed a continuity of radical urban youth movements in which radical politics merge with underground culture, libertarian principles prevail, and direct action is preferred.[34] This collection focuses on the development of autonomous movements after 1980, taking into account experiences from different European cities. When we compare the case studies in this collection, what similarities and differences can be observed? What are the main continuities and changes? What are the effects of these movements and what factors influence its development?

One continuity we see is the libertarian way of organising. In general, parties, trade unions, or other forms of institutional politics are dismissed in favour of small and local groups. Direct, participatory democracy is central and often political affinities and personal friendships overlap. This has been the case not only in 'traditional' movement cities such as Amsterdam or Copenhagen but also in 'new' places such as Poznań. This, however, does not mean that there are no leaders. Rather, there are informal hierarchies, as is shown in the chapters on Amsterdam and Poznań.

A second constant is the link between radical politics and subculture. The emphasis on specific political issues may shift from urban restructuring to anti-fascism. The form of organising may change from networks of squatted houses to an emphasis on rented social centres. The dominant music styles and subcultures of activism may change from punk to hardcore in the 1980s to acidtechno and freetekno 1990s to drum and bass and dub soundsystems in the 2000s. But the focus on the urban, on emancipatory politics, on youth and alternative lifestyles remains a constant. The Poznań squat, for example, started with a punk concert. The most recent protest wave in Copenhagen was triggered by the eviction of the Youth House that, along with others, functioned as an important scene for alternative music.

A third continuity is the localism of these movements, centering on urban development and a city for all. Squatting, therefore, is a central action method: it claims houses and social centres for public goals. But localism goes further. The movement in Vienna, for example, started with the Burggarten movement of 1979, which lifted the ban on walking on the grass in public parks. In Barcelona, squatters supported the construction of a local park and helped protect it against plans to build a sport complex. Similar protests also unfolded in Athens. In Brighton, a store in the city centre was squatted to protest high rent prices and gentrification.

The same goes, finally, for direct activism, and militancy. Autonomous movements tend to verge on the boundary between civil disobedience and confrontational politics. Here too, emphases may shift; for example from street fight militancy to more symbolic forms of confrontation. In Copenhagen, for example, autonomous activists refrained from engaging in violent confrontations for a while after a large eviction wave in 1990. Instead, they focused on forging alliances and peaceful demonstrations. However, after an anti-EEC demonstration met with brutal police force in May 1993, the movement again started to engage in intense confrontations with the state. Thus, while the movement acts more militantly at some moments than others, the goal remains to subvert traditional hierarchies and to question state authority.

THREE DECADES OF AUTONOMOUS MOVEMENTS

As the case studies in this collection show, some general lines of development can be observed in the movement culture from 1968 onwards. Compared to the social movements of '1968,' the youth revolts of the 1980s seemed more pessimistic and dystopian. Instead of pacifist 1960s flower children or radical activists fighting for a certain victory, disenchanted and disillusioned youths with 'no future' rose up, seemingly less organised and theoretical but more militant and embittered than their 1960s counterparts. The revolting youth seemed to have lost faith in society: in the welfare state, political parties, the economy, the trade unions, popular culture, etc. They denounced grand political programs and the idea of (workers') revolution and instead sought to establish small, liberated islands for experiments with autonomy and self-management.

Even though our collection takes the 1980 youth revolt as its starting point, the movements that emerged that year did not appear out of nowhere.

Rather, they built upon movements and experiences from the 1970s. Cities such as Amsterdam, Copenhagen, London, Berlin, and Frankfurt had seen the rise of radical urban and squatter movements in the early 1970s. The first documented squatter action in Germany took place in the run-down Westend neighbourhood of Frankfurt on September 19, 1970.[35] The first squatter action in Amsterdam had already taken place five years earlier: in January 1965.[36] As these movements picked up speed in the early 1970s, the foundations were laid for the movement that would fully develop from the 1980s onwards. The movements of the 1980s built upon previous experiences, networks, and knowledge. Furthermore, many characteristics such as the action repertoire, the merging of radical politics and underground culture, and the focus on direct action and anti-parliamentarism can be traced back to the 1970s and even earlier. It is thus not surprising that many of the contributions in this collection take the 1970s as their point of departure.

Even so, some significant shifts can be observed from 1980 onwards. In contrast to the movements of the 1970s, the squatters of the 1980s were not only more pessimistic, they also seemed younger and less theoretically inclined. One could even say that anti-theoretical attitudes were dominant in the movements of the 1980s. This was influenced by several factors, to start with, the fact that the activists were younger and often more proletarian than their forerunners of the 1968 student movement.[37] The movement also built upon radical feminist approaches that aimed at overcoming the divide between leftist theory and practice.[38] As a result, actions became more important than their theoretical underpinning. Furthermore, a revaluation of romanticist sentiments played a role. Most importantly because the squatters' movement resisted plans and governments that were still very much influenced by technocratic and rationalist ideas.[39]

But the anti-theoretical stance was in part also a reaction to the decline of the radical movements of the 1970s. Both those in Marxist-Leninist groups, groups supporting armed struggle, and radical student leaders of that era wrote long and often overly theoretical texts. By the end of the 1970s, however, these seemed to be written to draw attention away from the movement's trajectory towards insignificance or increasing moderation, rather than to prove a point. The frustration of younger activists with radical intellectuals was voiced, for example, in an influential song by the German punk band Slime, '*linke Spießer*': 'Always critical and political / Marx and Lenin on the bedside table / But you've got something against clashes / And you happily make room for the police. . . . And when we become aggressive / You are all suddenly conservative.'[40]

The lyrics of Slime seem to convey the aggression and lust for confrontation that was characteristic for the punk subculture and nourished by the 1980s squatter movement. This militant stance was also conveyed through the

Left: Graffiti on the former site of the Youth House/Ungdomshuset in Copenhagen—'69' references the street address of the squat, 2007. Photo: Josh MacPhee.

movement's posters and publications, which often showed lone street fighters with balaclavas facing large crowds of riot police.[41]

In comparison to the 'dark' and confrontational 1980s, the 1990s movement on the other hand seemed driven by new optimism. It has often been claimed that social movements suffered from the end of the Cold War. The Copenhagen movement, for example, felt driven under attack because 'everything that smacked of socialism and collectivist politics was on the defensive.' It does not appear so for Vienna. As Robert Foltin states, 'Rather, the fall of the so called "Iron Curtain" was followed by a flourishing of new social movements in Austria and Vienna.' Thus, the influence of the fall of the Berlin Wall seems rather mixed. In several places, the early 1990s witnessed a new wave of squats, while in other places such as East Berlin and Poznań, squatting became possible for the first time.

Punk and hardcore music remained important, but squats proved nourishing environments for experimentation. Electronic avant-garde music transformed into acid house and techno and in several places, the movement's infrastructure proved vital to the inception of new party scenes. In the summer of 1988, Britain's youth culture was hit by a sudden wave of illegal rave parties, in which ecstasy was widely available and used. This 'second summer of love,' referencing the first of 1967, soon resonated through to the rest of Europe and more hippie-like values counterbalanced the aggression and partly anti-social stance of punk.[42] Writing on the situation in Brighton, the Needle Collective and the Bash Street Kids even observe a current gaining influence in the movement called 'fluffiness.' This 'mystical belief in the transforming power of "positive energy"' was explained by one youth: 'It can't happen as a confrontational revolution, [but] a consciousness revolution. . . . If people can change the way they think, all these problems would suddenly lift.'[43] Even so, punk-like mentalities never fully disappeared, but rather found new ways of expression in darker more monotone music styles like tekno and hardcore.

This relative shift towards more pacifist values was also reflected in changing drug consumption. The 1980s had seen a steep rise of use of stimulants such as speed and cocaine among youths. In the squatter movement, speed had been more prevalent because of its price. Some youth cultures, such as punk and techno, explicitly flaunted the use of drugs. In Britain, an important 1980s punk magazine was called *Sniffin' Glue*. The 1990s on the other hand witnessed a tendency towards 'party drugs' such as ecstasy and in some circles LSD, both of which became very popular in the techno scene.[44]

In the 1990s, both gender relations and militant politics changed. In the 1980s, images of militant politics had traditionally focused on physical street confrontations that forced the police to retreat. This stimulated a masculine image of the ultimate street fighter. In the 1990s, this image changed, partly because of the growing influence of feminism and queer politics in the movement.[45] Already during the 1980s, radical women, lesbians, and gays had played a significant role in the movement and challenged traditional gender roles.[46]

Punk played an important role among others because of its dress codes: as male punks started wearing heavy make-up and leggings while women started wearing leather jackets, this tended to obfuscate the differences between male and female punks.[47] But in the 1990s, the influence of queer politics caused the movement to become more receptive to understanding homosexuality, transgender issues, and gender-based violence. In several places gender politics became a central issue within autonomous scenes.

A second factor influencing the changing form of militancy was the growing strength of the police apparatus that often made the 1980s tactics seem obsolete. It became less common, and more difficult, to carry helmets or other 'riot gear' to demonstrations. In several countries, even balaclavas were forbidden. The inflow of new activists in the 1990s through the alterglobalisation protests also influenced the tactics of the movement. In their chapter on Copenhagen, Flemming Mikkelsen and René Karpantchof show that letting go of the original militant attitudes was a prerequisite to forging links to this new movement. More recently, the same happened when Athens anarchists allied themselves with activists from the *indignados* movement. This only became possible after the first accepted the latter's emphasis on nonviolence. Even so, the black bloc has remained a central part of the autonomous movement and the black clothing style of many autonomous scenes still conveys a decisive militant stance.[48]

The 2000s witnessed a number of other significant developments. As the alterglobalisation movement and the rise of anti-summit protests led to stronger links between local movements. Grand international networks were fostered through international anti-summit mobilisations, social forums, and no-border camps. For relatively isolated movements such as the one in Poznań, these international contacts and gatherings were of great importance, stimulating global exchange of information and tactics. The political trends of 1990s developed further, as movements and scenes opened to strengthen already existing alliances and forge new ones with other social movements and organisations. This was in part due to the shrinking size of the movement in several places. As movements lost the power to mobilise independently, it became both easier and more necessary to cooperate. Again, this often influenced the militant stances of these movements. But the changing political climate in many European countries, showing a sharp shift to the right, also furthered this development.

RADICAL POLITICS, LIFESTYLE, AND SUBCULTURE

In autonomous movements, radical politics and youth subcultures are inextricably linked, though not always easily so. The range of possibilities for overlap were made visible again recently in the urban conflicts in Paris, London, Portugal, Spain, and Greece.

During the first two conflicts, no explicit political demands were made. This, of course, does not make these revolts unpolitical, as they are direct reactions

to the underprivileged position of migrants and migrant youth and more generally an underclass in both countries. Many politicians and observers, however,
have denounced these clashes as expressions of plain hooliganism and anti-social
behaviour.[49] Often the responses were openly racist. When in the UK a large
section of the looters and rioters turned out to be native British or 'white,' reality
was conveniently reinterpreted by one historian on BBC *Newsnight* to match the
nation's prejudice by exclaiming 'the whites have become black.'[50]

Other movements, such as those in Greece, Portugal, and Spain, have
taken a more openly political stance, in both cases against governmental austerity measures. The political character of these movements could be one explanation for the movements' longer periods of activity, in comparison, for example,
to riots in London and Paris, which subsided after a few weeks. But even here,
'non-political' youth cultures played an important role. In Greece, for example,
football hooligans took part in clashes with the police.[51] In Spain, political protest was linked to alternative party scenes.

The link with youth cultures thus does not render these movements less
political. Rather, a strong connection with youth subcultures is essential for political movements to move from a small group to a large movement. The 1980 Zurich
movement, for example, started only after political activists, demanding an autonomous youth centre, mixed with youths coming from a Bob Marley concert.[52] In
Amsterdam, punks played an essential role in the squatter movement's shift from
pacifism to militant politics.[53] Autonomous and social centres consciously cater to
both youth cultures by hosting or organising concerts and practice rooms and by
organising political meetings, debates, workshops, and so on.

But these links can also cause tensions, because youth subcultures can
be essentially apolitical and don't necessarily conform to the politics and norms
of political activists. Most youth cultures have a 'political' wing as can be observed with punk, hardcore, and techno, as well as football subcultures.[54] In
the 1980s, punks would go to demonstrations and activists to punk concerts.
But all the aforementioned youth cultures also have more 'hedonist' wings, in
which drug use, deliberately posing as political incorrect, machismo, and sexism
can play a role. This leads to conflicts in which activists attack others for their
unreflected attitudes, sexism, and anti-social behaviour, while the other party
denounces the politically influenced social norms of the activists as killjoys and
detrimental to the 'everything goes' and spontaneous nature of their subculture.
These conflicts happen time and again and are as old as the radical youth movements themselves and demand continuous engagement.

Historically, both radical movements and youth cultures have taken almost diabolical pleasure in appropriating dismissive terms assigned to them
by conservative journalists and politicians. The words 'punk' and 'queer,' for
example, have these origins. In a similar manner, German squatters dubbed
themselves as 'the people our parents always warned us about.' In more recent
times however, movements seem to aim more at presenting themselves as sta-

ble, politically conscious and worthy. Again, the stronger links with other, more moderate parties may have played a role in this.

POLITICAL OPPORTUNITIES AND URBAN DEVELOPMENT

The development of squatter and autonomous movements is influenced by several factors, such as legitimacy crises of governments that emerge out of financial scandals or political controversies. In West Berlin, for example, the city government lost its authority with regard to housing policy because of a fraud case in December 1980. The city government lost more than 125 million Deutschmarks when the fraudulent construction entrepreneur Garski went bankrupt and was then arrested. This situation furthered the rise of squatting, which took a big leap in subsequent months.[55]

Disagreements among or within ruling parties, such as was the case of West Berlin, during which the ruling social democrats were divided over the question how to deal with the squatters, can also be a factor. In this instance, a moderate wing wanted to resolve the issue by legalising most squats and opposing police repression. A more conservative wing, however, wanted to evict all squats and uphold the rule of law. Elections were underway, with the social democrats being challenged both on the left (by the Greens) and on the right (by the Christian Democrats). Only after the latter had won the elections, and a clear policy was formulated and implemented, did the squatter wave subside.[56]

Loss of authority and inner divisions among the governing can thus create space for political actors from below. Legal standings also play an important role, such as can be seen in the Netherlands. The importance of squatter law for movements is further explained by Lucy Finchett-Maddock in her chapter on the United Kingdom, in which she demonstrates that there is a gap between the law itself and how it is enforced 'on the ground' and that movements are often intensely occupied with the law, as squatter collectives offer legal advice and write handbooks on how to deal with the forces of law. Further, squatter groups often lobby to change laws already in place, block or change proposed laws, or lobby to change the way they are enforced. While Finchett-Maddock focuses her chapter on initiatives in London, similar cases can be observed in other cities.

The issue of ownership also plays an important role, as can be seen in Poznań, and the lack of clarity around the ownership of the squatted paint factory now called Rozbrat. A similar situation unfolded in East Berlin after the fall of the Berlin Wall, when the ownership of many buildings was unclear. In other cities too, ownership is important. In most cities, preferred sites of occupation are complexes belonging to large (international) firms or the (local) government, since both can be pressured with bad publicity. This provides activists with a stronger negotiating position.

Urban development also influences the opportunities and limits of squatting and autonomous movements. When squatters moved to the city centres in the late 1970s, cities across Western Europe had been in the midst of a prolonged crisis, struggling with a long list of socioeconomic ills, since the end of the 1960s. Industry and a substantial part of the middle class were leaving the city because of transportation difficulties and living conditions. As deinvestment led to decay and depopulation, poverty and crime increased. As a result, large urban areas were left empty, thus forming an ideal material basis for squatting. Autonomous activists turned to the inner cities as an arena for experimenting with autonomy and self-management. However, as squatters brought new life to the inner cities and deindustrialisation led to a definitive turn to service industries, the city centres became popular again and capital returned. Through the 1980s, Europe's inner cities became ever more intensely commodified, resulting in the often violent displacement of everything and everybody that did not produce a profit or fit the city brand.[57] As a result, in many cities, squatting moved from the city centres to the outskirts.

But not only external factors influence a movement's development, as the strength of a movement also lies in its capability to mobilise support and convince others of the rightfulness of their claims and demands. To be successful, movements must be able to form alliances with other political actors.

SIGNIFICANCE AND YIELDS

Radical youth movements have been a constant political factor in European cities since at least the 1970s. What has been their significance? What have they achieved? Traditionally, squatter movements have influenced urban development by their resistance to large urban restructuring plans. They have also influenced the cultural climate of many cities by using social centres and squats as facilitators for alternative music and art galleries. They have influenced the local political climate, by forming often sizeable activist scenes. And, at times, they have even played a role in national and international politics.

With regard to the movement's influence on urban development, the Dutch sociologist Hans Pruijt was one of the first to give a detailed and systematic account of the influence of citizen's protest against the Amsterdam urban redevelopment plans of the 1960s, 1970s, and 1980s. He assigns a central role to squatting in these protests. Initially, urban renewal plans foresaw the demolition of large parts of the houses in the city centre (with the exception of the mansions around the canals), the construction of broad roads through the city, and the construction of flats on the city's edge. The protest against these plans first caused significant delay, and then brought about a policy shift towards renovating the existing houses and preserving the historic city centre.[58] In Berlin, the squatters' movement has played an equally influential role.[59]

A great number of squats—according to Pruijt, at least 126 houses—were legalised in Amsterdam. In this sense, Amsterdam was exceptional. In most cities, the number of successful squat actions and subsequent legalisations has been much lower. In places where the conditions for squatting have been exceptionally negative, activist groups have often chosen to rent places and use them as autonomous social centres.

These autonomous social centres have often played a significant cultural role by providing performance spaces for underground bands and budding artists, such as the German bands Die Ärzte and Einstürzende Neubauten, and the British band Crass. A number of musical styles have their roots in squats and squatter bars, such as punk, hardcore, new wave, and various strands of electronic music.

In his chapter on squatting in Berlin, Alex Vasudevan raises an additional point regarding how the squatter movement has also heralded new styles and aesthetics of living and interior design. Characterised by functionalism, transparency, and do-it-yourself attitudes, both the interior and the furniture of squats were intentionally makeshift, 'raw,' and without unnecessary accessories. Squats were furnished with second-hand and self-made furniture and people painted directly on the walls rather than hanging up paintings; in this way, the interior (and exterior) of squatted houses and social centres gained their own particular style.

The K77 collective, for example, a house in former East Berlin in the early 1990s, aimed at creating a space with room for experimenting and constantly changing interiors. As one of the activists explained: 'New spaces were largely laid-out through flexible and self-built wallboards. Wall partitions were accordingly fitted with omissions. Light openings, room connections, or breaks in the wall were designed so that they can be closed and reopened at any time. Overall, design decisions were left to individuals.'

The squatters' style came to influence the mainstream. Grzegorz Piotrowski remarks that several commercial and high-end bars and cafés in Berlin have taken over the style of earlier squatter bars and some styles have been incorporated by large furniture chains.

While squatter movements have formed an important part of local activist scenes, at times they have also played a role in national politics through engagement in anti-nuclear and anti-apartheid actions in the 1980s, and the global justice/anti-globalisation movement in the late 1990s and 2000s. In Vienna, for example, left libertarian activists played an important role in the months-long protests against the first government with FPÖ ministers. Earlier, the movement was part of the alterglobalisation movement and its international campaigns. In a similar way, the movement has played an important role in the protests against austerity politics in Spain and Greece.

In sum, buildings have been saved and urban renewal projects blocked, delayed, or altered. Significant contributions have been made to local cultural life and at times the movement has played an important role in grand political campaigns, such as protests against apartheid, nuclear energy and arms, right-wing politics, international summits, and austerity politics.

There are, however, also critical voices that claim that the autonomous movement has unwillingly functioned as a forerunner of gentrification. Exactly those areas where the autonomous movement has been at its strongest have often become popular areas for yuppies and tourists. This goes, for example, for Kreuzberg in Berlin. As students, tourists, and yuppies move to these areas, both rents and prices rise. Or, as one observer put it, 'First come the squatters, then come the cocktail bars.'[60]

Saving run-down neighbourhoods from demolition and improving the living quality thus seems to be a double-edged sword. By adding value to the neighbourhood, eventually squatters get driven away by higher prices. Activists have noticed this problem, but formulating a solution proves to be difficult. Recently, the German left weekly *Jungle World* articulated the frustration in the face of these developments in an article on the successful defence of the Piranha squat in Cologne: 'Much praise in advance for the squatters who wish to leave their mark on the neighbourhood by organising workshops, artist studios and nonprofit cafés. But they will not be able to prevent that their mere presence makes the old workers' district Kalk more attractive for students and artists.'[61]

One of the results of this development is that squatter and autonomous movements are driven out of the inner city to the city's periphery. This is discussed in the case studies on Brighton and Barcelona. Activists have responded in different ways to this development. In Brighton, activists squatted a complex in the city centre to protest the high rents in the city centre. In Barcelona, squatters chose to move away from the city centre to the Sierra de Collserola mountain range just outside Barcelona. The running of a rural squat close to the city can create a new dynamic that retains its link to the city, while not being dependant on it. How this will play out in the long run remains an interesting question.

The causes and dynamics of gentrification have in recent years become a topic of heated debate.[62] Even so, the demands and action repertoire of squatters and autonomous movements seem to have remained more or less unaltered: they respond to gentrification by demanding a right to the city for all. In doing so, they join hands with tenants' groups, neighbourhood associations and others, and form broad political coalitions with a differentiated action repertoire ranging from petitions and moderate forms of action to direct interventions such as occupations. The protests are not only directed against rent and price increases but also revolve around the quality of living. Thus in Barcelona in the early 2000s, a park was occupied to resist the construction of a parking garage. Similar successful campaigns were organised in Athens as well, and Gregor Kritidis shows that these sort of struggle go back to the mid-1980s. Gentrification is thus intensely debated within the left, but has not significantly altered its politics.

CONCLUSION

A brief overview shows that squatter and autonomous movements are active within every larger city in Europe. Still, the existing literature is heavily influenced by the idea that squatter movements are mainly a phenomenon belonging to 1980s Northwestern Europe. To get a real sense of the scope of these movements, their evolution and potential, we must broaden the field of research both geographically and temporally. By doing so, local histories that have up to now received only scant attention are uncovered and larger comparisons can be made.

Such comparisons show a great number of continuities and similarities within squatter and autonomous movement history in Europe, ranging back to the early 1970s. They focus on the urban and demand a city for all; they organise informally, combine radical politics with underground youth cultures, and prefer direct action over parliamentary politics. Although the form and emphasis of the movements may shift, their basic structures remain the same.

Squatter and autonomous movements are active all over Europe and lastingly influence the cultural life within cities, playing an important role in local protest movements and at times gaining national or international significance. The development of these movements is influenced by political opportunities, legal situations, and capital flows, as well as how successful they are at mobilising sympathisers and forming alliances with other political groups.

In recent years, new protest movements have developed across Europe, directed against austerity measures and voicing the demand for 'true' democracy and a right to the city for all. Most of these movements are active within the urban landscape, and autonomous and squatter activists play an important role in them. This collection places these movements in their due historical contexts by covering the period from the 1980 protest wave to the most recent one. In doing so, it shows that radical protest movements are not something of the past or situated on the fringes of society. Rather, they are at the heart of it.

One
MYTH AND REALITY IN THE
AMSTERDAM SQUATTERS' MOVEMENT, 1975–2012
Nazima Kadir

INTRODUCTION

Antoine has been homeless in the Netherlands on and off for the past ten years. When he relates his housing history, it is difficult to ascertain a concrete narrative due to confusions, gaps, and his avoidance of answering some questions directly. He often sleeps illicitly in abandoned buildings. Sometimes, he moves on the next day. If he is lucky, he can stay in a spot for months, even years. His transient homelessness is clandestine and his existence is absent from all government records in the Netherlands. Is Antoine a Dutch squatter?

Rumours allege that squatting has existed in the Bijlmer for over forty years. The Bijlmer is a neighbourhood located on the outskirts of Amsterdam, originally built in the 1970s as a bedroom community for middle-class professionals who were to use the then newly constructed metro lines to commute to work. The plan failed miserably because, surprisingly, middle-class professionals wanted to remain in the inner city. Despite the intentions of city planners, the Bijlmer became known as the 'Black neighbourhood' of Amsterdam, featuring a mix of a vast array of immigrants from all over the world but defined mainly by its dominant population from Africa and the Caribbean.

One story is that newly arrived families from Suriname in the 1970s squatted entire blocks of apartment buildings. Other rumours contend that, years later, the original squatters rent spaces in those same buildings at exorbitant costs to undocumented immigrants. Do these practices constitute what is considered squatting in the Netherlands?

Mauricio recently moved to Amsterdam from Colombia. A convinced communist and veteran student activist, he fit easily into the fifteen-member international living group of the four-story squatted house where he resided. Within a few weeks, Mauricio's housemates suspected that he was psychologically unstable. He disappeared for a few days. There were rumours that he had been imprisoned for political activity.

This was somewhat true. Mauricio had walked into the Albert Heijn, a chain su-permarket, and left with a stolen piece of candy manufactured in Israel. He then re-entered the supermarket to announce to the manager that he had stolen the candy to protest the Palestinian occupation. He was arrested. A few weeks after this incident, his housemates learned that Mauricio was camping in the Vondelpark—the Central Park of Amsterdam—in a state of psychosis.

I BEGIN THIS ARTICLE with these stories of squatting that veer drastically from the dominant image of Dutch squatters—young, white, politically articulate, mili-tant, and skilled activists who heroically battle the police to defend their squats, which are symbols of anarchist, 'autonomous,' and 'free' spaces.[1] I do so to dem-onstrate the challenges of narrating a history and description of the Dutch squatters' movement that is both inclusive of the diversity within the movement and does not reproduce the exclusions of the movement's self-representation and its representations in social science literature.

Since the late 1970s, the Dutch squatters' movement—with its explicit images of political conviction, militancy, effectiveness, and anarchic heroism and its implicit reification of the archetype of the white male activist—has cap-tured the imagination of the radical left, in Europe as well as around the world. The movement has been highly mediatised for decades, the subject of count-less media pieces from newspaper articles, television news reports, and docu-mentary films to poems and novels in the Netherlands and abroad. This media attention—simultaneously cultivated and repudiated by the movement—has highly impacted both the continuing representations of the movement and the identities, practices, and self-imagination of activist squatters themselves. Thus, images from the 1980s—themselves made questionable by the focus on the actions of a tiny minority—swirl out of control, creating a funhouse mirror of ideologies, styles, and practices for activists nearly forty years later. Given this paradoxical dynamic, is it possible to describe this movement without acknowl-edging the impact of the distortions that result from these representations and the types of identities, meanings, and ideologies that people project onto the movement and themselves as activists?

Why is it so difficult for me to tell a straightforward story in contrast to those who have more easily penned the life of this movement from histori-cal, sociological, and political science perspectives? While most literature on the squatters' movement in the Netherlands is based on library research, mine is based on living and breathing the movement for nearly four years. Thus, unlike the rest of the literature in question, my research is anthropological and based on long-term participant observation and interviews. As I lived and worked in a squatters' community for three and a half years, these experiences formed the basis of my doctoral dissertation. During this period, I conducted hundreds of formal and informal interviews, worked as a cook in a squatted restaurant, and then as a housing campaigner for two successful anti-gentrification campaigns and the defences of two squatted houses where I resided. I lived in four squats and was evicted twice.

As a result of these experiences, I had to confront a number of persistent problems and contradictions that illustrate the disparity between the stereotypes of the movement and the reality of the movement in which I had immersed myself for years. While there were a number of people who more easily could be recognised as 'a real squatter' and identified themselves as such, most of the people in the movement did not. Many squatters were constantly negotiating with this imaginary ideal, while others, such as the examples of squatting highlighted in the beginning of this text, were so distant from it that they could not even be recognised within the framework of the Dutch squatters' movement.

Given these stark disparities, I constantly had to question what it meant to participate in this movement. This led me to distrust both the movement's discourse about itself and social science literature on the movement. Both have persistently failed to interrogate central hidden assumptions, such as the fact that only specific squatters with a set of particular tactics for taking over a space have been classified as part of the movement. Without making this explicit, this narrative endorses the assumption that squatting must be a public act of taking over, supported and enabled by an infrastructure of radical left subcultural spaces generally populated only by middle-class European youth.

These disparities have led me to conclude the following:

1. The mediatised images of the movement from the late 1970s and early 1980s, portraying a massive, heavily militant youth activist movement eagerly participating in highly televised riots, has created a myth that has captured the left radical imagination. However, in the 1970s and 1980s, when this myth was created, it only represented a small percentage of those who actually squatted, excluding the majority and failing to represent the diversity of squatters. This myth is reified by current historical and social science literature on the movement that has, on the whole, failed to interrogate the accuracy of this myth and only reproduced it uncritically.

2. The myth of the militant, organised, confrontational, anti-authoritarian, articulate, and 'autonomous' activist—usually represented as a thin, white man in his late teens or early twenties, wearing a balaclava and throwing stones from the roofs of squatted houses or confronting the police—has become a dominant ideological paradigm in the movement. The myth itself serves as a beacon that attracts many activists to the movement and fulfils unresolved identity needs.

3. The myth is dogmatic, exclusive, and so powerful that movement activists are regularly unable to go beyond the image and its limits. As a result, they are unable to address their complexity, diversity, motivations, and ideologies. Because they cannot confront who they are, they often cannot address what to do in the face of a completely different—and increasingly hostile—sociopolitical context.

KRAKERS MOETEN VOOR HANGEN SPECULANTEN BELANGEN

KOMITE JONGEREN HUISVESTING   LUTHERSE BURGWAL 1   TEL: 60 30 62

In order to integrate these analytical observations regarding the split between the myth of the ideal squatter and the reality of those who participate in the movement, as well as the role of this myth in the ideological discourse and imaginations of those who actively engage in the movement, I have structured this text in the following way:

The article begins with a historical overview. While I relate the events that compose what is accepted as the narrative of the Dutch squatters' movement, I continually question its accuracy. I critique four aspects of it: First, the narrative's emphasis on textual sources, which excludes non-verbal practices and the perspectives of those who are unable to represent themselves in written form. Second, the uncritical reproduction of the perspectives of male authority figures, which inherently contradicts the movement's self-representation as non-hierarchical and anti-authoritarian. Third, the teleological nature of the narrative. And, finally, its reification of a nostalgic white urbanity that excludes the impact of migrants on urban life.

The second section analyses the oppositional practices of the movement. I describe the main forms of actions directed against those identified as external enemies. These consist of (1) the squatting of houses and their protection through an organised, militant network; (2) the legal and political defence of a squatted house; and (3) the physical and spectacular defence of a squatted house at the moment of eviction. For those who define themselves as squatters, these practices are tacitly, but not explicitly, rituals and often, literally, rites of passage.

This description results from a specific methodology. Since this text is based on anthropological fieldwork, I focus on describing practices and how actions and networks are organised rather than reviewing and analysing social science literature and information from public sources. Following the description of the practices, I formulate a tactical critique, based on a wider consideration of contemporary challenges that face squatters. I argue that squatters' totalizing focus on violent resistance and confrontation is anachronistic and a denial of the contemporary challenges, which are more diffuse, difficult to confront, and less spectacular.

In the last section, I focus on debates and discussions within the squatters' movement. However, instead of presenting an extensive review and analysis of internal debates which are usually interpreted as written debates in movement media, I analyse a number of discourses of negative identification that circulate within the movement. I contend namely that the main debates are not explicit, but implicit and reveal themselves by the way several groups within the movement classify each other.

Here, too, practices are central rather than formal written and oral discourse, because oral and written formal discourse often reflects dogmas and imagined ideology rather than the actual struggles that define daily life. More often than not, people are more loyal to an ideological paradigm than to a

Left: Dutch squatters' poster, 1980. Courtesy of Interference Archive.

shrewd understanding of the diversity and contradictory nature of the movement. Hence, rumours and negative classifications more aptly reveal how this movement functions than do polemics on a squatters' website.

THE TELEVISED HISTORY OF THE DUTCH SQUATTERS' MOVEMENT

The squatters' movement in Amsterdam has its roots in a number of urban groups that sought to make social change. Some of these groups squatted to achieve symbolical goals to create 'free' spaces in what they perceived as a conformist environment. Others squatted for concrete and materialist reasons, such as to address the housing needs of young people and to fight urban planning measures by the state.

One major antecedent of the squatters in the mid-1960s was Provo, a group of anarchist, situationist, counter-cultural artists. They sought to challenge authoritarian and hierarchical social relations between citizens and the state and to question consumerism and the promotion of automobile traffic. They attacked symbols of authority through absurdist situationist weekly happenings. Provo was followed by the Kabouters (the Gnomes), a political party that continued to advocate for the issues that Provo raised on the level of municipal politics.

The subsequent squatter groups that emerged from these occupied houses gained notice through actions intentionally staged as media spectacles. They invited the media to record and witness the violence committed against the squatters by both the police and hired thugs. They also organised national squatting days in which they coordinated squatting actions all over the Netherlands to occur on one day. However, due to the almost immediate evictions of these squatted houses, accompanied by police violence, the squatting actions failed to provide a long-term housing solution.

Squatter groups that took over spaces for the sake of housing—instead of mainly sending out an anti-authoritarian, situationist message—were initiated by alternative youth support organisations that, ironically, received funds from the state. At that time, independent housing for young people was almost impossible to acquire. Young single people's desire to reside independently from their families reflected major shifts in youth lifestyles as a consequence of delayed entrance into the labour market.

This delay itself resulted from a number of social and political changes. First off, the access to higher education widened considerably beyond a privileged few. Everyone who enrolled in higher education received a living stipend and a scholarship that paid tuition. Secondly, young people delayed childbearing due to the women's movement changing assumptions about young women's sexual behaviour and the introduction and widespread use of the birth control pill. Finally, young people could easily obtain state unemployment benefits without restriction beginning at age sixteen.

Alternative youth support organisations recognised that housing presented a central problem for young people. They lobbied policy makers and politicians to solve the problem by creating independent youth housing. Since lobbying had limited impact, the organisations then became involved in squatting and transformed it from a symbolic tool to a viable means to both protest and provide housing. In Amsterdam, they began a voluntary organisation called the Kraakpandendienst (Squatted Houses Services Agency), to support the squatting of houses and the squats themselves. This organisation emphasised do-it-yourself principles from its inception. Outside of Amsterdam, the alternative youth service groups also initiated squatting actions and organised squatter groups. In Amsterdam, independent squatter groups and youth service organisations that squatted houses existed simultaneously. The independent groups often used a more radical rhetoric and promoted the use of violence more severely than the squatter groups associated with the alternative youth service organisations.

By 1970–1971, however, squatting as a practice was waning because of police repression, the short amount of time a squat existed before its eviction, and concessions made to the squatters' demands by the municipalities. Surprisingly, a higher appeals court decision reversed this decline in 1971. At the time, squatters relied on case law from 1914 that declared that someone could occupy or use a space without having legal entitlement to it. The practice of this case law translated into the requirement to display a table, bed, and chair to the police during the squatting action in order to establish residency in a property. In 1971, however, the court of higher appeals ruled not only that squatting was not punishable as a criminal act, but that squatters retained the rights to domestic peace in their residences. This decision meant that squatters possessed the same rights as renters and homeowners to refuse entry to anyone, including the police and property owners. Hence, only a court order, often obtained after a lengthy procedure, could evict squatters.

At this time, the squatting of houses through public takeovers had significant support: legally, through the change in case law; organisationally, buttressed by the state-funded youth organisations; and politically, by being embedded with the Kabouter party in the city council. Squatted houses became available as a result of the remaking of the urban spatial landscape planned during this period by the city government, beginning with the Nieuwmarktbuurt.

Urban renewal plans aimed at bulldozing eighteenth-century inner-city neighbourhoods to build highways and metros to ease transportation from newly built suburban housing complexes to the inner city in the first half of the 1970s (such as the Bijlmer, mentioned in the beginning of the article). In the Nieuwmarktbuurt, organised resistance rose against these plans. This organised resistance was composed of neighbourhood residents who refused to move from their homes and political activists who had experience from earlier movements. They protested the plans by squatting buildings that had been left empty for years and were slated for demolition, eventually leading to a large-scale riot when the final demolition was scheduled. The Nieuwmarkt campaign eventually succeeded in preventing a radical transformation of the eighteenth-century centre with its narrow streets and canals to a functionalist cityscape that privileged automobile access.

The Nieuwmarkt campaign enabled the squatters to transform from an array of disparate groups to a network of interdependent squatters' groups. The independent squatter groups and the *kraakspreekuren* (KSUs, the squatting information hour)—mainly neighbourhood based—formed the nodes of the network. The kraakspreekuren held significant authority since its members decided whom they supported in the squatting and maintenance of a house. During this period, the alarm list was instituted: a telephone tree that squatters use to mobilise to ward off attacks of *knokploegen* (groups of hired thugs) and police officers. In the same period, citywide and nationwide squatters' consultation meetings formed.

The Nieuwmarkt campaign culturally catalysed squatting, transforming it from mainly a symbolic protest tool to a lifestyle that combined activism and experimental forms of new left communal living. Sociologist Lynn Owens comments on the significance of the Nieuwmarkt campaign: 'Squatting had

A 1980 squatter poster stating, 'Their state of law is not ours.' Photo: Taco Anema.

become more than a way to simply put a roof over your head. It was a means of creating a better world, or at least a more livable city. Squatters began placing more emphasis not on the political message of squatting, but rather of the opportunities it gave to live an autonomous life, for self-development.'[2]

The period from the mid-1970s onward is collectively remembered as the so-called height of the squatters' movement in Amsterdam, referred to generally as 'the squatters' movement in the '80s. This period is discursively represented as a period of large-scale squatting in which the majority of the participants were idealistic, radical, left activists. The nostalgia of this period refers to a number of spectacular, mediagenic riots as well as a vibrant youth counter-culture that was enabled by the infrastructure created by a plethora of squatted spaces. The dominant histories of the movement focus on the tactics, developments, and confrontations related to the defence of a number of high profile squatted houses. These stories traditionally begin with the squatting of the Grote Keyser in 1978, after which the movement achieves its so-called height with the barricading of the Vondelstraat in March 1980 and the controversial riots on the coronation of Queen Beatrix in April 1980, and subsequently the discursive decline signalled by the violence following the eviction of the Lucky Luyk in 1982.

HISTORIOGRAPHY OF THE MEDIAGENIC AND TELEOLOGICAL NARRATIVE

Before relating a summary of the events that are accepted as the 'grand narrative' of the Dutch squatters' movement, it's important to list the endemic problems of this narrative and the ways in which it reifies a white, male activist archetype, and excludes the experiences of women, people of colour, immigrants, and those who resided in squats without a political agenda. While the narrative privileges the perspectives of a minority over the experiences of the majority of the squatters, my critique is based on my own research as a lens to interpret the historical treatments and reveal their distortions. Social historian Eric Duivenvoorden, who wrote a history of the movement and made an influential documentary film, transparently discusses his exclusionary focus:

> Young people occupy a house and sooner or later have to deal with an eviction threat from the government and/or the owner. In the overwhelming majority of cases, the squatters leave silently. In the following story, the only squatting actions that are described are the ones that contribute to a better understanding of the history of the squatters' movement. And there are plenty of such stories.[3]

Describing 'actions that contribute to a better understanding of the history' thus means concentrating on a minority of politically well-organised activists who articulate themselves in a manner that Duivenvoorden and others recognise as a legitimate form of squatter activism. Duivenvoorden writes that between 1964–1999, approximately forty-five to seventy thousand people in Amsterdam had some involvement with the squatters' movement, the overwhelming majority of whom were not activists and whose participation derived from a diversity of motivations. Consider, for example, that in this movement, there were macrobiotic squats, vegan squats, feminist squats that prohibited the presence of men, as well as squats whose inhabitants merely wanted free housing and lacked interest in politics. For squatters embedded in such households, the actions and conflicts that Duivenvoorden highlights as instrumental were most likely far removed from their social worlds.

By focusing on the 'politicos' and on mediagenic actions, the historical record gives excessive attention to branches of the movement that produced written text, without interrogating whether such texts resonated in the informal, non-written discourses and debates within the movement. The most textually verbose groups are those most often quoted, leading to a distorted view of movement discourse and giving excessive importance to texts with disputed relevance or that may have been only one voice among a cacophony. In my fieldwork, I noted many people who contributed to the movement but who did not feel comfortable expressing themselves verbally or in written form. Their work, which includes construction work, breaking down doors, renovating, cleaning, cooking, taking care of social spaces, and maintenance, is crucial to the movement's existence. Still, it is mostly ignored in social science literature since these individuals do not represent themselves in written form.

By focusing on actions, riots, and evictions to tell the story of the movement, social science literature creates an artificial linear progression as a means to create a tight narrative that requires a beginning, a middle and an end. Such a linear progression, also known as a teleological narrative, has an ideological agenda. It promotes the idea that movements come into being to tackle concrete, materialist issues, which, once achieved, then dissipate. Such a teleological narrative creates a false linearity and overly emphasises rational productive actions directed at external enemies. Social movements, however, are composed of human beings with a variety of motivations, some rational and materialist, and others that are emotional, cultural, and social. Such motivations are not concrete and are difficult to fit into a narrative of conquering materialist goals.

My own research reveals that the organizing and staging of events, protests, evictions, and actions is often circular and repetitious rather than linear and progressive. To insist that violent collective actions are events that transform history is an overly simplistic, teleological narrative. Instead, I assert that riots, evictions, and actions are not as instrumental for so-called larger movement goals as is often stated in social science literature and movement media. Rather, these events create cohesion in a fragile community. They present opportunities to advance towards the self-realisation of the ideal autonomous activist and serve to uphold this idealised image.

To illustrate this point, a number of squatter-made documentaries repeatedly present an action from 1978, during which squatters overtook a city council meeting. In this clip, a group of young, white squatters in their early twenties storm the city council meeting. A young man, tall, blond, wearing glasses, grabs the microphone from the chairperson, stands on a table, and makes a speech. The documentaries feature this clip because it portrays the behaviours which define the squatters' movement at its best: spontaneous direct action, anti-parliamentarism, lack of respect for authority figures, articulate public speaking, and bravery.

When I watched this clip repeatedly, I reflected on how this action was intended to give the impression of spontaneity, but that in actuality, to succeed, it must have been planned with meticulous attention to detail. I wondered, first off, about the brainstorming session that eventually led to this action being chosen as the one to pursue. How many meetings did the group hold to plan it? Who wrote the speech? Why did the group decide to pick this young man in particular to give the speech? How did they manage to videotape it? Did they invite the press? What were the hundreds of small details that they had to address to produce this action? These questions illustrate the contradiction between the necessity to plan intricately with the desire to leave an impression of spontaneity. This results in the discursive invisibility of the efforts required to create that performance.

Furthermore, the traditional narrative uncritically represents how authority functions in this movement and reifies the voices of male leaders. Such a practice renders invisible the participation of unnamed members who crucially enabled the production of actions. These unnamed members include people who may have been inarticulate or did not publicise their activities. For example, Duivenvoorden reifies the authority of male leaders by quoting from them extensively, both in his book and in the documentary. He fails to recognise that this method of historical narration—in which he privileges the voices of authority figures and represents actions as a consequence of their leadership—undermines arguments that these movements were anti-hierarchical and anti-authoritarian.

Finally, if one views the history of post-war Amsterdam through the lens of the squatters' movement, these texts present a misleading and nostalgic white urbanity that I find disturbing. They neglect the impact of the influx of non-white immigrants in the city. From the late 1960s to 2000, the population of Amsterdam radically transitioned from mainly white Dutch to over half 'foreign' (this percentage includes certain classifications of non-white people born in the Netherlands). In 1980, the official population of 'ethnic minorities' was 11 percent of the city, by 1986, it was 16 percent, by 1992, 27 percent, and by 1995, 32 percent.[4] By the time I conducted my fieldwork, the populations of the major Dutch cities had 50 percent or more non-white residents who were classified as foreign.

The shift in the composition of the urban population results from a number of factors. In the 1970s, the Netherlands had a guest worker policy leading to a substantial migration of labourers from Turkey and Morocco. Emphasised by every single government document that describes this policy, the Dutch state intended this policy to be temporary and never expected these workers to settle in the Netherlands. Regardless, the workers remained and reunited with their families, who immigrated to the Netherlands and began their own families. Furthermore, Suriname, a former Dutch colony, achieved independence in 1975. Consequently, a huge influx of Surinamese immigrated to the Netherlands between 1975 and 1980 (after which, Surinamers could no longer claim Dutch citizenship). The Hindustanis (Surinamese of Indian descent) mainly settled in The Hague, while the Creoles (of African descent) often moved to the Bijlmer neighbourhood. That the Bijlmer became a black Surinamese neighbourhood is ironic, since it had originally been constructed for white, middle-class people who were to commute to work in Amsterdam on the metro. This urban planning scheme was instrumental in the development of the squatters' movement and which the squatters had also partially succeeded in dismantling.

With the exception of the sociologist Virginie Mamadouh, who briefly mentions tensions between Surinamese squatters and white Dutch people in the Transvaal neighbourhood, the literature on squatting in Amsterdam wholly ignores the consequences of the radically changing face of the city's population.[5] By only focusing on a particular profile of white squatter activists, the historical texts present a misleading and distorted view. As I noted in the beginning of this article, there are rumours and assumptions in the squatters' movement that Surinamese immigrants squatted entire housing blocks in the Bijlmer in the 1970s, which have remained squatted until the present day. In fact, during my fieldwork, the most eviction notices published in the newspaper were for apartments in the Bijlmer that were squatted outside the movement. Yet, only one academic article from 1977 mentions this phenomenon.[6] Otherwise, all academic research on squatting in Amsterdam, including my own, has failed to analyse it in depth.

In terms of contextualizing squatters in the city and their relationship with their neighbours, the lack of discussion of immigration presents a problematic Eurocentricism and limited critical inquiry. The historical texts habitually present non-squatter neighbours as authentic, white, working-class residents who resist their displacement by urban renewal projects. However, looking at the figures for the population of the city further complicates this assumption regarding the locations of these 'solidaric' neighbours. By selectively focusing on certain sections of the city and particular types of people and lifestyle practices in exclusion of others in the immediate context, the classical literature constructs a fantasy of urban whiteness.

THE MYTHICAL 1980S

The Grote Keyser was a mansion on the Keizergracht, squatted in 1978. In the classic literature, the immense defence of this house against eviction symbolises the squatters' embrace of violence and the cultivation of a defiant attitude towards the so-called mainstream. For most of its existence, the squatters who inhabited the Grote Keyser primarily aimed to party rather than engage in political action. They often rented rooms to tourists and the key to the house was rumoured to float around Dam Square available to anyone who sought a crashpad. When the eviction notice for the house arrived, most of the residents moved out, but ten refused to leave and instead barricaded the house to protect themselves against the eviction attempts of the bailiff and the police.

The politicos from the Staatsliedenbuurt, a group of militant squatters around whom a tremendous amount of conflict would eventually develop, decided to take over the defence. They moved in, replaced the barricades of bed spirals with steel plates, and engineered a media spectacle around the house. They broadcasted a pirate radio station from within the house (called the Vrije Keyser, the Free Emperor), and produced a number of films that displayed endless rows of paint bombs and Molotov cocktails that the squatters had prepared for the eviction. I have watched countless documentaries and news clips from this period showcasing tall, thin, masked, young men engaged in various activities, from debating suited news reporters to walking on the roof of the house to guard it from potential evictors. The squatters were ready to fight, but Amsterdam's mayor Wim Polak refused to evict, claiming that an eviction was too dangerous for the police, the squatters, and public order. Instead, the city bought the building to create independent housing for young people.

The violent confrontation that the politicos sought came unexpectedly during the eviction of another squatted villa, the Vondelstraat, off of the Vondelpark, the Central Park of Amsterdam. The three-day riot around the Vondelstraat has since defined images of squatters and Amsterdam in the 1980s. The squatters set up burning barricades and removed stones from the street to throw at the police. In reaction, the riot police attacked the house with a force of 1,200 police officers, helicopters, several tanks, and water cannons. During the eviction of the Vondelstraat, over 10,000 people demonstrated against the city's heavy repression of the squatters, in particular the deployment of tanks against the city's own population.

After the Vondelstraat, the next defining and mediagenic riot took place during the coronation of Queen Beatrix on April 30, 1980. The coronation is widely considered both the height and the beginning of decline for the squatters' movement. For months, the squatters had campaigned against the coronation with the slogan, *Geen woning, geen kroning* (No housing, no coronation, a phrase that rhymes in Dutch). It posited the use of state resources to celebrate the excesses of the coronation against the lack of funds directed to solve the housing shortage in the Netherlands. To protest, squatters organised a nationwide squatting day during the coronation, opening hundreds of empty houses around the Netherlands. Simultaneously however, an anonymous group that called itself the Autonomen called for violent actions, resulting in a riot that lasted all day. For months afterward, movement participants debated the

Amsterdam squatters' poster, ~1990. Courtesy of Interference Archive.

riot: its impact on the squatters' public image, whether it had been fruitful, and who was responsible.

At the level of public and scholarly discourse, this point may have signified the beginning of decline. But culturally speaking, this period marked a renaissance of the squatters' subculture, which undermines the teleological narrative of decline. The squatters even succeeded in realizing the absurdist, parodying goals of Provo and the Kabouters to create a state within a state. If one participated in the movement, one could live entirely in it without interacting with the mainstream.

This subcultural infrastructure featured three important elements. First, squatters boasted their own media. There were fifteen newspapers for and by squatters, including one that related gossip, one intended for foreign squatters, and one for squatter children. *De Kraakkrant* (The Squatters' Newspaper) had a circulation of two thousand. Squatters ran the Vrije Keyser, a major pirate radio station, as well as a pirate television station, which they transmitted by regularly hacking the city's cable infrastructure. They formed printing press collectives to publish newspapers, pamphlets, books, posters, and other printed media.

Second, the squatters' subculture featured small, nonprofit activities that were staffed by volunteers and took place in squatted spaces, and thus had low fixed costs. These included: cafés, restaurants, bars, infoshops, give-away shops, bakeries, bookstores, bicycle repair shops, grocery stores, cinemas, welding workshops, dance clubs, performance spaces, medical clinics, rehearsal rooms, and a multiplicity of art initiatives and gallery spaces. A massive infrastructure existed solely intended for and created by predominantly young people who lived on low incomes derived from either state benefits or university scholarships. Everything that could not be produced from within the movement with a combination of voluntary labour and cheap and readily available products, such as building materials used in squatted houses to renovate and barricade, was stolen from the mainstream.

Third, the squatters' movement was composed of people involved in a wide assortment of radical left political issues such as anti-nuclear energy, anti-apartheid, anti-militarism, and anti-fascism. A differentiation existed between activists who mainly identified as squatters versus activists who resided in squats but primarily invested their time and energy in other radical left issues. Mobilizing these activists for actions related to squatting was challenging, since to be active in the squatters' movement meant primarily participating in resistance during evictions. Furthermore, in the left activist community, squatters had a reputation for violent, confrontational, and extremely rude behaviour.

Returning to the accepted narrative of the movement, the next major riot that is the subject of historical research was the eviction of the Lucky Luyk in 1982. The Lucky Luyk was a villa in Old South where previously a knokploeg had evicted the squatters. Despite the squatters' legal right to domestic peace, the police had refused to help the squatters retake the house. In reaction, the squatters organised a massive action to violently evict the knokploeg (hired thugs) and re-squat the space. With the media and political attention obtained from the squatters' campaigning, the city decided to purchase the house and convert it into social housing.

The city's decision proved controversial within the movement. A number of squatters felt content to leave the house because of its eventual conversion to social housing rather than remaining an object of speculation. However, the politicos from the Staatsliedenbuurt refused the offer, demanding that the city give social housing contracts to the house's squatter inhabitants since their efforts led to the house becoming social housing in the first place. Despite the internal debates, the politicos' stance was the answer to the city council's decision; they responded by evicting the squatters. Again, an enormous riot ensued during the eviction, during which an empty city tram, Tram 10, was set on fire. The media coverage, and in particular, the image of the blazing tram, led to the squatters' losing public support in Amsterdam.

The internal debate that followed from the riot calcified existing tensions in the squatters' movement. The 'politicos,' who were associated with the Staatsliedenbuurt neighbourhood, had for years advocated more radical and violent confrontations with the state. This group had also organised the most successful squatting actions and choreographed violence during evictions. Such tactics often led to material concessions from the state in the form of legalised squatted houses and social housing. The views and actions of the politicos—also called *kraakbonzen* (squatter bosses) by their critics—contrasted sharply with those of nonviolent squatters. They also differed widely from the views of people who squatted for the cultural opportunities enabled by the practice and the movement. The latter two often critiqued the politicos as authoritarian and for undermining the consensus-based decision-making within the movement (often established in the Stedelijk Overleg van Kraken (SOK, citywide squatters' consultation meeting). Meanwhile, the politicos considered squatters who failed to attend squatting actions and evictions, particularly artists who only wanted free space but lacked interest in the political activity that enabled the spaces to exist, as parasites.

Despite the sizable resentment of the kraakbonzen, those who opposed the politicos lacked their strategic acuity and skills. For example, deciding to eschew the authority of the politicos who dominated the kraakspreekuur (squatting information hour), one group squatted a building on the Prins Hendrikskade. When a vast police force arrived to evict the house, no squatters responded to the Prins Hendrikskade squatters' alarm. The police actions were broadcast live on the radio and on television. With the media spectacle, the politicos became involved. They succeeded in organizing a riot by mobilizing hundreds of squatters to fight the police, a deed that the anti-authoritarian squatters who resided in the house had failed to accomplish.

The burning of the tram and the condemnation of the Lucky Luyk riot as a failure by the majority of the activists shifted the movement's consensus regarding the use of violence to favour pragmatic negotiation with the state instead of confrontation. The politicos retreated to the Staatsliedenbuurt neighbourhood and fortified it into a fortress of the squatters' movement, featuring over five hundred squatted spaces. The police did not enter the neighbourhood and the politicos developed strong relationships with the renters. Furthermore, the politicos held strict standards for acceptable behaviour of the squatters in this neighbourhood, to the extent in which they evicted those who they considered problematic.

When Mayor Van Thijn announced his visit to the Staatsliedenbuurt in 1984, the politicos lobbied against his visit with the help of non-squatter neighbours. This culminated in a people's tribunal, composed of squatters and neighbourhood organisations. They proceeded to try and convict the mayor, in his absence, for his crimes against the city. The squatters demanded that the mayor apologize or they would refuse him entrance. The neighbourhood groups disagreed with the squatters' conditions for the mayor's visit and insisted on their rights to consult with the mayor if they wished. Despite the neighbourhood organisations' disagreement, the squatters blockaded the mayor's visit, which escalated into a riot.

Meanwhile, internal tension had calcified into internal strife. Isolated from the rest of the squatters' subculture, the politicos in the Staatsliedenbuurt became more militant and extended their gaze beyond empty houses, knokploegen, and police officers, onto other squatters. During a number of violent evictions, a few arrested squatters had identified other squatters. Informing on other activists is a taboo act, since this impinges on the mutual trust between activists involved in illegal actions. Instead, it is customary for activists in custody to remain silent for three days until their release (an expectation that continues today). To condemn this behaviour, the politicos formed a research organisation to find the 'traitors'—that is, those arrested who identified other participants—and then published posters with their names, photos, and addresses.

The politicos' methods became more draconian, to the point that they chased 'suspected traitors' through the streets of Amsterdam with cars and searchlights. The politicos' tactics proved intolerable for a number of squatters. They decided to eject one of the main politicos from the movement, Theo van der Giessen, by mobbing his house and beating him to the point of needing hospitalisation. After this attack, the rest of the politicos retreated, leading to the squatters' group in the Staatsliedenbuurt falling apart.

The historical surveys of the squatters' movement traditionally conclude with the defeat of the politicos and the ending of the movement due to overwhelming internal conflict. However, while the literature claims that the movement had died, it empirically continued. Again, this calls into question the stark contrast between the reality of the movement and its social science representations which tend to be removed from that reality, and more intent on

Following page spread: Police evicting a number of squats in Amsterdam, March 2006. Photo: Unknown. https://www.indymedia.nl/img/2006/03/35038.jpg

telling a story that narrates the movement's decline than one that views it as an entity that continues to live and change with the years.

While the movement did not end, a number of consequential changes in the social, legal, economic, and political context did occur which resulted in smaller numbers of participants in the movement. First, a number of laws changed the legal landscape for squatters.[7] In 1987, the Leegstandswet (empty property law) allowed the temporary renting of houses that were scheduled to be either renovated or demolished, whereas in the past, all rental contracts had been permanent. A second law changed juridical procedures that enabled owners to sue squatters anonymously, whereas previously, the owner had to possess the name of at least one inhabitant to evict. Before the law, squatters could potentially remain in a house indefinitely, as long as the owner lacked the legal name of the inhabitants.

Moreover, in 1993, article 429 went into effect, declaring that only houses that were factually empty for at least a year could be squatted, further reducing the number of spaces available. As a result, squatters had to provide documentation to the police that a squatted space had been empty for at least a year.

In addition, the availability and quality of potentially squattable spaces had reduced considerably. In the 1970s and 1980s, most squatted buildings were massive warehouses located in the city centre. These houses had been legalised into social housing and simply were no longer available to squat. Much of the abandoned properties that had dominated the urban landscape during these two decades had been renovated and rented or sold. Furthermore, 'anti-squatting' was introduced in the 1990s. Anti-squatting is an arrangement in which an agency contracts people to 'guard' a space. It serves as a temporary rental agreement without Dutch tenancy rights. The anti-squat system takes care of the housing needs of young, single, people, often students: the constituents whom the squatters' movement had previously attracted en masse.

Moreover, the social system that had supported a squatters' lifestyle radically changed. The squatters of the 1970s and 1980s had lived in a social welfare regime where the only preconditions to receive an unemployment allowance were to be the minimum sixteen years old and the ability to articulate one's incapacity to work. At the end of the 1980s, these preconditions became stricter, determining that one had to be twenty-three or older to qualify for public assistance and that the state could force someone to take a job in lieu of unemployment benefits. Moreover, the system of university scholarships had also changed, limiting the number of years one could study and receive a living allowance. Lastly, during the 1970s and 1980s, one could fulfil study credits through activism, while in the 1990s, working as an activist was seen as a diversion rather than as part of one's education.

OPPOSITIONAL PRACTICES IN THE CONTEMPORARY SQUATTERS' MOVEMENT

The main oppositional practices of the contemporary squatters' movement, which continue to constitute its self-definition, were established in the late 1970s and 1980s. Much of the movement's oppositional activities are directed towards owners of squatted houses and the state, while the daily practices of the movement revolve around the maintenance of solidarity networks and economies. Such solidarity networks ensure enough participants to secure the effectiveness of oppositional activities.

These oppositional practices are: (1) the squatting of houses and support of squatted houses through occupations, organised confrontations, and alarms to prevent the appropriation of the space by owners, their hired mercenaries, or the police; (2) strategic manipulation, which I define as the legal and political defence of a squatted house to circumvent eviction, including campaigning; and (3) the physical defence of a squatted house during an eviction. I will discuss these three practices in chronological order, before formulating a tactical critique.

The descriptions of practices that follow are from my three and a half years of fieldwork, in which I attended squatting actions nearly every week, participated in solidarity networks and actions, and worked in two campaigns for the defence of squats where I resided. I have experienced the evictions of houses where I lived and witnessed the evictions of my fellow squatters.

THE SQUATTING OF HOUSES AND THE SQUATTERS' CONFRONTATIONAL SUPPORT NETWORK

The first step to squatting a house is to thoroughly research an empty space as to its history and legal/bureaucratic status. To research a space includes searching for information on the internet, calling municipal agencies to collect information about a site, and approaching the space's neighbours and asking them deceptively about the space without revealing the intention to squat it. One should also observe a house to ensure that it's uninhabited. This means that the squatters have to diligently keep track of a certain location to ensure that it is empty for at least a few months, if not a year, using a number of tactics to determine if a space is in use.

Once the kraakspreekuur that the squatter has consulted with has determined that the house has been empty for a year or longer, then the squatter has to organise the squatting action itself. S/he should assemble a 'squatting kit,' consisting of a table, a chair, and a bed to establish occupancy. Usually, these items are found by searching throughout the city's bulk trash at night. Furthermore, s/he must collect barricading material from other squats or warehouses and construction sites. Also, an attorney should be arranged for the action. This demands obtaining recommendations from other squatters for which attorney to use and then assertively communicating with this attorney to retain his or her services. The squatter should compose a letter to the neighbours, which requires finding a model for a neighbourhood letter and help from someone who can write in

Dutch to translate the letter if necessary. Lastly, the squatters should publicise the action to ensure a large enough group—at least thirty people—to enable its occurrence. To achieve such a level of mobilisation, squatters create tiny flyers and distribute them throughout a number of squats and social centres since squatting actions can not be publicised over the internet due to fear of police surveillance. All of these elements have to be in place before the actual squatting of the house.

The squatting of a house begins with the group meeting at the assembly point. Once enough people have arrived, someone briefs the group about the location of the house, its history, and the plan of the action. During the squatting action, everything comes together: the door has to be broken open quickly before the police are called by the neighbours, the squatting kit of the table, bed, and chair are placed quietly in each floor (for houses of more than one floor), enough people should be inside the squatted space before the police arrive, the door must be barricaded strongly enough to keep out the police, hired thugs, or others who may want to evict, and enough people should stand outside the space to block the door to convince the police that they will violently resist if the police attempt to evict.

Meanwhile, a member of the kraakspreekuur negotiates with the police as the official spokesperson for the action. Assuming that the squatters successfully retain the house without eviction, everyone who participated celebrates. They drink beer together or, more elaborately, a meal is provided by those who squatted the house. After everyone has left, ideally, the newly squatted house should be continually occupied in case of attempts to evict by the police or the owner during the first few weeks after the action.

At one squatting action I attended, all the elements proceeded as planned. However, the spokesperson of the kraakspreekuur (who may have been drunk at the time) told the police that the house had stood empty for less than a year. The police then decided to evict. At the time, I stood outside with the group guarding the outside door of the house, but found myself moved with the entire outside group to crowd around the newly squatted flat and line the staircase inside the house to scare the police from evicting. Instead, the police called for backup, who—finding no squatters outside the building guarding the door—then surrounded the building and gained control of the entrances and exits. The kraakspreekuur then negotiated intensively with the police. The squatters decided to leave the house because the police could have easily tear gassed the inner staircase, arrested everyone, and evicted the flat. They also retreated because the squatters for that house included a family with a small child who the kraakspreekuur wanted to protect from the possible violence.

Immediately after the retreat, the squatters in the action met to discuss why it had failed. The spokesperson was conspicuously absent at this meeting. After a long discussion, the most experienced squatters present, who also spoke the most, decided that the combination of the lack of a barricading of the

Left: An eviction in March 2006. Photo: Unknown. https://www.indymedia.nl/img/2006/03/35037.jpg

outside building door, that the outside group had entered the building, and the spokesperson's error led to the failure. Except for one experienced female squatter, Dana, who criticised the spokesperson, the rest of the group of experienced squatters speaking in the meeting emphasized other missing elements over the spokesperson's error. For the next couple of days, I heard different members of the squatters' community discuss the action in which they criticised the tactical mistakes of the kraakspreekuur during the action, disparaged the squatters of the action for having bad luck and their disorganisation, and derided the spokesperson as an irresponsible drunk.

Another example of a failure was a house squatted by two immigrants with the kraakspreekuur. Although the action itself proceeded without incident, the two immigrants failed to continuously occupy during the first week. During a time when neither was home, the owner reclaimed the squat with police help. After this occurred, I ran into Dana, who confided to me, 'I feel sick about it. I can't even sleep knowing that they just left the house like that. They didn't have electricity for one night, so they slept somewhere else and now the house is lost.' Both of these examples show the tremendous effort and consciousness to detail required to successfully squat a house and how missing a few details can lead an action to failure. Moreover, these tiny details are crucial to the daily existence of a movement that is constantly under threat, yet none of the literature focuses on such dynamics. None of the print media of these actions feature the details that I have presented above, again, calling into question accounts of this movement based entirely on written sources.

In order for squatters to support each other during attempts to evict by the police, the owner, or a knokploeg, a phone tree is in place called 'the alarm.' The alarm is divided first by neighbourhood, because quickly mobilizing is easier on a neighbourhood than on a citywide level. A citywide alarm is only called during emergencies and is not particularly effective for quick mobilisation. A pre-alarm means that squatters are notified before a situation of potential violence erupts, so that they are prepared to go to a house in case an alarm is called.

Organised confrontations are situations in which squatters assemble a group of people to confront and intimidate their opponents. These can range from the construction workers employed by the owners to municipal civil servants who attempt to fine squatters for building safety regulations while they ignore the multiple violations that abound throughout the city. Social occasions often follow such confrontations.

STRATEGIC MANIPULATION

Strategic manipulation encompasses a number of activities intended to manoeuvre legal and administrative procedures to enable squatters to retain their houses for as long as possible. In the squatters' movement, to be strategic is to plan actions with an eye toward manipulating political and legal processes. Legally, such strategic manipulation is demonstrated, for example, when a squatter proves in the eviction case that the owner intends to leave the property empty rather than use it after the eviction as the owner claims. An example of administrative manipulation is when squatters arrange to have an owner's request for a building permit delayed, which would then prevent him or her from evicting squatters based on receiving such a permit.

Campaigning is strategic manipulation at a more intensified level in which squatters publicise a house in local political bodies, the press, and the neighbourhood by constructing it as a symbolic object of urban policy measures which lead to gentrification and the displacement of low-income people from Amsterdam. To campaign successfully requires having knowledge about the housing, legal, and administrative procedures that squatters use to their benefit. One should understand the court system, the rights of owners, and analyse larger housing policies and trends in Amsterdam. It requires an understanding that these processes are not fixed but flexible and that they can be influenced with enough public and private pressure, whether it is administrative, legal, or political lobbying. Campaigning tactics have been well within the repertoire of squatter activities for the past forty years. Many campaigns publicise the involvement of the mafia in real estate and the use of real estate to launder money, and construct narratives that play on populist sensibilities that hate real estate speculation. Such strategies have proved relatively successful for those who campaign for either the legalisation of their squat or the offer of legalised housing.

When the owner of the first house I lived in attempted to evict us, we embarked on an aggressive campaign to discredit him and pressure the neighbourhood council to politically and administratively block his efforts to evict. This campaign successfully delayed our eviction for a year. We 'created the following reality': that our owner served as a more legitimate front man for the former owner, who laundered money through real estate for the mafia. In order to 'create this reality,' we made a website for the house and posted a story on Indymedia (the news media website of the radical left in the Netherlands), alternative news networks, and internet squatter forums publicizing the history of the house in which we strongly hinted that the owner laundered money. We spread flyers throughout the neighbourhood publicizing this story. We lobbied the members of the housing committee, sent press packets to the neighbourhood council members, and organised actions at the neighbourhood council itself, in which a representative of the squatters' group declared the owner a mafia figure from whom the neighbourhood council should withdraw support. We cooperated with the renter in the house, an elderly woman who had resided in that house for over forty years, publicised her support of the squatters, and helped her speak at the neighbourhood council.

For the campaign, we courted the support of this elderly renter because we saw her as eliciting more sympathy from the public. As a working-class and elderly Amsterdammer, she seemed more authentic and vulnerable compared to ourselves, the squatters, who we believed appeared to the mainstream as self-serving in our manipulations to stay in the house. These tactics intended to interject the house into the news because once the house developed significance in the political and administrative consciousness, we could then exert pressure on the neighbourhood council to act more carefully, and thus, postpone the eventual eviction. 'For squatters, delaying is winning,' comments Jantine, a squatter with campaign experience.

After a year of campaigning, we received notice that the police planned to evict us in the next eviction wave. Eviction waves occur when the city contracts the riot police to evict all squatted houses with eviction notices on the same day to avoid the costliness of evicting on a more frequent basis. Because normal police are unprepared to handle the resistance expected from squatters, riot police must evict them. The eviction waves occur approximately three times a year.

In the last few days before the eviction, we tried numerous tactics to pressure the neighbourhood council and the mayor's office to cancel our eviction, including meeting with the chairperson of the neighbourhood council in the home of our elderly neighbour. We impressed upon the chairman that the squatters served as the only force to protect the neighbour from the bullying new owner who wanted to pressure her to leave her flat so that he could renovate and sell her apartment. We then organised an action on the city council in Amsterdam in which we occupied the main hall with hundreds of squatters and police sirens, surrounded by press, and demanded an audience with the mayor. Despite the squatters interrogating the mayor and the elderly neighbour pleading with the mayor for protection from the speculating house owner, he decided to evict our group of five squatters the next morning, with twenty trucks of police officers, a water cannon, and a remote flying robotic device that cost Dutch taxpayers several thousand euros. Meanwhile, our group of five stood outside the house and watched the police evict 'us.'

The vast majority of squatters do not defend their houses legally or politically. Instead, when they receive pressure from the owner or the state to vacate their squats, the majority leave their homes or make a deal. In the next section, I describe how squatters who will be evicted after having lost their eviction court case engage in a defence. Again, the number of squatters who practice such an eviction defence is miniscule due to such activities being arguably more symbolic rather than practical.

EVICTIONS

By the time squatters have received notice that they will be evicted, they can employ a delicate balancing act of strategic tactics to delay the actual eviction until the eviction wave. Again, just like with campaigning, the vast majority of squatters leave their houses after losing an eviction case. There are a small number of people who actually use the tactics that I describe below and 'defend their house to the end.'

Right: Resistance to eviction by squatters in Leidsestraat, Amsterdam, October 2006. Photo: Karen Eliot. http://www.flickr.com/photos/kareneliot/269663952/

The first action in this balancing act is to visibly barricade the squat to prevent the owner, the bailiff, and the police from entering the space and to maintain a perception that the squatters will act violently if anyone attempts to evict. As a result, a range exists between barricading that factually prevents entrance and 'symbolic' barricading which communicates a message of resistance to the police and the owners. Thus, if the bailiff and the police have the impression that squatters are prepared to violently resist an eviction attempt, they place the house on the list of squats to be evicted during the eviction wave.

Beyond 'symbolic barricading' is enacting the ideal of 'defending a house until the end,' which is to barricade a house to factually prevent entrance, notify the squatting community to prepare themselves for 'pre-alarm' in case of an attempted eviction, and to maintain an occupation schedule to ensure that the squat is never empty. Hermance, a veteran squatter, believes that such barricades give the movement a tactical advantage, 'Barricading is important for the movement because it forces the police to work hard to take a house back.'

Thus, instrumentally, resistance by squatters through barricading and violence during evictions serve a purpose for the movement. If regular police and bailiffs can evict squatters easily, then the city will stop conducting eviction waves. The eviction waves serve squatters because with sufficient calculation, squatters can reside in a house for at least three to four months; that is, if one squats a house immediately after an eviction wave, one can expect to remain until the next wave four months later.

Resistance during eviction waves is the most publicised and mediagenic form of conflict between squatters and their opponents. Squatters refer to this resistance as 'a show,' openly treating these events as performative rituals to communicate opposition with the police, the state, and the imagined mainstream. Furthermore, squatters are aware that resisting evictions will not result in their keeping their house. The 'riot' between squatters and police is highly institutionalised having occurred frequently during the past forty years of the movement. As a result, the primary performers comprise the squatters and the police, and the audience consists of members of the activist community, random observers, neighbourhood residents, and the press, who have expectations for the types of performances that they seek.

The following is a description of 'typical' resistance during a wave. First, the squatters stand either on the roof or inside the squatted house, wearing black clothes and masks. The mainstream expectation is that they throw Molotov cocktails or stones at the police although usually squatters use paint bombs. Before the riot police vans arrive, the area fills with undercover police officers who dress like football hooligans and photograph people in the area. Eventually, the riot police arrive with fifteen vans, including a truck with a water cannon to spray water on the squatters with high pressure to subdue them. The riot police wear shields, helmets, and wield batons. They clear the area, block a wide circle around the squat, and violently charge anyone standing in front of the house who attempts passive resistance. The police trucks surround the house and order the squatters to leave the house with a loudspeaker three times. Then the riot police leave the trucks and walk towards the house on foot, covering themselves with their shields to protect themselves from projectile objects. They spend an inordinate amount of time and effort breaking through barricading to enter the building. Once they enter the building, they ascertain if squatters remain inside hiding or have locked their bodies structurally into the house, called a 'lock-on,' which then requires more time and excessive physical force from the police to extract the squatters. Eventually, the police announce that they have cleared the building of squatters and return it to the owner.

If anyone who was sitting inside a squatted house is in jail, activist squatters organise noise demonstrations at the jail where the squatters are held. These demonstrations consist of a large group of people making noise at the jail and confronting police in a bullfight fashion at the jail itself. Eviction waves and noise demos are frequently featured in the Dutch press. In fact, journalists often embed themselves with squatters in houses or arrange beforehand interviews with squatters as well as trying to capture violent resistance on film if possible.

TACTICAL CRITIQUE

The tradition of violent resistance and riots between squatters and the police is a crucial part of the practices and self-definition of the contemporary movement. However, the participants' focus on violent resistance and confrontation as the main oppositional practices fails to grasp and address the movement's contemporary challenges. The most potent forces that threaten the squatters' movement in Amsterdam are not thugs hired by owners or police evictions. Rather, the movement is threatened overwhelmingly by: (1) anti-squatting; (2) a political climate that has turned against squatting, which results in the courts being more likely to evict than in the past, and in general, to sympathize with owners rather than squatters; (3) the wide-scale conversion of social housing into privately owned real estate, limiting the possibilities of legalizing squats into social housing due to the scarcity of spaces. This challenge results from a political and cultural shift which values housing as a market commodity rather than as a social good. Finally, (4) the prevalent xenophobia in Dutch public discourse impacts the movement since contemporary squatters are widely viewed as 'foreigners' who exploit a Dutch protest tactic and who lack the political ideals of squatters 'during the movement's height in the 1980s.'

To elaborate this point, the Dutch squatters' movement was composed of a mix of internationals and Dutch people since its inception. Hence, the xenophobic backlash against the movement does not result from new influx of internationals into the movement. Instead, this xenophobia is a continuation of

Following page spread: Protest against the eviction of a squat in the Steve Bikoplein in Amsterdam. Photo: Hans Bouton. http://hansfoto.wordpress.com/

racist discourse that abounds in Dutch public life that targets squatters with as much virulence as it strikes first- and second-generation immigrants who are held in contempt by the mainstream Dutch press.

With the exception of one or two squatter campaigns, most of the forms of action that define the movement have developed in a completely different sociopolitical context and have not evolved to address the threats and challenges to the movement today. However, the squatter campaigns that have evolved beyond the movement's action repertoire have successfully challenged some state practices. For example, the separation of arrested activists into Europeans and non-Europeans by placing non-Europeans in foreign detention—where they can remain indefinitely—with the eventual plan to deport them. This contrasts with a normal Dutch jail procedure, in which those who refuse to identify themselves can be detained for a maximum of three days. A number of squatters who have been arrested have refused to state their nationalities and have been placed in foreign detention. This practice of placing activists in foreign detention has been successfully challenged in court so that such discrimination can no longer occur without serious consideration on the part of the police.

INTERNAL DEBATES

This section is based on my anthropological research and, again, emphasises practices and informal discourses as more relevant for understanding internal debates than formal written and oral discourses. Before describing internal debates within the squatters' movement, it is useful to consider if it is one unified movement or an umbrella for several different movements with a wide variety of cultural and political intentions. Social movements scholar Francesco Alberoni argues that in all social movements, 'centrifugal forces,' of 'right' and 'left' wings exist.[8] He classifies these positions according to participants' orientations towards what they define as mainstream society. The right wing of a movement consists of people who primarily seek reform, while the left wing comprises those who want to break with and possibly destroy larger society.

Within the squatters' movement, how groups classify each other ideologically conforms to Alberoni's framework. A blunt oversimplification of the basic debate posits reformist housing activists who negotiate with state authorities versus radical anarchists who principally refuse to acknowledge the state's authority and promote the use of violence to combat the state and capitalism. Radical anarchists oppose discussion, participation, and negotiation with the state due to its inherent corruption. Thus, they discount housing activists as social democratic reformists who merely allow themselves to be co-opted into an inherently problematic and coercive capitalism. Housing activists, on the other hand, consider radical anarchists to be mainly concerned with performing symbolic acts of violence. They accuse radical anarchist squatters of being isolated in a style- and consumption-dominated subculture, unable to communicate with the rest of society, and ultimately only serving to promote symbolic issues rather than rectifying social injustices.

However, my analysis goes beyond the discourse of participants in the movement, based on observed internal dynamics and movement practices rather than polemics. I classify the internal groups of the movement based on a more complicated matrix of style, ideological commitment, and expression of political conviction. I highlight the importance of style—consisting of lifestyles and taste cultures—because it is often affiliated with and expresses particular ideologies.

Moreover, groups distinguish themselves by creating their identities in relation to other groups of squatters. Thus, the data for this section derives from how squatters informally classify each other rather than from debates and articles on websites such as Indymedia, which only reflect the points of view of those who comfortably express themselves in writing. While interviews are often biased and self-justifying, the combination of interviews and participation observation provides a more reliable source because of my accumulated knowledge of this community's functions and values.

CENTRIFUGAL FORCES

Other than a common act of public takeovers with a network of people and houses that support each other, there is a tremendous diversity of reasons and motivations for why people choose to squat. At one extreme, such motivations are embedded in radical politics, specifically in the desire to create 'free' spaces and lifestyles that are outside what is perceived as an authoritarian, hierarchical, and alienating mainstream. On the other, there are those who merely seek to reside in a house without paying rent and have no interests in politics whatsoever. With these extremes of motivations in mind, I will describe the range of groups according to the informal discourse of the movement, which I collected by living in squats and hanging out in squatted social centres, attending parties, and immersing myself in the cultural life of the movement. The groups are: wild squatters, crusty punks, baby punks, hippies, students, and campaigners/social democrats.

Wild squatters do not consult with a kraakspreekuur before squatting a house and locate themselves outside the solidarity network of the movement. Wild squatters stereotypically originate from Eastern or Southern Europe. They do not campaign or resist evictions, which in practical terms means that wild squatters occupy a space for as long as possible, but leave as soon as pressure arises. Despite not participating in the solidarity network, wild squatters often use the squatters' alarm list for emergencies. As a result, organised squatters debate if they should help wild squatters due to their lack of contributions.

Crusty punks exist in a separate category from wild squatters because they participate in the organised squatters' movement. Activist squatters use the word 'punks' to refer to an assertive posture and a clothing style, such as wearing

Following page spread: Squat action at the Eerste Oosterparkstraat in Amsterdam. Photo: Hans Bouton.

all black, ripped clothing, and sporting piercings and tattoos. 'Squatters with dogs' is another synonym for crusty punks.

To be crusty refers to being dirty on a bodily level by showering infrequently, laundering rarely, and residing in filthy spaces. The term summarises a whole set of assumptions. 'Crust,' 'crusty,' and sometimes 'punk' are codes to classify a lazy, disorganised, unreliable, and irresponsible person who is defined by a lack of care. A crust may be addicted to drugs, alcohol, or both. The stereotypical crusty punk spends the day drinking, partying all night, and intermittently earning a salary through wage labour. Crusty punks often feed themselves by dumpster diving. They eat and drink cheaply in social centres because crusty punks can often avoid paying for meals in such spaces.

Despite the lack of responsibility and accountability of crusty punks, many can organise themselves to squat houses with a kraakspreekuur. As noted earlier, squatting with the kraakspreekuur signifies that one complies with the multiple requirements to gather sufficient information before squatting a house. Although crusty punks generally lack interest in campaigning or research, many possess formidable building skills, invest in the movement by creating social spaces (especially bars), and demonstrate their solidarity with other squatters through mutual aid and sharing resources.

Crusty punks who see themselves as activists are known for their willingness to participate in potentially violent actions, their enthusiasm for rioting, and the pleasure that they experience in fighting the police. The skill to riot is highly valued in the movement. However, for people who organise violent actions, relying on the participation of crusty punks in an action proves challenging due to their lack of dependability.

Baby punks, some of whom are also crusts, differ from crusty punks. Baby punks are defined by a combination of their lifestyle and their identities as political activists while crusty punks are mainly known for their behaviour. While a crusty punk may be identified as crusty out of laziness—for example, by failing to connect the water pipes and build a shower due to a lack of interest—a baby punk may claim to be crusty out of political conviction by stating that its unhealthy to shower frequently and harmful for the environment to waste water.

Baby punks refer to people who are young, either adolescent or barely adolescent, and chose to become squatter punks. They enthusiastically learn and inhabit the tropes of the squatter world, and then reify this identity confrontationally by verbally criticizing those who do not share consumption decisions that symbolise political convictions (vegetarianism, veganism, animal rights).

A baby punk's life is entirely in the movement. It consists of anti-fascist and other political actions, noise demonstrations, getting arrested, sitting in jail, evictions, the labour- and time-intensive process of squatting a house and making it habitable, parties, *vokus* (*volkskeuken*, that is, people's kitchens—restaurants run by volunteers and funded by donations), information evenings, giveaway shops, day cafés, and generally participating in the social infrastructure of the movement. Lastly, like crusty punks, baby punks are well-known for their enthusiasm for potentially violent actions.

Hippie activists and student squatters are openly transient participants in the squatters' and activists' social world. The stereotype of hippies is that they tend to originate from outside the Netherlands, dutifully attend political and squatting actions, have a hippie fashion style (colourful and loose-fitting clothing, Indian fabrics), are radical environmentalists, may work to support refugees, and promote vegetarianism and veganism. Such people may work at small NGOs based in Amsterdam that offer low-paid or volunteer jobs in which the staff often live in squats and integrate into the radical left social scene of activists and squatters.

Although the social world of radical left activists and squatters seem to comprise 'the scene,' a division exists. The activist scene is more international in addition to the core of Dutch people. It is transient with a constant flow of people coming and going. Although hippies form part of the squatters' movement because they often squat for housing, they identify primarily as part of the international, leftist, anti-globalisation network. They organise benefit parties for various autonomous groups in the Global South in squatted social centres, attend parties, work in social centres, and regularly populate vokus. The Dutch squatters' scene (versus the Polish and Spanish) is comparatively more stable. Dutch squatters (including non-Dutch people) share years of history through the intense cycles of squatting a house, living together, creating communities, campaigning, and getting evicted.

Traveling is a constitutive aspect of being classified as a hippie. They often travel to attend action camps, or to riot in immense anti-globalisation summits, and to visit places in the Global South, such as the squatted, organised areas of post-economic crisis Argentina and Oaxaca, Mexico, which the European radical left laud as autonomous. Latin America, with its history of leftist popular movements, attracts hippie activists. In a course of one year, a hippie activist may spend three to six months in Amsterdam and travel around the world during the rest of the time. Furthermore, the gentler and kinder demeanour of hippies distinguishes them from punks. They are almost entirely women, tend to act more physically affectionate, and strive to treat others more inclusively.

Student squatters belong to the second category of openly transient members of the movement. A separate student kraakspreekuur serves the university population. Squatters are classified as students due to their style and habitus more than the actual fact of studying, since many punks also study in the Dutch higher education system. The stereotype of student squatters are that they are directed, ambitious, and, by default, only temporarily part of the movement, since by studying they will move on to another phase of professional life. Despite the fact that most squatters' involvement in the movement is short-lived, student squatters are characterised by the transparency in which they and others understand that they will be squatters for a short time of their lives and then move on to middle-class professions, with secure housing.

Student squatters who work as movement activists are valued members of the movement versus those who squat to solve their housing problem without contributing. In comparison to baby punks, student squatter activists do not need to perform their conviction because the mere fact of participating in the movement attests to their commitment, since the majority of students in the city choose to anti-squat.

Campaigners are the last group, also known disparagingly as 'the social democrats' because of their willingness to engage with political parties. This community has a reputation for conducting campaigns by engaging in local housing politics, lobbying politicians, maintaining relationships with the press, and for having a less punk style than other squatter groups. They are also well organised and have a tight solidarity network in their neighbourhood.

CRITICAL VIEW OF INTERNAL IDENTITIES AND POLITICAL NORMS

This overview demonstrates the distinctions between groups based on a matrix of ideology, style, habitus, and performance of political conviction. Furthermore, group identities are often created in relation to each other. However, beyond internal differences, the main point of identity making occurs between a general squatter identity versus the imagined mainstream, which is constructed as the external Other. This external Other in informal squatter discourse is further distinguished into a number of stereotypical groups: yuppies, neighbours, anti-squatters, and immigrants. How squatters classify and imagine these groups is contradictory, tense, and related to the larger political, social, and legal context in which squatters exist.

For example, during my fieldwork, to sign an anti-squat contract was an absolute taboo among politically minded activist squatters. My interviews and informal, private conversations revealed, however, that this practice was common. The squatters who had signed such contracts kept it secret from the community as a means to preserve their reputations. The contempt of squatters for anti-squatters is on one hand practical: anti-squatting undermines squatting. It is also ideological in the hatred of middle-class lifestyle and consumption choices: squatters imagine anti-squatters as white, Dutch, middle-class university students who embody the conformity that they reject. Yet, with the increasingly draconian political and legal climate turning against squatters as well as the squatting ban being passed into law, an anti-squat contract has become less taboo. Hence, the practice of signing an anti-squat contract has slowly become more accepted as other means of retaining squatted houses have diminished. This example reveals how the larger context in which squatters operate impacts ideological norms, political practices, and group identity within the movement.

CONCLUSION

The Dutch squatters' movement has been monumentalised in the landscape of Amsterdam. The movement saved the exquisitely beautiful inner city from being bulldozed in the 1970s. Legalised squatted buildings are also spread throughout the city as both housing and cultural institutions that enable the movement's collective memory to live on. However, the collective remembrance and ensuing nostalgia has had a paradoxical effect on internal dynamics in the movement and how activists imagine themselves and their participation.

Due to the critical inquires opened by post-colonial theory and subaltern studies, anthropologists have viewed historical texts that present a straightforward narrative with suspicion. Anthropologists focus on detailing and analysing informal and unwritten daily practices. Hence, we understand the limits of narratives that are based entirely on written sources since they present partial perspectives of those privileged enough to feel comfortable textually representing themselves. The field of social movement studies, exemplified by the literature on the Dutch squatters' movements, has been particularly noteworthy for its uncritical uses of grand narratives and lack of analysis of internal dynamics of movement subcultures.

A teleological narrative, with its artificial emphasis on creating a beginning, a middle, and an end, is inappropriate for understanding the Dutch squatters' movement. This is especially the case because the discourse of decline has been ever-present since its inception. If one views the collection of squatter-made documentaries, one sees that the movement's end has been declared on countless occasions. In the late 1970s, the mid-1970s was authentic. In 1980, 1978 was the height of the movement. In 1981, the movement was at its peak in 1980, and so on and so forth until the contemporary nostalgia about 'squatting in the '80s.' Yet, the movement lives on despite the repeated announcement of its decline.

To understand the movement's persistence more fully, it is more useful to view it as an amalgamation of an anachronistic and myopic European youth subculture, housing activism, and a trajectory of individual self-realisation in a high-pressured urban space. With these elements in mind, one sees that the pronouncement of the movement's death more aptly describes the end of participation in the biographies of those who make such declarations. To view the movement in such a way, then the circularity of actions that fail to address contemporary challenges, the repetition of political slogans that have not changed for nearly forty years, and the movement's persistent whiteness and lack of diversity despite being located in a highly multicultural city can be better understood.

The recent emergence of the Occupy movements and the public squatting of empty properties by people who are left homeless due to the massive foreclosures resulting from the financial crisis demonstrate a need for the types of skills and resources offered by the Dutch squatters' movement with its forty years of expertise. Can the movement move past the heavy nostalgia and the weight of the 1980s to address contemporary, diffuse, and less confrontational challenges? Can the movement tackle prevalent xenophobia in Dutch public life that attacks it discursively and legally? Is the movement fated to continue as an isolated subculture of radical left European youth or will it evolve to engage with the challenges of multicultural urban life and potential post-crisis squatters who may not ascribe to a specific set of radical left taste cultures?

FURTHER READING

There is a sizable literature on the history of the Amsterdam squatters' movement, both in Dutch and in English. For the history of the movement in English, I recommend Lynn Owens's *Cracking under Pressure: Narrating the Decline of the Amsterdam Squatters' Movement* (Amsterdam: Amsterdam University Press, 2009). Owens studies the decline of the Amsterdam squatters' movement to contribute to social movement studies, which has been dominated by resource mobilisation and political process approaches that focus on how social movements originate. Rather than a broad sociological analysis, Owens focuses on analysing the emotions expressed in narratives of squatters in reaction to a number of high-profile events that he argues are crucial to the development and the eventual decline of the movement.

Owens's primary sources were the Staatsarchief, the squatters' movement archive, which is housed in the International Institute of Social History in Amsterdam and comprises over seventy-five meters of material, including films, posters, and sound documents. In addition, Owens based his study on the full transcripts of interviews conducted with twenty-eight squatters active in the movement in the 1970s and 1980s. These interviews were recorded for the documentary *De stad was van ons* (dir. Joost Seelen 1996) which can be viewed with subtitles on YouTube.

If you read Dutch, I recommend examining the website of the Staatsarchief: http://www.iisg.nl/staatsarchief. Two other major historical texts are Virginie Mamadouh's *De stad in eigen hand. Provo's, kabouters en krakers als stedelijke sociale beweging* (Amsterdam: Sua, 1992) (The City in Our Hands), and *Een voet tussen de deur. Geschiedenis van de kraakbeweging (1964–1999)* (A Foot between the Door) (Amsterdam: Arbeiderspers, 2000) by Eric Duivenvoorden. The latter text can be downloaded in full from the Staatsarchief website.

Mamadouh is mainly concerned with utilizing the framework of 'urban social movements' established by Manuel Castells and testing its relevance to the development and characteristics of four social movements in Amsterdam: the Provos, Kabouters, the Nieuwmarkt campaign, and the squatters. Mamadouh argues that Castells's definition of urban social movements is overly Marxist in its dependence on class conflict. Mamadouh contends that the influence and impact of urban social movements is difficult to measure in terms of class conflict. Instead, these movements were directed towards creating and enacting a vision of the city that challenged the types of municipal policies and the social norms of urban lifestyles at the time.

Duivenvoorden's book, *Een voet tussen de deur*, is the most comprehensive and detailed of the three. Duivenvoorden relates a popular history, the result of meticulous archival research, intended for an audience of members of the educated Dutch left who possess considerable knowledge of major figures in Amsterdam politics and leftist social movements since the 1960s.

For scholarly analysis of the contemporary Dutch squatters' movement, it is best to read the work of sociologist Hans Pruijt. Pruijt, a former squatter, has an unromantic and sober view of squatting which can be refreshing in social movement studies, a field dominated by an uncritical fetishism of activists.

His articles include: 'The Impact of Citizens' Protest on City Planning in Amsterdam,' in *Cultural Heritage and the Future of the Historic Inner City of Amsterdam*, edited by Léon Deben et al. (Amsterdam: Amsterdam University Press, 2004): 228–44; 'Is the Institutionalization of Urban Movements Inevitable? A Comparison of the Opportunities for Sustained Squatting in New York City and Amsterdam,' *International Journal of Urban and Regional Research* 27 (2003): 133–57; and 'The Logic of Urban Squatting,' *International Journal of Urban and Regional Research* 37 (2012): 19–45. Some of these texts can be found on Pruijt's personal homepage: http://www.eur.nl/fsw/english/sociology/profiles/profiel_mis/10750/.

Two

THE RISE AND CRISIS OF THE ANARCHIST
AND LIBERTARIAN MOVEMENT IN GREECE, 1973–2012

Gregor Kritidis

INTRODUCTION

IN THE EARLY 1980S, Athens was confronted with a series of dramatic riots. On November 17, 1980, riots unfolded when a demonstration—marching from Athens Polytechnic to the U.S. embassy—passed the Greek parliament. During these riots, the student Iakovos Koumis and the worker Stamatina Kanellopoulou were killed by the police. Less then a year later, in 1981, a concert of the Irish blues-rock artist Rory Gallagher ended with riots. As this was the first performance of a well-known international star in Greece since a Rolling Stones concert in 1967, the concert attracted thirty-five thousand people. The authorities could not deal with crowds this large and the event got out of hand.

Thirty years later, the Greeks would return en masse to the streets, this time to ward off extremely drastic cuts under the pressure of the EU.

To understand these and other social and political conflicts in modern day Greece, and the role of the anarchist and anarchist-inspired movements within these conflicts, it is necessary to trace back the roots of this movement in the country's recent history.

ANARCHISM AND THE WORKERS' MOVEMENT UNTIL
THE END OF THE COLONELS' REGIME (1967–1973)

RADICALISM AND ANARCHISM IN THE EARLY WORKERS' MOVEMENT

The Greek workers' movement that emerged in the late nineteenth century was profoundly influenced by anarchism: it was organised in local and federal associations and was often militant. This was partly due to the position of labour in Greek politics. Until the 1970s, labour was never completely pacified or in-tegrated in the political system, resulting in continual violent confrontations.

Even so, in the wake of the Russian revolution, Marxism-Leninism became the most influential ideology on the left. The recently formed so-cialist party changed its name to the Kommunistiko Komma Ellados (KKE, Communist Party of Greece) and became the dominant political party on the left. For most anarchist and socialist activists, the turn to Leninism posed no big step. Impressed by the events in the East, it was evident to them that the Soviet Union set the example of how to make and win a revolution.

The KKE has often been criticised for its lack of party democracy and its aggressive and repressive attitudes towards other left currents in the workers' movement during this first period. Even so, a positive side to the party's emergence was the fact that it was the first political organisation that represented class interests instead of the clientelism characteristic of the earlier political parties.

In 1918, the Geniki Synomospondia ton Ergaton Ellados (GSEE, General Confederation of Workers of Greece) was founded. The strength and radicalism of some of its local and regional branches—like the workers-cen-tre in Athens, the iron miners on Serifos Island, and tobacco-workers in the north—prompted the state to intervene. Radical leaders were excluded, and by exceptional law a new right-wing leadership was installed which tried to curb and control the radicalism of its rank and file members in the 1920s. This re-sulted in a divide between a 'moderate,' state-controlled trade union leadership and a radical membership base.

In the following years, political struggles raged on within the GSEE. Conflicts took the form of political confrontations, so that no one could get a position or leadership function if he was not backed by a political organisation. In the end, the trade unions became dominated alternately by state authorities or political parties—a situation that has remained unchanged up to the present day. After 1974, PASKE (Panhellenic Socialist Workers Organisation), con-trolled by PASOK (Panellininiko Sosialistiko Kinima, or Panhellenic Socialist Movement) became predominant, while the KKE was the dominant factor on the left for a long time. While industrial sectors and construction remained under communist influence, and unions in the education field tended to euro-communist Synaspismos (the former KKE Interior), public sector unions were controlled by PASKE.

PRE-WAR COUNTER-CULTURE: REMBETIKO MUSIC

In the 1920s, the majority of the population consisted of peasants, artisans, and people working only half a year or less in industries. Even though a small section of all labouring men and women could be characterised as industrial workers, living exclusively from industrial labour, the communist party became

---

Previous page spread: Militant demonstrations in Athens in December 2008 following the death of a young protester. Photo: Murple Jane/Possibly Maybe. https://www.flickr.com/photos/murplejane/3098761766/

the dominant political force in the Greek workers' movement. The majority of the urban population was living in conditions that can be described as 'sub-proletarian': people lived off casual work, small day jobs, and the like.

This situation intensified after more than a million refugees migrated from Asia Minor to Greece in 1922 as a result of a lost war against the newly established Turkish state. In these circumstances, a politics focused exclusively on organised industrial workers was destined to fail.

In the following years, it was not so much the political *ideology* of Marxism and its different forms that came to unite the subaltern classes, but rather an authentic product of proletarian *culture*: rembetiko music. Rembetiko was a musical style created by proletarian and sub-proletarian artists living in Greek metropolises. For this reason, it has often been compared to blues. Its lyrics revolve around issues such as drug use, petty crime, sex, love, sorrow, violence, trouble with police, prosecution by authorities, and imprisonment. While rembetiko was in most cases not explicitly political, it did express the pursuit of freedom and a better life beyond the misery of sub-proletarian existence.

It is not surprising that the communist party looked upon this socio-cultural milieu with suspicion. For the communist KKE, the 'rembetes'—as the rembetiko artists and fans were called—were an incalculable factor that did not feel obliged to adhere to party discipline. The KKE revised its position during the 1940s, when rembetes actively took part in the resistance against the German occupation. But after the liberation, this position was again reversed. In the areas controlled by the communist party, all opposition that did not follow the party line was prosecuted and marginalised.

THE SECOND WORLD WAR

German occupation of 1941–1945 caused profound social and political transformations in Greece. While parts of the political and military elites had gone abroad, many business people collaborated with the occupiers. Communist activists soon grew to become the most important factor of resistance and within a few years, the KKE-led Ethniko Apeleftherotiko Metopo (EAM, National Liberation Front) was the dominant political and military power in the country, organising nearly half of the Greek population.

Unlike the Yugoslav partisans, the KKE leadership did not set out its own course, but strictly followed the orders coming from the Soviet Union. For this, the communist movement paid a heavy price. The Soviet Union had formed an alliance with Great Britain and the United States. Thus, the KKE aimed for cooperation with the British army. This even led to the KKE accepting British troops to land in Greece in autumn 1944, a decision that was backed by Stalin.

However, as conflicts broke out between the communist forces and right-wing groups that had collaborated with the Nazi-occupants, the British chose to side with the latter. In December 1944, the communist movement lost the battle of Athens. A long and brutal civil war followed, which lasted until 1949. In the end, the communists were defeated by a coalition of right-wing middle-class forces, backed by the British and, later—after proclamation of the Truman Doctrine in 1947—U.S. financial and military aid.

FROM 'STEERED DEMOCRACY' TO THE COLONELS' REGIME

In the following eighteen years, Greece functioned as a 'steered democracy,' while the communist party was officially forbidden. Even so, this did not lead to a distancing from communist party organisation within the workers' movement, or a turn back to anarchist ideas. Rather, the communist party remained dominant, as did the Leninist way of organizing even in non-Stalinist groups. Activists who left the communist party disagreed with parts of its political ideology and praxis as in the Hungarian crisis of 1956, but did not overcome it in general.

The 1950s were politically relatively quiet in Greece. But the post-war order was destabilised in the 1960s, when the left-liberal Enosi Kentrou (Centre Union, EK) became a relevant factor in Greek politics. Under the leadership of Georgios Papandreou, the party gained the backing of a mass movement. Even though EK was a middle-class party, it became the centre of political mobilisation, including for radical currents of the previously defeated left. The EK was elected to government in 1963, but after a conflict—instigated by secret service infiltrators—the party split and Papandreou was dismissed in 1965. Reacting to continuing political turmoil and social struggles, a group of army colonels, backed by the United States, staged a coup d'état in 1967. They remained in power until 1974.

During this period, the communist KKE split. Political differences between the party's leadership-in-exile situated in Bucharest, on the one hand, and activists in the Greek underground, on the other, caused a party split in 1968. Dissidents founded the KKE Interior that soon turned to eurocommunist ideas and renamed itself Synaspismos (coalition). For the first time since the 1930s, the position of the communist 'church' was contested by several dissident currents. In retrospect, this turned out to be not simply a temporary crisis of party communism, but a historical turning point. From this moment onwards, every subsequent generation of activists and social movements has shifted further away from party communism and Leninism. In search of new forms of fighting and organising, libertarian and anarchist ideas have come to the fore again.

THE REVOLT OF 1973 AND AFTER

THE 1973 STUDENT REVOLT

The military coup d'état of 1967 heralded seven years of dictatorship and repression. The regime was relatively stable, because although the junta never gained mass support within Greek society, the old left was not able to organise a strong resistance movement.

At the same time, the new and radical Western youth culture caused youths to shift to the left. Jimi Hendrix and the Doors were much more attractive than military marches. Screenings of the film *Woodstock* even turned into open demonstrations against the junta in cinemas of Athens.

The counter-cultural and radical ideas of late 1960s also travelled to Greece via students who studied abroad and brought their experiences from England, France, and Germany back to their home country. These experiences merged with situationist ideas from Paris and 'Guevarism.' The Argentinian/Cuban revolutionary, Ché Guevara, seemed to be the embodiment of a spontaneous, revolutionary people's struggle. It was youths influenced by these experiences and events that occupied the university in 1973.

The occupation of Athens Polytechnic and the business school in Athens in November 1973 marked the beginning of a new era, even though the action was defeated on November 17, when the military attacked the university campus with heavily armed forces and tanks. The action was a turning point, because it was the first time in Greece that public buildings were occupied and transformed into centres of social and political mass protest. Eventually, the action caused the end of the military dictatorship.

Athens Polytechnic became the epicentre of democratic self-organisation and had a nationwide impact. From here, activists distributed pamphlets, flyers and posters, and even started an independent radio station. The revolt had a lasting influence on Greek youth culture because it showed new forms of organisation and action, while at the same time revealing the powerlessness of the old left. In the past seven years, they had not been able to effectively undermine the dictatorship.

The occupation of the Polytechnic and of other universities was not organised by party-activists, but by a widespread coalition of other left-wing currents. This alliance ranged from Leninists of all types (Trotskyists, Maoists, etc.) to libertarian socialists. Together, they played a crucial role in organising mass-resistance against military dictatorship. But just as before the war, counter-culture played an important role uniting the activists from different political currents. This was illustrated by the release of a record of rembetiko songs in 1974 by the famous radical artist Giorgos Dalaras. It was the first time since the German occupation that these songs were distributed legally.

CRISIS OF THE NEW MOVEMENT AFTER 1973

The revolt against the junta had been carried out by small numbers of activists in combination with mass mobilisations. But after the fall of the dictatorship, the activists were not able to effectively obstruct the return to parliamentary democratic 'normality' and the new radical protest movement quickly disintegrated into a great number of smaller groups and organisations. In 1974, the conservative politician Konstantinos Karamanlis returned from France, where

Following page spread: Demonstration in Athens, December 2008. Photo: Murple Jane/Possibly Maybe. http://www.flickr.com/photos/murplejane/3089330615/

he had lived in exile. With the slogan 'Karamanlis or tanks' an effective campaign was set up to bring the old political powers back in charge and to restore the formally democratic institutions. Attempts by activists to question and de-legitimise these authorities and institutions were unsuccessful. The radical movement was isolated.

The isolation of the activists and their inability to effectively oppose the new authorities was above all illustrated by the murder of libertarian Alexandros Panagoulis in 1976. Panagoulis had been one of the most popular political activists of the era, known for his attempt to kill the leader of the Greek junta in 1968, after which he had been arrested and tortured. His burial was accompanied by a memorial march of several hundred thousand people. But it was a demonstration of mourning, instead of the beginning of a new wave of struggle.

THE RISE OF PASOK

Authoritarian political groups and parties resurfaced, but neither the Moscow-orientated KKE nor the dissident KKE Interior—which had split off from the KKE in 1968—could win the struggle for hegemony within the left. Instead, the newly founded Panhellenic Socialist Movement (PASOK) became the dominant political force on the left.

PASOK was a social democratic party that combined radical social rhetoric with elements of third world national liberation movements, and a modest policy of social reform. The different currents, some of which were far more radical, were held together and kept in check through a strong party hierarchy with Andreas Papandreou as a charismatic, unifying leader.

PASOK soon became a popular party. In 1981, the party won the elections and formed a government. For some, this victory signalled the social and political integration of the subaltern classes in Greek society. PASOK promised *Allaghi* (Change), and in the first legislative period health-centres and new schools were established, self-organisation in cooperatives was supported, and trade union's rights were strengthened. But this model of social emancipation soon reached its limits.

First of all, the traditional system of clientelism was not dismantled. Instead it was transformed: loyalty was no longer linked to persons, but to the party. PASOK enforced clientelism by creating jobs in the wider public sector. Whoever wanted to get employed in the public sector had at least to join PASOK's trade union federation PASKE. Thus, political power was assured by public employment as a method of controlling both the labour market and the trade unions.

On top of this, the party soon made a sharp turn to the right. After four years of rule, the PASOK government imposed its first austerity programme in 1985. Increases in taxes, cuts in social spending, liberalisation of job protection, and other measures led to a wage reduction of 8.6 percent. An economic recession prompted the government to economise. And even though this policy was not successful in revitalising the economy, it did mark a long-term change of political direction for the party. From a left reform party, the PASOK developed into a market-friendly neoliberal party.

With this change, the party leadership's relationship to the subaltern classes changed. In the early 1980s, the PASOK government had achieved a fragile integration of subaltern classes in Greek society. Now, the ties to this stratum were questioned by the party's own leadership. This development can be illustrated by the career of Kostas Simitis, the minister of economic affairs in 1985. He was dismissed after mass protests against his policies, but ten years later succeeded Papandreou as party chairman.

Because of the party's development, political space was opened up for more radical groups and movements that had always opposed PASOK's model of socialism. In 1985, the libertarian movement in Greece gained a new impetus.

ANARCHISM FROM THE END OF THE JUNTA TO THE BEGINNING OF THE 1990S

ANARCHISM IN THE 1970S

The anarchist movement appeared for the first time on the Greek stage as a true political force in the mid-1980s. It was not of course the first time that radical activists agitated and executed actions without relying on party-organisations. From the mid-1970s, there had been a number of anarchist groups who had published anarchist literature from classic authors such as Mikhail Bakunin and Peter Kropotkin to more recent thinkers such as Guy Debord and Murray Bookchin.

But for most, anarchism represented more a way of life and a youth culture than a coherent political programme. Artists like the singer-songwriter Nikolas Asimos opposed the culture of capitalism by his way of life, and his way of making and distributing music. Following in the footsteps of the rembetes of the 1920s and 1930s, he lived like an outlaw and was more than once put in prison. His music combined Western European and U.S. rock music with more classic Greek musical styles. He refused to bring out his work on commercial labels, and instead distributed his music through self-made tapes. More than any other, he challenged middle-class ways of living and values and instead propagated alternative forms of living and working together.

There were thus small circles of anarchist intellectuals as well as a libertarian youth culture. However, only a few of the newly politicised youths in the early 1970s considered themselves to be anarchist. The term had a negative connotation because the KKE used it to denounce all other movements of the radical left. Radicals who were active outside of party structures instead were called *agria neolaia* (wild youths). These youths often combined a nonconformist lifestyle with radical politics, and there were regular confrontations with the police over issues such as public order, drug use, and boisterous behaviour.

VIOLENT CONFRONTATIONS AND THE RORY GALLAGHER CONCERT OF 1981

In the years following the end of the dictatorship, these confrontations grew ever more numerous. Because of this, the authorities started their first 'anti-terror campaign' in 1976, after the First of May celebrations had given way to massive riots involving thousands of young people clashing with the police. These clashes became a mass phenomenon in the late 1970s and early 1980s. The annual anniversary of the 1973 student revolt became an almost traditional day of riots.

The largest of these riots was the one mentioned at the start of this chapter, which happened during a student demonstration on November 17, 1980, that commemorated the '73 uprising of students against the colonels' regime. Protesters tried to march to the U.S. embassy, but riot police attacked the demonstration. In the resulting street fights, two protesters were killed. The authorities had little experience in crowd control, which was revealed during the events surrounding the aforementioned Rory Gallagher concert. They were nervous about the presence of such a large crowd, which was twice as large as the organisers had expected. In this setting, it was almost inevitable that the situation would escalate.

The tensions were even greater, because the concert took place just before the national elections. The political divides between the left and the right in parliament were great. The left had been strengthened by the mass struggles of the 1970s. For the elections of 1981, it was expected that PASOK would win a big victory. Both the political right and large sections of the middle class feared a 'revenge' from the subaltern classes and the right feared losing its influence after more than thirty years of control. Thus when the police started to attack the crowd, widespread riots occurred.

The riots of 1981 had not been planned in advance. By many, they were interpreted as a radical protest by youths against the elections and the parliamentary system. This gave the emerging anarchist movement, which was still small and of little influence, a new impetus. Young activists, especially school and university students, were increasingly attracted to it.

GROWING ANARCHIST MOVEMENT IN THE EARLY 1980S

Soon, anarchists started organising and executing their own actions. One of the first political actions of activists who called themselves anarchist was the attack on a neo-fascist conference in Athens in 1984. One of the speakers at the conference was Jean-Marie Le Pen of Action Française. Anarchist groups clashed with the authorities, fought back the police, and subsequently drove the participants out of the hotel in which the conference was taking place.

The action was an important moment for the movement, not because it was a militant action, but because the anarchists for the first time succeeded in overcoming the culture of pacifism and legalism that the communist party had always propagated and practised since the end of civil war. At the time, the Greek left and right had different traditions of using violence. For the Greek police force as well as for neo-fascist groups, using violence never had been a questionable means. Brutality had been part of their political tradition. The communist and socialist left on the other hand, had always accepted the use of force only as a means of self-defence, a last resort. It was not something that should be used in an offensive way. This unwritten rule was now broken, and the anarchists now appropriated an aggressive, offensive, and militant style for themselves.

Next to this, the action marked the rise of a new generation of anarchist activists. This new generation was influenced, on the one hand by, the wave of squatting and autonomous action that had swept Western Europe in the years 1979–1981. On the other hand, it was influenced by the new punk subculture that developed in Great Britain, Germany, and Italy. Bands such as Adiexodo (Dead End Street), Panx Romana, and Genia tou Chaous (Generation of Chaos) became popular.

More and more, the idea and practice of 'insurrectionism' became characteristic for the metropolitan anarchist movement in Greece. More than any other issue, questioning the state's monopoly on violence and provoking clashes with the police distinguished the anarchists from other left radicals. Most anarchists wanted to combat the state, its institutions, and ruling parties in a direct way. They preferred militant and direct activism. Slogans like 'the most important lessons are learned on the barricade' became popular and illustrated that theory and theoretical debate played a minor role within the movement.

At some periods during these years, violent confrontations became a daily phenomenon. Certain dates, such as the First of May and November 17, the anniversary of the students' revolt, remained volatile.

The police were unable to control the anarchist subculture in central Athens, but its attempts caused a lot of conflicts. Often, the appearance of police officers was, in itself, enough to cause trouble. In fact, there was an going conflict for social control of the urban area.

THE ANARCHIST MOVEMENT AND THE PROTEST WAVE OF 1985–1986

When PASOK formed a government in 1981, it had no ambition of radically reforming society, even though the right had been very afraid of this. On the contrary, PASOK wanted to bring about stability and economic growth and end the mass struggles and class conflicts that had ravaged Greek society since the fall of the colonels' regime. In their attempt to repress and pacify radical movements and conflicts, PASOK occasionally received help from the KKE. More than once, student branches of the KKE attacked radical-left activists during university occupations, thus acting as substitute police while the police were not allowed to enter the campus because of the university asylum from 1973.

Even though PASOK's rise to government in many respects posed a historical development, often seen as indicative for the integration of the subaltern classes in Greek society, the party was soon also criticised for its authori-

tarian political style and conservatism. Many activists, like members of several Trotskyist groups, who had joined PASOK in the beginning soon left the party.

Tensions also emerged within other left parties. Many activists of the traditional left—KKE and KKE Interior—were disappointed by their organisations for not opposing the new government in a consistent manner. As a result, they soon found themselves alongside the more radical anarchists in their opposition to the PASOK-government.

Because of this development, the non-party radical left grew significantly in the early 1980s. By the mid-1980s, the movement had grown to a considerable size and strength and for the first time many called it 'anarchist,' thus turning the negative term into a political statement.

The movement was further strengthened by a national wave of protest that followed upon the first austerity measures that the PASOK executed after their second election victory in 1985. During 1985 and 1986, radical youths mobilised and staged a number of militant demonstrations, inciting in part extreme police repression.

Repression and counter-violence soon became important mobilising issues for the anarchist movement. During a November 17 anniversary in 1986, the young militant Michalis Kaltezas was killed by the police in Athens. This incident caused riots all over Greece that could only be repressed by massive police mobilisation.

A LARGE ARRAY OF ACTIVIST ISSUES

Other political issues, such as ecology and the protection of the environment, became especially important on local and regional levels. The industrialisation of agriculture caused ever more problems on a local level, while on the other hand, the quality of life in many large Greek cities sank drastically because of overpopulation and bad construction projects. After the civil war, ten thousand dissidents had moved to Athens to escape the political repression in their villages. Because of this, the city grew rapidly without any planning. This development combined with the growing number of cars cost Athens a great number of former green areas. Besides the smog, the so-called *tsimentopiisi* (cementation) became an important political issue.

A great number of local conflicts revolved around illegal building activity in green areas or even public parks. In these conflicts, anarchist activists played a significant role. Activists blocked the demolition of green areas or planted new trees in destroyed parks. Between 1984 and 1986, ecologists worked together with anarchists and libertarians in the Green Alternative Movement.

Another important issue was the support of prosecuted conscientious objectors. In fact, only libertarians like the group around the magazine *Arnoumai* (I refuse) picked up this issue. It was important for anarchists, because it provided a way of expressing their criticism of the army, nationalism, and cultures

Left: Riots in Greece, Dec. 2008. Photo: Unknown. https://libcom.org/gallery/greece-riots-2008-photo-gallery

of obedience. Because there was no legal possibility of objecting to military service, people could avoid conscription if they had 'psychological problems.' Even religious reasons were not accepted, and for a long time, Jehovah's Witnesses were the only organised group of conscientious objectors.

The taboo against non-religious conscientious objection was broken in 1987, when the first group of activists declared in public their refusal to enrol in the army and were sentenced to four years imprisonment. After a series of hunger strikes, accompanied by an impressive solidarity campaign, these sentences were reduced. Although a great number of young men changed their place of residence to avoid prosecution, the number of men who openly objected to military service was very low. At the beginning of the 1990s, it was around one hundred in all.

Anarchists and libertarians were among the first to deal with issues of sexism and gender. They also attacked virulent nationalism and racism, especially their actions against the discrimination of Slavic and Turkish minorities. No left current opposed nationalism more consistently than the anarchists. For this reason, the anarchist movement was the first to fight against racism, when it re-emerged in the beginning 1990s, as a result of increasing immigration and the wave of nationalist violence that shook the Balkans.

A prominent new form of action that emerged in this era was the squatting of vacant buildings in order to turn them into self-managed social centres. These centres provided room for the movement's counter-culture and also established an infrastructure for radical political groups and currents. One of the first successful squats in Greece was the Villa Amalia in the centre of Athens, near Athens Polytechnic. A second important squat was Lelas Karagianni 37, only about a kilometre further away. Both neoclassical buildings had been abandoned for decades and became central meeting points for the anarchist and punk scene in Athens from the end of 1980s.

Through these squats, the movement established for the first time permanent locations in the city of Athens and thus became a sort of institution of social sub- and counter-culture. This development was of great importance, because social movements and student protests such as the one between 1986 and 1988, were met with heavy repression. Even pasting posters or writing graffiti was prosecuted and many activists were subsequently received prison sentences. Anarchists had experience in defending assemblies, demonstrations, and other collective actions against police attacks. This experience became very helpful in the defence of squats and other locations.

MASS STRUGGLE IN THE ERA OF NEOLIBERALISM (1990–2007)

CHANGING POLITICAL CONTEXT IN THE 1990S
At the end of the 1980s, the context in which the anarchist movement had been active changed radically as a result of both national and international developments. Internationally, the collapse of the Soviet Union marked the end of the

Cold War. This event had major consequences because it changed the international economic consensus. With capitalism reigning triumphant, economic policy turned away from classic welfare state policies, towards a new neoliberal mainstream. The stronger focus on free market economics meant the privatisation of former government sectors such as public transport and telecommunication, and the downgrading of social security benefits.

In Greece, all major parties, especially PASOK, which governed during most of the 1990s, supported the neoliberal economic policies. This change of politics and the broad political consensus on these issues radically changed the conditions for political action. The media landscape changed as well, after the lifting of state control on the television and radio market new private media companies emerged in the early 1990s and gained control over large sections of it. By and large, these companies supported neoliberal currents in all parties and promoted consumerism and a more business-minded culture. This helped shift public opinion to the right. In the 1990s, the neoliberal consensus stimulated individualist and consumer-oriented lifestyles. Meanwhile, labour rights were dismantled step by step and state-owned companies were privatised.

Most of all, neoliberal policies affected the labour market. While trade unions in the public sector were able to defend their status, labour conditions in the private sector worsened. Permanent jobs became scarcer, wages as well as benefits decreased, and working conditions worsened. Young people, women, and immigrants were particularly affected by these developments.

These changes were also felt by leftist parties, many of which fell into crisis. PASOK was shaken by a number of scandals. The attempt by PASOK's leadership to strengthen the party's profile on the economy and the media failed in 1988, when the former director of the Bank of Crete, Giorgos Koskotas, fled to the United States after plundering the bank, naming senior PASOK members as co-conspirators. For a few years, PASOK lost power. The Greek communist party KKE entered a deep crisis even worse than PASOK. On the one hand, the fall of the Berlin Wall caused an ideological crisis within the party: it became clear that party communism had failed. On the other hand, the KKE's decision to enter into an all-party coalition government in 1988—without PASOK, but with the conservative Néa Dimokratía (ND)—led to heavy criticism from young communist activists. In the subsequent years, the KKE lost nearly all of its youth members and a great number of its cadre and voters.

MASS STRUGGLES IN 1990–1991
In 1990, the conservative ND was elected into government. It was a sign of the rise of neoliberalism. ND's government plans foresaw new austerity measures, deregulation of the labour market, and de-industrialisation. This, however, sparked a wave of mass protests from trade unions and workers. Through a series of strikes and demonstrations, often accompanied by violent clashes

with the police, the trade unions were able effectively to block most of these measures, including pension cuts and the privatisation of public companies like the refineries, Telecom Hellas, Skaramangas-Shipyards, and Olympic Airways. Especially important in this respect was a wildcat strike of Athens' bus drivers in August 1992, which culminated in the battle of Votanikos, a suburb of Athens, where five hundred drivers and neighbourhood residents clashed with the riot police. The privatisation of public transport was successfully stopped. But in some important sectors like the textile industries, the movement suffered defeat. The biggest textile company on the Balkans for example, Peiraiki-Patraiki, closed down, resulting in the firing of ten thousand workers.

The second wave of protests was directed at the school and university reform bill of 1990. Individual professional advancement was one of the essential neoliberal promises to young Greeks in the 1990s. Because advancement is traditionally achieved through education, this became a central field of social struggle. In 1990, however, the government proposed reforms to drastically reduce the number of school and university graduates by raising the bar for university access combined with strict requirements of discipline. This caused a wave of protest.

In the following months, dozens of universities and thousands of schools were occupied nationwide. It was estimated that about 60 to 70 percent of all school and university students took part in the movement. Often, parents supported their children by joining in actions, providing food and support.

The protest campaign ended dramatically when Nikos Teboneras, an activist of the teachers' union, was killed by a right-wing thug, while defending an occupied school against a fascist attack in Patras, in the west of Greece, in January 1991. The killer was a local councillor for the ruling ND party and a member of its youth organisation ONNED. The incident caused three days of riots and across the country. In Patras, more than twenty-five thousand people took part in the demonstration the next day. In the following days, the minister of education, Kontogiannopoulos, resigned and the reform bill was withdrawn.

Through mass mobilisations and protest, both the reform of the labour market, and that of the education system were halted. The frontal attack on living conditions of the ND-government had ended in complete failure. In 1993, PASOK returned to office.

RADICALISATION OF THE STUDENT MOVEMENT

The events of 1990–1991 caused a radicalisation of the student movement, which came to be influenced by libertarian and anarchist ideas. Concepts such as direct action, self-organisation, and social insurrection became ever more popular among school and university students. The occupation of school and university buildings without setting any demands but seeking a direct confrontation with teachers and police was a frequent phenomenon. The Zapatistas' uprising in Mexico in 1994 had a big influence on the movement, an inspiring and concrete example of a radical non-Leninist movement that realised a number of anarchist ideas.

More and more *aftonomi steki* (autonomous centres) were established in several neighbourhoods of Athens and other Greek cities, thus providing new meeting points for those who did not want to get involved in party activism. In the beginning, most of the stekia were situated in the quarters around the city centre, especially in a neighbourhood called Exarcheia. Often they had a specific political or cultural character, like the steki of anarcho-syndicalists or stekia of communities of migrants. But more and more stekia were established in other parts of Athens, like Keratsini, Galatsi, Kallithea, Zografou, and Kaisariani. For the anarchist movement, these stekia were an important backbone providing the infrastructure for meetings, concerts, movie screenings, and all kinds of political and cultural activities.

RADICAL ACTION AT THE UNIVERSITY

By 1990, the struggle for access to education and knowledge had become an important issue for activists. The conflicts, however revolved not only around access to these institutions, but also around the social relations within them, especially at high schools. On the one hand, there was frustration about the pressure to acquire high grades necessary to get enrolled at a university. On the other hand, students criticised the teaching methods, which focused on memorising facts, rather than process information, and were often referred to as *papagalia* (from the word 'papagalo,' parrot). Schools and universities seemed to resemble factories, rather than pedagogical institutions.

From the beginning of the 1990s, the occupation of schools and university buildings became a central means of political action for radical youth. This form of action was used not only during protests against school and university reforms but also to protest neoliberal reforms in other fields. The occupation of schools and university buildings became one of the cornerstones of radical youth protest that aimed less at emphasizing specific political demands, and much more at the interruption of everyday life and the creation of a social sphere beyond institutional control: an autonomous space. In an interview with the conservative *Kathimerini* newspaper, a high school student explained the meaning of their action. 'The relevance of occupying a school,' he said, 'is to learn how to occupy other places and institutes.'[82]

Even so, only the occupations of university buildings—and not of high schools—gained an explicit anarchist character. One of the more spectacular occupations in this line was the occupation of Athens Polytechnic during the anniversary of November 17, 1995, terminated by the police who arrested more than five hundred activists in an especially brutal way. To express their solidarity, other militants subsequently occupied the Panteion University and burned the Greek flag on top of the building, an incident that sparked controversy and outrage and broad debate in mass media.

All these confrontations in and around the schools and universities did not go uncontested, but they often led to heavy confrontations: not only with police forces but also with fascist groups. These struggles were not limited to youths, as parents and trade unionists got involved in the actions and subsequent violent clashes. This happened for example in 1998–1999, when more than 160 school students were arrested in different schools all over the country.

MASS MOBILISATIONS IN THE FIRST YEARS OF THE NEW MILLENNIUM

In 2000, Greek society was again shaken by a wave of social conflicts and mass demonstrations. This time, a PASOK government tried to implement a pension reform, which mass demonstrations organised by the trade unions largely forestalled.

But more than this, the rise of the anti-globalisation movement in the late 1990s and first years of the millenium gave anarchist currents a new impetus. The anti-globalisation movement was a broad movement that comprised anarchist and libertarian groups. But it also included the parliamentary Marxist party Synaspismos (Coalition of Left Movements and Ecology), which was an offshoot from the KKE Interior, and other radical Marxist groups.

In its wake, a large number of new libertarian and anarchist groups and organisations were founded, such as Indymedia Athens in 2001 and the first nationwide autonomous organisation Antiexousiastiki Kinisi (Anti-Authoritarian Movement, AK) in 2003. The formation of AK marked a new development within the anarchist movement: a growing interest in social issues and a turn towards wider parts of subaltern classes. In that same year, the social centre Yfanet, a former textile-factory, was squatted. It now is an important political and cultural centre in the city of Thessaloniki.

As in other countries, the anti-globalisation movement mainly mobilised around international summits and social forums. The Greek anarchists played an important role in the protests against the EU summit in Thessaloniki in June 2003, which involved battling police forces like in Goethenburg, Genoa, and Prague. Through these mobilisations, Greek activists came into contact with anarchist groups from all over Europe. When the European Social Forum took place in Athens in 2005, more than seventy thousand people participated in the closing demonstration.

In 2006, another education bill was introduced by Prime Minister Kostas Karamanlis of the conservative Néa Dimokratía. Again, this incited a student mobilisation. But this time, a broad protest movement emerged that also included workers. In the mass mobilisations that followed, anarchist groups and organisations played an important role. Several radical Marxist groups were also active in the movement, like the New Left Current (Neo Aristero Revma, NAR) and the Coalition of the Radical Left (SYRIZA). The first was an offshoot of the communist youth organisation from 1989, the second a coalition of Synaspismos and several other organisations formed in 2004, but the role of anarchist ideas within the movement was clearly growing. Blocs of anarchist groups became more visible at occupations and demonstrations, and left parties had too little influence to gain control over the coordination of activities.

The tactics of the communist youth organisation, KNE, indicated the fading influence of the traditional left. The communists traditionally opposed occupations during general assemblies, but when they could not prevent an occupation because anarchists and left radicals were in the majority, they took part in order not to lose contact with their social base. They could not control the decision-making any more.

In general, the adoption of direct action tactics by other groups and organisations can be seen as an indicator of the growing influence of anarchist ideas. The teachers' unions were among the first to approve such tactics in 1998, when teachers with long-term experience but without tenure were forced by the government to undergo examination again. Activists of the union blocked and occupied examination centres and clashed with police forces. In 2006, the conservative government tried to dispose of university asylum and academic self-administration. Furthermore, they wanted to open higher education to the free market. During the subsequent mass mobilisations of 2006 to 2007, civil disobedience and militant activism became widely accepted means of action. Unions of teachers and university staff were openly hostile toward the education bill. Instead of resorting to traditional forms of trade union campaigns and compromise, they now openly and uncompromisingly fought the authorities. These tactics proved successful: nearly all measures mandated by the Bologna-treaty were blocked completely.

THE REVOLT OF DECEMBER 2008

A NATIONWIDE UPRISING
In December 2008, events got completely 'out of control' when the sixteen-year-old school student Alexandros Grigoropoulos was killed by a police officer in Exarchia. His only 'fault' was to be in the wrong place at the wrong time: after a quarrel between two police officers and some youngsters, one of the officers opened fire. A video recorded by a neighbour shows that instead of giving first aid, the police simply returned to their patrol car.

This incident caused a massive wave of violent protest that shook Greek society to its very core. During these protests, for the first time, anarchist networks formed the backbone of mobilisations against the 'government of murderers.' The influence of anarchism was clear at the occupied Athens Polytechnic and the business school in Athens, and also at the School of Drama at the University of Thessaloniki. In the coordination of the occupations and decision-making, horizontalism and participatory democracy dominated. These occupied university buildings became the central points of coordination within the movement.

The Marxist left, on the other hand, played only a minor role. Only the Athens law school was occupied by a coalition of radical Marxist groups and members of SYRIZA. The KKE's stance towards the militant movement was predictably negative. The statement of KKE General Secretary Aleka Papariga was characteristic in this respect. She declared that during a true revolution, not even one window would be broken. In a similar vein, KKE officials criticised the left party SYRIZA for their sympathetic stance towards the militant protesters. They denounced this stance as opportunistic. Very soon, Indymedia Athens gained the position of the central mobilising medium, while other radical sites emerged rapidly.

THE CRISIS OF PARLIAMENTARY POLITICS

The December Uprising laid bare the crisis of the social order and its political legitimacy that had been growing for years. To a large extent, this crisis was not specifically Greek, it was part of a much broader development. Since the collapse of the Soviet Union, neoliberal reform and austerity measures have become the only legitimate policy not only in Greece but also in the whole of the West. As these politics became the consensus among all ruling political parties, political discontent moved away from the parliamentary arena. The size and growth of the anarchist movement was an expression and a product of this crisis of parliamentary politics.

As political parties seemed unwilling and unable to listen to the public and respond to their needs and desires, party politics lost their legitimacy. They became ever more identified with striving for power, corruption, and the interests of all sorts of lobby groups. The neoliberal slogan 'there is no alternative' had produced an anti-political stance among the public and caused a decline of traditional political participation on a large scale. As political parties lost influence and appeal, as the declining attendance rates at elections showed, 'antipolitical' movements such as the anarchist movement grew. The extent of distrust of party-politics was illustrated by the fact that even the parties of the left were unable to attract supporters and activists.

CHARACTERISING THE ANARCHIST MOVEMENT

There is little reliable data on the social composition of the anarchist movement, though it is clear that the movement is composed mostly of youths and is not distinctly a working-class movement. Even though there are older active anarchists, most of the militants are between fifteen and forty years old. The movement of the 1990s recruited mostly among high school and university students, and other well educated youth. Still, the clashes in December 2008 show that the movement attracts youths from all classes. The mass protests and confrontations also attract working-class people and football hooligans, but a significant portion of the riots occurred in middle-class suburbs. When the police raided social centres and squats, several children of PASOK politicians, and those of other leftist politicians, were arrested.

The mass media and left political parties traditionally face the anarchist movement with deep suspicion and incomprehension. The militant *koukouloforoi* ('hoodies') are equated with indiscriminate violence and political criminality. Certainly, violent confrontations with anti-riot police forces and solidarity campaigns for imprisoned comrades have become a kind of trademark of the movement. But anarchists and libertarians are involved in far more activities, campaigns, and actions than this.

Anarchists have not only focused on militant confrontations: they have also initiated or taken part in protests against the destruction of public parks or against the privatisation of beaches. Even though they had to undergo occasional intense police repression, they have been successful in changing car parks into proper parks in the neighbourhood of Exarcheia and other parts of Athens. Others have started a free camping movement claiming free access to beaches, proclaiming the 'undeniable right to enjoy nature,' and opposing commercial forms of tourism. Sometimes, free camping has been combined with ecological protest such as that in a valley near Trikala against the construction of a dam.

Anarchists have also started collective soup kitchens and taken part in organising citizen's assemblies on a local level. In many suburbs of Athens, citizens' assemblies preceded the occupation of Syntagma Square in the summer of 2011. Besides ideas of self-organisation, direct action, anti-racism, and anti-fascism, anarchists were among the first to discuss de-growth economy and to criticise Stalinist misdeeds, as many publications on Indymedia Athens in the last years show.

Still, issues of sex and gender have so far received little attention, and when fascists set fire to a Jewish library in the city of Chania in Crete, this received only minor attention from anarchists. Open anti-Semitism in Greek society, even on the left, is prevalent, and only a few organisations, such as the anarchist magazine *Evtopia*, are concerned with it.

In contrast to the traditional left and notwithstanding the Anti-Authoritarian Movement, anarchists have not founded their own organisations or interregional federations. This is in part due to the fact that they cannot be considered a homogeneous bloc. In fact, the Greek anarchist movement is a pluriform whole of different currents and groups, circles of friends and organisations, and corresponding networks of all kinds. The anarchist politics are embedded in a counter-culture in which music plays a crucial role. In recent times, hip-hop has become popular, but punk, new wave, and rembetiko-influenced music are equally popular. This subculture explains the link between mass mobilisations and radical politics.

Since the late 1990s, websites are the most important media for communication and the circulation of information. Before, this was mainly done through meetings in squatted buildings and autonomous centres, magazines and newspapers and self-managed radio stations. Within a few years after its launch in 2001, Indymedia Athens acquired the role of a central information platform. It is used not only by anarchists and libertarians but also by Marxist organisations. The authorities have repeatedly tried to shut down Indymedia Athens, hosted on Athens Polytechnic's servers, by threatening university authorities with prosecution. To date, all attempts have failed, because the constitution protects the freedom of ideas and their circulation, and police authorities are prohibited from entering the Polytechnic campus. This so-called university asylum was repealed in the autumn of 2011, but it is still unclear if this new law can be implemented. At the same time, there is strong resistance from both students and university staff, which up to now could not be successfully suppressed.

AN ANTI-THEORETICAL MOVEMENT?

Although there are no academics in Greece who concentrate on anarchist theory, and the movement has traditionally been little interested in theory, theoretical discussions about anarchism have recently intensified. These discussions mainly take place outside academic institutions among students, publishers, writers, and self-educated activists, centering on classical anarchist authors like Pierre-Joseph Proudhon, Max Stirner, Mikhail Bakunin, Errico Malatesta, and Peter Kropotkin.

In addition, libertarian currents such as German and Dutch council-communism and Spanish anarcho-syndicalism have gained importance. Finally, anarchist forerunners of the ecological movement like Murray Bookchin and the autonomous movements of Italy and Germany are now discussed.

Takis Fotopoulos's concept of inclusive democracy has also to some extent inspired local movements in Greece.[83] The same goes for the works of Cornelius Castoriadis, which have received renewed interest, and also more conservative

'Social and Class Counterstrike,' a call for a demonstration on October 19, 2011. Poster: Gathering of Anarchists for Social Liberation. http://opseutaras.blogspot.dk/2011_10_01_archive.html

thinkers such as Carl Schmitt, Carl von Clausewitz, and Friedrich Nietzsche, are discussed.

The question of how to organise and fight under conditions of today's 'social war' is especially central in anarchist debates. But while these theoretical discussions have reached an almost scientific level, the focus has remained on confrontational politics and clashes with the police, the main characteristic of anarchism in Greece.

THE CRISIS OF INSURRECTIONALISM

With regards to the violent confrontations, it is important to note that in most cases the use of violence was anything but indiscriminate, as the mainstream media claim time and again. In fact, most violence is meant to cause material damage and targets symbols of capitalism and consumer culture, such as shopping malls and banks. A classic illustration of these tactics was the 'attack' on the Athens Christmas tree at the central Syntagma Square in 2008. Student activists of the college of art first 'redecorated' the tree with rubbish and later others burned it down. After this, the tree was replaced by a plastic tree—ironically called the tree of Kaklamanis, after the mayor of Athens—and had to be protected by special police forces day and night. Even clashes with the police never aim to kill police officers, but rather question the state monopoly on violence and political power. Traditionally, there has been a relatively clear consensus as to which kinds of violence are acceptable and which are not. When a small shop was burnt down during a riot in Thessaloniki, anarchists collected money to compensate for the damage.

Even so, small sections of the radical left as well as anarchist-inspired groups have been attracted to underground actions and armed struggle, and most

Call for forty-eight-hour general strike on October 19–20, 2011. Poster: Gathering Resistance and Solidarity Kypseli/Athens. http://sakakp.blogspot.com

anarchists never denounced these forms of struggle. There was, for example, the November 17 movement, which executed a number of attacks on political and military leaders of the former junta. Other groups committed bank robberies or theft. Anarchists were active in solidarity campaigns and the prison struggle of political—as well as 'ordinary'—prisoners. Yet, most of them did not execute these sorts of actions.

Since the mid-1990s, riots and violent incidents have at times become an almost everyday phenomenon in Athens and Thessaloniki. In December 2008, after the killing of Alexandros Grigoropoulos by police officers, these clashes grew explosively. Even high school students were involved in attacks on police stations and for days parts of central Athens were no-go areas for the police. However, soon after the December uprising of 2008, the movement was confronted with a pressing problem concerning the central tactics of insurrectionary anarchism. The violent clashes grew ever more alike and usually involved the 'usual suspects,' who took recourse to the same practices time and again. Because of this, the clashes became predictable and began to lose their political impact. Becoming ever more radical and violent obviously became a dead end street. Thus, the tactics of insurrectionalism had reached their limits.

The main problem of insurrectionalism was not the violence, but much more the lack of popular power that sprang from these confrontations. This problem was most vividly illustrated during the December riots. Even though thousands of people took part in demonstrations, marches, and riots, social change remained out of reach. Police forces could not control the city of Athens, because the revolt was simply too massive—as even the president of Attica's police department had to admit—but the revolt was not translated into social power, or direct influence on government policies. A second problem that anarchists had to face was that in the face of the size of the confrontations, and the involvement of non-activists such as students, youth, migrants, and football fans, the political side of the uprising tended to fade.

REORIENTATION: LABOUR AND DIRECT DEMOCRACY NOW

For this reason, many militants have started looking for new forms of collective action and new political themes. This development commenced around 2009. One option that was tested involved a stronger focus on labour issues. This reorientation had its roots in the solidarity movement for Kostantina Kouneva, an activist of the Athens cleaners' trade union, who was attacked by company thugs with acid and badly injured. After this, workers defence against employer violence and workers' organisations became more central in the view of many anarchists. These issues had been subject of campaigns before, for example during solidarity campaigns for fishermen from Egypt, but now activists tried more systematically to establish anarchist trade unions. Activists in Athens above all aimed at organising dispatch riders, waiters, and cooks. In the end, these attempts had only little success, because job insecurity and high unemployment rates severely limit the possibilities to pressure companies.

At the same time, violent confrontations continued. A tragic incident during mass protest against austerity measures was the burning down of an office of the Marfin Bank in May 2010, during which three clerks were killed, one of whom was pregnant. It is unclear who exactly was responsible for this incident, but there can be no doubt that insurrectionist attitudes cultivated a political climate in which such murderous incidents could take place. The incident caused massive outrage among both the public and anarchists and demoralised many activists. In the weeks that followed, mass protests declined.

In the period that followed, the anarchist movement lost part of its vitality and political initiative. The movement was still involved in radical actions, such as the local protest against the construction of a rubbish dump in the town of Keratea, which would process rubbish from the whole Attica region, or the six-week hunger strike of North African immigrants demanding legal status, a campaign that was partly successful. The Greek government gave them legal status for six months, promising to simplify access to long-term legal status.

But when the uprisings in Tunisia and Egypt, and the protests in Spain inspired the rise of a new movement of so-called 'apolitical' *'indignados'* (*aganaktismeni*) and previously unpoliticised youths started occupying central squares in major cities all over Greece in May 2011, one of their main positions was not to use violence. They thus clearly demarcated themselves from the anarchist politics of insurrectionalism.

Even so, anarchist and radical left activists could join the movement without significant problems. They were accepted to the general assemblies and introduced ideas of autonomous self-organisation. As a result of the occupations, conflicts with the authorities, and defamation in mass media, the movement soon became more political. After a brief period, the indignados changed their name to 'direct democracy now.'

Within the 'direct democracy now' movement, people from all parts of society experimented with participatory democracy and propagated direct democracy without the influence of party or union professionals. Of course, activists of all political traditions and even conservative people took part in the movement, but the shared goal was to fight the rigorous austerity measures dictated by the EU, IMF, and European Central Bank.

For three weeks, mass demonstrations—involving more than three hundred thousand participants at their peak—were not overshadowed by violent confrontations. And in the middle of June 2011, the Greek government resigned because of these protests. Only the backing of the German and French government brought the retired prime minister Papandreou back into office. The protests had finally regained political influence. Without a doubt, the experiences of the Tunisian and Egyptian democratisation movements inspired this 'miracle of Athens.'

3 χρονια μετα την εξεγερση

Απο την χ των δολοφόνων

στην ς των φασιστών

6
ΔΕΚ.

12:00 συγκέντρωση
προπύλαια

18:00 Διαδήλωση
προπύλαια

αντιεξουσιαστική κινηση αθήνας

However, this nonviolent movement soon came to an end when both police forces and fascist thugs attacked the protesters occupying the Athens Syntagma Square with tear gas and shock-grenades. This happened on June 15. But the movement could not be deterred so easily and within a few hours, the square—which is situated in front of the Greek parliament—was reoccupied. For the first time, a mass demonstration was able to fight back against police forces and defeat the authorities. Again the influence of anarchist and radical activists was of great importance, as they are seen as the most resolute part of the movement.

Although the next wave of mass protest against austerity measures in autumn 2011 was more powerful, the result was contrary to what was intended. The PASOK government resigned, but the new administration was formed by PASOK, conservative Néa Dimokratía, and fascistic LAOS under the leadership of Lukas Papadimos, formerly of the European Central Bank. This bourgeois bloc had only a weak basis in society, but the full backing of the EU and the Troika: a commission made up of the EU, the European Central Bank, and the IMF. The Troika was formed in May 2010 to grant loans in order to avert Greece's bankruptcy and to ensure that the austerity measures—which were the preconditions for the loans—were executed.

Under the pressure of mass protests, elections were held again in May 2012. The result was a collapse of the traditional parties and the rise of SYRIZA, the coalition of the radical left. SYRIZA is not a typical Greek party, although it has its roots in the communist left. As the name shows it is a coalition of different organisations that was founded after mass protest against European Summit Conference in 2003.

But again the effect was an even more right-wing interim government, because no political party or party-coalition was able to form a majority government. Even though SYRIZA got even more votes in the subsequent elections of June 2012, Néa Dimokratía became the biggest party with the votes of people from small towns and the countryside. The new government was formed by ND, PASOK, and the newly founded Democratic Left.

Without a doubt, most people active within the mass protest movements—and probably even most libertarians—voted for SYRIZA. Though politically active, they are still a minority within Greek society. With most Greeks paralyzed by the austerity measures, only 62 percent of the people entitled to vote took part in the elections.

The new government formed after June 2012 and soon started an aggressive campaign against the weakest part of the population: migrants without legal status, who are now threatened with imprisonment in detention camps. Next to government policies, migrants are also ever more threatened by gangs related to the new fascist party Chrysi Avghi (Golden Dawn), which gained almost 7 percent of the vote during the last elections. Parts of

Left: '3 years after the revolt—from the government of murderers to the government of fascists,' December 2011. Poster: Movement Against Authority.

Athens have become increasingly dangerous for migrants, while others have become centres of conflict between fascists and anarchists. Such is the case in the quarter Aghios Panteleimonas, where fascists established their own regime of control while anarchists from nearby squatted centres attempt to undermine their position with anti-fascist motorcycle convoys and other forms of mobilisation.

One incident related to this, however, shows how the political climate has deteriorated and how government policy strengthens the position of Nazi gangs. In September 2012, a group of anti-fascist motorcyclists were arrested by the police and subsequently tortured at Attica's central police department. As Greek media ignored the incident, it was the British newspaper *The Guardian* that reported on the case.[84] After this, Greek journalists from the public television channel ERT discussed the events in a popular morning show, but calls for the minister of interior, the strong man of Néa Dimokratía, Nikos Dendias, to resign were ignored.

The next waves of protest in autumn 2012 and January 2013 caused a deepening of political divisions. On the one side, the ruling bloc, represented by the Troika and the governing coalition, imposed further austerity measures and often reacted violently to opposition. They are generally assisted by the mass media, which is controlled by big business, and by the fascist Golden Dawn party. The latter do so in parliament and on the streets: by voting in favour of privatising government firms and exempting ship-owners from taxation, and by organizing street gangs that attack migrants and protesters. More than ever, Golden Dawn represents the economical and political interests of the 'deep state' in Greece.

On the other side, there is the mass movement rooted in all parts of subaltern classes and represented by SYRIZA, the organisations of the radical left including the KKE, and of course anarchists of all sorts. While austerity measures have effectively knocked down working-class incomes to a point where tens of thousands of people survive only through public aid and soup kitchens, self-organisation through cooperation has become the most popular concept of solidarity. These cooperatives have increasingly become the backbone of social and political resistance. Next to collective kitchens and consumer-cooperatives, social health centres have been founded to remedy the collapse of the public health system. Some of these health centres have existed for years, initially helping predominantly migrants without legal status. Others were founded more recently by neighbourhood assemblies or self-managed cultural centres. Most of them want to overcome traditional forms of medical care and are also involved in other activities like flea markets or anti-fascist mobilisation.

One of the most successful examples of a recently founded coopera-tion is the *Efimerida ton Syntakton* (Newspaper of the Editorial Journalists). This newspaper was founded by journalists after the closedown of the biggest left-liberal daily newspaper of Greece, the *Eleftherotypia* (Free Press). The can-celling of a bank credit led to financial difficulties and a labour conflict. After *Eleftherotypia* folded, the journalists started a self-managed newspaper. Even more interesting is the first self-managed industrial company: the construc-tion material plant Vio.Me. It started in February 2013 with the support of an enormous countrywide solidarity movement. Vio.Me is an outstanding ex-ample of the impact of anarchist ideas. Within the traditional Greek workers and communist movement, there are no precursors or earlier examples of this way of organizing. It is not amazing that KKE follows the activities of Vio.Me workers with suspicion, while SYRIZA backed the movement as a new form of class struggle.[85]

Greek authorities try to break the spirit of resistance and self-organ-isation through police brutality. The goal is to defeat the most unruly and active parts of society. In January 2013, militant strikes of bus and metro drivers and sailors were suppressed by emergency laws that threatened the strikers with five years imprisonment. In December 2012 and January 2013, the oldest squats of Athens, Villa Amalia, Villa Lelas Karagianni, and Villa Skaramangas were attacked and evicted by the police. In April 2013, Athens Indymedia and the independent radio station, 98 FM, both hosted at the server of Athens Polytechnic, were shut down. Even so, the government campaign against the anarchist movement has up to now been of limited success. Both Indymedia and 98 FM are broadcasting again, and the an-archist movement remains capable of mobilizing large numbers of people. Still, the Greek government continues efforts to destroy the structures of the opposition.

INSTEAD OF A CONCLUSION

Libertarian currents have become important in Greek society the last thirty years and have partly replaced the communist radicalism of former times. This radi-calism has never been pacified as it was done in the countries of Northwestern Europe. One reason for this could be the weakness of the party-organised so-cialist movement. This is of course due to its early defeat by authoritarian rule, but it is also linked to the low level of industrialisation. Finally, just like the social democratic parties in other European countries, PASOK has turned to neoliberalism and no longer poses a real alternative to the conservative parties. This has opened up a comparatively large political space for more libertarian and anarchist currents.

When the crisis hit Greece and subsequently the state was forced into dramatic and humiliating budget cuts, Greece seemed to be on fire for a moment. The political situation in Greece remains turbulent to this day. For this reason, it is difficult to draw conclusions from the current events. At this moment, it is still unclear if the social movements in Greece will be able to withstand and fight back the new forms of authoritarianism and austerity politics implemented by the European Union. But the anarchist movement plays an important role in this process by supporting broad protests and stressing the importance of autonomous self-organisation and direct action for mass movements.

A main problem of Greek anarchism is the lack of a wider perspective and an effective strategy. As long as there is no real discussion about the next steps of social and political change, anarchism can give no answer to the question of how to transform society on a local or international level. The riots of December 2008 marked the end of a political and social order that had been established after the fall of dictatorship. However, it is one thing to destroy the old social forms of society. To build up new ones is another.

FURTHER READING

Since the Greek revolt of December 2008, a sizable amount of literature has appeared on the contemporary situation and the recent past of radical protest in Greece. Two important English-language publications are: *We Are an Image from the Future: The Greek Revolt of December 2008*, edited by A.G. Schwarz et al. (Oakland: AK Press, 2010); and *Revolt and Crisis in Greece: Between a Present Yet to Pass and a Future Still to Come* by Antonis Vradis and Dimitris Dalakoglou (Oakland: AK Press, 2011). In 2013, Costas Douzinas published *Philosophy and Resistance in Crisis: Greece and the Future of Europe* (Cambridge: Polity Press, 2013).

Studies have also been published in other languages. Two of my articles analysing the present situation were published in German: 'Irgendwann nehmen die Tränen Rache. Zur Renaissance des Anarchismus in Griechenland,' *Das Argument* 289 (2010): 826–38; and 'Die Demokratie in Griechenland zwischen Ende und Wiedergeburt,' in *Krisen Proteste. Beiträge aus Sozial.Geschichte Online*, edited by Peter Birke and Max Henninger (Berlin: Assoziation A, 2012). See also: Kostas Lampos, *Amesi Dimokratia kai Ataxiki Koinonia* (Thessaloniki: Nisides, 2012).

Futhermore, two noteworthy German language publications include: Willy Baer et al., *Schrei im Dezember. Griechenland 2008. Ein erschossender Demonstrant* (Hamburg: Bibliothek des Widerstands, 2010); and Erik Eberhard, *Revolution und Konterrevolution in Griechenland* (Vienna: Arbeitsgruppe Marxismus, 2005).

For people able to read Greek, the following studies are recommended: M. Charitatou-Synodinou, *Stachty kai burberry. O dekemvris 2008 mesa apo synthimata, eikones kai keimena* (Athens, 2010); and D.T., *Gia mia istoria tou anarchikou kinimatos tou elladikou chorou* (Melbourne, 2008), available online at http://ngnm.vrahokipos.net; and I. Hobo, *2011: I ektropi ton ekdochon. Kinitopoiiseis ton plateion kai katastasi ektatis anangis* (Athens, 2011).

Studies on social movements in Greece during the 1980s and 1990s are relatively rare, especially in languages other than Greek. Besides Dimitris Charalambis, *Gesellschaftliche Klassen, politische Krise und Abhängigkeit. Die politische Strategien der herrschenden Klasse in Griechenland und die innerbürgerliche Widersprüche (1952–1974)* (PhD thesis, 1981); two Greek publications include K. Moskof, *Eisagogi stin istoria tou kinimatos tis ergatikis taxis stin Ellada* (Athens, 1988); and S. Priftis, *EAM—ELAS—OPLA* (Athens, 1984).

Three

¡EL CARRER ES NOSTRE!
THE AUTONOMOUS MOVEMENT IN BARCELONA, 1980–2012

Claudio Cattaneo and Enrique Tudela

THE PRECURSORS OF BARCELONA'S AUTONOMOUS MOVEMENT: THE LATE 1970S

THE SPANISH CONTEXT of the early 1980s, Barcelona in particular, was strongly influenced by the transition from Franco's dictatorship and the heritage of the social revolution of 1936. For this reason we need to take a step back in history and talk of the workers' and neighbourhood movements of the 1970s, before we can talk about squatting and autonomous action in the 1980s.

Until the late 1980s, Barcelona did not harbour a sizeable autonomous youth movement like other European countries with a longer democratic tradition. But Barcelona did experience radical workers' protests from the early 1970s onwards. Franco's industrial development policies had heavily influenced Barcelona and its metropolitan area, which was already characterised by a strong industrial concentration. A large number of factories were constructed and a new working class formed in the area as a result. This consisted largely of migrants coming from the impoverished rural regions of Andalusia, Extremadura, Aragon, and Galicia. They often lived in self-built slums.[1]

Because of this, a strong workers' movement, characterised by autonomous tendencies, had already emerged at the beginning of the 1970s. Here, with 'autonomous tendencies' we do not mean counter-cultural youth, but the workers' dedication to direct action and wildcat strikes, and horizontal decision-making at the workplace through assemblies. These traditions indeed influenced the next generation of young autonomous groups, but it has to be acknowledged that, in comparison to Italy and the Italian Autonomia youth movement of the 1970s, these early movements were a minority.

Most of the workers' activism was oriented towards the legalisation of trade unions and political parties, which were illegal under Franco.[2] Still,

this movement was quite independent from anti-Franco political organisations and from official trade unions mainly controlled by the Partit Socialista
Unificat de Catalunya (PSUC), the Catalan branch of the Spanish Communist
Party. The struggles of the movement found some of their theoretical inspiration from small intellectual groups composed of students and workers already established by the end of the 1960s and beginnings of the 1970s, such
as Circulos de Formación de Cuadros, Plataformas Anticapitalistas and the
Grupos Obreros Autonomos. However, their main reference was big wildcat
strikes, such as the one that took place at the Harry Walker factory, at the
Maquinista or, in 1976, the wildcat strike at the port of Barcelona.[3] We define these movements as autonomous because they referred to themselves in
this manner, because they were independent from political parties and trade
unions, and finally because they used direct action and organised horizontal
decision-making through assemblies.

Next to workers' activism, neighbourhood struggles played an increasingly important role. The era was characterised by strong urban development
and the promotion of Barcelona as a conference and trade-friendly capital. The
city and its population grew at a steady pace, leading to massive construction of
apartment blocks and of entire neighbourhoods in the peripheral rings to sup-
plant large zones of barrack huts.[4] Most of this urban restructuring generated
strong neighbourhood resistance. Due to the fact that Barcelona was by that
time a heavily polluted city, many of these struggles were focused on reclaiming
more green parks and the elimination of factories settled next to working-class
neighbourhoods. Sometimes, these struggles were controlled by leftist parties, mainly the Communist Party. But since its vertical organisation was often
criticised by the neighbours involved, many struggles developed independently,
using more democratic dynamics. They did not refer to other European neighbourhood struggles even if the issues at hand were in general similar. Women
played a very important role in these neighbourhood struggles. By the beginning of the 1980s, the neighbourhood movement had become more important
than the workers' movement.

This was also the result of the decline of autonomous workers' actions
after the so-called Moncloa Agreements of 1977. This pact was directed towards economic stability and was signed by the government, most political
parties represented in the National Congress, and the trade union Comisiones
Obreras. Those radical tendencies that did not agree with this institutionalisation of workers' power were effectively excluded, and subsequently, these groups
became isolated and the workers' movement lost its vibrant dynamics.[5]

In Barcelona, the years between the death of the dictator and the beginning of the 1980s were particularly intense and paved the way for a long-desired
tawakening of counter-cultural and radical political activities and a recovery of
the libertarian and anti-fascist past of Barcelona. This was evident in the found-

Previous page spread: Squat symbol welded to the peak of the 'rurban' squat Can Masdeu, 2009. Photo: Josh
MacPhee.

ing of several magazines, in the search for the heritage of the 1936 revolution, and in the opening of libertarian self-organised counter-cultural centres, called *ateneus* (athenaeums). These had already been established in the nineteenth century, in opposition to cultural centres of the bourgeoisie, in order that the working class could also have its own places where culture was understood as a means for people's emancipation. These libertarian ateneus can be seen as popular universities, with their own libraries and programmes to improve literacy among Spanish people. In addition to this, they also produced leaflets, books, and pamphlets, and organised excursions, conferences, talks, theatre plays, poetry or other cultural performances.

This experience was, and still is, so vivid in the collective libertarian memory because it represented a real and concrete opportunity to radically change the entire society after a civil war and four decades of dictatorship. Between 1976 and 1979, activism was also directed at an attempt to re-establish the anarchist syndicalist trade union, CNT, a project that failed at the national level because of the strong divisions within anarchist circles, but also because of a criminalisation campaign against the new libertarian movement. The infamous Scala incident is a good example of this. After a protest against the Moncloa Agreements, a discotheque was set on fire, claiming several lives. Prompted by an agent provocateur, this incident provided the first opportunity to criminalise the CNT as a terrorist organisation, as it strengthened the old Franquist myth of evil and murderous anarchists.[6]

At the local level, some libertarian ateneus remained active. They often collaborated with neighbourhood associations, which helped to maintain a connection with the people and with the struggles they faced against the remodelling of their neighbourhoods imposed from above to satisfy the plans of an ever-growing city. They were organised in the Libertarian Assembly of the Barcelona area, which would become the supporting base for many of the autonomous projects of the 1980s. Their activism focused on politically hot issues, such as abortion rights, anti-militarism, the struggle against prisons, and anti-nuclear activism. In the summer of 1977, thousands of people gathered in Park Güell for the Jornadas Libertarias Internacionales (International Libertarian Meeting) with speakers coming from across Catalonia, and eager to advance libertarian and anarchist debate, which was particularly vivid in those years after Franco's death. It was one of the most inspiring happenings of this new anti-authoritarian generation that would be the protagonist of the social and political struggles in the following years.[7] Also in 1977, the Ateneu Popular de Nou Barris was created, following a campaign of direct actions to stop a poisonous asphalt plant next to blocks of flats. The campaign included sabotage actions and occupations. The aim of the Ateneu Popular was to start a much-needed self-organised cultural centre for this working-class neighbourhood. The centre still exists and is generally considered a lasting example of successful self-organisation on a neighbourhood level.[8]

Despite several actions and campaigns in the second half of the 1970s, the 1980s began in Barcelona the same way as they did in the rest of the country. Caused by the general process of social demobilisation that occurred at the end of the transition period and the beginning of the new parliamentarian democracy, political disenchantment was widespread. The dominant sectors of the anti-Franco opposition were incorporated into the public administration, while the most radical proponents got sidetracked.

The victory of the social democratic Partido Socialista Obrero Español (PSOE) in 1982 did not bring about any major change in the living conditions of the population. Besides this, an economic crisis occurred which caused unemployment to grow, particularly among young people. It was a period in which heroin consumption peaked among youth in working-class neighbourhoods. In addition to this, robberies and other forms of crime increased, followed by police repression. The overall result was a high death toll among young people during this decade. The era witnessed the rise of a number of popular personalities like El Vaquilla, a delinquent from Pomar, a poor neighbourhood of Badalona, next to Barcelona. He became famous for being considered a social bandit: robbing banks and distributing the loot.

Politically, however, the young people of Barcelona did not feel they had many options to satisfy their needs for socialisation, for learning or for self-expression. This disenchantment caused them to flee into counter-cultural scenes.[9] In this atmosphere, the first punk bands were formed, the precursors of the first squatting activity in Barcelona. At the same time, some of the currents within the workers' movement of the 1970s switched from a labour-centred vision of social struggle to a general resistance to paid work. This was a precursor of the counter-cultural attitude that characterised most of the Barcelona autonomous movements of the following decades. However, they did not succeed in converging with other critical movements. It took a few years for this convergence between different currents of theoretical and practical autonomous struggle to occur.

¡PATADA EN LA PUERTA! (KICK IN THE DOOR!): THE FIRST SQUATTERS OF BARCELONA, 1984–1994

If we define the autonomous movement proper as a combination of a cultural critique of consumerist society, a DIY mentality, and, finally, a subversion of traditional political routines,[10] then this type of movement arises in Barcelona only towards the mid-1980s together with the first punks. Before this time, the autonomous workers' fights of the 1970s already represented an attempt to delegitimise traditional power structures and political routines. However, these young workers did not develop a proper counter-cultural movement that could be comparable to the rest of the European context.

At the beginning of the 1980s, young radical punk movements had only just come to the fore. They were composed of teenagers, mainly inspired by the music and aesthetics of the already well-established English movement. This early scene was, however, not yet politicised.

There was a strong institutional effort to crush what remained of the libertarian struggles of the previous decade. This included the different anarchist 'commandos' dedicated to robbing banks in order to fight the capitalist system and eventually support workers' strikes in the Barcelona area. Because of police repression and lack of a social base, these groups had all disbanded by 1983. Meanwhile, fanzine culture began to develop among youngsters along with free radio stations. Examples of the latter that have survived up to the present are Radio Pica, which was founded in 1981 and shut down by police between 1987 and 1991, and Radio Bronka, established in 1987. The 'do it yourself' philosophy that was connected to the punk scene started to flourish. This subculture identified itself as autonomous: independent of (and hostile to) political parties and trade unions, and supportive of horizontal forms of organising and decision-making through assemblies.[11]

The politicisation of this young scene was largely inspired by the arrival of hardcore and punk music and of activist groups, such as MDC from the United States, Razzia from Germany, Impact from Italy or BGK from the Netherlands. These bands used to translate their lyrics into Spanish, print them on flyers, and distribute them before their concerts among the public. Concerts were mainly organised in private establishments or youth centres. This, however, became increasingly difficult to sustain due to the damages that occurred during the concerts.

Concert venues and places for band rehearsals, workshops, and concerts became more and more scarce. Even though the cafés and bars in the city centre remained important for the social life of the youngsters, bigger non-commercial and self-managed spaces, like those that existed in other European cities, were needed. A need felt more keenly by youngsters from Barcelona and Madrid who had visited Amsterdam, Berlin, or Milan.[12] The punk fanzines also voiced the need for better organisation and a merging of the punk and the libertarian movement. Finally, in December 1984, the first squatting action occurred in Barcelona. It was organised by a group of youngsters named Colectivo Squat de Barcelona (CSB), and took place in the Torrent de l'Olla, in the Gràcia neighbourhood.[13] The action had been prepared a few months in advance, in order to create publicity and raise money and support. Important support came from the neighbourhood association of Gràcia and particularly the libertarian ateneu of Gràcia. The latter provided expertise, such as organisation for the press conference. The ateneu activists were a generation older, but felt closely connected to the libertarian militancy and their novel antagonist practices. This was probably the first politicised and public squatting action ever in the whole Spanish state. The action on the one hand tried to fill the need for autonomous space but was at the same time a critique of everyday consumerism. To cite one of the squatters:

We used to do everything. One time, in 1984, we realized that punks in (western) Europe had their own spaces and that squatters or krakers, occupied houses, so we also decided to try to get our own place for rehearsals. From then on, it was like a tornado: squatting, repression, contact with the libertarian 'Ateneus,' street protests, new occupations, jail, more protest, arrival of nazi skins, self-defense, fight against military service, further repression, till this day.[14]

This first squat was evicted within a few hours and nineteen people were arrested, but it nonetheless presented the opportunity for young punks to connect with the older generation of the libertarian ateneus from Gràcia and Poble Sec, who helped organise the press conference and legal support and showed the youngsters how to better defend themselves next time.

In February 1985, a second squatting action occurred in Calle Bolívar in the Vallcarca neighbourhood, which lasted just over a month. During the eviction, five arrests were made. The activists spent five days in jail because they were considered recidivists. This wave of repression caused the dissolution of the CSB. During the following short break in the squatting activities, several places in Barcelona served as social centres. Kafe Volter, established in October 1985, for example, served as a meeting point for many youngsters to hold assemblies, round tables, and to organise campaigns. This place, however, lasted only a year and became the stage for several violent confrontations between punks and Nazi gangs. These Nazis, with skinhead aesthetics, so called boneheads, became more visible and staged multiple violent attacks in the streets and against different places where punks gathered, like Kafe Volter.[15] These confrontations influenced an entire generation of young autonomous punks and squatters in Barcelona.

One of the most intense social struggles that was fought in this period, and in which many squatters and punks were involved, was the struggle against militarism. A milestone in this campaign was the protests against the referendum on Spain joining NATO on March 12, 1986, which was proposed by the socialist government. In the case of Barcelona, the anti-militarist mobilisation began in 1986 with a massive carnival parade through the city. The event was organised ad hoc in order to promote the refusal to join NATO. It was followed by rallying in support of a massive demonstration against the referendum in Madrid. But despite the widespread protests, the government eventually won the referendum. This struggle and eventual defeat was an important moment in the dynamic of the anti-militarist movement, which involved students, social movements, and radical left parties. The mobilisations contributed to the spreading of autonomist and anti-militarist ideas to large parts of the younger generation.[16]

In April, a month after the defeat in the referendum, an unauthorised street protest was organised against compulsory military service. The demonstration was attacked by the police from the start and ended in major riots in the city. On the following day, April 26, another protest was organised in support of the thirty-three people who had been arrested in the two squatting actions that occurred in the previous year, and who now stood trial. This was the first time the punk and squatter movement became visible to the broader public. After the protest, groups of people attacked the town hall and the building of the Catalan government, both in the central San Jaume square. A few hours later, in retaliation to these events, the local police attacked the Concentrik, a bar frequented by leftists and now filled with protesters. This resulted in further riots between the protesters and the police, ending with many people injured and fourteen arrests, seven of whom spent almost a month in jail. This unforeseen action by the police provoked a sudden widespread reaction among the young people of the city, marking a new stage in the social struggles of the time and resulting in the politicisation of many people. The most radical and dynamic sectors of the autonomous scene of Barcelona had finally been able to break out of their marginality. Large gatherings were organised in front of courthouses, prisons, and the town hall, which is a typically Spanish way to manifest rage as well as to provide support for repressed comrades. Members of the autonomous scene also participated in the general First of May demonstration, organised by the major trade unions, but as a separate bloc. They organised the symbolic action of burning a puppet resembling a policeman. This participation contributed to the building of solidarity networks with other sectors of the social movement.[17]

The movement protested against increased government control and police repression and for this they received support from neighbourhood associations, feminist and homosexual groups, radical parties from the extra-parliamentary left such as the Liga Comunista Revolucionaria, and civic associations. The youth presented themselves as the Plataforma Unitaria Anti-represiva de Jovenes (PUAJ, Youth United Against Repression) a heterogeneous and widespread association of politically active people from all over Barcelona. This surge in activism was unprecedented in scale since the transition. However, police attacks against gatherings in bars continued throughout the decade.

In October of this same year (1986), Barcelona was designated as the organiser of the Olympic Games of 1992, which had a profound impact on the city's history. This turn of events resurrected long-held plans of the elite to completely transform the city. Plans had been developed during the time of a Franquist mayor called Porcioles (1957–1973), who was in favour of the development of a 'Great Barcelona' and formulated the Plan General Matropolitáno (PGM), which is the guiding document for urban development still in force today. In this plan, it was foreseen that the metropolitan area of Barcelona could grow to a population of eleven million people, thus requiring new infrastructure and a complete overhaul of the city's landscape. During his rule, Porcioles became notorious in the working-class neighbourhoods, among leftist groups, and in ecologist circles for his aggressive plans of urban expansion and remodelling.

The Olympic Games were seen by leftists and ecologists as an excuse to invest an enormous amount of public money into new infrastructures that served to transform the city in ways that were detrimental to the living conditions of most of population. The idea behind it was, and still is, to remodel the old industrial structure, as industrial production had entered a crisis during the previous decade. The old city was to give way to a new fashion-designed post-industrial metropolis, characterised by a flourishing tourist industry and an advanced tertiary sector.[18] Barcelona was to be transformed into an investment-friendly city, resulting in a massive influx of international capital. Most of this capital was aimed at the development of the tourism industry in the area. In the process, employment became increasingly precarious.

At first, propaganda, prompted by the local governments (both the city's and the Catalan region's) was able to generate widespread consensus among Barcelona's citizens. The vision of a modern Mediterranean metropolis with high living standards, a social equilibrium, and the aspiration to become the economical capital of Southern Europe was appealing. In the end, however, people realised the dramatic impact these macro-projects had on the city and on society. The urban renewal process created a city divided by highways, with increasing social and economic inequalities, and police control. All this was done in the name of commerce. This became especially evident years later, in 2008, when the official Barcelona slogan was selling the city as the *botiga més gran del mon*, 'the biggest shop in the world.'[19]

The years 1986 and 1987 witnessed a steep rise of activism and protest. Firstly, there was an explosion of student protests. Massive student strikes were organised, both in high schools and universities, often ending in violent riots against the police. This constituted a good opportunity for a generation of youngsters to come together in open assemblies, were they could experience and practice horizontal processes of decision-making.[20] These actions were organised independently and were therefore beyond the control of the recently created student syndicates of Marxist inspiration, which were connected to the youth sections of the PSOE, and ruled instead through a hierarchic processes of decision-making. Years later, many of the students who had joined the strikes joined the growing struggle against militarism.

At the same time, also in 1986, there was the wildcat strike in the port of Barcelona, which we would define as an autonomous strike because it was organised through horizontal assemblies and without the support of the main trade unions or any other established institution. The organisation of this strike was coordinated spontaneously by workers, who came together and defined themselves as the Coordinadora de Estibadores Portuarios (Coordination of Port Stevedores). The strikers managed to take control of the port and launched a series of very radical and powerful direct actions, such as refusing to load weapons to be exported to Chile, taking the huge port cranes in a march to St Jaume Square or throwing 'blacklegs,' workers who were not joining the strike, in the sea. The strike rapidly spread to other parts of the country. From the trade union perspective, the strike clearly showed the friction between the generation of the early 1970s and the radicalised workers of the mid-1980s. The first had fought for democratisation and trade union legalisation. The latter had developed a strong fighting capacity—at a time when workers' struggles in general were weak in Spain and the country was joining the European Economic Community (EEC)[21]—which the workers now directed against the macro-economic policies of the new Spanish democracy, in which the Socialist Party and many of the former anti-Franquist activists played an important role.

Despite all the social unrest and criticism, Barcelona was designated as the host of the 1992 Olympic Games. The fight against this event was not a priority for most of the radical movements of Barcelona. Unlike other European cities like Amsterdam, where the autonomous and radical movement managed to effectively sabotage the city's nomination by radical and militant actions, in Barcelona resistance was small. One of the reasons for this could be the confusion caused by the defeat of the anti-NATO campaign. Another reason was that the squatter movement, as well as the fight against urban development, was still in its early phase though it would gain much more prominence later. Furthermore, the Catalan Socialist Party's (PSC) campaign was simply very convincing. It told the citizens of Barcelona that the games would be a boost for modernity in the city. Or, as the urban historian Joni D. stated: 'The Olympic Games signified the death of one city and the birth of a new one: the city as a shopping mall, the city as a theme park, the city as a tourist route. In those times, few people realised this and when we tried to react it was already too late: they did with the city what they wanted.'[22] In 1987, squatters again tried to create a social centre and this time they had more luck. In June, a two-story house was squatted at 10 Cros Street, in Sants district. It was thus named Cros 10. The squat was to be used by the libertarian assembly of Barcelona for meetings and organising campaigns and became the alternative and libertarian ateneu of Sants. It was used, among other things, for the campaign to boycott the political elections.

The squat action had an enormous impact. Before this event, squatting seemed impossible given the usual swift evictions by the police. For this reason, social centres were established in non-squatted buildings, sometimes rented, sometimes in buildings administered by the local council. Between 1987 and 1988, militant people close to the libertarian ateneus established two social centres. These places were useful to foment counter-cultural exchange and to provoke a subversive environment similar to the one represented previously by Kafe Volter and similar to the Amsterdam Info-Cafés. They were El Lokal in Cera street, in the Raval neighbourhood, and Anti in the Libertat street of Gràcia, close to the libertarian ateneu of Gràcia. Both constituted small safe zones for the movement.[23]

Towards the end of the decade, anti-military struggles became more intense and resistance against the alternative civilian service increased. At the same time, the cultural distance from the workers' movements of the previous decades grew as counter-cultural elements became more prevalent within the movement. Towards the 1990s, these characteristics had become so strongly rooted in the movement that we can speak of an 'autonomous movement' in the classic sense of the word: a radical urban youth movement. This became obvious because of the movement's participation in 'the international day of sabotage,' that has occurred annually on April 30 since 1987. The day was characterised by direct actions against banks, political parties, and enterprises. This attack on paid work and mainstream trade unions was repeated on other occasions, as when general strikes were being called. On December 14, 1988, the main trade-unions organised a general strike against the reform of the labour market prompted by the socialist government. During the day, different autonomous and libertarian groups organised in a decentralised way in different neighbourhoods, and executed direct actions such as closing bars and shops that had not joined the strike and informing passers-by and shop tenants of the reasons for the strike in the mornings. In the afternoon, the groups came together in the city centre for a joint street demonstration.

Towards the end of 1989, following the example of the Cros 10 squat, several groups and people in the city squatted various buildings. This activity culminated in the squatting of Kasa de la Muntanya, a building still occupied today. This famous squat was instrumental in extending this practice across the city, in particular to Gràcia and Vallcarca—the neighbourhoods where Kasa de la Muntanya is located, which became prime neighbourhoods for squatting after 1990.

The urban development plans of the authorities of Barcelona and its surrounding towns continued inexorably, notwithstanding violent riots by locals that tried to resist them. An example of this was the fight of the residents of El Besòs against the construction of more apartment blocks instead of previously promised social facilities. The protests culminated in battles with the police. In the same year (1991), both Editorial Virus, an autonomous publishing company, and Radio Contrabanda, a free radio station were founded. Both soon became important players in the autonomous-libertarian scene in the city. In the same period, another wave of sporadic encounters with Nazi skins occurred.

As a consequence of the support of the First Gulf War by the Spanish Army in 1991, the number of objectors to military service across the Spain increased dramatically. Many youngsters obliged to undergo military service did not agree with the war, much less could they imagine themselves being actually called into battle. The objectors were supported by associations like Mili KK (Mili Shit), Movimiento de Objeción de Conciencia (MOC), and Colectivo Antimilitarista Pro-Insumisión (CAMPI), and organised in Barcelona in the organisation Casal de la Pau.

In the summer of 1992, the Olympic Games were held and apart from some minor actions, nothing was done. In the period just after the Olympic

Games, a number of squatting projects in the city became well-known to a broader public. These were Casal de Guinardo, Kasa de la Muntanya, Ateneu de Korneyà, Adokines in Santa Coloma, and Vaqueria in L'Hospitalet. The last project in particular became more open and inviting and was not just focused on the punk movement that continued to dominate the movement in Barcelona, as well as in the rest of Spain.[24]

Between 1993 and 1994, several initiatives were undertaken to organise better coordination between the squatting projects in Gràcia and Guinardo, and between 1994 and 1995 the first squat assembly of Barcelona was organised. This assembly remained active throughout the rest of the decade, formulating a response to the development plans of the city government. The motive behind this sudden coordination was the establishment of a new penal code in 1995, according to which both civil disobedience and squatting would be considered criminal behaviour. In 1995, the Casal Popular of Guinardo organised the first squatters' gathering, in which two hundred people participated and several working groups were formed. *Info Usurpa*, a weekly agenda for the social centres' activities was printed on an A-3 paper format and stuck to the doors of squats or glued to street walls; this was the first internal media of Barcelonese squats.[25]

CINE PRINCESA AND THE EXTENSION OF THE AUTONOMOUS MOVEMENTS (1996–2006)

Towards the middle of the 1990s, the first street protests against real estate speculation were organised, mainly in response to municipal government plans such as the gentrification of the central district of Ciutat Vella under the auspices of the Olympic Games. During one of the protests against real estate speculation—and against the fake consensus that had been created in Barcelona around the Olympic Games—something important happened: on March 10, 1996, the Cine Princesa was squatted.[26] The occupation of the building, situated in the very centre of Barcelona (on Via Laietana), can be seen as the libertarian/autonomous movements answer to real-estate speculation. It was conceived during the Spanish squatters gathering, the Jornadas de Okupación Estatal, held in the squatted social centre Casal del Guinardó. The action had been preceded by careful preparation and the choice of the building was very symbolic. The cinema had been the place of the first trade union meetings after the death of Franco between 1976 and 1977. The older generation, that of the autonomous workers of the seventies, helped in the action. This cooperation of two generations of militant people, inspired by different ways of conceiving autonomy, somehow anticipated the influence that this squatter action would have on many social movements in later times. In fact, militants who came together constituted what we now understand as the autonomous and libertarian movement of Barcelona. This movement, which by 1996 had already emerged as a very broad and diverse

one, longed to find physical places for expression, and understood the strategic role of squatting. In fact, squatting was an ideal method of criticizing the logic of the established system and, in particular, real estate speculation.

During the seven months of its existence, the Cine Princesa served as a central social space where all sorts of different gatherings were held and organised: anti-repression meetings, the anniversary of the gay liberation front, the assemblies of the neighbourhood movement, and concerts in support of the Zapatista rebellion. After the occupation of the Cine Princesa, other emblematic buildings were also occupied, such as La Hamsa in the Sants district. In September 1996, after the local government threatened to evict the squatters, a number of artists and famous musicians expressed their support. Despite this, the squatters were attacked by the police on October 28; the social centre was closed and forty-eight people were arrested and subsequently beaten and maltreated by the national police. Such infamous and illegal practices as beating detainees; keeping them under arrest and in isolation and without communication for longer than the legal limit; not providing them with basic necessities such as water or food; psychologically threatening them; verbally abusing non-whites, immigrants, and women; and taking them to repeated, unannounced interrogations still occur in police stations throughout Spain.

In the afternoon of October 28, masses of enraged people from various neighbourhoods protested in solidarity with the youngsters who had been beaten up. During the protest, the police station in Laietana Street was attacked by stone-throwing protesters. For many people involved, this was an important experience, because it was their first experience with violent forms of protest.[27]

Despite the tough approach by the authorities, many new people now joined the movement and in the spring of 1997, in the central Borne neighbourhood, a music festival was organised, combined with a protest for the decriminalisation of squatting. Finally, on April 6, ten houses were occupied simultaneously all over the city. Among the places that were squatted were El Palomar in Sant Andreu and the Casal de Joves in Gràcia.

The political situation at that time was beneficial to squatting because the conservative Partido Popular had won the general election of June 1996, while in Catalonia and Barcelona the Catalan nationalists of Convergencia i Unió (CiU) and the Catalan socialist party were governing, respectively. This political contrast created a certain kind of tolerance towards the social movements of Catalonia and Barcelona, since the local rulers maintained a certain sympathy for 'fellow victims' of the central Spanish government. The Catalan popular leftist movements were often inspired by a sense of cultural regionalism and shared with the libertarian movements an aversion towards the central government. The best example of this was the different way the local governments of Madrid and Barcelona treated the protests of 2003 against the Iraq war supported by the Partido Popular government. Moreover, during a short

Left: Graffiti at Can Masdeu, 2009. Photo: Josh MacPhee.

period of time, the PSC and the mass media showed some sympathy towards the practice of squatting.

In December 1996, Kan Pasqual, located in the Sierra de Collserola area, a mountain range between Barcelona and the Vallès county was squatted. This was an old holiday camp house in a rural environment which represented the beginning of a new squatting model that from then on developed in the fringe space between the city and the country: a combination of rural and urban characteristics, referred to as 'rurban' (rural-urban) squatting.

In 1997, squatter actions extended all over the city and many people began to participate actively in squatting projects. Places like Can Vies in Sants or Les Naus in Gràcia were established and the existence of a network within the city became evident in the summer of 1997, when actions were organised at different places to celebrate the second conference for humanity and against neoliberalism, promoted by collectives in support of the Zapatista rebellion. Since 1994, a movement in support of the Zapatista rebellion had emerged under the leadership of El Lokal, an autonomous space which became known across Europe for its close relationship with the Mexican rebels, and which also contributed to the thinking about autonomy and the necessary means of obtaining it. Many people in the decades of the 1990s and beginning of the twenty-first century—once the strength of the movement of conscientious objectors decreased—participated in social struggle through support groups for the Zapatista rebellion, including sending brigades of international observers to the area.

By this time, squatting had brought together a wide range of different libertarian groups around Barcelona. They started to coordinate themselves through the squat assembly that gathered on a monthly basis and created their own media for communication and coordination, such as the *Info Usurpa* and the *Contra Infos*. Both were weekly newspapers printed on three A-3 sheets to be hung outside doors or on street walls. The first showed the weekly agenda of each squat, while the latter published alternative and independent news from and about social movements and campaigns. Both were published on Tuesdays and distributed from Espai Obert (Open Space), a social centre initially rented in the central Poble Sec neighbourhood and nowadays located in the Sants district. The goal of Espai Obert was to be used as a service space for the squatter movement and related social movements; it thus had computer facilities and rooms for occasional meetings. Soon, it became a node in the network of various left-wing libertarian groups in the city.

At the same time, during the Spanish squatters' gathering at Les Naus, some women from the squatters' movement began to claim their own spaces to share their experiences as women participating into the movement. Following this initial example, the Coordinadora Feminista Autónoma was created, joining together many women's autonomous collectives that had been formed during the 1990s. These new groups were influenced by the lesbian and feminist autonomous groups of the early 1980s, which had not been directly involved in the early squatters' movement, but were nevertheless horizontally organised and had developed independently from institutionalised feminist groups. The new groups created during the 1990s on the other hand, were constituted by women who were usually involved in the squatter movement. Some of them were the Unides i Enemigues del Patriarcat, La Chalás, Les Tenses, Les Ovariques. They started to work together in the Coordinadora Feminista Autónoma for a campaign against sexual violence in the winter of 1997–1998. They also organised weekly meetings related to feminism and anti-fascism, anti-capitalism or counter-information in the squatted social centre Kan Titella in Gràcia. This also led to the foundation of *Mujeres Preokupando*, a magazine dealing with feminist issues and squatting. *Mujeres Preokupando* was produced by autonomous women's collectives from different parts of Spain, each of which was in charge of editing an issue every one or two years. In Barcelona, the Coordinadora Feminista Autónoma was a site of convergence for women participating within the squatters' movement until its dissolution in 2002.[28]

The year 1999 was important for several reasons. First, the Jornadas de Lluita Social 'Trenquem el silenci' (Gathering of Social Struggle 'Let's break the silence') were organised in Barcelona, as well as in Madrid and in Córdoba (Andalusia). Many autonomous groups from Barcelona participated in them and organised direct actions in order to make numerous social inequalities and problems visible.

In October of the same year, a confrontation unfolded in the Sants neighbourhood between anti-fascists and the police, who were protecting a demonstration by Spanish fascists. This annual demonstration in the Sants neighbourhood traditionally involved riots. This year however, the conflict reached a critical level. Because of the size of the confrontation and the following repression, a new generation of autonomous activists in Barcelona, in particular the Sants district, was forged with support of the local social centres.

But the big increase in criminalisation that resulted from the local law enforcement's claim that links existed between squatters and the Commando Barcelona, the local branch of the Basque ETA, had even more impact. The news created widespread divisions within the broader political left as well as within the autonomous movement. The autonomous left was divided because ETA resisted the central government because of its regionalist/nationalist ideology. Some activists were sympathetic to this, because most squatters are anti-state, whether Spanish, Catalan or Basque. Most however rejected the ETA's ideology. The news had a very negative impact on public opinion and prompted the movement's increasing criminalisation. It marked the end of an expansive phase of the movement between 1996 and 1999. After this, it would not return to its former strength.

In the following year, 2000, a series of large mobilisations against big events began. The first of these was a grand military parade in May. It was

assemblea de
joves de gràcia

okupar és resistir,
resistir és vèncer!!

promoted by the right-wing central government because, since the abolition of compulsory military service in 1998, the army had become a professional service, which needed to promote its image among the population. As a protest against this march, a protest camp in the streets was formed and several groups connected to, or part of, the independent left proclaimed boycotts of the event. In support of the protest Plataforma Unitària per la Pau (Unitary Platform for Peace), a platform composed of anti-militarists, Catalan independence supporters, and other social movements distributed a one-time-only newspaper to support the mobilisations.

For the first time in several years, the squatter movement was not leading the protests: new spaces, which were not squatted, were beginning to take the lead, such as the Espai Obert, a large and centrally located building founded by the Libertarian Ateneu of Poble Sec. At the same time, the anti-globalisation movement—emerging from the Seattle protests of 1999—started to gather strength. Actions were being prepared for protests against the international summits of the coming year.

The new millennium marked the development of activism targeted at more global structures. The anti-globalisation movement, which reached its peak at the beginning of the decade, held massive protests in Barcelona. It brought together people from radical groups with more moderate and 'broad' left people and organisations. For instance, during the World Bank meeting of summer 2001 and the EU meeting in the spring of 2002, hundreds of thousands of people turned out to protest, partially answering the call from several left-wing political parties and the main trade unions. In addition, decentralised actions were organised by affinity groups, which were a part of the squatter movement and other direct-democracy social movements.

After the G8 meeting in Genoa in 2001—during which the activist Carlo Giuliani was killed—the anti-globalisation movement began to decline and change; in Barcelona, it started focusing more on local struggles. The first one of these was the protest against Spanish participation in the Second Gulf War in 2003, the second against a massive urban renovation plan in 2004. Both brought together many different parts of the population. The most important campaign was the movement in 2003 against the Iraq invasion. While the right-wing Spanish government supported the Iraq war and even participated in it, Catalonia and Barcelona, both governed by a central left coalition, opposed the war. Several hundred thousand people marched against the war. Again, this was accompanied by direct actions by affinity groups. To a lesser extent, the autonomous groups of the city united in 2004 to protest against the Forum de les cultures (Forum of the Cultures), a cultural event that was regarded as a cover for a massive renovation plan with public money and at the same time the privatisation of the post-industrial area on the waterfront, which has been turned into a tourist attraction.

Left: A mural marking a squatted social center, 2009. Photo: Josh MacPhee.

Info Usurpa

"i no anem amb compte
els mitjans de comunicació,
s faran estimar l'opressor
i odiar l'oprimit"

Malcolm X

MARÇ 18
...RESES POLÍTIQUE...
...CATALU...

Visita...
www.si...

la G...
un
TIENDA
"tot

50 MILLO
I IMP...
HASTA CUAND...
NO A LA...

JUAN ALEX I...
1 ANY SEGREST...
EN UN MUNTATGE DE...
MANIFESTACIÓ 4 DE FEBR...
PL. UNIVERSITAT 18:00...
CONCENTRACIÓ A JUTJATS PEL PROCÉS...
26 DE GENER 9:30H...
27 DE FEBRER 9:30H...
www.s...

LA LLEI D'ESTRANG...
PROU DISCRIM...
MANIFESTA...

In 2005 and 2006, again many people mobilised in protests against the establishment of the Civic Law in Barcelona, which curtailed many freedoms of use of public spaces, criminalizing—through extremely high fines—a wide range of youth and lower-class behaviour, such as skating, spray painting, sticking posters on public walls, the drinking of alcohol, ball games, prostitution, unauthorised street selling, begging, peeing, and spitting.

PER TOT ARREU (ALL OVER THE PLACE): EXPANSION AND DECENTRALISATION

Squatting continued. The movement became more diverse as more buildings were occupied. With the increase in rents and the popularity of Barcelona as a destination for young Europeans, the squatting phenomenon has grown to include many places that are squatted for housing purposes and not necessarily as social centres. This contributes to the movement's openness and diversity but also signifies that the movement is less unified than in the previous decade.

Info Usurpa, the autonomous weekly bulletin and agenda of the movement, shows an increase in the amount of entries on its list. The number of squatted social centres offering public activities has increased from less than thirty in the 1990s to more than sixty at the time of this writing. The geographical reach of the squatting movement and the wider activist scene has increased to include the wider metropolitan area in a forty-kilometre radius around the city centre.

As the Barcelona squatter scene became well known in Europe, an influx of people from other European countries followed. On the one hand, this increased the amount of squats and social centres while causing the movement to become more diffused on the other. Due to this diffusion, the Barcelona Squat Assembly has only been active sporadically in the last decade.

Squatters from foreign countries have often been less connected with the issues of the different localities, because they often lack contact with local people, neighbourhood movements, and the struggles of their neighbourhood, and also because of language barriers. They often stick to their own national language or, at best, speak English, leaving them isolated from locals, who—like most people on the Iberian Peninsula—have a hard time understanding foreign languages.

Following the brutal eviction of the Cine Princesa—which brought the squatters popularity and sympathy—the movement experienced a period in which the social centres were few, the squatters' assembly had just been established, and everyone knew each other. As the movement kept on growing and the number of squats increased, massive evictions became common, which contributed to conflicts becoming more visible.

In July 2000, the National Police, after evicting Kan Ñoqui, also evicted the squatters from the nearby Kasa de la Muntanya, but the latter without a

Left: *Info Usurpa* weekly calendar wheatpasted to the front of the squat Miles de Viviendas, 2009. Photo: Josh MacPhee.

court order. This incited two days of street riots and protests, during which one person lost his eye due to a rubber bullet. The protests ended in the reoccupation of the historical squat. Between April 30 and May 2, 2002, authorities attempted to evict Can Masdeu. In response to this, more than three hundred people were mobilised for more than sixty hours. Eleven squatters hung off the walls of the building as a form of resistance against the eviction. It was an example of how evictions could be stopped without a violent defence. In 2003, four major squats in the Barcelona area—the Ateneu de Viladecans, Ateneu de Korneyà, Kasa de la Muntanya, and Can Masdeu—were under threat of eviction. The squatters' assembly organised fifteen days of events in support of the squats which led to a partial victory; at least for the time being. Kasa de la Muntanya, which was under the most imminent threat of eviction, managed to hold on. Ateneu de Korneyà, however, was lost after a few months of resistance.

After the eviction of La Hamsa in August 2004, two direct actions were executed in order to show that the conflict was still going on. The first consisted of occupying La Pedrera, the famous building designed by Gaudí and a real tourist attraction in the city centre. The other was a symbolic re-occupation of La Hamsa: symbolic, because the building had been destroyed in the meanwhile. In 2007, La Makabra was evicted. This was an artists' squat that, together with other squats, had introduced the tradition of squatting places for developing artistic activities such as circuses, theatres, dances, and skating. The large abandoned industrial estates of the Poble Nou provided the opportunity for the squatting of larger buildings that could be used for cultural activities, such as La Nave, ArtKatraz, and La Makabra. The (attempted) evictions of these buildings showed that the city administration had designated the area for the development of a business district. Autonomous or cultural activities were deemed unwanted.

In 2008 and 2011, Can Vies, in the Sants district, won two civil cases against the owner, the Transport Metropolitans de Barcelona. This allowed the historically important social centre to remain in the heart of this traditionally active neighbourhood.

Squatting in Barcelona has mostly been centred in specific neighbourhoods because the existence of a cluster of squats located close to each other reinforced local resistance and forged solidarity and mutual aid. Gràcia/Vallcarca, Sants and San Andreu have been the central neighbourhoods where the first wave of squats and social centres were established. Up to a century ago, when Barcelona comprised only what is now known as the Old Town district, Gràcia, Sants and San Andreu used to be independent municipalities, separated from Barcelona by fields, and were only later incorporated into the Barcelona municipality. Nowadays, these neighbourhoods still show some resemblance to old villages, and harbour a great number of people who have been living there for a long time. Perhaps these urban and social characteristics can explain why squat-

Right: Squatters prepare for an eviction attempt at Can Masdeu. Photo: Unknown.

ting has emerged here. On the other hand, it did not succeed in the Old Town because repression has always been much more strident against attempts to set up a social centre in the city's heart, as the case of the Cine Princesa in 1996 emblematically showed.

Still, it is hard to explain with accuracy why squats have emerged particularly in these areas, and not at other places. Other city districts and neighbourhoods lacked squats and social centres altogether. In the most recent years, the clustering phenomenon has become even more evident: while the total number of squats in the city has increased dramatically, their presence is much less spread out. The eradication of squatting from some neighbourhoods, which is also difficult to explain, seems to imply that other neighbourhoods, such as the Clot neighbourhood, have emerged as squatting centres. Some activities have also shifted to neighbourhoods on the city's periphery.

The first squats of the 1980s and 1990s were created mainly out of a desire for social and public spaces where young people could realise their dreams and interests. These places brought with them a DIY culture and harboured the punk scene. Within these spaces a radical discourse developed that was critical of 'paid work' and consumer society, mostly because of the time constraints imposed by maintaining a full-time job. In the following years, the demand for decent housing became more prominent as rents soared. This contributed to a rise in squatting activities for housing, instead of social spaces that performed a public utility. A popular movement against real estate speculation also gained strength, culminating in the creation of a platform named Barcelona contra la Especulación in 2002.[29]

This platform fought urban projects, such as El Forat de la Vergonya. In the crowded area of Santa Caterina, in the proximity of the cathedral, the local government planned to build a massive sports complex, complete with an underground car park largely paid for by the EU. The local community, however, was told they were going to build a park. When the latter found out they had been cheated, they built their own park. Eventually, the authorities constructed a wall around the self-built public park in order to start construction. This wall was subsequently destroyed during a popular protest.[30] The entire project was cancelled after a successful appeal to the EU by the platform. The self-created park continued to exist until 2006, when the municipal authorities decided to install their own infrastructure. The site is now managed by the community.

The more institutionalised federation of neighbourhood-associations of Barcelona (Federació de Associacions de Veins i Veines de Barcelona, FAVB), initially supported the platform, but later withheld its approval. This resulted in a weakening of the movement. Despite this, the platform has continued to be active until the present day and has engaged in several successful campaigns, all with the objective of preserving public space.[31]

The movement for decent housing was of a less radical nature, but adopted throughout the country. It worked with the slogan, 'No tendras casa en la puta vida' (You will never own a house in your fucking life). Since 2006, this movement organised several large demonstrations across Spain to demand the right to decent housing, guaranteed by Article 47 of the Spanish Constitution. This culminated in the formulation of a list of demands, including a proposal to cut housing rents to a maximum of 20 percent of a person's salary.

In Barcelona, the movement was represented by the Taller contra la Violencia Inmobiliaria y Urbanistica (workshop against urban and real-estate violence), an info-point in defence of tenants' rights. Its office was on the ground-floor of Magdalenas, a squatted building in Carrer Magdalenas, which rather than a squat defined itself as part of the PHRP network (Promoció d'Habitatge Realment Públic, promotion of really public housing). PHRP campaigns consisted of squatting empty blocks of flats for housing purposes. PHRP Magdalenas furthered the legalisation of its squatting projects through active negotiation with the city council. This caused a rupture with the Barcelona Squat Assembly.[32] There is no history of legalisation of squats in Barcelona. Squatters tend to reject every form of dialogue with the authorities, especially dialogues aimed at legalisation. Activists fear that legalisation would create a precedent for authorities to offer the possibility of legalisation to some squats while evicting others.

There was, however, one previous case of legalization in 2000, which involved the Torreblanca squat in the neighbouring town of Sant Cugat. This caused a conflict within the Squat Assembly that resulted in the exclusion of Torreblanca from the *Info Usurpa* list. PHRP Magdalenas was legalised in 2008. This squatted block of flats—in which two flats were still legally occupied by their rightful tenants—was under threat of being transformed into a hotel by real-estate developers. After a prolonged struggle, an agreement with the authorities was reached. The occupiers received a space to continue their political activities and the plan to convert the building into a hotel was cancelled. These two cases, however, do not seem to have affected the general tendency of squatters to refuse negotiations with governing institutions. This attitude is mutual, as the government is not eager to start any legalisation processes. Agreements are, however, often reached between squatters and private owners.

UNA FINESTRA AL CAMP (A WINDOW LOOKING AT THE COUNTRYSIDE): THE RURBAN MOVEMENT

Parallel to developments in the city, and partially connected to them, a new type of autonomy emerged in the new millennium. It came from the 'rurban' squats established on the Collserola hills surrounding central Barcelona.[33] The project of Kan Pasqual, a social centre and community housing project of about ten to fifteen people, and its surrounding 'neighbourhood' of smaller houses was developing on the secluded hills of the southwest side of Collserola. In late 2001,

Can Masdeu, a larger community home of roughly twenty-five people, with an active social centre on the north of Collserola, very close to the Nou Barris working-class neighbourhood, was squatted as well.

The rurban practice is an original take on the typical squatting principles oriented towards autonomy, horizontal self-organisation, DIY practices, and a critique of the established system. This is not only clear from the illegal occupations of abandoned buildings and the realisation of social and housing projects, but also from the use of the land and its produce in a typical squatters' way. The result is a unique relationship with the rural space in the form of collective production, ecological organic agriculture, care for the environment, and the establishment of a political-ecological discourse that considers market capitalism and the established forms of power and control as detrimental to normal life. Alternatively, the people involved can live in closer connection to nature and higher autonomy from industrial forms and human-made means of production.

One of the members of Kan Pasqual was inspired by the visit of Al Gore to Barcelona. He described the project as follows:

> I live in a rural squat with 15 adults and three kids. We have a relatively low level of CO_2 emissions, similar to that of a poor country. But poor we are not. We have a very rich and diverse lifestyle; every week is a cycle of visits, fiestas, assemblies, farm and kitchen tasks, all kind of workshops. We organise counter-information, meals, street protests, concerts, popular meals, games for kids and, again, fiestas. We live as in a creative tornado, set free by a squatting movement that still they have not managed to control.
>
> Most of what we do is difficult to apply in general: a couple with children living in a flat, and both working to pay rent or a mortgage, will not have time to use wood to cook or recycle groceries. We recycle a lot from the recycling point, where we are given anything that is thrown away by others. Our friends give us things that do not fit in their flats. Recycling extends the lifecycle of products and no CO_2 is wasted in its production and neither is money. Even our house is recycled! If it wasn't for us, it would already be a ruin and to build a home for 15 people would release hundreds of tons of CO_2. It is always better to renew an old house.
>
> We are not connected to the electricity network. After a few years of working with candles, we got solar panels and we have now constructed a windmill. There is not enough electricity for a washing machine and we can recharge the laptop only on sunny days.
>
> We heat the house with wooden stoves and, in part, cook with wood. We only collect fallen wood, leaving something to regenerate the forest. Not everybody can use wood, and a lot of fallen wood is not collected, thus making the forest very flammable. We tend to 11 orchards, some of them very big, and we use the manure of two retired horses. We have some permaculture, mulching to keep moisture, foment biodiversity with mini habitats and a pool. We do two

jobs in one.

We do not get water from the water network. Instead, we collect it from roofs and paths storing it into deposits and reservoirs and pump it (with diesel, it's true) from a well. We use a deposit as a swimming pool!

We have chickens and ducks eating the remains of our food, dry bread and some grains. The city used to be full of chickens and orchards and, in time, could be again. We make beer, conserves, jam, crafts, medicinal creams, spirits, wine, magazines; we have a massive library, workshops for wood, mechanics, mycology, natural health, astronomy, etc.

We have a super compost toilet built by German carpenters. We hope that what we do in Kan Pasqual could continue to inspire practical changes, whether as a mini orchard on the terrace or to foment social revolution! The best would be to come for a visit and participate.

The rurban discourse is spread through entries in leftist newspapers such as *La Directa* and *Diagonal*, and also through neo-rural fanzines such as *La llamada del cuerno*. It is an object of debate in the movement, which organises meetings on rural squatting and rural re-population. The discourse places great emphasis on ecological forms of production, such as low-energy intensity, a reliance on renewable energies, the employment of renewable organic materials and the closing of water and material cycles. The rurban projects try to show that, in an era of increasing scarcity of natural resources, the urban lifestyle is unsustainable. As an alternative, they propose practices more in harmony with the natural environment.[34]

They thus represent an innovative combination of anti-capitalist practices with the construction of real alternatives. They also create a link between the urban and the rural reality. Barcelona, with its prominent Collserola hill, shows dramatically how close these two realities are connected. They are separated only by a few kilometres.[35]

The rurban movement of Barcelona has contributed to a new wave of activism, combining environmentalism with general aspects of anti-capitalist resistance. Examples are the Catalan movement against GMOs (genetically modified organisms), that established an agro-ecological network, and the European-wide Reclaim the Fields movement.[36] Apart from this, the squats have also participated actively in the defence of the Collserola Park, which is now a Natural Park, but which is under constant threat of the ever-expanding city. The most prominent example of the new activism has been the establishment in 2007 of a network of people and groups defending the side of Collserola facing Barcelona, which was under threat due to urban development.[37]

¡NINGÚ ENS REPRESENTA! (NOBODY REPRESENTS US!): THE PRESENT

Following page spread: Gathering at Can Masdeu. Photo: Unknown.

Currently, the squatter movement in Barcelona is more heterogeneous than ever. New topics and forms of action, beyond squatting, are becoming visible.

First, organisations such as Te kedas donde kieras (You stay where you want) and Observatori de Drets Socials (Socials Rights Observatory) have formed to support non-documented immigrants, a vulnerable group suffering from ever increasing repression, exclusion, and deportation.

Additionally, widespread resistance has flared up against fines leveed as punishment for direct actions such as squatting, mobilisations during strikes, and so on. Instead, these groups have opted to go to jail for the number of days equivalent to the value of the fine.[38] In 2009, a person was sentenced to prison for not paying the fine related to the protests against Pla Caufec: a massive urban real estate project on the hills of Collserola near the south entrance to Barcelona.[39] The person suspended himself from a nearby skyscraper for three days, in protest against this project.

Since the dissolution, in 2002, of the Coordinadora Feminista Autónoma, the feminist autonomous movement has moved into the Mambo squat. This house was squatted in 2006 and is situated in the centre of Barcelona. Here, activists have created a social centre exclusively for women, a space where different currents of autonomous feminism converge. Focal points for the autonomous feminist movement are the relation between art and politics, the struggle against heteronormativity, fighting harassment of sexual workers in the centre of Barcelona, and criticism of institutionalised feminism.[40] This Mambo collective—an acronym for Autonomous Moment of Audacious Women and Lesbians—was evicted in 2007, but continues to be active and contributes to the cooperation and communication between various radical feminist collectives in Barcelona.[41]

Other groups also focus on gender issues and the fight against transphobia, such as the Stop Trans Pathologization campaign. Some of these groups are organised around social centres like La Revoltosa, in the Clot neighbourhood, or the Feministas Indignadas, who were formed after the 15M movement in 2011. Since 2011, various feminist collectives organised the Jornadas Feministas Autónomas (the autonomous feminist conference) every March under the name 'Se va a armar la gorda' (we are going to make a racket). The conference consists of workshops in squatted houses, and a nighttime, torchlight demonstration on March 7.

In 2008, students of the University of Barcelona occupied the rectorate of their central building for several weeks to protest the Bologna Plans to reform the university system in the EU. After the students were evicted from the building, major street protests occurred, followed by the usual police repression. However, the students did not lose their motivation and occupied La Rimaia, an old building, in order to create an independent space that was declared a Free University. Despite two evictions, the project survived until May 2012 in a different place: La Rimaia III. In 2013, the project moved again after another eviction: to La Base, in Poble Sec, this time in a rented space.

Several autonomous radical groups have become more and more integrated, as is shown by the formation of the Assembly of Barcelona, made up of people from the Squat Assembly and neighbourhood movements, which—during the last general strike in autumn 2010—squatted, although temporarily, an abandoned bank in the most central square of the city.

Because of this cooperation, the overall picture of the movement today is quite heterogeneous: the past years have seen a flourishing of many collectives dealing with an enormous variety of issues. The autonomous movement has become an important part of Barcelona's left-wing milieu, as can be illustrated by a few more examples.

La Pinya, for example, is a free kindergarten/pre-school that brings together young parents of various movements, who are interested in educating their children according to an alternative pedagogy and different values from those of the typically patriarchal family structure. The school, where children are already trained in the practice of the assembly, is located in Cal Suis, a squatted building in Esplugues, a town bordering with Barcelona.

On October 17, 2008, the activist Enric Duran announced that he had committed fraud against more than thirty credit institutions. Duran—who soon become known as Robin Banks—is a Barcelona-based activist who holds that the infinite growth of the financial system (based on the constant creation of virtual money, made by credit institutions) is detrimental to society and the planet. He therefore sought to attack capitalism at its very core: by falsifying documents, he managed to borrow €492,000, which he never paid back. Instead, he used the money to fund other activities that would promote a new society. His statement was among others published in the Catalan free newspaper *Crisis*, which was distributed by activists. Duran was arrested and has spent two months in jail. Court cases are still ongoing, at higher courts.

Following his line of reasoning, a number of groups that promote degrowth against the idea of constant economic growth are increasingly present in street protests. A practical way to conceive a degrowth society is through the Cooperativa Integral: a project that seeks to bring together tenants, producers and consumers. At this moment, there is such an attempt in progress in Ca La Fou, a former industrial colony in the province of Barcelona. Those involved aim at reviving traditional industrial production in a cooperative manner.

The neo-rural movement, which focuses on life in the countryside and serves as an inspiration for the rurban tendency in cities, is increasing stable. Inspired by the values and the style of rural life, it does not just develop in the countryside as activists engaged in the tiring struggles of urban movements are increasingly turning towards this way of life. The rurban environment—such as on the Collserola hills of Barcelona, a natural park of over eight thousand hectares with many abandoned country houses—is an excellent area for this,

Following page spread: 'Everything is possible.' http://oscarmateos.wordpress.com/2012/05/11/5-reflexiones-sobre-el-15m/15m-barcelona-644x362/

but not the only one: Can Piella, a vibrant rurban squat active in the pan-European movement Reclaim the Fields as well as in the integration of local eco-alternatives in the Vallès county, is located ten kilometres north of Barcelona and is preparing its resistance against an imminent eviction at the time of this writing.[42] As the spread of community gardens shows, the urban milieu can also provide for a similar lifestyle, and several gatherings have been organised by these groups since 2009.[43]

A number of radical autonomous groups are also inspired by an anti-industrial mentality, and see a close link between capitalism and the colonisation of the physical environment. According to them, the territorial expansionism of the state and capitalistic enterprises needs to be fought, a struggle that does not just take place in cities and their urban sprawl but also outside the cities, far away from the eyes of the multitude. These collectives have come together in anti-industrial gatherings, such as in July 2010 with the Acampada de Resistencies (Resistance Camps) in the province of Girona. Recently, they have also organised actions of direct resistance against major infrastructure projects, like the MAT project (Very High Voltage Power Line). This project is supposed to deliver electricity at four hundred kilovolts from Africa to Europe and will pass through Catalonia. During winter 2010, a three-month long protest tree camp was organised in the province of Girona. The forest where the tree camp was situated would have been felled to let the line pass.

There has also been clandestine resistance against GMOs, a movement apparently inspired by French popular movements. There have been some cases where experimental and illegal GMO fields have been destroyed, with a first case in 2004 and the latest one in 2010. It is, however, difficult to determine who is behind these actions, because of the activists' reluctance to communicate with the mass media.

On May 15, 2011, the movement for Real Democracy emerged. This movement simultaneously occupied the main squares of several Spanish cities, giving rise to a widespread movement that spread to Greece and the United States. After the dissolution of protest camps in the main squares—some with violent evictions, such as in Plaza del Sol, Madrid—the movement has continued to work through local assemblies, mainly at the neighbourhood level but also through the network. For its first anniversary, protest marches all over Spain have been organised as well as temporary reappropriation of the squares (in Barcelona during three days), where public debates and workshops have been held, thus contributing to maintain the visibility of the movement.

A novel phenomenon bridging autonomous movements and institutional politics is now taking place all over Catalonia, with the successful entrance in November 2012 to the Catalan parliament of three MPs from the CUP (candidacy for popular unity), a mainly Catalanist and pro-independence movement that, however, was born as a people's movement and in contrast to the logic and functioning of more conventional political parties, promotes direct participation in political decision-making.[44] Time will tell if this popular anti-capitalist movement will increase its presence in the parliament, as well as maintain its grassroots ideals and practices and its distance from the conventional logic of representative democracy.

QUALSEVOL NIT POT SORTIR EL SOL
(ON ANY NIGHT THE SUN CAN RISE): CONCLUSIONS

The autonomous movements of Barcelona came into being later than in most other European cities. The reason for this could be the dictatorship that lasted until the mid-1970s, and which brutally repressed opposition movements and any visible forms of protest. In the late 1970s, the installation of a democratic system, the existence of multiple political parties, and free elections gave many people the illusion of having achieved freedom. This, too, counteracted the development of autonomous forms of organisation beyond official political parties.

During the 1980s, the autonomous movement remained very marginal, a fact that contributed to the wide support for Barcelona hosting the 1992 Olympic Games. However, the games also marked the destiny of Barcelona for the following decades. The city's main focus became attracting foreign tourists, business investments, and transforming the Mediterranean city into a cosmopolitan market-oriented metropolis. These efforts have worked in several ways. In autonomous scenes all over the world, Barcelona is also seen as an attractive place. Its attractiveness is just not limited to them, however, and the attraction of tourists and foreign investments has heralded a process of gentrification for the city.

Resistance to urban redesigning and remodelling, which had already began before 1992, unfortunately came up too late and was too small: it was not until the Forum of the Cultures in 2004 that a large part of the population realised the senselessness of such plans imposed from above. Because of protests, broad neighbourhood movements, and squatter actions, many people have become more conscious of the colonisation of everyday life, the creation of living alternatives inspired by ecological autonomy, and a constant critique of the local municipal policies.

Every movement in the past few decades has operated from one or more specific physical spaces. In the early 1980s, the Libertarian Ateneus were a prominent centre. Later, there was Kafe Volter, where the embryonic punk and young autonomous movements took shape. The original squatting movement in the 1990s, had Cine Princesa, Kasa de la Muntanya, and La Hamsa as principal exponents, while the new millennium saw the emergence of Can Masdeu, closely related to the anti-globalisation movement and to the widespread concern about serious environmental crisis. El Forat de la Vergonya can also be seen as an example of local resistance against one aspect of the Barcelona model, characterised by real-estate speculation, rising rents, and a growing housing problem. PHRP Magdalenes can be seen as the most important representative of the movement for the constitutional right to decent housing. More recently, the Free University La Rimaia, squatted in the wake of the student protests against the implementation of the Bologna Plan, has opened up the practice of squatting and self-organisation to students.

The temporary occupation of the Credit Bank building—located on the Plaza Catalunya in the very centre of Barcelona—in the context of the general strike of September 2010, and the occupation of the Catalonia square during May 2011, show how autonomous movements can strike at the symbolic and physical heart of Barcelona.

The 15M movement has incited similar actions all over the world. In the couple of weeks that the movement existed, it helped to structure and establish the democratic mechanisms that are now considered its most important tenets. The movement has left central squares and is now evident in de-centralised operations on a neighbourhood level, while at the same time staying connected with other Spanish cities.

As we have tried to demonstrate in this article, Barcelona has been a fertile ground for many autonomous experiences during the last few decades. It has always been strongly linked with its libertarian history, while remaining open to experience new forms of urban revolt and the construction of alternatives in search of social transformation.

The present challenge for Barcelona activists is to extend autonomous practices to a wider spectrum of people. An example of this lies in the realm of decision-making, characterised by openness, horizontalism, and consensus mechanisms, which became visible during the popular assemblies in the squares of the local neighbourhoods. Taking things a step further—and more closely connected with the disposition for direct actions so typical of the autonomous movement—is the popular and organised expropriation by impoverished families of blocks of flats that have remained unfinished or unsold after the crisis. This form of struggle could spread widely, as the case of the 15M building demonstrates.[45] We look forward to seeing these developments.

FURTHER READING

There is a sizable body of literature on radical urban movements in Barcelona since the 1960s. Unfortunately, for non-Spanish speaking people, most of it is in Spanish. A general analysis of the autonomous social movements in Barcelona (from 1975 to 2005) is provided by: Enrique Leyva, Ivan Miró, and Xavier Urbano, *De la protesta al contrapoder: Nous protagonistes socials en la Barcelona metropolitana* (Barcelona: Virus, 2007)

Two texts on autonomous and libertarian movement in the 1970s are: Felipe Pasajes, 'Arquelogía de la autonomía obrera en Barcelona, 1964-1973,' in *Luchas Autónomas en los años setenta,* edited by Espai en Blanc (Madrid: Traficantes de Sueños, 2008), 73–113; and Joan Zambrana, *La alternativa libertaria (Catalunya 1976–1979)* (Barcelona: Edicions Fet a má-CEDALL, 2000).

There is not yet much literature on the 1980s. But there is one study on the autonomous and punk scene in the 1980s: Joni D., *Que pagui Pujol Una crónica punk de la Barcelona dels '80* (Barcelona: La Ciutat Invisible, 2010).

On squats in the 1990s, there are two good reads: Antoni Batista, *Okupes, la mobilització sorprenent* (Barcelona: Plaza & Janes, 2002) and an overview of critical and autonomous resistance to the Barcelona urban model in late 1990s and early 2000: Unió Temporal de Escribes, *Barcelona marca registrada: un model per desarmar* (Barcelona: Virus, 2004).

Even though most studies about the movement in Barcelona are in Spanish the following doctoral dissertation is in English: Claudio Cattaneo, *The Ecological Economics of Urban Squatters in Barcelona* (Barcelona: UAB, 2008).

For information on current developments, there are a number of journals and websites. *La Directa* is a weekly movement newspaper. There is also the monthly *La veu del carrer*, which is published by the neighbourhood coordination FAVB (Federació de Asociacions de Veins de Barcelona). Important websites are barcelona.indymedia.org and usurpa.squat.net/.

Four
AUTONOMOUS URBANISMS AND THE RIGHT TO THE CITY: THE SPATIAL POLITICS OF SQUATTING IN BERLIN, 1968–2012
Alex Vasudevan

INTRODUCTION

THE ORIGINS OF THIS CHAPTER can be traced back to the violent eviction of squatters from twelve houses on Mainzer Strasse in the Berlin district of Friedrichshain on November 14, 1990, after three days of street battles with over four thousand West German police officers.[1] The fall of the Berlin Wall a year earlier had marked the beginning of a rapid process of 'spatial redefinition' for the entire GDR. East German housing policy had meant that much of East Berlin's nineteenth-century housing stock was never properly maintained and had, by the late 1980s, slipped into serious disrepair.[2] With the reunification, formerly nationalised property was seized and quickly transferred to private ownership, while planning imperatives prioritised the urbanisation of capital and the creative destruction of previously socialist space.[3] At the same time, the fall of the Wall offered a rare opportunity for various social groupings to create radically new and *autonomous* spaces of collective and common property. If a first wave of squatters had earlier moved into the West Berlin district of Kreuzberg in the late 1970s and early 1980s, a second wave now moved east into abandoned tenement blocks. At one point in 1990, over 130 buildings were occupied in various districts of East Berlin, though the violent clearing of Mainzer Strasse represented, in many respects, the beginning of the end of the squatter movement, and the transformation of the scene into a multitude of new autonomous geographies.

Yet, neither the collective 'composition' of new zones of autonomy and solidarity nor the tactics and performances deployed by activist communities in Berlin in the 1990s were themselves new. Squatting and other occupation-based practices formed only one important part of a more complex historical geography of resistance in West Germany that came to reimagine the urban as a space of refuge, gathering, and subversion. From the student movement and the extra-parliamentary opposition (*Außerparlamentarische Opposition* or APO) of the 1960s, to the new social movements and violent struggles of the 1970s, a broad repertoire of oppositional strategies were developed which actively explored the possibility of forging an alternative public sphere and a renewed right to urban life.[4]

In this chapter, I wish to retrace the contours of this oppositional milieu as one historically specific example of an *autonomous urbanism* where theoretical ideas about politics and place were transformed into methodologies for assembling 'times and spaces for alternative living.'[5] In particular, I will focus on the role and significance of the *Hausbesetzerbewegung* (German squatter movement) from the 1960s onwards. Despite a growing body of literature on the role of '1968' as a watershed moment in the evolution of new social movements in West Germany, there remains little empirical work on the role of squatter movements within a broader matrix of protest and resistance.[6] To what extent was the squatter movement in West, and later a reunified Germany, successful in articulating a creative reworking of the built form and urban space? In what way were these counter-claims to the city expressed as a form of architectural activism? How might urban squatting be seen as an autonomous form of 'world-making'?

In the following pages, I attempt to answer these framing questions by retracing the historical development of the squatter scene in Berlin. I will argue that the very techniques and tactics mobilised by various elements of the APO in the 1960s (from happenings and teach-ins to new forms of theatre and agit-prop) were crucial to the 'dwelling perspective'[7] that would later come to characterise the spatial practices of squatters in both West and former East Berlin. By focusing on the relationship between squatting and the built form, I would like to suggest that to squat was to make a spatial commitment to producing a new set of affective and autonomous geographies of attachment, dwelling, and expression. I am inspired here, in part, by the recent work of Lauren Berlant on the fashioning of 'intimate' publics and the affective investments involved in practices of sociability and world-building that move beyond conventional formulations or bracketing of the 'political.'[8]

While the squatting movement attracted those who wished to protest the lack of affordable housing, rampant property speculation, and the negative effects of post-war urban redevelopment, it also offered an opportunity for many to quite literally build an alternative *habitus* where the very practice of squatting became the basis for producing a common spatial field, a field where principles and practices of cooperative living intersected with juggled political commitments, emotional attachments, and the mundane materialisms of domesticity, occupation, and renovation. Yet to remain alert, in this respect,

Previous page spread: Georg von Rauch Haus, 2010. Photo: Alex Vasudevan.

to the micro-practices of squatting, is not only to dwell on the quotidian but to conjoin these registers with wider debates about the *practice* of urban politics and the emancipatory possibilities of the built form. A thick description of the squatting scene in Berlin is thus itself an enquiry into new ways of thinking about and inhabiting the city. In the remainder of the chapter, I will move through a discussion of the historical development of the German squatting movement, drawing specific attention to the role that the built form has come to play in the everyday practices of squatting. The chapter will culminate with an examination of K77, a squat in former East Berlin that has since become a legal experiment in 'architectural activism' and through which wider questions surrounding housing autonomy and the reinvention of the 'commons' in the contemporary city are examined.

THE ARCHITECTURE OF PROTEST:
SPATIAL POLITICS AND THE WEST GERMAN CITY

As recent geographical scholarship has shown, cities have perhaps become the key site for a variety of spatial struggles, many of which turn on the politics of property, from state attempts at regulating homelessness and panhandling, to development-driven displacements, such as gentrification.[9] While such struggles over urban space have dramatised the interarticulation of neoliberal norms with an increasingly aggressive approach to urban regeneration, as urban geographer David Harvey has recently pointed out, they also remind us of the 'intimate connection between the development of capitalism and urbanization.' For Harvey, crises of capitalist accumulation are necessarily incomplete and recurring and ultimately essential for the geographical expansion of 'profitable activity.'[10] Moreover, as Harvey makes clear, this is a relentlessly violent process driven by displacement and the 'dispersed and distributed exploitation of living labour.'[11]

If the urbanisation of capital has come to be dominated by what Harvey refers to as 'accumulation by dispossession,' geographers have, in recent years, attempted to supplement Harvey's work by both identifying and attending to those 'moments of interruption in the circuits of capital that can further elucidate the tasks of resistance for political action and writing.'[12] The bulk of this chapter concentrates on the significance of squatting as one example of a wide range of practices that over the past few decades has prioritised the development of value-creating activities in the city that are not subsumable to or simple expressions of capital. The role and significance of the German squatting movement from the 1960s onwards may thus be profitably understood as a complex social formation through which the relentless logic of accumulation was actively contested and creatively interrupted.

I will attempt to retrace the historical development of the German squatting movement as a series of 'imaginative acts of social agency enacted

through architecture.' I will do so by focusing on the rich set of 'spatial practices' developed by squatters in Berlin over the past thirty years. I suggest that it is important to examine the squatting scene as a way of attending to the relationship between 'architecture and agency.' In this way, I hope not only to reflect on the dynamic nature of the built environment but to the 'processes through which the everyday "tactics" of creating livable places are themselves tied to particular forms of empowerment.'[13] If squatting relocates and embeds the material possibilities of contestatory experimentation and practical political change in new ways of *performing* architecture, it also offers, as I ultimately argue, important insights into the production of what Jenny Pickerill and Paul Chatterton have elsewhere described as *autonomous geographies*—'those spaces where people desire to constitute non-capitalist, egalitarian, and solidaristic forms of political, social, and economic organization through a combination of resistance and creation.'[14]

SQUATTING THE CITY

The recent historical geography of squatting in West Germany does not have its origins in Berlin but rather in Frankfurt, where an abandoned *Jugendstil* apartment on the Eppsteiner Strasse in the city's Westend district was re-occupied on September 19, 1970. Houses on the nearby Liebigstrasse and Corneliusstrasse soon followed. It was ultimately, however, West Berlin that came to occupy a privileged position within the squatter scene. As Belinda Davis has recently noted, the broad spectrum of 'New Left' activism in West Germany promoted a popular spatial imaginary of protest that situated activism squarely within West Berlin.[15] For many young people in particular, West Berlin acted as a kind of geographical correlate to a whole host of alternative political activities that shaped and were, in turn, shaped by the city's physical and symbolic fabric. 'Activists,' writes Davis, '"made" West Berlin; West Berlin in turn made the activists.'[16]

  The first squat in Berlin began on July 4, 1971. On that day, over three hundred students, activists, and youth workers occupied two floors of an abandoned factory at 13 Mariannenplatz in the district of Kreuzberg with a view to creating a centre for disadvantaged and unemployed youth and 'where we,' as a pamphlet published by the activists declared, 'can determine for ourselves what we do in our spare time.'[17] Despite initial clashes with the police, municipal authorities eventually supported and legalised the initiative that included plans for a metal and wood workshop, a studio, a clinic, and a theatre space. This was followed by further agitations in December 1971 after a teach-in at the Technical University to protest the shooting of the militant activist Georg von Rauch. Many of the activists involved in the creation of the Kreuzberg youth centre a few months earlier now took the opportunity to squat the nearby, aban-

Left: Regenbogenfabrik social centre, Kreuzberg, Berlin, 2009. Photo: Alex Vasudevan.

doned Martha-Maria Haus. This was a former residence for nuns and a part of the Bethanian Hospital complex at Mariannenplatz, built between 1845–1847 and closed in 1970. Further police intervention and brutality notwithstanding, negotiations with municipal authorities led to official approval and legal sanction. Contracts were drawn up and squatters moved into what was now called the Georg von Rauch Haus.

The history behind the founding of the Georg von Rauch Haus has admittedly acquired something of a mythical status within a broader history of squatting in West Berlin and was famously celebrated at the time by the famous radical left band Ton Steine Scherben in the cult hit 'Das Rauch-Haus Lied.' Indeed, performances of various kinds were crucial to the repertoire of social practices and direct action political tactics first developed by student activists and other members of the APO and later adopted by participants in the squatting scene. As a number of theatre and performance historians have recently argued, the emergence of an alternative public sphere in West Germany in the late 1960s relied in no small part on a new range of tactics whose provenance can be attributed to the performing arts themselves.[18] Happenings, teach-ins, and street theatre were an integral part of a 'new political pedagogy' and testified to a performative milieu characterised by the blurring of boundaries between the traditional place of theatrical performance and public space. The making of new public geographies, however, was short-lived and emergency laws banning public political demonstrations in the mid-1970s prompted a move by many activists towards the creation of less 'exceptional' spaces.

While early experiments in alternative forms of communal living coincided with the agitations of the late 1960s (for example by the notorious Kommune I), the 'crackdown era' of the 1970s exacerbated a shift in the geography of activism and protest in West Germany. What some historians have described as a retreat from the public sphere constituted, in fact, a new preoccupation with *Innerlichkeit* (innerness) as activists looked 'inside' and turned to the emotional geographies of everyday life as a means of achieving 'broad movement visions.'[19] Intimate settings—cafés, pubs, alternative presses, bookstores, youth centres, and parties—offered an expanded counter-geography through which alternative support networks were created, friendships made, and solidarities secured. The debate about what constituted a common 'form of life' was not, however, limited or reducible to inward-looking collectives or militant forms of political extremism. It was a key source of debate and disagreement across all branches of the left and contributed to the growth of more modest forms of activism such as the *Bürgerinitiativen* (BIs), 'citizens' initiatives' that grew to prominence in the late 1970s and were to provide an organisational framework for the development of the Green and peace movements in West Germany.[20]

'Site occupation' was an important tactic adopted by the BIs, most importantly of construction sites of nuclear power plants, highways, or airport runways. It is thus perhaps not surprising that various forms of communal living (including squatted houses) were to remain key territories within the activist community, offering a space for 'non-hierarchical' living and open political debate. While it would be misleading, in this respect, to suggest that the squatter movement in Berlin was untouched by disagreement, eviction, or violence, I want to underscore the degree to which squatting came to offer a specific environment for the adaptation, rehearsal, and domestication of existing modes of political action. The manipulation of the built environment played a crucial role here, though 'architecture' was never simply the container or the context for the creation of 'existential territories' to borrow Félix Guattari's useful phrasing.[21] If anything, many if not most took the active materiality of a building as axiomatic—from its basic form to the socio-materials that went into its making—as a necessary condition for experimenting with 'new forms of collective living.'[22] The possibility for social change was to be found therefore less in traditional politics than in the kind of 'molecular revolution' advocated by Félix Guattari among others.[23] For Guattari—himself a talismanic figure of the new social movements of the 1970s—change required a new micro-politics that sought to redraw the boundaries between 'activism' and 'the political.'

Indeed, the work of Guattari figured prominently in the evolution of the counter-cultural left in West Germany during the 1970s, especially as more orthodox forms of extra-parliamentary opposition were challenged by *Spontis* (Spontaneists) and various other groupings that identified themselves with a vibrant undogmatic left and drew inspiration from other forms of political organisation and practice. These new developments culminated in a three-day TUNIX (Do Nothing) congress of the oppositional left in Berlin in January 1978 that was organised by the Spontis and was attended by Michel Foucault, Félix Guattari, and Jean-Luc Godard, among others. At stake here was a determinate concern for generating 'alternative modes of living that attempt to exist beyond existing social power relations and, in so doing, begin to redefine the city.'[24]

In this way, activism, resistance, and subversion still hinged on pressing context-bound imperatives. The squatting scene, which first emerged in West Berlin in Kreuzberg in the early 1970s and flourished briefly after 1979, was a direct consequence of an endemic housing crisis that had its origins in the vagaries of post-war reconstruction.[25] In order to address enormous housing shortages in the immediate aftermath of the war, a host of major planning programmes were rolled out by local municipal councils in West Berlin. These initiatives prioritised the building of large-scale housing estates on the outskirts of the city, offering cheap rents through direct state subsidy. The economic recession in the 1960s, however, quickly brought an end to the building of massive modernist satellite cities. High rents and expensive financing prompted the transfer of capital back into inner-city districts. To lower the costs of construction, 'public housing developments were transplanted into previously multipurpose *Gründerzeit* districts [such as Kreuzberg] "replacing" those historic districts with monofunctional modern districts.'[26] Yet, this process of wholesale destruction and displacement—what became known as Kahlschlag oder Flächensanierung (clear-cut or area renovation)—was never designed to be especially cost effective and, if anything, only exacerbated an existing housing crisis through rampant speculation and local corruption.

The above-mentioned developments, coupled with the building of the Berlin Wall in 1961, turned the district of Kreuzberg into a 'depopulated cul-de-sac' characterised by falling housing prices, top-down planning initiatives, and a pro-development lobby preoccupied with 'shifting margins of profitability and revalorization.'[27] Semi-derelict housing stock from the nineteenth century, abandoned factory spaces, and vacant tracts of land remained underdeveloped while low-income residents struggled to find affordable housing.

Effective resistance to this new model of urban 'redesign' did not really take off until the late 1970s and found its most concrete expression in the so-called SO 36 district of Kreuzberg. As the activists who set in motion a new wave of squatting in Kreuzberg in the winter of 1979 made clear in a widely distributed flyer:

> In our district, hundreds of apartments are empty and falling apart. Cheap apartments are demolished because landlords no longer put them up for rent. This is against the law. On the 3rd and 4th of February, the citizen's initiative S036 (after the local post code) wants to restore the lawful condition of rental accommodation. Starting at 10 o'clock we will occupy and restore one apartment in Luebbener Strasse and another on Goerlitzter Strasse.[28]

Without wishing to homogenise a variegated history of occupation, eviction, reoccupation, and further eviction, the period between 1979 and 1981 represented a high point for squatting in Kreuzberg in particular and West Berlin more generally. Squatters in Berlin often confronted abandoned spaces that required significant renovation. They relied on DIY maintenance and repair and quickly adopted the motto *Instands(be)setzung* as a slogan for the movement; the term itself a clever combination of the German words for maintenance (*Instandsetzung*) and squatting (*Besetzung*). By April 1980, various squatter groups had even decided to come together and form a *Besetzerrat* or squatter council to coordinate activities across what was still a loosely connected scene that brought together militant activists that favoured political confrontation with other citizen action groups that supported more modest forms of mediation and negotiation. The squatter council adopted a wide range of tactics from grassroots campaigning and mass public demonstrations to press conferences and 'open house' performances.

As much as such grassroots activism may have helped squatters to generate publicity and support for a new politics of housing, 1981 marked another turning point for the scene. The violent crackdown by the police on activists who were attempting to occupy a house at 48 Fraenkelufer on December 12, 1980, in Kreuzberg (what became known as the 'Schlact am Fraenkelufer') served as a catalyst for the scene and the wider autonomous movement. At its peak on May 15, 1981, 165 houses were occupied in West Berlin though only 77 had been successful in securing some form of contractual arrangement with local municipal authorities. A new hard-line policy was quickly rolled out by the Berlin Senate (the *Berliner Linie der Vernunft* or the 'Berlin Policy of Reason'). It proscribed and vigorously policed any further attempts to squat in West Berlin. As a result, squats unable to secure legal sanction were cleared out. Many 'projects' that were able to guarantee long-term use of a building fell under the *Behutsame Stadterneuerung* (Cautious/gentle urban renewal) programme later ratified by the Berlin House of Representatives in 1983. Under this programme, houses could apply for public funds to repair and modernise their properties through what became known as the *Bauliche Selbsthilfe* (Structural Self-Help) initiative.

If legalisation served to intensify the criminalisation of 'hard-line' activists and the marginalisation of the squatting scene, in the view of many, it also led to the institutionalisation of squats. The programme was widely perceived as a form of 'pacification,' and recriminations quickly circulated within the movement as up to eighty houses accepted an offer for funding even if it meant using public funds to support attempts at creating non-speculative alternative spaces. Amidst widespread feelings of anger, failure, and loss, it is perhaps not surprising, then, that the movement had splintered by the mid-1980s despite the consolidation of the autonomous scene in West Berlin. The last squat without a legal contract, the iconic KuKuCk (Kunst & KulturCentrum Kreuzberg), was cleared in July 1984. Despite the brief flourishing of an 'open-air' squat in a strip of no-man's-land west of the Wall, a second wave of squatting was able to revive the scene in districts of former East Berlin only after the fall of the Berlin Wall.

The hard lessons of the 1980s had been learned. Notwithstanding the massive protests surrounding the eviction of squatters from Mainzer Strasse in November 1990, a more pragmatic form of negotiation was taken on board by activists keen on reconciling the tensions between institutional political structures and practical forms of 'self-rule.' Squatting now demanded a trade-off between existing political institutions and new 'insurgent' forms of urban citizenship, though it would be misleading to conflate realistic political ambitions with a sense of diminished commitment.[29] The very task of asserting a 'right to the city' simply demanded a form of activism that attempted to balance and extend claims for self-determination with broader participation in local politics. In this context, to turn to the unfulfilled potential of the built environment was a recognition of the challenges facing activists who remained committed to new ways of thinking about and living in the city.

REBUILDING THE POLITICAL

Traditional accounts of the squatting movement in Berlin have tended to track the very different histories that have come to differentiate two successive generations of squatting.[30] In contrast, it is equally important to think how both moments—taken together—marked just the latest episode in the social life of a particular architectural form: the Berliner *Mietshaus* or tenement house. As Werner Hegemann's impressive political history of architecture and housing in Berlin famously argued, the tenement house was, in many ways, a defining architectonic symptom for the deleterious consequences of unfettered modernisation.[31] First conceived in the late eighteenth century by the Prussian King Frederick II to house soldiers and their families, the Berlin tenement house was itself intimately tied to successive rounds of creative destruction from at least the middle of the nineteenth century.

Most commentators, including Hegemann himself, have singled out the Hobrecht plan of 1862 as *the* key moment in the transformation of Berlin in the second half of the nineteenth century.[32] The extension plan for the city of Berlin, the plan drawn up by a then-inexperienced engineer James Hobrecht, focused on the circulation of traffic and future development outside the built-up core of the city. The final result was a vast and regularised grid of city blocks linked to existing roads and property lines. As Brian Ladd has argued, state officials attempted to regulate the acquisition of land where streets were planned, but the plan did not provide any provision for controlling 'what was or not built on the privately owned land that the streets traversed.'[33] A land speculation boom ensued as landowners sought to maximise windfall profits. The result was the construction of massive tenement blocks (*Mietskasernen*), traditionally five stories high, that extended to the back of the lot and were only broken up by a series of tiny courtyards that could be as narrow as fifteen feet, the minimum necessary to comply with fire regulations. Poor living conditions, disease, and overcrowding were commonplace.

Whereas recent historical scholarship has attempted to offer a more balanced picture of the development of the Berlin tenement house up to the Second World War and with a particular view to retracing the everyday lives of its inhabitants, the story of the Mietshaus nevertheless carried with it a sedimented historical geography of protest from riots over the provision of housing in the 1860s and 1870s to widespread strikes over rising rents in the early 1930s.[34] The stigma surrounding crowded apartment blocks further intensified during the war as inner courtyards quickly became death traps in times of aerial bombardment.[35] Yet, where a first generation of post-war planners saw the widespread demolition of Mietskasernen as a much-needed solution to a pressing housing crisis, squatters would later come to see the same buildings in light of the creative possibilities they offered. In their eyes, the city was nothing less than the 'conjunction of seemingly endless possibilities of remaking' where the built form offered openings onto different forms of autonomous urban living.[36]

'Capital,' writes David Harvey, 'represents itself in the form of a physical landscape created in its own image, created as use values to enhance the progressive accumulation of capital.' But if this very process of accumulation, as Harvey also reminds us, 'builds a physical landscape suitable to its own condition,' it often does so 'only to have to destroy it.'[37] The Berlin tenement house would seem, in this respect, to anatomise the very forces of creative destruction. For many squatters, however, it became an instrument of resistance and creative reappropriation. 'A hallmark of the *Mietskaserne*,' writes Brian Ladd, '[is] its flexibility.'[38] The many dilapidated and decaying Mietskasernen of post-war Berlin offered the potential for squatters to cultivate new forms of sociality and, in so doing, reconcile a ruinous artefact of urban modernity with alternative expressions of human collectivity.

As the former squatter and now architect Dougal Sheridan made clear, reappropriation was itself shaped by the basic task of improving or repairing old buildings and relied on 'a large degree of collective action and decision-making.'[39] Often the material circumstances of abandoned buildings meant that the rules of occupancy, DIY maintenance, and regeneration were fluid and that 'the division and distribution of space and facilities [was] not . . . predetermined.' Squatters responded to normative assumptions about living and the 'home' through the questioning of its more basic spatialities. This took on a number of forms and embodied a broad range of spatial practices. At the most rudimentary level, architecture served as a guiding frame for the breakdown of the traditional public/private divide and the prioritisation of various forms of communal space, though Sheridan's own experience with the squat at Brunnenstrasse 6/7 in Prenzlauer Berg during the mid-1990s highlights the complex gradations of private and public space that were often made possible by the existing building structure. Here, the permeability of the building was increased and re-engineered to suit the changing needs and wishes of the squatters. Walls were removed in order to increase the size of social spaces while stairwells were created to produce a new geography of movement through the building, now connected and held together by an interspatial network of doors, passageways, courtyards, and vestibules.[40] These experiments with the built form became a key process for exploring a new micro-politics of alignment, interdependency, and connection.[41]

In other instances, more trenchant forms of occupation were mobilised with a view to creating particular spheres of identification that would encourage forms of interaction 'that other deliberative spheres [would otherwise] constrain or censor.'[42] The former chocolate factory of the firm Greiser und Dobritz at Mariannenstrasse 6 and Naunystrasse 72 in Kreuzberg was squatted in 1981, for example, by a group of women who 'were looking for rooms where they could live undisturbed and meet freely with each other without the unwanted attention of men and without being restricted solely to their own private apartments or the routinizing spatial demands of domesticity and social reproduction.[43] Renovation and modernisation of the 'Schockofabrik' was undertaken by the occupants and focused on a process of participatory architecture and sustainable redevelopment.

While former squatters reflected positively on the ways in which they were able to forge an emotional field of commitment and solidarity, they also drew attention to the negative consequences—the 'grind'—of shared living. In the words of one former squatter: 'life . . . was often difficult, external and internal "enemies" had to be confronted. There were tears and some comrades and principles had to be left behind. The motto, "to live and work together" led to a delicate balancing act between happiness and emotional breakdown which at times was rather sobering.'[44] Another former squatter, 'Ingrid,' who moved to West Berlin in the late 1980s to study, talked about the strong sense of loss that accompanied her choice to squat and abandon existing friendships and familial dependencies.[45] 'Karen,' who came to the scene in 1990 as a punk from the former GDR, described in turn how the intense affective atmosphere of a squatted house was often less a product of political activism than the everyday negotiation of shifting subjectivities. As many others highlighted, everyday life *inside* a house was 'suffused' with '*outside*' politics as sectarian political divisions were quickly mapped onto the performance of daily activities. Indeed for some, it was difficult to even imagine 'sharing a bathroom and a kitchen with someone who didn't think the same way . . . [as one] did.'[46]

But far more commonly these were spaces of cooperation and collective action where the 'dream of self-determination' and the 'symbiosis of living and working' was fulfilled.[47] This was always, to be sure, a precarious process punctuated by continuous deliberation, disagreement, and dissent. Yet, to reconfigure the built environment was to make *common* cause and amplify the creativity and durability of everyday living arrangements, behaviours, and performances. As Marx reminds us in the *Grundrisse*, 'really free working, for example, *composing*, is at the same time precisely the most damned seriousness, the most intense exertion.'[48] In the remainder of this article, I will narrow my focus to and explore the case of K77, a former squat and now communal housing project where a host of tentative and sometimes experimental practices for composing autonomous urban socialities have been developed over the course of the last fifteen years. While there were and remain today a number of squatted houses in East Berlin that have gained more critical attention (Eimer, Köpi, Tacheles), K77 exemplifies the particular role that architectural experimentation has come to play in the performance of alternative political practices.

SQUATTING AS 'SOCIAL SCULPTURE': THE CASE OF K77

The fall of the Berlin Wall set in motion a new wave of squatting in East Berlin. Between December 1989 and April 1990, over seventy houses were occupied in districts such as Mitte and Prenzlauer Berg. They were dominated, for the most part, by East German youths who had come out of the various alternative subcultures that had sprung up in the German Democratic Republic during the late 1980s. By July 1990, the centre of the scene had further shifted to the district of Friedrichshain and now included a large number of Western activists. If the eventual police crackdown on squatters living on Mainzer Strasse in November 1990 served to further radicalise a new generation of squatters, for a number of students studying at the Hochschule der Künste it seemed clear that new forms of practice were needed in the face of a revivified version of the 'Berliner Linie.' Claims for a 'transformed and renewed right to urban life'[49] did not simply depend on entrenched forms of militancy but would ultimately turn to less confrontational tactics and greater cooperation with local authorities. Housing autonomy was, in this context, less a desired state than a constant process of negotiation.

Recalling earlier links between activist practice and the performing arts, a group of students at the Hochschule adopted a new form of site-specific practice which, as one former squatter noted, served as a 'catalyst for the occupation of abandoned buildings.' On December 16, 1990, they occupied an empty apartment in Friedrichshain and turned its spaces into a temporary gallery space housing the First Mainzer Art Exhibition. A second exhibition was held on February 25, 1991, in various rooms of a gallery in Kreuzberg. Further 'happenings' and occupations ensued until June 20, 1992, when a number of activists dressed as doctors and nurses occupied one of the oldest buildings in Prenzlauer Berg at number 77 Kastanienallee.[50] The building had been empty for six years. Originally built in 1848, the three-story building predated the Hobrecht plan and sat on an unusual 10 x 100 m lot. The 'complex' consisted of three houses separated by three interior courtyards. To squat here, as the group would later proclaim, was to respond to a 'medical emergency,' and save 'the heart of the house, dress and heal its wounds, and fill it with life.'[51]

Drawing explicit inspiration from the work of the German artist Joseph Beuys, the group which took over Kastanienallee 77 (hereafter K77) in 1992 deliberately recast the act of squatting as a form of *unbefristeten Kunstaktion* (continuous performance) or installation art. K77 became in the words of Beuys, a *social sculpture*, a location for 'non-speculative, self-defined, communal life, work, and culture.'[52] According to Beuys,[53] his objects were to be understood as 'stimulants for the transformation of the idea of sculpture . . . or of art in general. They should provoke thoughts about what sculpture can be and how the concept of sculpting can be extended to the . . . materials used by

Following page spread: Performing 'Occupation' at K77, June 1992, from a pamphlet produced by K77.

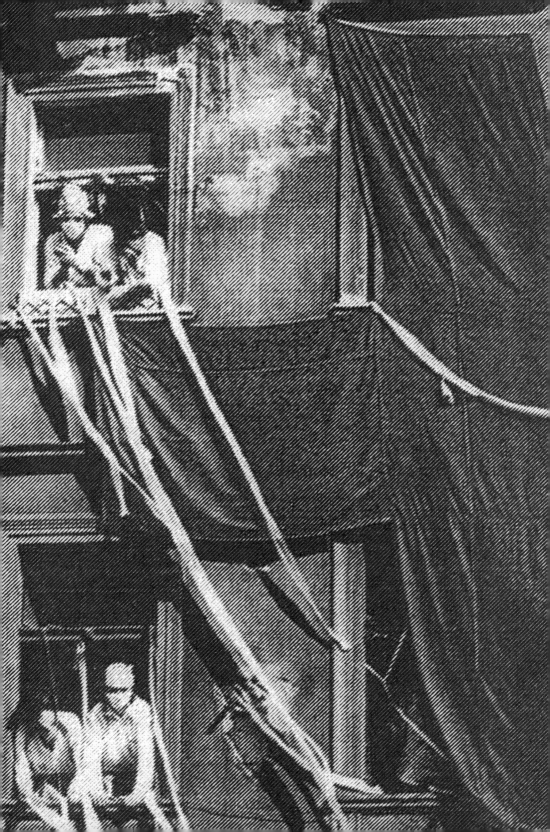

The 'Art' of Squatting, from a pamphlet produced by K77.

everyone.' To think of sculpture as constitutively *social* was to therefore draw attention to the different practices through which 'we mold and shape the world in which we live.'

Beuys's working methods became something of a credo or manifesto for the group of activists that had come to work and live in K77, and it is perhaps not surprising that over the course of the summer of 1992, a number of varied performances, exhibitions, and installations were created. '*Wir haben Theater gemacht*' (we made theatre) were the words of 'Georg,' one former occupant while another described the occupation as a *Theaterstück* (theatre piece) that built on recent developments in performance art. As 'Georg' pointed out, 'there was no plan or set of rules governing the squat.' 'Every space could be played with,' added a founding member of the house. 'The possibilities were endless.' For many, these were possibilities that transformed the building into a '*Freiraum*' or 'free space' that demanded creative experimentation.[54] It was only with late summer rain and colder weather that the realities of living in a building that did not have a roof, proper windows, or water, gas, and electricity, set in.

Experimentalism quickly shaded into pragmatism. Without any financial or legal support, producing a 'social sculpture' depended upon the constructive use of 'found materials' as well as improvisatory 'improvements' to the building's existing form. At the same time, to secure more permanent residency, the group worked hard to acquire legal status, which they attained in 1994. A fifty-year lease was signed and a communal, 'non-property oriented solution to ownership' was also resolved through the creation of a foundation through which profits were channeled into a number of sociopolitical projects, both in Berlin and the developing world.[55] The foundation running K77 was also successful in securing public funds via the Structural Self-Help initiative. But this only covered 80 percent of the reconstructing costs. As a former inhabitant recalled, 'the remainder was made up through our own contribution. We all toiled up to fifty hours a month over three long years on the building site.'[56] The building was, in this way, painstakingly renovated. Sustainable planning principles were used, recycled building materials adopted, and strict conservation laws closely followed.

Over a hundred people have lived in K77 over the years since its initial reoccupation. Today, approximately twenty-five adults and children still live together 'in one flat' across six levels in three different buildings. Seventy percent of the complex is now devoted to living arrangements. The other 30 percent includes a nonprofit cinema, a ceramics workshop, studio space, and a homeopathic clinic. The core of the project remains the negotiation and transgression of boundaries (political, social, cultural) and the creation of what Mathias Heyden, one of the original occupants of K77, has described as an 'architecture of self and co-determination [that] questions the right to the design and use of space.'[57] For Heyden, K77 remains something of an architectural laboratory

for user participation and self-organisation. Heyden's own description of the project indeed highlights the role of the built form in creating new modes of dwelling that are themselves dependent upon the unpredictable evolution of spaces. According to Heyden,

> Every two years, the inhabitants [of K77] sort out who wants to live where and in which constellation, so that the usage and interpretation of available spaces is constantly renewed. . . . In the process-oriented planning and building stage, a broad variety of forms of participation and self-organization came about: the new spaces were largely laid-out through flexible and self-built wallboards. Wall partitions were accordingly fitted with omissions. Light openings, room connections, or breaks in the wall were designed so that they can be closed and reopened at any time. Overall, design decisions were left to individuals.[58]

A number of former occupants singled out in turn the kitchen as the key 'socio-spatial centre of the house.' The same floor also contains a communal dining room, a room for children to play, and a 'bathing landscape.' More general issues relating to the *ongoing* and collective redesign of K77 from floor layouts to infrastructural 'improvements' are discussed and agreed on by all members of the house. Such attempts to foster a sense of collective property and economy coincides with a strong commitment to overcoming 'particular conditionings of the individual and the self.'[59] To do so is to work towards the construction of a new *habitus*, to borrow Bourdieu's now overworked term.[60] In the particular case of K77, it is the very performance of architecture itself that has become, in this context, a key source of inspiration for a whole host of self-organised and collective everyday practices.

K77 can therefore be seen as the spatial manifestation of 'a much broader understanding of self-empowered space.'[61] It was also part of an informal network of squatted houses, all located in former districts of East Berlin, and to which the development of shared cultural spaces was a common cause. The network included K77 and houses at Augustrasse 10 ('KuLe'), Kleine Hamburger Strasse 5, Lychenerstrasse 60, and Rosenthaler Strasse 68 ('Eimer'). If the history of these houses must inevitably be set alongside the recent and intensifying gentrification of neighbourhoods such as Mitte and Prenzlauer Berg, it also carries with it a form of 'architectural activism' that has come to offer a critical point of purchase on new strategies for participatory architecture, housing autonomy, and community design.[62] For Mathias Heyden, the 'emancipative social sculpture' of K77—and for that matter the tactics and practices of squatting more generally—represent only one example or possibility of how an embodied and practical understanding of the built environment is crucial to the design of potential spaces for future commons.[63] Indeed, there are a number of projects, groups, and networks in Berlin that have begun

Left: Part of K77, former squatted space in Prenzlauer Berg, Berlin, 2009. Photo: Alex Vasudevan.

to explore these issues across a range of sites from 'guerrilla' Turkish gardens (*gecekondu*) to sculpture parks, temporary event-based installations to more systematic attempts at community design.[64] It is with this growing field of practice in mind that I wish to offer a few concluding comments on the historical significance of the squatting scene in terms of ongoing claims to the building of autonomous forms of urban living.

CONCLUSION

In this chapter, I have retraced the historical development of the squatting scene in Berlin as a way of rethinking contemporary scholarship on the built environment as a point of departure for a renewed form of emancipatory urban politics. Central to this argument is the relationship between the articulation of an alternative 'rights to the city' and the micro-political appropriation of the built form. As David Harvey has recently reminded us, 'The right to the city is far more than the individual liberty to access urban resources: it is a right to change ourselves by changing the city. It is, moreover, a common rather than an individual right since this transformation inevitably depends upon the exercise of a collective power to reshape the processes of urbanization.'[65]

This process of 'reshaping' has taken on a number of forms in the Global North and South and I have concentrated my own attention on the recomposition of 'affective' publics as an active architectural project. My main aim has been to understand the practice of squatting as one important example of commoning in the contemporary city. To the extent that theorisations of community and the common have received renewed political attention, the spatial performances of squatters represent an attempt at the creation of autonomous urban spaces—both precarious and durable—and the development of new possibilities for collective enunciation.[66] Yet, as the eviction of squatters on with which I began this chapter also suggests, this is a history marked by violence and it would be misleading to underestimate its significance for the squatting experience. While these are issues beyond the compass of this chapter, I have argued elsewhere that the very intensity of investment and commitment made by squatters in developing an alternative 'form of life' can be seen as an active rejection of the violence experienced and sometimes practiced by the squatting movement. Perhaps it is the very memory of such violence that has ultimately prompted the inhabitants of K77 and many others to never relinquish *in toto* the utopian practices of their predecessors or the desire for constructing new ways of thinking about the city. And perhaps it is with this in mind that a particular configuration of architecture and performance can become a way of thinking, describing, and theorizing social change in a present tense in which we can still imagine the possibility of an 'autonomous city' and it is still possible to forge other different spaces.

FURTHER READING

There now exists a body of literature on the history of squatting and autonomous urban politics in Berlin. Key studies are in German and have tended to focus on specific aspects of the squatting scene and were often closely connected to the experiences of activists.

The most important of these studies are: A.G. Grauwacke, *Autonome in Bewegung. Aus den ersten 23. Jahren* (Berlin: Assoziation A, 2008); Amantine, *Gender und Häuserkampf* (Münster: Unrast, 2011); Susan Arndt et al., eds., *Berlin Mainzer Strasse: Wohnen ist wichtiger als das Gesetz* (Berlin: Basisdruck, 1992); Stefan Aust and Sabine Rosenbladt, *Hausbesetzer. Wofür sie kämpfen, wie sie leben und wie sie leben wollen* (Hamburg: Hoffmann und Campe, 1981); Heide Kolling, *Honig aus dem zweiten Stock: Berliner Hausprojekte erzählen* (Berlin: Assoziation A, 2008); and Bernd Laurisch, *Kein Abriß unter dieser Nummer* (Giessen: Anabas, 1981).

A few studies have also attempted to situate the squatter movement in Germany within a wider geographical matrix. For this perspective, see: Harald Bodenschatz et al., *Schluss mit der Zerstörung? Stadterneuerung und städtische Opposition in Amsterdam, London und West-Berlin* (Giessen: Anabas, 1982); and Andreas Suttner, *'Beton Brennt': Hausbesetzer und Selbstverwaltung im Berlin, Wien und Zürich der 80er* (Münster: Lit Verlag, 2011).

The literature in English is relatively small with a few important texts. Of these, I wish to mention: Andrej Holm and Armin Kuhn, 'Squatting and Urban Renewal: the Interaction of Squatter Movements and Strategies of Urban restructuring in Berlin,' *International Journal of Urban and Regional Research* 35 (2011): 644–58.

Less has been written in English on the German autonomist movement though it is worth consulting Geronimo, *Fire and Flames: A History of the German Autonomist Movement* (Oakland: PM Press, 2012).

Five
EBB AND FLOW:
AUTONOMY AND SQUATTING IN BRIGHTON, 1973–2012
Needle Collective and the Bash Street Kids

INTRODUCTION: WELCOME TO BRIGHTON (AND HOVE)

Squatting is a disease which breaks out at intervals.
—Brighton Evening Argus, *1973*

WE CANNOT REALLY TALK of an autonomous movement in Brighton in the same way as it existed in European cities such as Berlin or Amsterdam. Radical politics in Britain have followed a rather different trajectory, which makes the term something of a continental import. Besides, Brighton simply never had the numbers of people necessary for building a coherent movement.

Nevertheless, the town has a longstanding reputation (deserved or undeserved), for being a 'radical' place. It is, for example, a centre of higher education with a youthful population and has a large gay scene. Its proximity to London enhances links to activities in the capital (though also leading to a certain amount of 'brain drain'). All these factors have resulted in a vibrant direct action milieu, if not quite a movement. As we shall see, this scene's politics are not always clear-cut or universal, but they do revolve around ideas such as activism for social change, non-hierarchical decision-making, and a DIY ethos.

Brighton's history also includes a tradition of squatting, both for living space and as connected to campaigning. (Of course, much squatting is focused on immediate housing needs and so tries to stay invisible.) The extent and nature of squatting can therefore be a useful barometer to study the fluctuating nature of the autonomous milieu. Just as the sea rises and falls against our stony beach, so too this radical scene has experienced ebbs and flows, affected by both local and national events.

Our alternative to the tours that clog the town centre in the summer will take in everything from students of post-autonomist theory to dumpster divers, encountering ravers, and environmental activists along the way. We, the authors, are a group of people with experiences of squatting and activism in Brighton from the 1980s to the present day. This is a story told by people who were there, but it is worth noting that everyone's history is different and this amalgamation will be influenced by our own interests and biases.

Inevitably, throwing the focus on one area pushes others into relative darkness. Travelling, student occupations, and many other forms of activity overlap considerably with squatting. Certainly, some would argue that Britain's squatter scene is smaller than it might have been due to time and energy instead going into the travelling circuit. While these other areas are important, they shall not be our focus here.

Currently, although squats exist everywhere, the only remaining places in England with identifiable squatter communities are Brighton, London, and Bristol. From a continental perspective, this may seem strange. After all, in what was described by the BBC as 'a peculiarity of English law,' squatting is not illegal in England and Wales. (Different legal systems in Scotland and Northern Ireland forbid it.) However, it is unlawful, meaning that officially it is a task for the owner, not the police, to evict squatters via the courts. An owner's ignorance, procedural delays, and legal dodges are what make squatting viable. Quite often, a building can be evicted only then to stand empty again, so it is not unknown for a crew to leave somewhere, wait for the eviction order to expire, and then move back in again.

The radical left milieu is (as elsewhere) characterised by sporadic bursts of activity which we shall follow through a roughly chronological path, as we examine various squatter groups in order to trace a hidden history. We have listed information about collectives, texts, and films in the further reading section.

THE 1970S: SQUATTING HITS BRIGHTON

The squatting movement has hit Brighton and this time it's here in a really big way.
   —Brighton Voice, *1975*

Waves of squatting broke out in Britain after both world wars, mostly organised by families of ex-servicemen combating housing shortages—and Brighton was no exception. A key organiser during the first wave was the chimney sweep and social activist Harry Cowley, who swiftly became something of a local legend. The second wave was the most significant; not only was it bigger, but it began in Brighton (through the Secret Committee of Ex-Servicemen, aka the Brighton Vigilantes) before spreading round the rest of the country. Each wave

---

Previous page spread: Community garden. Photo: Unknown.

lasted a couple of years before succumbing to the familiar mixture of concessions and repression.

The modern squatting movement was established in East London in December 1968, when the London Squatters Campaign installed working-class families in disused council properties, usually offering to pay rent after occupation. This was soon succeeded by, and sometimes came into conflict with, hippie squatting by the alternative youth who wished to live communally 'outside' the system. Both practices were usually countered by a pincer movement of media vilification and illegal evictions, sometimes ending in arrests. In some cases, defences against illegal eviction were themselves deemed illegal and used as a pretext for eviction.

Ron Bailey of the London Squatters Campaign gives Brighton's start date as May 1969, when Andy Wright of Brighton Rents Projects (BRP) visited him and took up these working methods. Bailey later described Brighton as having 'outside London, the longest and most determined squatting campaign.'[1] The trigger was housing need: just like East London, Brighton suffered from the problems of unscrupulous landlords and slum housing.

One quote may sum up both the strengths and weaknesses of this movement. In a statement to the *Brighton and Hove Gazette* the BRP explained 'the idea is to place families into empty houses and for the "squatters" to go in, defend and look after them.'[2] Squatting was a means to meet immediate needs and challenge sacrosanct private property. But there was also an implicit division between working-class families and 'squatter' activists.

The largest BRP squat was a row of houses owned by the Army in Wykeham Terrace, which were occupied in July 1969. The action then expanded into the adjoining Queens Square—housing twelve families in all. However, following a firebombing of the local Army Information Office, the addresses were raided, explosives found, and some places evicted.[3]

This was a setback, but squatting continued. In general, following negative publicity in London, heavy-handed eviction methods were not used. This was part of a shift from heavies to court orders. As ever, supposed 'legal rights' exist only in the abstract until insisted upon by political activism.

Masthead for the *Brighton Voice*, 1987.

An invaluable resource for the subsequent era is the *Brighton Voice*, an alternative newspaper published from 1973 to 1989, describing itself as 'the only community paper serving the whole of the Brighton area, with a readership of three to four thousand people.' The very first issue had a cover story concerning the saving of six hundred houses which had been proposed for demolition to make way for a road scheme.

In 1975, a Brighton Squatters Association was set up, with an estimated eighty members. The association had two aims: to provide instant accommodation for homeless people in Brighton and to publicise the generally dire housing situation. The latter was deemed necessary because squatting had become (not for the first or the last time) a controversial issue in the media:

> All over Britain in the last month, the squatting movement has been under attack. Not from the armed bailiffs of five years ago but from the worthless inarticulate hacks of many newspapers. The *Sunday People* [newspaper] recently carried out a four week group-probe into the London squatters, during which [time] reporters infiltrated squats and then wrote stories portraying them as the next cell of the revolution.[4]

There were to be more shows of force. Later on in 1975, a squat at 2 Temple Gardens withstood six attempts at illegal eviction, with three squatters arrested and charged. They were later fined between £25 and £50, as well as being given a conditional discharge. The *Brighton Voice* commented 'as the week long trial dragged on it became obvious that . . . the men were really standing trial for being squatters.'

Yet squatting continued, with the *Brighton Voice* reporting both evictions and successes. Most likely it was only the tip to the iceberg of what was really going on. In *Squatting: The Real Story* Steve Platt estimates that Brighton had 150 squats in the mid-1970s.[5] While it is impossible to say what sort of politics (if any) drove these squats, clearly there was a politically motivated element. One activist wrote:

> Of course squatting is an attack on private property: it should be. Not an attack on the houses themselves or destruction of walls, windows or floors, but a principled attack on the iron law of property which rules our society, making it lawful for some people to have two, three or twenty houses and others to have none at all. It may be the law but it is not justice. Squatting is one way of bringing a little bit of justice into this ruthless society. *More people should squat.*

Certainly, some degree of success was achieved by the squatters: various families were eventually rehoused by the council after first squatting properties. And in 1978, Michael Elbro (Brighton and Hove Council Housing Manager) commented in the *Voice*: 'I think that squatting is a symptom of the problem, it's not a problem in itself. . . . As squatting becomes more vociferous then we need to sit up and think that there's a lot wrong with the housing situation as it is.'[6]

THE EARLY 1980S: A THOUSAND EMPTY WINDOWS

There are many empty properties in Brighton, which are being left to rot, most of which would make excellent squats. Why should we put up with living in expensive, tiny often damp bedsits on our own, lining a landlord's pockets?
—Brighton Bomber, *1986*

By the early 1980s squatting was at its most widespread, the centre of a perfect storm of factors. The town was then in transition between the 'old economy' of industry and warehousing, and what was to become its modern base in 'leisure' industries and new media. Combined with a deep recession, this left a large number of properties empty.

Moreover, the largely Victorian centre held many 'historic' old properties, their façades given legal protection. Landlords sometimes deliberately left these empty, hoping they would fall into such disrepair they would then have an excuse to pull them down. Many of these places were too large and too run-down to live in, but they added to a general sense that space was not 'privatised' but up for grabs. The streets were lined with a thousand empty windows, which were taken by many as an invite.

Widespread private letting, which often meant shelling out for squalor, continued to sow dissent. The anarchist newspaper *Brighton Bomber*, for example, ran a regular 'Scum Landlord of the Month' feature. But it was not so much the large private properties in the city centre that were occupied. English towns with large squat numbers normally had plentiful amounts of council-owned properties. Publicly accountable councils were obliged to respect squatters' rights more than private landlords. Unlike the defended fortresses of somewhere like Berlin, squats were typically small, domestic properties. Council properties that existed in Brighton were out on the estates, far away from the town centre. Often these were clumped together, allowing for whole areas to be occupied.

This led to a scene of young people squatting, so they could live with mates and without bossy landlords, and endless flux. Eviction would hit (usually between three and six months), then people would find somewhere else to live and move on. Places would open and close, people would move in and out, faster than anyone could count. This volatility and short-termism excluded the working-class families who had originally been the squatters.

The result was a scene for 'job-free,' alternative youth. In an atomised society, squatters lived communally, shared dole money, took food from supermarket bins, and made money busking. But squatting was less about establishing a political base, or even primarily about housing need. In many cases it was a lifestyle statement. Squatters would meet not in social centres but gang together at the right pubs and parties, a grubby cognoscenti. Beneath contempt were those with jobs and mortgages. Sign on and sport an alternative haircut and you would be a face on the scene. Squatting was the necessary next step up on the anti-property ladder; though it was trumped by travelling, the crown of alternative lifestylism.

The main incubator was anarcho-punk, with its fervent—if ill-defined—hostility to 'the system.' As the Bash Street Kids said of this era, 'For most anarchism remained a "look" and attitude first, and a set of political ideas second (if at all).'[7] Everyone professed they were against the state, but only a few were politically active. Some were so permanently wasted and self-destructive as to be a liability. While at its broadest, squatting was in many ways at its shallowest.

Of course it was not always an easy ride. The police had come to regard squats as beneath their notice, yet they could equally turn a blind eye if landlords hired heavies to throw people out. Evictions were sometimes resisted, usually by delaying tactics designed to cost the bailiffs time and money. But with little prospect of holding out long term, licensing not barricading remained the common hope for living security.

This could happen. The Peoples State of Trumpton (named after a kids' TV show) squatted a group of terraced houses, some of which are now owned as a housing cooperative. In 1984, places on Gloucester Street were legalised and the Nook on Lover's Walk was even bought by the squatters with the help of Two Piers Housing Cooperative. However, there was often a tension between these attempts to gain licenses and a tendency to exhibit a punky fetish for confrontation.

With rare exceptions (such as a café in the summer of 1987), squats were living places with no infrastructure. People would regularly hitch up to London to visit the 121 Centre, with its printing press and bookshop. Backpackers would return with glorious tales of mighty squat centres in Amsterdam or Barcelona. These holiday tales were fine stories, but were never thought to have any bearing on daily life.

 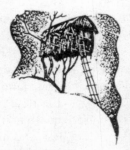

LORGAN
SHORT LIFE HOUSING CO-OP.

Letterhead/logo for the Lorgan Housing Co-op.

Then again, at the time squatting felt more a given than a priority—a base from which one better focused on other things. If evictions were frequent, there was normally somewhere else to move to. If there was no squat centre to meet, there were other venues (such as the council-funded Unemployed Centre). The *Brighton Voice* now featured less squatting stories than in the 1970s, a situation echoed in the more explicitly anarchist *Brighton Bomber*. When there was mention, it was often when a promised license for a place fell through.

THE LATE 1980S: A SEA CHANGE

> *Squatting should be acknowledged as a viable and necessary option to a problem with no immediate solution . . . not a threat but an alternative.*
> —*Anonymous squatter, in the film* Justice in the Courthouse

By the late 1980s things had turned on their head. A countrywide property boom had been exacerbated in Brighton, which was now established as a desirable location for the affluent. Streets once littered with enticing empty windows were now packed with 'desirable' renovated flats populated by yuppies and their ever-alert burglar alarms.

One infamous incident marked the changing of the tides. A group of houses in Portland Road, squatted by thirty people in May 1985, had been

Brighton in the late 1980s. Photo: Unknown.

licensed through the charity Brighton Housing Trust (BHT). However, the following year the electricity board disconnected them, alleging meter tampering. Claiming safety concerns, BHT then gave notice to evict. There was extensive support campaigning, including a symbolic squat and banner drop on a prominent town centre building. Yet in October 1986 the houses were still evicted.

The immediate response was a more concerted attempt at licensing. Three short-lived housing co-ops were formed, Brighton Rock in 1986, Watch This Space in 1987, and Lorgan (in 1989, following the successful short-term licensing of a large squat on a private road). As Watch This Space put it, in the community guide *Brighton in the Nineties*, 'we formed in response to a situation where decent affordable accommodation was no longer available to a large section of our community.'[8] These co-ops had some successes, securing grants and occupying properties.

Yet overall the lifeblood slowly drained from the scene. Despite threats there were no legal assaults on squatter's rights. In fact the 1988 Housing Act, which eroded tenants' rights while deregulating rents, might have even encouraged squatting. But there were other pushes, chiefly greater difficulty in drawing the dole. Commitment, which had in many cases only been hairstyle-deep, evaporated. A once-lively scene was whittled down to a hard core, operating in a much more antagonistic environment.

On the cusp of the decade, a fresh burst of political activism erupted against the Poll Tax. This was a 'flat tax' to be paid at the same rate by everyone,

Logo for the Watch This Space Housing Cooperative.

rich or poor, later abandoned due to opposition.[9] But there was no corresponding rise in squatting. If anything, the size and urgency of the struggle against
the Poll Tax sucked attention away from other matters. With no longstanding
squats, it was an activity quickly wiped from the collective memory.

THE 1990S: GOVERNMENT ON TRIAL

We've set this centre up in three days. We can do it ourselves. Fuck the politicians.
—Anonymous squatter in the film Justice in the Courthouse

Yet the 1990s would see the biggest squat in Brighton's history so far. This again
arose out of a subculture, but a different one to the previous eras of hippie or
anarcho-punk—it was the free party scene.

This had found an ideal base in Brighton from the late 1980s onwards,
thanks to its largely young and 'alternative' population. If there were not as
many empty buildings as before, they did not need to be so habitable for a
night's partying, and some were reoccupied weekend after weekend. The seafront and nearby South Downs were also handy venues. Police at first took a
hands-off approach.

These parties were in many ways similar to the old free festival scene,
and were adopted by many stalwarts of that era. You had to be in the know to
hear of them, but once you were there they tended to be socially inclusive and
often run for voluntary donations. However they were more explicitly centred
around hedonism than the festivals, their trance-out experience quite individu-
alised, and aside from the organisers most participants were apolitical to the
point of being anti-political.

Politics, however, proved to be equally against them. The Conservative
government, which had seemed impregnable throughout the 1980s, was now
in the dying days of its power. The Criminal Justice and Public Order Act
(CJA) was concocted as a means to shore up core support. It was not just
an explicit attack on direct action tactics but also on alternative culture in
general, introducing (or strengthening) laws against squatters, ravers, hunt
sabbers (anti-hunting activists), and New Age travellers. As with the earlier
Public Order Act (passed in 1987), this had the immediate effect of uniting
everyone affected and the government stepped into a hornets' nest of nationwide opposition.

But the biggest recruiter was the notorious section which effectively
criminalised free parties. It gave police the power to disperse groups of twenty or more people listening to music which 'includes sounds wholly or predominantly characterised by the emission of a succession of repetitive beats.' In
Brighton these coalesced around the group 'Justice?'

Among other actions, a sizeable building directly opposite the Royal
Pavilion, a tourist icon, was turned into a social centre. In a reversal of al-

most all previous squats, no one lived there permanently. After five years of standing empty it was in a sorry state—but that just gave the large volunteer army something to do, refurbishing and decorating it, making it theirs. As it had been previously used as a court, it was dubbed the Courthouse. Home Secretary Michael Howard, architect of the CJA, was invited to open it for 'uniting our culture like never before.' When he failed to show, a stand-in in a Howard mask did the deed with a golden crowbar. The government was subjected to a theatrical show trial in the old courtroom for conspiracy to violate human rights with this Bill.

The party crowd's anti-politics soon crystallised into an ideology nicknamed 'fluffiness,' an initially disparaging term, which its adherents then took up. This went beyond tactical nonviolence or philosophical pacifism into a mystical belief in the transforming power of 'positive energy.' In the Undercurrents video *Justice in the Courthouse*, one participant elucidated, 'it can't happen as a confrontational revolution, [but] a consciousness revolution. . . . If people can change the way they think, all these problems would suddenly lift.' A group such as the police should not be seen as the police, but as a collection of individual consciousnesses awaiting enlightenment.

Ructions ensued, with fluffiness facing two main antagonists within the scene. The first was a group of Earth First! activists, a radical environmental movement which had recently spread from America to Britain. This group was associated with the periodical *Do or Die* ('voices from the ecological resistance') and had mostly been involved in the then-widespread land occupations against road building.

Meanwhile Brighton Autonomists, as their name might suggest, were more influenced by continental Autonomism. Having evolved from a University of Sussex society, they would feed into the radical journal *Aufheben*. A secret memo from the university from 1994, later leaked to the student magazine *Uni Undercurrents*, observed the students' 'connection with the "anarchists" of 1982–86,' probably 'through some of the latter still being around and active in Brighton,' and concluded 'our main problem vis-a-vis violence and disruption rests with the "anarchists" rather than the "SWP" [the Trotskyist Socialist Workers Party] et al.' Despite the loose application of the term 'anarchist,' their estimation is largely correct. Inter-generational fraternisation expanded knowledge and experience, and broke the normal cycle where the wheel of radical opposition constantly needed reinvention.

Despite strong differences, the Autonomist and 'fluffiness' groups worked in a loose alliance. The Autonomists mounted an exhibition of squats in other cities like Copenhagen and Berlin, showing examples where such a movement could exist in defiance of the law. Also political debates were staged with the fluffies, which were always well-attended and always acrimonious.

The late Conservative politician Harold Macmillan once observed that the greatest obstacle to political achievement was 'events.' As it transpired, events scuppered fluffiness. In a short space of time, the Courthouse was served with its eviction order and (in November 1994) the CJA passed with not one clause modified. The united opposition was defeated.

This new situation led to deep and bitter arguments over whether the eviction should be resisted. By an uneasy consensus, it was agreed that—after a series of delaying barricades—the attic should be secured and the roof occupied—visibly but nonviolently. On November 10, 1994, this tactic was put to the test—and worked so successfully that an early headline of the local newspaper *Argus*, stating that the eviction had happened, was later rewritten much more sympathetically and acknowledging the still-resident squatters. At nightfall, the roof occupation voluntarily ended. The building had been lost, but for those involved it felt like a victory.

Still, fluffiness was a busted flush. Fluffiness had been the inchoate feel-good factor which held the group together. A combination of a more radical critique and the intrusion of real world events shattered this feeling. As *Aufheben* observed, what made these groups 'such hate targets of the government is that, although they may be a long way from consciously declaring war on capital, they share a common refusal . . . of a life subordinated to wage labour.'[10] But radical critique did not succeed in replacing fluffiness. Instead, nothing did. Finding their ideals in conflict with reality, most chose to abandon reality. Group numbers started to fall.

But 'Justice?' did not simply fade away. They spawned the 'information for action' newsletter *SchNEWS*, which has been published weekly to this day. *SchNEWS* was an important source of news on direct action and radical politics, in the days before widespread use of the internet and mobile phones. It was read out weekly at the New Kensington, a crusty pub in the then-alternative North Laine area. While providing a place for people to meet and socialise, there could be tension between using the pub as a site for organisation and its inherently commercial nature. For example, those attending meetings, often unemployed and short of money, would be expected to buy drinks, while the pub's staff did not always appreciate the police attention their clientele brought.

More buildings were occupied, such as CJs and the derelict office block Anston House, which was cracked several times, including once for a national direct action conference. Later actions organised by 'Justice?' included a Squatters Estate Agency in 1996, as a reaction to National Homelessness Week. ('Better than wearing a badge,' as one participant recalled.) This unexpectedly became a national media story. The group also put out *SchLETS*, an occasional newsletter listing empty buildings in Brighton and the surrounding area.

The opposition to the CJA was a galvanising factor to the squatting scene for the next few years. However, the average life of a squat had been reduced to about two months, which meant that a lot of energy was swallowed up by fighting eviction, looking for new places, and moving, in a constant repeat.

Following page spread: The Anarchist Teapot, two storefronts down from McDonald's.

What was once a given was now almost akin to full-time 'job.' Yet, there were various groups which cohered around different projects and stuck together from one location to the next.

House prices continued to rocket upwards and the shops in the bohemian North Laine mutated from scruffy independents into gleaming and generic chain stores. From 1993 to 1996, some abandoned beach chalets were occupied on the seafront near to the West Pier. There's an amusing YouTube clip about the occupation. When the squatters were evicted, they moved onto the derelict West Pier—a wreck which could only be reached by water—and lived there for the rest of summer. This area is now packed with nightclubs, restaurants, and twee shops catering to tourists, indicating in microcosm how Brighton has changed.

Next to this, there was the Anarchist Teapot, which was a collective which began squatting shops and other empty buildings to set up vegan cafés which served free tea. It was similar to other projects in Norwich, Leeds, Worthing, and Nottingham. They occupied eight places in rapid succession from 1996 to 1998. These included an old doughnut store whose racks were filled with radical literature, an eighty-room hotel, and an ex–Burger King two doors down from a McDonald's (complete with a 'don't eat there, eat here' banner).

Through favouring more prominent locations and by making their cafés as welcoming as possible, the collective extended attendance beyond the usual alternative ghetto. One collective member commented that 'smelly dogs, loud music, cider and tie-dye wall hangings were purged . . . we realised that Anarchist Teapot has actually changed a lot of Brighton people's perceptions of what anarchists are like.'[11] Their politics tended to the 'post-leftist' anarchism of radical eco-action, counter-summiting, and affinity groups. The collective later morphed into a field kitchen inspired by the Dutch group Rampenplan, cooking at protests and gatherings.

The SPOR collective were another active group which organ-

Poster for a SPOR festival, May 1999. Poster: SPOR.

ised two major happenings in Brighton. In 1999, they squatted a severely di-lapidated row of shops—plus the flats above—right in the centre of town for a month-long art event. According to *Sporzine*, 'working day and night it took a small crew of dedicated frontliners two weeks to sort the place out.'[12] The first visitors were an Armed Response Unit (which left after establishing that the only guns present were part of large metal sculptures) swiftly followed by alter-native sorts from all over Europe. It all ended in a riotous party. 'Underground networks in resonance,' declaimed one flyer.

They later took over the old Cooperative bank on Ship Street in 2001, providing 'free community space to individuals and groups who share the vi-sion of an environmentally sustainable future' in the words of *Sporzine*—which termed itself an autonomous production, incidentally.[13] In a film about the bank called *Rhizomatic #1*, one member declared, 'Without somewhere to be free in, the concept of freedom actually doesn't exist.' The evicting bailiffs were met by sock puppets talking to them through the letterbox and then spent some time forcing entry into the building, only to find it deserted.

Dismissive of politics and seen by some 'traditionally radical' activists as drop-out lifestylists, SPOR came from a different strand of autonomy with roots in the travelling circuses of the free party scene (Spiral Tribe, the Mutoid Waste Company, etc.). However, SPOR did end up cross-breeding with more explicitly political groups, for example hosting activist meetings such as the Rebel Alliance and organising a one-day party/occupation—the May Bug Ball—of a town centre site earmarked for yet another supermarket. This thir-teen-acre location next to the main railway station was later squatted for a short period (the Harvest Forestry squat, 2002).

2000S: EVERY SPACE A COMMODITY

The darker side of yuppification is the crackdown on untidy second-class citizens like squatters, travellers and street drinkers.
—Rough Music *10, May–June 2006*

In 2003, activists opened a new social centre. It was named the Cowley Club, after squatting pioneer Harry Cowley, but ironically the building had been bought! The Cowley consists of a café and private members bar with a book-shop and library, plus a four-person housing cooperative living above. Around this time, similar projects linked through the UK Social Centre Network opened in other towns, such as the London Action Resource Centre, Sumac in Nottingham, and the Common Place in Leeds.

The question arose whether legal spaces, as opposed to squatted ones, marked a retreat from the anti-capitalist struggle or a tactical advance.[14] When the Gamer Heaven—an old computer games shop—was cracked by the Freespace collective, their website quoted from *325* magazine: 'Every space is a commodity to be consumed or capitalised upon. We believe for a space to be truly autonomous it must first be liberated.' Debates raged over whether a legal space could be autonomous or not. While challenges have certainly arisen from maintaining a space such as the Cowley, which plays the legal game yet remains oppositional, arguments have tended to take the form of the ideological opposing the pragmatic. Holding a squat, particularly a social centre on a prominent street, for more than a month or two had become virtually impossible in Brighton. In illustration, projects such as the Ray Tindle Centre, the old Bingo Hall in Hove, and Terra Audio at the ex-Territorial Army barracks on Lewes Road—which is still derelict today—were quickly evicted.

It was now certainly harder to squat than before. In general, evictions might be legal, with a Protected Intending Occupier form (PIO) or a court-issued Interim Possession Order (IPO). They also might be illegal, with builders kicking the door in, faked PIOs enforced by the police or as a result of the police themselves raiding the squat on dubious legal grounds. Favourite suspected crimes are abstraction of electricity—using the power supply without having signed up for an account, although police have been known to ignore proof of payment in any case—or criminal damage, such as taking off a lock or repairing the water supply. Charges are rarely made for these 'crimes,' but after having been held at the police station, squatters frequently find the owner has retaken possession of the building and their stuff is on the street.

Set against the above, the usefulness of having a stable place from which to organise is clear and many groups use the Cowley Club to meet and fundraise. However, the flipside of this is that the Cowley has become in some ways an anarchist ghetto, centralising everything in one space—which is not always open if there are not enough volunteers—and activists have their time taken up with management issues. Nevertheless, the Cowley remains open as a volunteer-run, self-organised social centre with similarities and links to a range of projects across Europe. The question of ghettoisation is a thorny one. Since most squatted projects did not emerge from their self-imposed isolation from society at large and the gentrification of Brighton continues, other previously alternative spaces (such as the Kensington) have closed down or changed ownership.

With both the *Brighton Voice* and the *Bomber* gone, and *SchNEWS* taking on a more national focus, squat stories have mostly come from *Rough Music*, 'Brighton's trouble makin', dirt diggin' monthly' (2005–present). This has detailed the increasing clampdown on squatting, for example:

Rough Music knows of several incidents where trivial arrests have been made so as to evict squatters and board up properties. In one particularly blatant example, a man was arrested in his home for the fictional offence of 'being in an enclosed space' and immediately 'de-arrested' as soon as he was out of the house. . . . Top cop Nev Kemp has stated in the *Argus* that 'squatting will not be tolerated in Brighton.' He has no legal authority to make such a statement because squatting is not illegal. Another ugly face of the campaign to clean up Brighton for the yuppies?[15]

Evictions in the 2000s and later were rarely resisted (with some exceptions which we will mention). If suspecting any opposition, police and bailiffs normally came once with the eviction papers and then waited for numbers to dwindle before suddenly pouncing in overwhelming force—a tactic they tended to find effective.

However, the old Methodist Church on London Road did resist several eviction attempts before being eventually relinquished. It was occupied in solidarity with the European-wide Days of Action in Support of Squats and Autonomous Spaces in April 2008 and later re-squatted as a convergence space for an anti-arms trade demo. A spokesman for the squatters the first time round said, 'Within the church, the main area is going to be a community centre open to not-for-profit groups and offering things such as self-defence and yoga classes, language exchanges and classes in circus skills.'[16] The squatters discussed using the building as a community resource with the owners, but they were rebuffed and the church is now partly converted into flats.

Sometimes, the short-term nature of a squatted space can create a burst of energy, with new conglomerations of people forming to sort out the building and put on events. Evictions can then almost be a fitting end, providing a time for people to regroup. Temporary Autonomous Art (TAA) events set out to harness this power and followed in the footsteps of SPOR. Brighton has seen three TAAs. A short film on YouTube about the first Brighton TAA in Portslade (2008) shows both the amount of work put into the building and the numbers of people which came. Obviously inspired by Hakim Bey's writings on pirate utopias and temporary autonomous zones, the TAA events began in London in the early 2000s. A loose group of artists mainly connected to the burgeoning underground squat party scene began organising art events, in an attempt to release the creativity that could sometimes be stifled by the drugs and noise of a party. Typically, the events would last a week in a reclaimed space and then became the focal point of many activities such as workshops, films, and performances. There would be an open call-out for artwork and people would be free to put up their work anywhere they wanted, or to make something from the trash they found in the building.

Through the 2000s, other campaigns, such as the Titnore Woods landsquat on the edge of Durrington just outside Brighton, used squatting or occupation as a tactic. People were living in treehouses from the summer 2006 onwards to protect the ancient woodland from a plan to build a Tesco supermarket and eight hundred houses. A victory of sorts was won in 2010 and the treehouses were taken down. Though a new Tesco supermarket was built next to the old one (which was demolished for an expanded car park), at least for now the woods and the adjacent farmland have been saved. A revised planning application is in the works, and would see development up to fifteen metres away from the trees.

As in previous decades, university occupations continued to occur regularly and the Autonomous Society still linked students with activism in Brighton—however it now defined itself along the hallmarks of People's Global Action.

Short-term squats were still occasionally used for parties, but in the main were quickly busted by the police for abstraction of electricity or because of complaints about noise. There have still been some successful fundraising parties, such as the 325/ABC party in the old Sainsbury's supermarket on London Road and the SmashEDO rave against a local arms factory at the school on Old Shoreham Road. In the case of the school, the benefit was a leaving party before eviction. The squatters had maintained decent relations with the neighbours, in part because the local community was unhappy at the plans of unscrupulous developers to let the school fall down in order to build more yuppie flats. The buildings are still standing empty while the developers try to persuade the Council to let them build seventy-two flats on the site, next to Hove Park.

Unfortunately, instead of criminalising emptiness, the government now seems intent on criminalising one solution to emptiness.

THE PRESENT: MORE EBB THAN FLOW

Fact: squatters cause damage, are frequently anti-social, delay buildings being developed and avoid the daily expenses we all have to pay. They are usually politically motivated and anti-establishment.
—*'Mad' Mike Weatherley, MP for Hove, 2011*

The Cabinet first considered outlawing squatting during the wave following World War II. Currently (September 2011) the government has a consultation period open on 'Dealing with Squatters' and it is possible that this will come to pass. One cheerleader for criminalisation is the Conservative MP for Hove, Mike Weatherley, who suggested it in a Private Members Bill in early 2011. (Since 1997, Hove and Brighton have been combined into a unitary authority.) Equally, matters may simply continue as they have been, with the authorities fast-tracking legal evictions and curtailing legal dodges by the defence, while preserving squatting's ostensible legality. Whichever way, in Brighton squatting is treated as though already effectively criminalised—both by the police and the mainstream media.

Despite this inauspicious environment, actions continue. A few squats have been existing quietly for years. Other squatters move from place to place every few weeks or months, still existing by busking, dumpster-diving, and part-time work. The Wildkatz have squatted various spaces including Home Farm in Stanmer Park (2010) and a shop at Churchill Square (smack in the middle of the shopping district, 2011). The latter was a successful short-term social centre protesting against public spending cuts. While some consumers were scared to enter a free zone, the brave were greeted with a freeshop, tea, and radical literature.

Another successful project was the Lewes Road Community Garden, which was occupied for about a year between 2009 and 2010. A long-empty and rubbish-strewn lot, once an Esso petrol station, was occupied and swiftly converted into a guerrilla garden. The concrete space was transformed with raised beds, pots, and colourful graffiti. Despite sympathetic media stories and the support of Caroline Lucas—now the UK's first Green MP, for Brighton Pavilion—the garden was evicted for a new building development. Part of the success here lay in taking action where it was most needed—at a notorious pollution hotspot—rather than in the alternative ghetto of the Lanes. The popularity of the project was shown by the numbers of people who came out to resist several attempts by bailiffs to get onsite. When the eviction was being resisted it was revealed that Tesco planned to open a supermarket.

A subsequent effort to make a garden in the centre of town on a lot which had been empty for fourteen years was quickly scotched, although it was evicted on grounds of trespass. The more liberal elements of the group had declared that squatting the land might offend the neighbours and thus it was easy for the development company to regain possession. The raised beds were completely destroyed by a mechanised digger and the site is now a mess of humped earth.

Another protest against supermarkets was launched in 2011, when it was discovered that an 'actually local' Taj supermarket would close down and reopen as a 'Sainsbury's Local' store. The building was squatted by a group called Sabotaj and received huge public support. In its short lifetime, the squat hosted well-attended meetings and a guerrilla art show. A court order for eviction (IPO) was quickly sought and granted. The squatters at first refused to leave, but then as the days dragged energy levels dropped and the building was eventually retaken in a massive police operation. The action was claimed to have resulted in one arrest, even though there was actually no one in the building. Much in the same way as the Courthouse inspired people in the 1990s, a new generation of squatters have been fired up by the Sabotaj and the Churchill Square projects.

SNOB(AHA), the Squatters Network of Brighton (and Hove actually), has recently formed as an umbrella group for solidarity between projects, providing legal advice, media liaison, and coordinating opposition to criminalisation and illegal evictions. It has also published an incomplete history of squatting in Brighton.

Following page spread: Sabotaj squat in Brighton, 2011. Photo: Squatters Network of Brighton (and Hove Actually). https://network23.org/snob/history3/

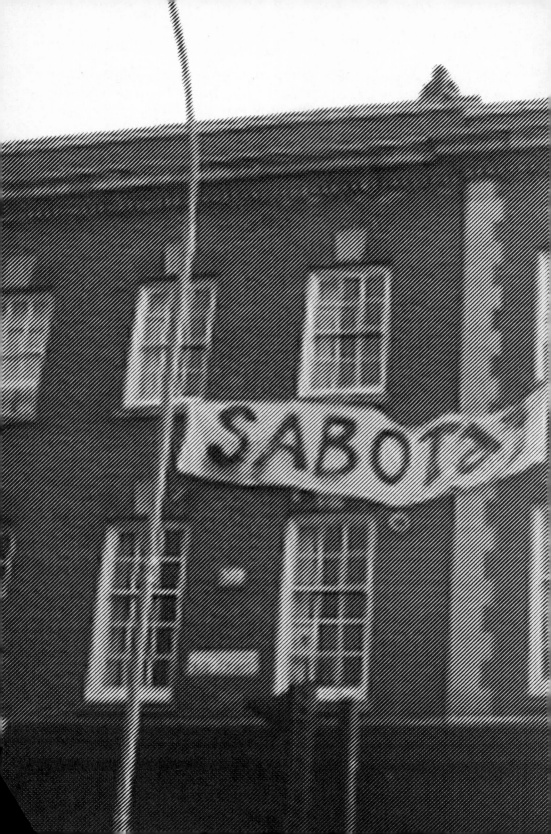

CONCLUSION: EVERYTHING IS POSSIBLE, NOTHING IS CERTAIN

Strike Resist Occupy!
        —*Banner on Churchill Square squat 2011, and elsewhere*

If Brighton has never contained the numbers to create a strong autonomous movement, there has been a longstanding tradition of radical protest around which a scene has loosely cohered. From the many forms this has taken, we have chosen to use the squatter groups as a focus.

It may be worth asking at this point, what is meant by the term 'autonomous'? As our short study demonstrates, there have been many and varied currents, too inchoate to call a movement. Despite this, the milieu could be said to have oriented itself around two poles. We might call the first 'autonomy from,' where a personal niche or subcultural space is established, a bubble floating inside but separate from capitalist social relations. Examples of this are busking instead of working, dumpster-diving instead of shopping and so on. There is also 'autonomy against,' which sees 'autonomy from' as insufficient and holds that the desire for autonomy inherently involves contesting capitalism. While it is impossible to be completely autonomous from capital, this does not invalidate the struggle itself, since autonomous practices may well challenge the hegemony they are embedded within.

Squatting in Brighton involves people and groups situated in various positions relative to these two poles. Those holding to 'autonomy against' want to build oppositional communities and have tended to see attacks as almost advantageous, a push towards their pole, purging drop-out tendencies and galvanising people into self-organisation. While this has tended to happen in the past, the effect has usually been short-term and insufficient to prevent the attack. While resistance has come in waves, assault has been relentless and perpetual. Moreover, it could be argued that squatting demonstrated the limitations of 'autonomy from' at its very beginning; theoretically a legal right, it was only made possible by mass campaigning.

The ebb in squatting is just one signifier of the way just about every aspect of autonomous living has been severely beaten back in recent years. It used to be possible not only to squat in Brighton but to subsist on paltry dole cheques or bad wages by plugging oneself into a low-cost alternative scene. This is still possible, but a diminished scene makes daily life harder for the non-wealthy. Squatting as direct action against private property is certainly an effective tool, providing a means to avoid paying rent, supplying organisational spaces and acting as inspiration to others, but it is also time-consuming. From the 1990s onwards, the average lifespan of a squat has been six weeks. Some last a few days. The tide has turned.

As squatting fights to exist in a way similar to its establishment in the early 1970s, this might make its story seem somewhat circular. However, mention of circularity is not meant to suggest squatting is necessarily coming to an end. In fact, the opposite might be true. Perhaps it is a new beginning, in a freshly configured struggle. When squatting was criminalised in Spain in the mid-1990s, there was a subsequent upsurge in activity. Here, it is conceivable that coming caps to Housing Benefit could result in a rise in squatting. High rents in the UK, and Brighton in particular, means a wide demographic group depends upon this benefit, including low-paid workers.

Here we are approaching a wider question of whether austerity measures will provoke unrest—which in many ways seems the most vital of current questions. But, of course, attempts to answer it should not fall into a black-and-white model where repression simply equals resistance. Squatted projects will undoubtedly play a role in this new social movement. Indeed, the lesson of this squatting history is that, with an inspired bunch of people, much can be accomplished. The future is unwritten. There are 3,600 vacant properties in Brighton. To reprise the name of one of the 1980s housing cooperatives, Watch This Space.

ADDENDUM

Since the writing of this article, the move towards the criminalisation of squatting has accelerated. The consultation referred to above closed on October 5, 2011, and just five days later Kenneth Clarke (Secretary of State for 'Justice') announced an amendment to the Legal Aid, Sentencing and Punishment of Offenders Bill which would make it a criminal offence to squat in residential buildings. John McDonnell MP called this an attempt to 'bypass democracy.' The amendment states: 'The offence would be committed where a person enters a residential building as a trespasser (having entered as such), knows or ought to know that he or she is a trespasser, and lives (or intends to live) there for any period.'

Mike Weatherley proudly claimed victory for his campaign to criminalise squatting in a speech the day before the amendment was announced by Clarke, stating on his website, 'To all the squatters out there: get out and stay out.' It is perhaps worth noting that of the 2,200 respondents to the consultation, more than 2,100 were against changing the current laws. Homelessness charities (such as Shelter and Crisis), the Criminal Bar Association, the Law Society, the National Union of Students and High Court Enforcement Officers all advised against changes, while Caroline Lucas (Brighton Pavilion's Green MP) spoke in support of squatting in the House of Commons. The bill is currently (January 2012) under discussion in the House of Lords.

Why criminalisation is happening now is an interesting question. One possible explanation would be that it is because squatting's 'threat' level is currently low. Just as forceful campaigning established the de facto right to squat in the 1970s, the police have recently been able to act as though squatting is already illegal and thus the government now feels able to put the final cherry on the cake. Another perspective is that squatting is actually gaining in strength, once again forming a vital cog in a growing anti-capitalist movement. The government then wants to crush this resurgent force as part of its repressive drive against so-called domestic extremists. In illustration, three squats in Hove were raided by London's Metropolitan Police before the Royal Wedding in April 2011; despite seven arrests there were no charges, but all three squats were illegally evicted. To finish on the local level, the Brighton squatting scene is at its strongest in recent memory. The ebb and flow continues.

FURTHER READING

Not a lot of literature focuses on the squatter and autonomous movements in Brighton, though a number of interesting texts and other sources are available.

Two London-focused books on the squatters' movement in the UK in the 1960s and 1970s are *The Squatters* by Ron Bailey (London: Penguin, 1973) and *Squatting: The Real Story* (London: Bay Leaf Books, 1980), written by a collective including the anarchist philosopher Colin Ward, lawyer David Watkinson, and journalist Steve Platt.

There is also a critical examination of the anarchist scene in 1980s Britain, 'Nostalgia in the UK,' written by the Bash Street Kids (1998, http://www.uncarved.org/music/apunk/nostalgia.html).

Regarding Brighton itself, there are several sources such as *Brighton in the Nineties. A Community Guide* (1990)—a community information guide which contained advice on squatting and information about housing co-ops—and *A Brief History of Squatting in Brighton* (2011), a pamphlet published by the Squatters Network of Brighton (and Hove Actually) (https://network23.org/snob/history/).

Alongside many updates on the Freespaces section of Indymedia (indymedia.org.uk/en/topics/freespaces/), articles on specific projects include 'The Harvest Forestry Squat'—a *SchNEWS* article on the short-lived squat opposing the construction of yuppie flats and a Sainsbury's supermarket in central Brighton, below the train station, and *The Sabotaj Story* which describes a later anti-Sainsbury's occupation at the Old Steine (2011, http://brighton.squat.net/the-sabotaj-story).

The Brighton scene has produced and continues to produce a number of small print publications. *The Brighton Voice* (1973–1999) was an alternative newspaper with a libertarian left slant, while the *Brighton Bomber* (late 1980s) was—according to Wikipedia—a 'more extreme anarchist paper.' Both frequently featured articles on squatting. In the 1990s, *Uni Undercurrents* was a short-lived magazine produced by the Autonomous Students Society at Sussex

University. *SchNEWS* is a direct action news-sheet published weekly since its formation at the Courthouse squat in 1994. Given out for free at alternative events and in the street, it's also available online (http://www.schnews.org.uk). *Rough Music* is a sporadically published news-sheet which focuses on local campaigns, civic corruption, and yuppification (January 2005 onwards, http://www.roughmusic.org).

Brighton-based journals that reference squatting are the occasionally published *Do or Die* (1992–2003, eco-action.org/dod) and *Aufheben* (published annually, 1992 onwards, http://www.libcom.org/aufheben).

Next to this, there are a number of films available on the history of squatting in Brighton. Examples are *Justice in the Courthouse* (1994) and *Squatters' Estate Agency* (1996), which recount two actions by the group Justice? *Rhizomatic #1* (2001) is a twenty-minute film which aims to convey the philosophy behind the reclamation of a Cooperative Bank building for an art event by the SPOR collective (which also published several zines). In a similar fashion, *Temporary Autonomous Art Brighton* (2008) documents the effort that went into a weeklong squatted art event in Portslade, near Brighton. All these films can be found on YouTube.

Six

YOUTH, SPACE, AND AUTONOMY IN COPENHAGEN: THE SQUATTERS' AND AUTONOMOUS MOVEMENT, 1963–2012

René Karpantschof and Flemming Mikkelsen

INTRODUCTION

'DANGEROUS YOUTH'

On the 23rd and 24th of September in 2006, about three thousand young people marched through the streets of Copenhagen, built barricades, and clashed with the police. On December 14, 2006, five thousand took part in a peaceful demonstration in front of the City Hall. Two days later, however, many of the same demonstrators, together with foreign sympathisers, turned parts of inner Copenhagen into what the public media called 'a war zone.' But the worst was still to come. From the 1st until the 3rd of March 2007, peaceful rallies with more than ten thousand participants were followed by riots and violent confrontations with the police. A variety of projectiles were used, cars were set on fire and more than 850 people were arrested. Thus March 1–3, 2007, turned into days of all-out riots in which the Copenhagen night sky was marked by columns of smoke from big fires in the streets, burning cars, and tear gas. Unaffected by around a thousand arrests, the protests continued in a daily basis throughout the month with peaceful and not-so-peaceful rallies. Why this anger and ferocity?

It was the reaction of thousands of young people to the decision of the municipality of Copenhagen to close and, a little later, to bulldoze one of the last squatted buildings in the city. It had turned into a collective symbol and a popular rallying ground for young activists. But to fully understand how the above-described situation came into being, we must go back to the mid-1960s, when the first squatters appeared on the social and political stage.

We start out with a brief introduction of key concepts and theoretical considerations, before concentrating on a detailed analytical narrative of the most prominent squatter movements since the 1980s: their organisational structure, activities and protest repertoires, claim making, opponents, and allies. At the end of this study, we conclude with a number of reflections on youth in Copenhagen, city space, autonomy, and democracy.[1]

MOBILISATION, SPACE, AND AUTONOMY: THEORETICAL CONSIDERATIONS

Our theoretical position starts with concepts of organisation, interaction, opportunity/threat, identities, space, and autonomy.[2] It is argued that local as well as national and international political opportunities, transnational connections, and relationships with opponents and allies play a major role in determining the social, cultural, and political infrastructure of the squatter movements. However, to really understand the dynamic of the successive squatter movements we must discuss the meaning of *space* and *repertoire of contentious action*.

To begin with, we distinguish between a top-down and a bottom-up approach to the construction of space, more concretely referred to as *place*. Roughly speaking, power holders create public places to support and regulate a specific hierarchical political system, including the distribution of wealth and power. Ordinary people, on the other hand, try to carve out safe places to defend local interests and specific forms of social organisation and identities. According to the sociologist William H. Sewell, we should be especially attentive to the ways in which 'spatial constraints are turned into advantages in political and social struggles and the ways that such struggles can restructure the meanings, uses, and strategic valance of space. . . . Insurgents produce space above all by changing the meanings and strategic uses of their environments.'[3]

From a position of constant opposition to the established political order, safe spaces do not only insist on freedom from political and economic constraints and control from authorities. They also depend on the capacity to launch and innovate a repertoire of contentious action in the form of protest demonstrations, violent direct actions, meetings, public hearings, political communication, as well as peaceful negotiations and conciliations. The argument has been presented in Figure 1, which adds two additional concepts concerning the reaction of authorities, often the police, and the impact of international inspiration and transnational communities.

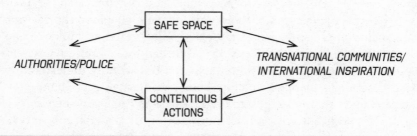

Figure 1, above: Safe space and contentious actions between national and international agents.
Previous page spread: Cutting unions in the squat Ryesgade 58, 1985. Photo: Jesper Holst.

Youth movements and especially squatter movements regularly negoti-ated with the *authorities*, especially with regards to the legalisation of occupied houses or the right to arrange happenings or other alternative rallies. However, bureaucrats were seldom eager to decriminalise house occupations, and instead often handed over the problem to the *police*. According to the political scien-tist Michael Lipsky, 'Police may be conceived as "street-level bureaucrats" who "represent" the government to people. And at the same time as they represent government policies, police forces also help define the terms of urban conflict by their actions.'[4] In other words, police forces have a certain freedom of action in confronting squatters and autonomous groups. This ranges from a defen-sive, tolerant style (cooperation and dialogue) to an offensive, zero-tolerant style (show of force).

Youth movements often operate in an international context and work through *transnational links*. These ties may be more or less durable and intense, and include among other things forms of organisation and action on particular issues, similar goals and slogans, and on some occasions it results in regular concerted transnational campaigns.[5]

Equipped with these tools, we are now in a position to embark on an analytical narrative of squatter movements, autonomous groups, and other youth movements in Denmark—predominantly in Copenhagen—from the early start in the mid-1960s until the present.

BIRTH OF THE SQUATTER MOVEMENT AND EARLY TENANT PROTESTS, 1963–1980

A major innovation of the repertoire of contentious performances in the post-war era in Western Europe was the occupation of public and private places. From the start, this practice included squatting as a means to secure cheap residence, and autonomous and safe spaces.

The first real occupation of a house was carried out by a left-wing group called Gruppe 61 on February 24, 1963. The respective house was designated for demolition. Two years later, groups of youngsters, most of them students, seeped into an old vacant house in the old city centre of Copenhagen. Within half a year, around sixty people had moved in. With the approval of the owner, they took over the administration and formed an autonomous community, which they called the Republic Sofiegården. From here, they expanded and tried to spread this way of living to other students. The decision of the local authorities to demolish Sofiegården in 1968 was initially successfully countered by the resi-dents. But after the resistance had been suppressed with the help of the police, the house was lost and the former residents departed in two directions. One group decided to cooperate with the municipality on projects creating new stu-dent residences out of run-down houses. The other group decided on a tactic of new occupations and, together with new activists, developed into what became known as the first real squatter movement (Slumstormerbevægelsen).

In the succeeding two to three years, the squatter movement occupied newly abandoned houses and attracted students, political activists, drug offenders, and young people with social problems. Inspired by the Black Panthers in the United States, the thinking of Mao, and several urban movements in other European countries, the left-wing faction of the movement pleaded for a better environment and traffic-free cities but first and foremost for self-determined and autonomous areas that would serve as 'a revolutionary island in a capitalist ocean.' In September 1971, they launched a 'tenant revolt' campaign with new squatter actions, symbolic blockades, and demonstrations. Shortly after this 'September offensive,' however, the squatter movement broke up and split into three factions: one group turned into a dogmatic Marxist-Leninist front organisation while the second decided to stay in their own neighbourhoods to improve the general living conditions there. The third faction moved into Christiania. In this context, especially the latter two are of interest, because they constituted the continuation of the early squatter movement.

The Freetown Christiania, sometime in the 1970s. Photo: Unknown.

In the summer of 1971, a local group of activists destroyed a fence and set up a playground in the corner of a recently evacuated old barrack complex. They were soon followed by a vast number of other young people, who established themselves in the empty buildings. From there, they tried to organise a new society known as the Fristaden Christiania (Freetown Christiania). This huge area comprised approximately eighty-five acres in the centre of Copenhagen, and has, since 1971, obtained a specific legal, social, and political status. At the outset Christiania was facilitated by the irresoluteness of the Ministry of Defence, which had no plans for the site. In the following years, Christiania secured widespread support from the general population, and especially from the left-wing parties in parliament. In 1973, the government acknowledged Christiania as a temporary 'social experiment' tantamount to a de facto recognition of the occupation.

Besides a flourishing black economy and hashish market, Christiania became the centre of alternative life-styles, alternative forms of decision-making, cultural activities, shops, public houses, restaurants, and production cooperatives. The police have intervened on several occasions to put a damper on the drug market, the black economy, and illegal housing, and the relationship with the political authorities has sometimes been very tense. Nevertheless, the Freetown has managed to survive on the edge of society, and though it has adjusted to changing social and political situations, Christiania has maintained many of the original ideas and alternative modes of organisation.

But Christiania was not the only squatter/tenant movement in Denmark. In some of the larger provincial towns, young people and students protested against high rents and organised rent boycotts. And in the old districts of Copenhagen, tenants formed associations in order to raise the standards of their neighbourhoods. One of the most well-known and well-organised tenant associations, named Nørrebro Beboeraktion (NB), emerged from the early squatter movement and existed as an independent organisation during the 1970s. It was situated in the old working-class quarter of Copenhagen, and could draw on ideological and organisational elements from the communist part of the labour movement, the 'new' left-wing parties, and the specific local political culture.

NB tried to preserve and fireproof the old buildings in the area, many of which were purposefully left empty. They also formed block protection units, cooperation committees against freehold flats, and provided a lot of different social activities such as a football association, recreational grounds, and a playground for children called Byggeren. However, NB was not the only player in the area. It faced a social democratic majority in the city council and powerful construction companies, which wanted to carry on with the urban renewal plans. The conflict escalated and reached a climax in 1980, when the municipality of Copenhagen ordered workers, under police protection, to remove the playground Byggeren. To the local inhabitants, Byggeren was of high symbolic value because it demonstrated the self-determination and resistance of the inhabitants, and because it was a rare open space in an otherwise crowded neighbourhood. The demolition of the playground resulted in a two weeks' long confrontation with the police, barricades, demonstrations, several wounded, and arrests. During the riots, young people from all over Copenhagen joined the protest. Several of them later took part in actions and squats in 1981, actions that heralded the inauguration of the second squatter movement in Denmark: the BZ-movement ('BZ' is a phonetic abridgement of the Danish word for squatting that has turned into a symbol).

THE BZ-MOVEMENT IN THE 1980S

EMERGENCE AND EARLY DEVELOPMENT OF THE BZ-MOVEMENT, 1981–1983

This second wave of squats did not just emerge from battles in the streets. Similarly to the first generation of squatters, it was also inspired by international events. The second wave began in the Netherlands or, to be more precise, in Amsterdam during the first months of 1980. From there it spread to Zurich, reaching cities in Germany during the first quarter of 1981. Young people in Copenhagen began to occupy buildings in the succeeding months.[6]

The BZ-movement started with several occupations of buildings in the inner city of Copenhagen. In October 1981 a group of young people called Initivgruppen occupied an old disused monastery in central Copenhagen, and turned it into a social centre. The Initivgruppen consisted of around thirty people from socialist youth organisations, youngsters from Christiania, women from the feminist Red Stocking movement, some punks, and students from the Free Gymnasium.

The decision to occupy the old monastery was not a spontaneous one. The groundwork had been laid during meetings with other youth groups and discussions with local residents. Secondly, the Initivgruppen had negotiated with the municipality to acquire a space to set up a social centre. The social democratic city council, however—which for years had supported heavy-handed reconstruction plans with the deployment of police forces—resolutely rejected the idea of a youth centre. So, on October 15, youth occupied the unused bakery Rutana, which was designated for demolition. The action was peaceful and lasted two hours. Two days later, a demonstration in front of Rutana resulted in a violent confrontation with the police and the first arrests. Several demonstrations followed, which again led to confrontations and arrests, while the police took its recourse to heavy use of tear gas.

Following this course of events, on October 31, youths occupied the above-mentioned monastery, Abel Cathrinesgade. Here, the squatters built an open house free of rules and leaders, and with only a few guidelines. However, after three and a half months, they voluntarily left. Because the group of inhabitants had been too unstable and the house had attracted too many outsiders with social problems, it had become impossible to manage everyday social life in the squatted complex.

For some this was a defeat and they left the movement. Others, however, had established close social networks and were still possessed by the desire to realise the idea of living together in an autonomous community. Thus, the occupation of houses went on, and though the squatters were often confronted with hastily gathered police forces and evicted, they succeeded in holding on to quite a few houses for several months. These squatted houses became the backbone of the early BZ-movement. Here they experimented with new ways of life and interior design, and set up music cafés, pubs, and workshops. The squats were also the place from which the activists organised and mobilised for demonstrations, happenings, and new occupations.

It was squatting and direct confrontations with the police that delineated the ascending phase of the movement. Sustained confrontations gave rise to a veritable spiral of violence followed by mutual rearmament. The police availed themselves of new equipment and more flexible forms of organisation, while the BZ activists also extended their striking power: they learned to build barricades, to mask themselves, and to use slingshots. However, they also executed less violent radical actions such as collective theft from supermarkets, followed by distribution to the poor and passers-by. Finally, they also organised nonviolent actions such as happenings in public places.

A turning point for the BZ-movement occurred in the autumn of 1982, but especially in January 1983, when the police evicted and bulldozed most of the occupied buildings. Deprived of their homes and scattered throughout the city, the squatters vented their frustration and anger through vandalism. The situation seemed to signal the end of the movement. But during the summer and autumn of 1983, the movement seemed to reconsolidate as the remaining BZ activists slowly oozed into a new building, Ryesgade 58.

AFTER THE FIRST PHASE: CHANGING ACTION REPERTOIRES IN THE 1980S
The above description of the ascending phase of the BZ-movement in many ways seems to support the conventional idea of a squatter movement: a loose collection of young people, some of them with left-wing sympathies, who occupy empty houses to acquire cheap living spaces and eventually experiment with alternative lifestyles. When their way of life is opposed or thwarted, they react with violence. In other words, the squatter movement is seen by many as being a social and cultural phenomenon—for some even a social problem. Our position, however, is that the squatter movement is first and foremost a political phenomenon: besides confrontations with the political authorities, the prelude to the BZ-movement was rooted in formal and informal organisations with connections to left-wing civil organisations, and inspiration from international socialist currents. To substantiate this argument, we have arranged the following Figure 2, which shows the number of BZ actions from 1981 until 1994.

The figure confirms on the one hand that the BZ-movement was rooted in squatting and housing problems. But it also shows that the movement soon developed into a multilateral political organisation with a strong international commitment. In chronological order, non-housing issues took precedence after 1983. In particular, demonstrations and violent assaults on representatives of the apartheid regime in South Africa and their their collaborators and commercial partners in Denmark, dominated the agenda until 1990. Manifestations of solidarity with squatters and autonomous movements in other countries also took place these years. From 1991, anti-racism, actions against right-wing groups, ecology, and the plight of immigrants became dominant issues. It is also worth noticing that direct confrontations with the police, demonstrations against police violence, and the authorities' treatment of arrested people were a constant source of anger and activism.

Against this background we can divide the entire period into four phases: the first cycle lasted from 1981 until 1983, and was dominated by squatting, peaceful happenings and demonstrations, and by violent confrontations with the police. It was succeeded by a time of more diffused and direct confrontational actions, which lasted from 1984 until 1986. During the period 1987–1990, international issues and small-scale disruptive actions became dominant. The protest repertoire changed once more during the final years from 1991 to 1994, when new people joined the movement, and the BZ-movement splintered into an array of different factions and small independent action groups.

But before we unfold this story we must return to the occupied house in Ryesgade 58.

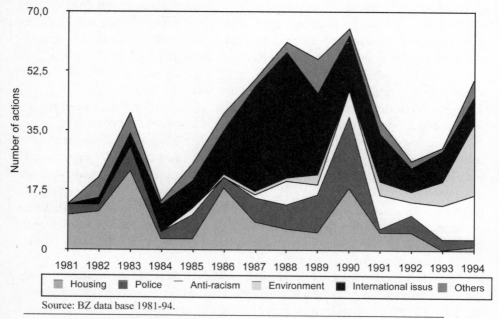

Source: BZ data base 1981-94.

Figure 2: The BZ-movement—Actions and Issues of Contention, 1981–1994.

FROM DEMOBILISATION TO NEW ACTIVISM, 1984–1986

In the occupied house in Ryesgade—and from 1985 onwards in several other new squats—the BZs tried and further developed their idea of an autonomous community. The absolute absence of rules within the squats, which had been characteristic of the early BZ-movement, was replaced by regular house meetings and rules. Each single person was obliged to take part in cooking, night watch, discussions of common problems, and, of course, defence of the house. Occasionally large meetings were organised for the whole movement.

In 1984 and 1985, the BZ activists got caught up in protracted negotiations with the city council in order to obtain financial assistance and legal rights to the remaining and newly squatted houses. It was during the weekly talks and peaceful encounters with representatives of the city council that the BZ activists explicitly formulated their idea of direct democracy and principles of syndicalist organizing. However, these could not be reconciled with the interests of the city council. New evictions seemed inevitable.

To forestall the expected eviction and demolition of Ryesgade 58, BZ activists chose a spectacular form of protest. From September 14 to September 22, 1986, they occupied, barricaded and held a large area around the Ryesgade. The occupation received widespread media attention. After several clashes with the police ended with victories for the activists, the latter left the barricades after one week of occupations. They did so unannounced and quietly, leaving the police and media baffled.

Contrary to the situation in 1983, when the BZ activists were nearly erased from the city map, they emerged from the battle with renewed strength and courage. They had stood up to the police and received an enormous amount of press coverage, but the main reason for their success was that hundreds of sympathisers joined the movement and were organised in barricade gangs. From this, there emerged a spirit of solidarity that increased mobilisation and renewed activities. The remaining and newly squatted houses became the basis for demonstrations and attacks on foreign embassies and foreign and Danish-owned firms trading with totalitarian regimes.

International cooperation was not new. Already from the start of the movement there had been personal contacts with squatters and left-wing radicals in Germany and the Netherlands. Squatter activists met during international meetings, joined in international campaigns, and took part in each other's demonstrations. Besides this, several BZ activists visited Nicaragua and formed solidarity brigades that protested against representatives of the apartheid regime in South Africa.

BZ-INTERNATIONALISM AND ANTI-IMPERIALISM, 1987–1990

The decline in movement activities 1984 to 1985, which we can observe in Figure 2, gave impetus to the idea that the opening of a new international front would benefit the movement. The anti-imperialist strategy of the German Rote Armee

Fraktion (Red Army Faction)—especially as it was formulated in their strategy paper *Guerilla, Widerstand und antiimperialistische Front* from 1982—served as an ideological point of reference and rallying point. The newly squatted houses and renewed recruitment to the movement, during and in the wake of the Ryesgade-revolt at the end of 1986, made it possible to put these ideas into effect.

Looking at the movement's action repertoire in this period, it appears that only a few actions were aimed at occupying buildings. The vast majority of actions consisted of attacks on foreign embassies, foreign-owned firms, Danish firms, banks, and other institutions representing international financial interests in Denmark. The streets were used for demonstrations against apartheid in South Africa, the United States, Israel, the EC, and other representatives of 'capitalism and imperialism all over the world.' Between 1986 and 1991, the BZ-movement generated two distinct forms of action: well-organised militant demonstrations and sabotage actions. During militant demonstrations, the majority of the protesters were dressed alike—in black—and carried helmets, clubs, and fireworks. They managed to keep the police away from their demonstrations and, sometimes, to free arrested comrades. Sabotage was often conducted by small groups who, under the cover of darkness threw stones, paint, stink bombs or Molotov cocktails at embassies or multinational corporations. Sabotage also included spectacular, well-organised raids and campaigns, as when twenty-seven Shell stations were damaged overnight in November 1986, or when 150 activists completely smashed the South African Consulate in 1989. These and other campaigns were often succeeded by public demonstrations, debates, and newspaper articles.

In 1985, after a town festivity 350 Danish locals, most of them young men, assaulted a group of Iranian refugees who had been lodged in a hotel in the town of Kalundborg. It was a major incident that directed the attention of the public towards a new dimension of conflict in Danish society: xenophobia. Since 1980, politicians and the media had been fuelling an increasingly aggressive xenophobic, right-wing populism by focusing on refugees and immigrants as a threat to the maintenance of law and order, and welfare in Denmark. At the same time, new types of racist youth gangs and White-Power groups emerged. These groups not only targeted migrants and refugees but also left-wing groups and BZ activists. Thus, in 1985, a White-Power gang known as the 'Green Jackets' carried out attacks on BZ-houses using incendiaries and a shotgun. This was the beginning of a series of violent confrontations and in the late 1980s, Green Jackets and left-wing activists clashed on several occasions. Anti-racism became a prominent theme within the left. When, in 1987, the anti-immigrant Den Danske Forening (Danish Association) was founded, it soon became the target for a broad coalition of left-wing organisations (Fællesinitiativet Mod Racisme), which included the BZ-movement.[7]

The broadening interests and field of action of the BZ-movement caused the activists to choose the term 'autonomous movement' over 'BZ.'

The latter term referred too much to the practice of squatting, which had become less prominent. In their renaming, the activists followed the German example, where the activists also dubbed themselves autonomous. Their isolated position—a result of the constant clashes with the police combined with a lack of potential allies due to a general demobilization of other movements—caused the BZ activists to search for moral and strategic support among like-minded groups in other countries, who were exposed to similar police repression. They arranged hearings and meetings with comrades and prominent people from abroad, including ex-prisoner Roland Meyer from the Rote Armee Fraktion. They also attended the annual New Year's meeting in Hamburg and started close collaboration with autonomous activists from the Hafenstrasse, also in Hamburg.

Though the police had given up wholesale arrests after 1984, and were forced onto the defensive after Ryesgade, they did not retreat. Rather, they engaged in a war of position. Instead of frontal attacks on occupied houses, the police mounted pinprick actions. They searched houses and raided organisations with connections to the BZ milieu. Occasional arrests and putting people into solitary confinement with little reason intended to frighten sympathisers away from the movement. The BZ activists reacted with minor raids on police patrols and police stations and larger demonstrations in public places against police violence. Sometimes they marched to prisons and courthouses in sympathy with arrested comrades. They also arranged some very spectacular and provocative 'action-weeks' such as Week 19 (1988) and the Robin Raid-Week (1989). During these weeks BZ activists occupied public places in an attempt to raise debates on issues such as pollution, pornography, poverty, oppression of people in third world countries, etc. or they would distribute food to the needy which they had previously 'stolen' from the supermarket. The police often reacted with arrests and brutality but also developed a more long-term policy after Ryesgade.

A new law ordered owners to make empty buildings unfit for occupancy, if necessary with the help of the police. The police availed themselves of better equipment, including long-range tear gas guns. But, more importantly, they improved their logistics. Their ability to quickly mobilise hundreds of riot-equipped forces increased considerably after 1986. This modernisation campaign culminated in the eviction by the police of the most active squats in 1990: Mekanisk Musik Museum, Sorte Hest, Baghuset, and finally Kapaw. The BZ activists retaliated with riots, futile attempts at resquatting the houses, and the organisation of demonstrations that attracted thousands of sympathisers. But it was of no consequence. The BZ-movement collapsed, primarily because it was deprived of their central places. In short, the political authorities had embarked on a strategy of repression: no negotiations, the demolition of potential squats and, ultimately, police force.

Following page spread: Activists with captured police shields at the Baldersgade 20-22 squat, 1989. Photo: Unknown.

THE DISSOLUTION OF THE BZ-MOVEMENT AND
THE FORMATION OF THE AUTONOMOUS MOVEMENT, 1991–2005

The loss of most of the squats and two of the most important outlets to the wider world, the cafés and meeting places at Kapaw and Sorte Hest, strongly reduced the power and the mobilizing potential of the movement. On top of this, the media attention to anti-imperialist actions diminished. Finally, after the fall of the Berlin Wall in 1989, everything that smacked of socialism and collectivist politics was on the defensive. The movement was politically isolated and without central places. Because of this, some activists left the movement, while others collectively bought houses and settled down in communities in the inner city of Copenhagen, not far from their old bastions. From there, they began reconstructing their political network, and were integrated into larger fields of political activities rooted in anti-racism, environmentalism, anti-imperialism, socialist youth networks, and the resistance to the European Economic Community (EEC).

On November 30, 1991, several BZ activists met during a large successful anti-fascist blockade in Lund in southern Sweden. The renewed contacts were transformed into concrete organised political activities after the young anti-racist campaigner, Henrik Christensen, was killed by a bomb on March 16, 1992; an act attributed to neo-Nazis. This led to the formation of Anti-Fascist-Action (AFA), a mix of former BZ activists, that same year. Around the same time, the Anti-Racist-Network (ARN) was formed, a coalition in which several left-wing groups took part. Besides several demonstrations against right-wing organisations and neo-Nazis, AFA and ARN rallied in Sweden, and participated in European anti-racist cooperation.

After the evictions of 1990, most BZ activists refrained from squatting and looked for alternative forms of action. In general, they also avoided direct confrontations with the police. Together with other young left socialists they founded a new organisation called Rebel, and on May 1, 1993, they opened a new activist centre: Solidaritetshuset, in the Nørrebro neighbourhood. But despite the formation of AFA and Rebel, the movement remained fragmented and politically disoriented, and seemed ostensibly on its way towards dissolution. Manifest activities dropped to the same low level as last time the movement was on its way to breaking up, after the evictions of 1983. May 18, 1993, however, would prove to be yet another turning point, bringing new life to the movement.

The tide had already begun to turn on June 2, 1992, when a small majority of the Danish voters rejected the EEC referendum, the so-called Maastricht Treaty, much to the annoyance of the leading politicians. In the following months, they negotiated a compromise with the other EEC countries that was approved by the Danes in the second referendum on May 18, 1993. The same evening, demonstrators blocked a road in the inner city of Copenhagen and put up a banner 'EEC-free zone.' The police intervened with tear gas, and during the subsequent uproar drew their pistols and shot and wounded eleven persons, both demonstrators and bystanders. In a single blow, this incident gave the otherwise languishing movement wide publicity as a militant left-wing opposition force. In the following months, the movement engaged in intense confrontations with the state and in vigorous disputes with left-wing parties and the public. It led to new recruitment and increased internal solidarity and mobilisation: the BZ activists of the 1980s had given way to the autonomous movement of the 1990s.

While anti-racism and anti-Nazism were still growing in importance, other issues were coming to the fore as well.[8] Prior to 1993, only few actions focused on environmental problems. But with the decision of the government to build a bridge over the Sound to Sweden, the anti-capitalist movement acquired a concrete and ideological rallying point. Together with local residents affected by the plans and people affiliated with the Stop-the-Bridge-Network, groups of autonomous activists blockaded the construction site and demonstrated for a more ecologically sustainable economy. They also levelled their anger against Danish firms working for the Sound-consortium, and launched a campaign against the entry of McDonald's in the inner city of Copenhagen. This group of autonomous environmentalists had their meeting place in the Solidaritetshuset and the adjoining anti-fascist café, Kafa-X, where they gathered with other like-minded youth groups. The autonomous activists also introduced the international campaign Reclaim the Streets, and joined forces with other foreign activists to try and block the EU summit in Gøteborg 2001.

Contrary to the BZ-movement, the autonomous movement attempted to achieve more political impact through alliances with established organisations and parties. As a result of this new tactic, the number of disruptive actions declined, fewer houses were occupied, and only conflicts in Christiania now and then gave rise to confrontations between occupants and the police. It took until 2006, before youths again built barricades and clashed with the police, as shown in Figure 3.

THE BATTLE OF UNGDOMSHUSET AND OTHER CAMPAIGNS, 2006–2010

THE BATTLE OF UNGDOMSHUSET 2006–2008

After many years without major collective violent incidents, Denmark was again confronted with a youth rebellion in 2006. But it was not just any kind of youth rebellion: thousands of young people, and some older people as well, mobilised against the decision of the municipality to close, and later tear down, one of the last squatted buildings in Copenhagen: Ungdomshuset (The Youth House). In the previous decades, the building had turned into a collective symbol and a popular rallying ground for young activists.

The battle for Ungdomshuset actually goes back to 1982, when the municipality—after serious confrontations in the streets—surrendered a disused building to the BZ-movement. Under the slogan 'No thanks to the system,' the activists moved in, and since then the Youth House has been inextricably linked to radical political and cultural youth milieus. As was the case with most of the occupied houses, the Youth House was managed through a weekly meeting, which decided on the daily routine of the house. In case of important political issues, which affected the whole movement—such as the threat of eviction of houses or negotiations with the officials—activists from all occupied houses were called together. Many of these general meetings took place in the Youth House, which was the only squat with an old ballroom, where several hundred people could be gathered at the same time. The ballroom was used for concerts and parties. For the general public, the House was known as a leading stage for alternative rock and punk bands. It also became the location for numerous political meetings, some even with representatives of rebels and revolutionary movements from all over the world. The Youth House also sheltered a low-price public kitchen, a café, and a cinema.

During the first half of the 1990s, when the second generation of the BZ-movement became fragmented and disoriented and the transformation into the autonomous movement was on its way, the Youth House became isolated and was left without support from the veteran activists. New and inexperienced young activists tried to bring new life to the place, but without much success, and when the House was hit by a fire in 1996, the opponents in the

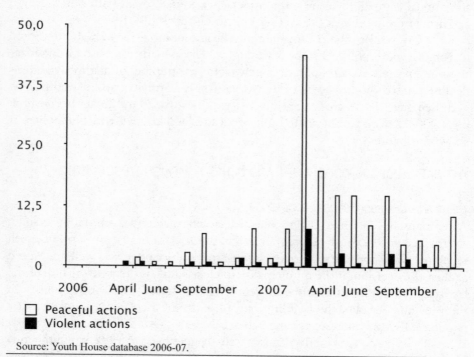

Source: Youth House database 2006-07.

Figure 3: Peaceful and violent Youth House actions, 2006–2007.

city council saw their opportunity to shut down the former BZ stronghold. However, when the politicians decided to close down the House in 1999—a decision which was put through in 2007—the House gained renewed strength and thousands of sympathisers reacted with massive protests as we can see from Figure 3.

On March 1, 2007, a Danish anti-terrorist unit forced its way into the Youth House and paved the way for the demolition of the whole house, which took place five days later. Although the activists and supporters of the Youth House had lost the 'final battle' for the squat's preservation, they had not lost the struggle for an autonomous centre. After three days of revolt from March 1, 2007, onwards, the protesters started a campaign of seemingly endless demonstrations, actions, and happenings, including more clashes with the police. These were fuelled by a profound anger at the loss of the House but also impelled by a spreading sympathy and understanding among ordinary Danes of the need for free spaces in a city like Copenhagen.[9] After several peaceful demonstrations, five thousand activists surprised the otherwise well-prepared forces of law in a squatting action of an unprecedented scale in October 2007. The tactic was to launch a low-risk mass action in order deliberately to push the police back without using violence. And so they did. The police lost control and temper, and reacted with massive use of batons, tear gas, and police dogs, and several activists were wounded. The episode was much discussed in the public media, and the otherwise stalemate situation began to loosen.

Police leaders and politicians seriously began to fear where this apparently uncontrollable situation was headed. The persistent protests had exhausted the police, who on several occasions had to mobilise reinforcements from other cities. Consequently, the responsible politicians of Copenhagen city council started what they had long refused: negotiations with the protesters. In June 2008, they finally gave the activists a municipal building as compensation for the old Youth House. Ironically, this decision was met by protests and a demonstration by the neighbours of the new Youth House. Led by Liberal Party politicians—that is, politicians with conservative views—they marched through the city centre of Copenhagen with bricks made of styrofoam in their hands. They carried these bricks to show 'how people get their way in Copenhagen.'

The battle for the Youth House not only evoked strong feelings among the citizens of Copenhagen and the rest of Denmark but also engaged young people in many other countries. From August 28, 2006, until October 6, 2007, there were eighty-one solidarity demonstrations scattered all over the urban world from the nearby city of Malmö in Sweden to Moscow in Russia and Seoul in South Korea. However, by far the most demonstrations took place in cities in Germany, followed by sympathy actions in the Netherlands, Norway, Sweden, Finland, Italy, France, Spain, and Greece, etc. In general, the number of participants was small, but on March 10, 2007, nearly three thousand young

Following page spread: Youth House supporters clashing with riot police in Copenhagen, December 16, 2006. Photo: Hans Jorgensen.

people gathered in Berlin for a solidarity demonstration. A week earlier, hundreds of supporters of the Copenhagen Youth House had clashed with police forces in Hamburg.

SPREADING ACTIVISM: CHRISTIANIA AND OTHER CAMPAIGNS 2007–2010

One of the consequences of the eventful and partly victorious battle of the Youth House was a renaissance of radical left ideas and street-level activism. Not only had the conflict proven that street-level activism was still possible and even effective, it had also mobilised scores of hitherto passive youngsters eager to continue and widen the struggle to other societal issues.

One such issue was the fight over the old squatted hippie site, the Freetown Christiania. Since the appointment of a liberal-conservative government, supported by the nationalist Danish Peoples Party, in 2001, tensions between inhabitants of Christiania and the authorities had increased. In 2004, the government had cancelled an existing agreement between Christiania and the state—an agreement, in existence since 1991, by which the city government accepted the special Freetown culture and way of life—in favour of a plan to 'normalise' the situation in Christiania. By normalisation, the right-wing parties meant replacing the self-determination and collective use of the area by commercial principles such as private ownership and authority-controlled procedures and regulations for Christiania. When the pressure on Christiania started to rise, Youth House sympathisers and Freetown followers united and mobilised ten to fifteen thousand participants for a big march through Copenhagen. On March 31, 2007, the march was held, led by a banner calling for 'Free spaces for everybody! Defend Christiania! More Youth Houses now!' From 2007 until 2009, Christiania supporters and many of the newly mobilised Youth House activists joined forces to resist the riot police that were frequently sent into Christiania to enforce the governmental normalisation plan. Subsequently, the government, despite its earlier declarations, gave in. It allowed Christiania more time and made a revised offer, which in 2011 resulted in a new agreement that seemingly secured Christiania a future on its own terms.[10]

Yet, the new activist milieu, emanating from the Youth House battle, was also fighting on other fronts. In October 2008, two thousand protesters once again outmanoeuvred a large police force and achieved their objective of tearing down a fence around a disputed camp for asylum-seekers. And in August 2009, thousands participated in a series of peaceful protests and dramatic sit-in blockades to prevent the police from expelling a group of asylum-seekers that had been seeking refuge in a church. Just one month later, fifteen hundred activists attempted an assault on a big coal-fuelled power station as part of a campaign preparing for the imminent COP15 climate summit in Copenhagen in December 2009.

These events were the most spectacular among many activities that signalled the emergence of a new milieu of vigorous and self-confident activist groups in the wake of the Youth House mobilisations. On several occasions these new groups took the authorities by surprise with their innovative tactics and highly mobilizing 'expectations of success.' But by the end of 2009, the movement had lost momentum again, not least because the police—with adjusted counter-tactics and escalated repression—managed to control and recapture the streets during the COP15 summit in Copenhagen. After this, the activist milieu demobilised and reverted to a condition of fragmentation and disorientation.

CONCLUSIONS

THE STRUGGLE FOR CITY SPACE AND AUTONOMY, 1963–2010

What we can learn from this analytical narrative of three generations of squatters is that occupations were a new form of collective action at the beginning of the 1970s, one that could later be used by many different groups in many different settings. Occupations put immediate pressure on authorities and caught the attention of the public. However, it was also a risky business because authorities often reacted with brute police force followed by arrests and fines.

The first generation of squatters in Denmark had their centre of gravity in the inner city of Copenhagen, in the old working-class districts where a vast number of vacant and badly maintained houses were marked for demolition. The squatters were not alone but emerged on the political scene at the same time as many other left-wing parties and social movements. And in spite of the fact that the squatters occupied several condemned buildings, they seldom became involved in lasting confrontations with the authorities and the police. Instead of formulating a coherent left-wing ideology—as was the case with many other contemporary movements—the early squatters set up community-based organisations, arranged social activities, and talked about changing mentalities.

The squatters of the 1980s and the 1990s adopted an anti-capitalist and anti-imperialist frame, occupied houses, and struggled with the police primarily in the same districts as the early squatters. However, what really distinguished them from the first generation of squatters was their unique national and international political engagements, and their willingness to engage in direct actions, acts of sabotage, and confrontations with the police. They were more radical but also more isolated from the rest of the political community and other movements. In the long run, however, squatting as a social and political action was losing momentum.

From the early 1990s onwards, attempts to occupy new houses by and large have ceased to be a prominent or successful means of action. Instead, the defence of earlier conquests and positions has become more important. Two factors can explain this development. First of all, there were simply not many buildings left to occupy. From the 1960s until the 1980s, urban renewal plans generated many empty houses; they were left empty in order to be demolished or renovated. When the slum clearances were brought to an end during the 1990s, these opportunities to squat faded. That not only reduced the number of buildings suitable for occupation but also made it more difficult to legitimise new squats. The second reason for the decline of house occupations was that occupation as a form of action no longer took the authorities by surprise. They had learned to tackle the phenomenon politically and through the deployment of police force. On the threshold of the 1990s, the authorities were much more willing and prepared to bring the far better equipped police forces into action, and to accept disturbances and possible critical media coverage in the wake of evictions.[11]

Confronted with state repression and deprived of most of their houses, the second generation of squatters split into several minor political action groups and more or less disintegrated. Only inspiration from the new global social movements, and the attempt of the authorities to get rid of the last major autonomous rallying ground for young people—the Youth House—started a new wave of mobilisation that lasted from September 2006 until December 2009.[12] The combination of violent street fighting with peaceful demonstrations resulted in a new Youth House not far away from the old one, and fostered a renaissance of direct action and radical mass protests in Denmark—at least for a while.

DIRECT ACTION, SQUATTING, AND DEMOCRACY

The last issues to be addressed here are the political impact of the squatter movements and the connections between direct action, squatting, and democracy. In the public media it is often held that illegal occupations do not produce concrete and lasting results. But this is a myth. Besides Christiania, which has existed for forty years, a lot of communal dwellings, tenants' houses, cultural centres, student hostels, youth houses, and outdoor facilities thank their existence to this practice and have managed to resist political and commercial interests for many years. In recent days, the example of the Youth House confirms that it pays to mobilise in the streets and indeed to use some form of violence. The sometimes violent resistance from squatters has forced political and economic authorities to negotiate with the activists and pay due regard to the interests of local residents. In view of the second-generation squatters especially, militant actions were deemed necessary to preserve the movement—'no violence no movement'—and participation in violent actions gave prestige to some individuals. But it also resulted in disagreement and disruption within the movement, causing people to leave. At the same time, the movement's focus on violent confrontation isolated it from other left organisations, groups, and movements.

During the years that followed, collective violence and especially the victorious confrontations with the police became part of the grand narrative of the squatter movement. These stories are being retold again and again. But the squatter movements were about much more than illegal house occupations and collective violence. The squatters were involved in national and international political campaigns. The occupied houses functioned as the movement's back-bone and provided the necessary infrastructure. They served as homes, rallying grounds, and safe spaces for generations of young people. Next to this, they became important meeting places for political debates and the preparation of new occupations. Above all, they were movement centres from which political campaigns were launched concerning racism, radical feminism, environmental issues, town planning, and urban politics. Also, solidarity actions for immigrants and radical movements in other countries were of great importance.

The action repertoire of the squatter movements alternated between direct actions, peaceful demonstrations, and public debates with established or-ganisations and authorities. And though the squatters were often accused, by the authorities, of using violent means and thus bending the democratic rules, it is also possible to interpret their repertoire of action and political engagement in a more positive way.

Authorities, political parties, established organisations, and economi-cally privileged groups tend to freeze the structure of a society, and to extend their power via the market and via routine politics; underprivileged groups do not have these possibilities.[13] Demonstrations and direct actions, including squatting, have the potential to challenge the powerful and to mobilise espe-cially young people. It has promoted dialogue with politicians, and, for a period, transferred power and control over urban space from the market and the con-ventional political system to the underprivileged, which in this way obtained access to resources and opportunities for self-expression from which they would otherwise have been excluded. In this sense, youth movements are rational po-litical actors who strategically alternate between violent actions, peaceful dem-onstrations, and negotiations when they think it will help their cause.

Young activists accept, but also challenge, the principles of representa-tive democracy. At the general level of society, they recognise the notion of lib-eral democracy. But when it comes to the community level they strongly argue for direct democracy.[14] The squatters and other youth movements see poverty, inequality, and privilege as barriers to democratic incorporation, and therefore stress the social, cultural, and economic empowerment of marginalised groups. In other words, the squatters feel connected with new ideas of participatory de-mocracy fostered by of the New Left, the student movement in the 1960s and 1970s, and the feminists' emancipatory approach to democracy.

From a general point of view, young people are in line with the over-all trend in political participation and development. However, it has become clear that they also sometimes broke new political ground, innovated the rep-ertoire of political performances, and brought new political issues to the fore. This happened during the 1960s and the 1970s, and the significance of 1968 for the women's movement, the environmental movement, and the squatters' movement can hardly be overestimated. These and other protest movements

---

Following page spread: Zombies proclaiming, 'You cannot kill us – Youth House now!,' Copenhagen, August 9, 2007. Photo: Svend Espensen.

attempted to go beyond the formal political system and to build up new political communities based on autonomy and self-determination. In many respects the Danish squatters actually managed to find a balance between democratic political procedures, acts of dissent, and 'participatory democracy.' However, a minority among them did move away from democratic ideals into authoritarian Maoist and Leninist splinter groups. In other words, the successive squatter movements mirror the attitudes, ideologies, forms of organisation, and action repertoire of the New Left, but they do deviate from all other movements in one important way: where all other movements ceased to exist after a few years, the squatter movements have survived for nearly forty-five years so far, and in that way have maintained a spatio-political network and a critical voice on the fringe of mainstream society.

FURTHER READING

Although squatter movements and other youth movements in Denmark have been the subject of numerous articles and several books, there are very few academic publications.

One of the first books that took a close look at some of the early occupied buildings in Copenhagen was Turi Rye Madsen et al., *Ungdom 80—Ungdom som social bevægelse* [Youth 80—Youth as Social Movement] (Copenhagen: Forlaget Politiske Studier, 1982). Bolette Christensen's *Fortællinger fra Indre Nørrebro. Solidaritet og handlekraft i det lokale* [Narratives from the Inner Nørrebro] (Copenhagen: Jurist- og Økonomforbundets Forlag, 2000) describes the struggle for urban space and portrays the organisational infrastructure of squatter groups and tenants associations in central Copenhagen during the last forty years.

In 'Youth as a Political Movement'—published in *International Journal of Urban and Regional Research* 25 (2001)—Mikkelsen and Karpantschof analyse the development of the squatters' and autonomous movement in Copenhagen, also named the BZ movement. The article is based on a detailed statistical mapping of collective actions, issues of contention, and number of occupied houses during the years 1981–95.

The anthology *Kampen om Ungdomshuset. Studier i et oprør* (Copenhagen: Monsun og Forlaget Frydenlund, 2009) [The Struggle over the Youth House: Studies in a Revolt], edited by René Karpantschof and Martin Lindblom, examines the background, historical unfolding, and anatomy of the urban uprising in Copenhagen in 2007. The uprising resulted in more than 2,500 arrests, an unprecedented police campaign and, in the end, a victory for the activists.

Finally, the anthology *Space for Urban Alternatives? Christiania 1971–2011* (Stockholm: Gidlunds Förlag, 2011), edited by Håkan Thörn, Cathrin Wasshede, and Tomas Nilson, provides a historical account of the biggest and most lasting squat in Denmark: the Freetown Christiania.

Apart from books and texts, there are also several multimedia sources on the movement. Two films worth mentioning are *BZ'at—Ni dage bag barrikaderne* [Nine days behind the barricades] (dir. Bent Erik Staalhøj, 1987) and *69* (dir. Nikolaj Viborg, 2008). The first is a forty-six-minute documentary about a sensational squatter-uprising in Copenhagen in 1986. It can be found online, both in Danish and in German. The second is a sixty-minute award-winning documentary about the struggle over the Ungdomshuset. It is available in Danish and in English.

There are a number of interesting websites. The site http://www.ungdomshuset.dk is hosted by the new Ungdomshuset collective and contains some English-language information. The site http://www.christiania.org is hosted by Christiania. The latter site, which is an older one, contains some information in English.

Seven

SQUATTING IN LONDON:
SQUATTERS' RIGHTS AND LEGAL MOVEMENT(S)

Lucy Finchett-Maddock

INTRODUCTION

If you see a house, take it and let the law do its damnedest.
    —Gerald Dworkin[1]

Remember—trying to stop squatting is like stamping on a greasy golfball.
    —All Lambeth Squatters[2]

TRYING TO UNDERSTAND HOW the law is interlaced within the actions of squatters is an emotional, historical project. To put this in context, in 2010, 'The Library House,' a social centre in Camberwell, London, was evicted. Not concerned for themselves but for the previous tenant, the social centre collective used their knowledge of the law and their rights in order to ensure that a single, black mother could return to her previous home.[3] The council had illegally evicted the lady mentioned while she was away (in prison). The collective used the argument: 'You are not entitled to evict us, because we believe that you evicted the previous tenant illegally and she is the one who should take us to court.'[4] The council, after a while, dropped her case and took her back as a secure tenant.

Despite this, the library building remained boarded up, the social centre collective's use of the law in the name of housing a single mother, was taken over once again by the abandonment of property rights. Nevertheless, a clear use and interference of law had become part of the daily lives of the squatters, and the importance of using the court process to result in a benevolent outcome, is indicative of the ambiguous role that law has played over the last decades within the practices and beliefs of squatters, and carried within the discussions of this work, too.

This is an analysis of the path that the law relating to squatting has taken in the UK in the last forty years. While the focus of this collection of essays is squatting movements that have developed since 1980, the focal characteristic of what can be described as the *legal* movement in the UK, as we know it, emerged after 1968 and during the 1970s.

Given this juncture in legal history and where it sits with regards to this collection, it would be wrong to begin the legal history of UK squatters' rights from 1980. Thus there will be a relaying of the legal genesis of squatters' rights that occurred during the 1970s, prior to a reflection on the legal and political atmosphere surrounding squatting around 1980, which will be illustrated through the presence and activities of the Advisory Service for Squatters (ASS). In order to place the relevance of the developments during the 1970s and 1980s in the context of today, the current climate regarding squatting in the UK will be looked at, including the recent change in law relating to squatting in residential buildings.

The focus of this essay is to highlight the experiences of squatting movements in various locations and through the use of various case studies. Of particular interest is the interplay between the law changing within the courts and parliament, and the actions of squatters on the ground. Is there what can be described as a 'legal movement' expressed through the actions of the squatting movements? What is the law reflecting in its development, or is it reflecting anything at all? The focus on the importance of law is to understand whether the legality or illegality of squatting is something that, firstly, effects the practices and actions of squatters, and secondly to understand how law reacts and responds in turn to the actions of squatters, not forgetting the endemic role of politics and the policies of political parties at specific times. The focus is specifically on squatting movements in London.

Any presence of a 'legal movement' (and this concept shall be explained shortly) can be understood in two ways:

—The legal and political decisions taking place within parliament and the courts, constituting the characteristics of a movement of politics and policy since 1968 to 2011 and beyond. This is looked at in comparison and contrast to those movements constituted by squatters themselves, and whether there is a legalistic and institutional movement that has worked in tandem and infiltrated into political, social, and subcultural occupations.

—The practices and actions or reactions of squatters to changes in law, whether their legal awareness and organisation alternates depending on the movement of state law itself. This could be seen as an expression of 'legal activism.'

Previous page spread: Squatting buttons from the 56A Archive. Photo: Josh MacPhee.

What is to be assessed are the characteristics of the interpenetrating nature of squatting law and the actions of squatters, within the UK (and London specifically), and how this interplay has been incorporated within the practices and actions of the squatting movements themselves, at the same time as its expression with the events and historical manoeuvres of the UK's legal and political institutions throughout the 1970s, up until today.

The Advisory Service for Squatters (ASS) has been chosen because of its historical significance in relation to the squatting movement in London during the 1970s and around 1980, at the same time as their proposed exemplification of legal activism, such as their offering advice on the legality of squatting in the face of changes to the law, as well as practical guidance. 'Squatters' Action for Secure Homes' (SQUASH) has been chosen as a second example of where squatters (and their affiliates) can be seen using their legal knowledge as a form of legal activism, and at the same time being an extant example of the development of the squatting movement in London and the rest of the UK in 2011–2012. Both have been chosen in order to assess whether they were expressing the changes in law during the 1970s, to display a snapshot of the situation in 1980, continuing through to changes in UK squatting law after 2011. Do these groups illustrate the effects of any state institutionalised legal movements in squatting law, and the presence of any movements of legal activism within the squatting movement itself? Or is there a phantom 'mirror' between the law and the effects on the ground?

The chapter will be structured as follows. First, the concept of 'legal movement' will be introduced, followed by a brief history of UK squatting since the Second World War, and on into the legal developments during the 1970s. The year 1980 shall be taken as a juncture of reflection on the previous actions during the 1970s through the example of the ASS and its composition at the time. Changes in the law that followed from 1980 to 2012 shall be discussed, with the campaign organisation SQUASH as a second example of a squatting movement, as felt on the ground. The role of social movements, violence, and human rights shall be discussed in relation to squatting and law to conclude. It should be noted that at this point, the majority of the piece was written before the change in laws relating to squatting in 2012 in England and Wales, whereby as a result of the Legal Aid, Sentencing and Punishment of Offenders Act 2012 (hereinafter LASPOA), squatting in a residential building became an act of criminal trespass.

LEGAL MOVEMENTS

Legal movements happen throughout history and act to change the way in which we deal with the social and political, through the use of legislation and resultant measures attached. Without legal movements for change, it is argued that the law is not a 'mirror' of society, the very basis for a constantly

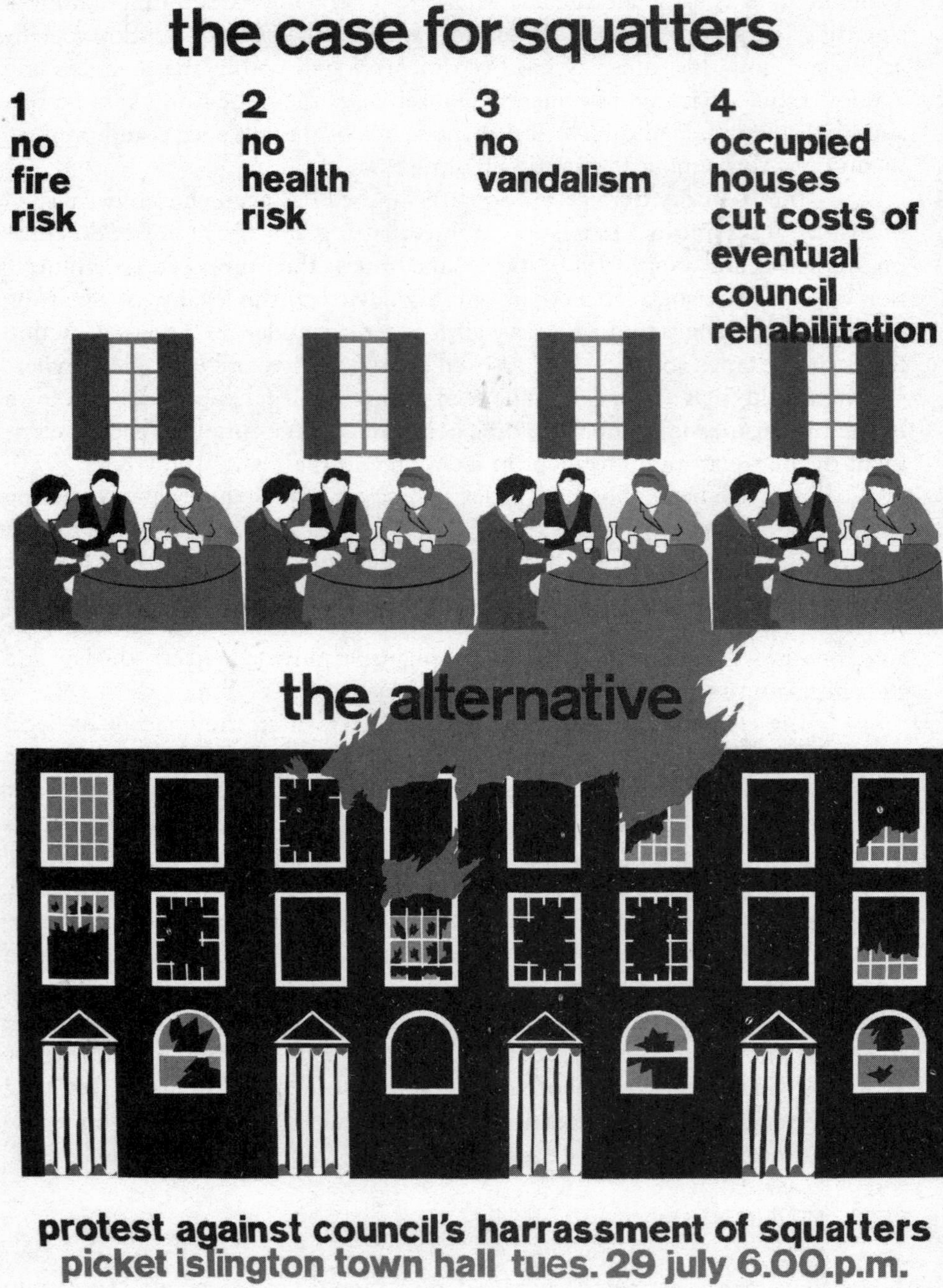

the case for squatters

1
no
fire
risk

2
no
health
risk

3
no
vandalism

4
occupied
houses
cut costs of
eventual
council
rehabilitation

the alternative

protest against council's harrassment of squatters
picket islington town hall tues. 29 july 6.00.p.m.

Pro-squatting poster from Islington, London, 1975. Courtesy of Interference Archive.

changing and representative constitution being the need for alteration.[5] But is this mirror possible at all? And ultimately, is it something that is desirable at the same time? Within constitutional theory, German constitutional theorist Carl Schmitt concludes that a nation's constitution must be constantly upheld, at the moment at which it is not, it no longer has its constituents, or its 'constituent power.'[6] This is a very abstract understanding of legal movement, and it is widely acknowledged that law does not reflect, indeed cannot reflect, the will of all at the same time, at a given juncture.[7] And thus when there are legal movements, they are in effect, 'keeping up' with the social, political, and social machinations that are taking place outside the legislature and the courts. At the same time, the majority of laws made are lacking in their constituent power, they lack a legal movement that gives impetus for change however many months or years in hindsight.

This is of significant relevance when considering the legal remit of squatting which lies within a juncture of land law, the middle ground of adverse possession, and the law relating to trespass. Reforms of English land law have been affected since 1925,[8] with the aim of a complete tabular register of all estates in land within England and Wales, following from the 'Torrens system' as seen in Australia and other common law as well as civil law jurisdictions.[9] This would enable an exact 'reflection,' as such, at a specific juncture in time, of all the estates and plateaus of ownership in England and Wales as one record: the mirror of law in action so to speak. Nevertheless, and specifically in relation to the role of squatters, this has not proved entirely successful, and this shall be discussed later.

Taking inspiration from social movement theory, legal movements act in a similar fashion. Legal theorist Gary Minda analogises trends within jurisprudence that have been affected by theories from economics, sociology, philosophy, literary criticism, and anthropology, and in the same sense, this is a helpful way of seeing how the movements within squatting law and squatters can be seen to operate.[10] Speaking of the manner in which legal movements have been altered by supposedly 'outside' events, Minda states: 'Academic trends in legal scholarship do not occur in a vacuum, nor are law schools and legal scholars autonomous. To understand what has been going on in contemporary legal theory, one must look to what has been going on [elsewhere].'[11] There is a recycling and repetition of movements and themes, 'always reproducing the same common argumentative and normative structures.'[12] Thus, there is a symbiotic relationship, but does this relay to the legal developments and squatting practices of the UK? As an example, it is now illegal to squat in a residential building in England and Wales (and arguably always has been under the Criminal Law Act 1977), yet there is a very strong tradition of squatting within the main cities in the UK. So does it really matter that one cannot squat legitimately in the eyes of the state? In fact, in many instances there is a clear element of 'breaking the law' that encourages squatting. The hope is to offer an insight into these conflicting relations.

Squatting as a legal right has been a controversial area of law, and its bracket of adverse possession has developed as a result of the synchronous development of the regime of property rights overall. Within the history of English law relating to property rights, the task is to ascertain whether a cyclical motion that can be observed within the development and recession of the regime of squatters' rights, and the effects this has on the social and political (squatting itself), and whether this results in a form of the squatters themselves 'practising' the law on the ground, so to speak, and whether there are legal movements as such within their practices and actions, which can equate to a form of 'legal activism.'

Legal movements are fuelled by the practices and actions of given sets of actors and participants themselves. In order for squatters to gain access and produce their space, a squat must be sought within the realm of the law, thus they must have knowledge of the relevant law in order for the space to be 'legitimate.' According to recent opinion, 'the new generation of squatters has a greater understanding of the law and how it can protect them, helped in part by sophisticated legal advice available on the Internet.'[13] In order to ensure that the regime of squatters' rights is kept legal in the UK, those who need to use alternative housing are aware of a need to respect the law, and therefore it is important to understand whether and how those involved in squatting movements, whether of radical political backgrounds or those purely seeking housing, in general, have a sound or 'professional' knowledge of squatting-related law (or are aware of the need for good legal advice by the likes of the ASS and SQUASH).

To pinpoint a form of legal activism within squatting is not something that is confined to the actions and strategies of squatters and land reclamation movements within the UK. According to writer and activist Anders Corr, this is a mechanism used worldwide, particularly within liberation movements of the South. In the words of Corr: 'Authorities exclude land and housing activists from effective use of the law in official legal channels to some extent, but activists can extend the use of law beyond the courtroom and appeal to public opinion. To buttress their legitimacy, indigenous nations use treaty rights, rent strikers cite building codes, and squatters appeal to land reform laws. Broadcasting government failure to follow its own laws strengthens the legitimacy of direct action in the eyes of the public.'[14] Thus, as a definite 'tactic' within social movements dealing with land issues throughout the world, it is prescient to consider the role of law within the UK squatting movement, and the manner in which legalism is manifested within the participants' activities. Again, a reminder that this piece speaks to the legal situation by and large before the onset of residential squatting coming under the remit of criminal trespass in 2012, it is hoped nevertheless that this analysis will be of relevance to understandings of illegality and legality overall and the effects of this on the squatting scene in the UK.

HISTORICAL BACKGROUND

The law doth punish man or woman
That steals the goose from off the common
But lets the greater felon loose
That steals the common from the goose.
        —Anonymous[15]

The squatting movement in the UK that began in 1945, taken within the last century, was directly linked to the housing shortage after the Second World War.[16] This began as more of a direct housing action movement for the homeless, the levels of which were heightened due to the effects of the war on population and the lack of social housing for returning soldiers and their families. There was an out-and-out reaction to the 'Homes fit for Heroes' policy that was put forward by the government at the time, which in the words of Ron Bailey, was, 'enough to say that "homes fit for heroes" just did not exist; returning servicemen successfully seized empty properties to live in—to the astonishment and rage of the government of the day.'[17] It was clear that houses were not going to be provided unless militant action was taken.[18] According to political and moral theorist Gerald Dworkin, the 'Ex-Servicemen's Secret Committee' (one of the many groups of ex-servicemen who installed homeless families into properties by night),[19] had got so desperate they resorted to the adage, 'If you see a house, take it and let the law do its damnedest.'[20] This is a phrase that resounds in light of section 144 of LASPOA relating to squatting as a crime of trespass in residential buildings. As the movement spread, it became an early version of an attack on speculation, 'on the right of landlords to keep property unoccupied for any reason.'[21] Old army camps started to be occupied, and squatters' protection societies and federations were formed.[22]

According to Steve Platt, writing in *Squatting: The Real Story*, the post-war squatting movement was essentially quashed in 1946, among other reasons, due to political alignment with the Communist Party and lack of support from the trade unions.[23] But in 1968, a new squatting wave could be observed. According to Platt, 'The main impetus for the 1968–69 squatting campaign came from a loosely knit group of radicals, many of whom had been involved with the Committee of 100 [British anti-war group] and the Vietnam Solidarity Campaign.'[24] It was from the end of the 1960s that squatting enacted its role as, 'a harbinger of a new style of social and political activity that changes demoralised and helpless people from being the objects of social policy to becoming active fighters in their own cause.'[25] The London Squatters Campaign was set up in November 1968. Those gathered there with the aim of, 'the rehousing of families from hostels or slums by means of squatting,' in the hope of sparking off a 'movement' of such in radical re-housing.[26] This was a response to the continuation of the shortage of housing and the dire work of councils on the provision of re-homing the homeless, and providing adequate services overall.[27] Direct housing action became a viable, if the *only* viable option, whereby homeless families and individuals were taking the 'law into their own hands' and rehousing themselves. A leading figure in the movement, activist and lobbyist Ron Bailey, recounts how on a morning in 1968, he felt the urge to take housing action: 'All this went through my mind on that evening of the third showing of *Cathy* [*Come Home*]. By three o'clock in the morning I had become convinced that a new squatters campaign was both necessary and realistic. I woke up some friends who were staying in my house, they too were enthusiastic and we immediately began to discuss ways and means to initiate the campaign. On 14 November 1968, the London Squatters Campaign came into being.'[28]

This practice has continued on through the various squatting groups, particularly characteristic of the movement in London, such as the 'Brent Homeless Families,' and more recently, the 'North East London Squatters,' among many others. After the 1960s and 1970s, there was a move away from families specifically and to individual and group squatters. During the 1970s, the Family Squatters Advisory Service (FSAS) was set up, which then re-grouped and formed the ASS.

This historical narrative is very much one in response to the social needs and deprivation of the time, yet out of this came the prevalence of punk squats and autonomist movements within London, such as 'The London Autonomists.'[29] Given this, the political background to the history of squatting holds an ambiguous link to the understanding of the reasoning of the law that governs it, and therefore the resistance on the ground. Given the infamous history of the 1970s as deep in social and financial difficulty in the UK, the Thatcher era of the 1980s followed with its boom for some, and not for others. How the political atmosphere, from left to right to left again, affected the law on squatting (and the resultant squatting activities on the ground), is of concern.

THE LAW

As mentioned, the law on squatting in England and Wales has recently changed. As of September 1, 2012, under section 144 of LASPOA, it became illegal in England and Wales to squat a residential building. The act defines illegal squatting:

> Offence of squatting in a residential building (1) A person commits an offence if—(a) the person is in a residential building as a trespasser having entered it as a trespasser, (b) the person knows or ought to know that he or she is a trespasser, and (c) the person is living in the building or intends to live there for any period. (2) The offence is not committed by a person holding over after the end of a lease or licence (even if the person leaves and re-enters the building).

Previously, it was not a criminal but civil offence. Traditionally, the UK has had 'squatters' rights.' Section 12 of the Criminal Law Act 1977, as amended by the Criminal Justice and Public Order Act 1994, laid out the distinction that underlies a trespasser and a squatter through whether the said adverse possessor had knowledge of there being a resident living in a said property. As long as there were no clear signs of the owner of the property living there, then Section 6 of the Criminal Law Act 1977 could be used, acting as the legal document through which squatters' rights are upheld. The avoidance of any damage to the property would maintain the entrance into the property as a civil offence, and not as that of a criminal nature. If there was evidence of criminal damage, then the police would have the powers to remove squatters. Occupants had to ensure there was someone in the building at all times, as it was illegal on the part of owner, or anyone else for that matter, to enter a building while it is occupied. In order to ensure legal occupancy, squatters had to have sole access to the property, and thus had to ensure access through replacing the locks and securing the building entirely, with no broken windows or doors. Eviction could only legally take place after a 'Possession Order' ('PO') had been made by the owner, to remove the unwanted residents from the property. The squatters then had the right to remain until this Order was agreed by the local or High Court. Thus, eviction could only take place after it has been agreed civilly within the courts. This is still operative with regard to commercial properties, but not those of a residential nature.

The changes that have taken place with regards to squatters' rights are only just coming to light, and therefore the effects of the law have not been fully felt at the time of this collection's publication.

In September 2011, legal academics, solicitors, and barristers in the practice of housing law, wrote a joint letter stating how they were concerned that a significant number of recent media reports had been exaggerating and misrepresenting the incidence of squatting in the UK, stating: '[These statements are] legally incorrect, as the guidance published by the Department for Communities and Local Government in March [2012] makes clear. We are concerned that such repeated inaccurate reporting of this issue has created fear for homeowners, confusion for the police and ill-informed debate among both the public and politicians on reforming the law.'

Despite the fact that the change in law effects only residential properties, this triumph of mis-information arguably lead to the assumption of all squatting to be a criminal and not civil offence. According to the Advisory Service for Squatters (ASS) in 2011, 'It will be difficult for those squatters who are using commercial properties to remain where they are despite the fact that they are still perfectly in their rights to do so, as the public will assume that squatters' rights have been outlawed entirely.' Yet the social utility of squatting was arguably to be overlooked at a time when 720,000 homes are unaffordable to those on low incomes in England, 60,000 in Scotland, and 30,000 in Wales due to caps on local housing allowance.[30] Squatting as a legal right has not always been a controversial area of law, its bracketing under the remit of adverse possession saw the synchronous emergence of property rights overall. Were it not for the stop valve of adverse possession and the taking of land by seizure, it would have been difficult to balance competing claims to land overall. Time limits on claims to land date back to as early as the Limitation Act 1623 and earlier, introducing arbitrary time limits on the assertion of claims. As a result, there developed the novel area of possession by successful taking. The bringing in of Limitation Acts saw possession based on the effluxion of time as one of the foundational concepts of English land law, at once enclosing one's right to land and at the same time opening out the beginning of another's based on a system of relativity of title.

Adverse possession remains a central paradox within English land law, statutory limitation as that which presses the relativity of title to its extremity. Seizure of land is therefore the basis of individual property rights, and the claim to an understanding of ownership. The mixing of labour with the land and the curtailment of the true owner's rights through abandonment and misuse is a very Lockean proviso, and given the fundamental role of adverse possession and squatting (as the control of land) as shaping property rights overall, legislators could have considered what the removal of this doctrine means to the strength of rights to property in sum. At the same time, the social utility to squatting is removed with swift, undemocratic changes to the law and misrepresentations of squatting on the ground.

Actually keeping track on the number of squatters in the UK is not an easy task, as the police and many local authorities do not keep records. In 1979, there were estimated to be 50,000 squatters throughout the UK, with the majority (30,000) living in London. Present day (from the mid-noughties), the ASS, believes there are now roughly 22,000 people living in squats, increased from 15,000 seven years ago. In 1995, there were an estimated 9,500; the figures are believed to be a modest estimate.[31] This is an increase in England and Wales of 25 percent.[32]

LEGAL MOVEMENTS IN THE 1970S

What is a squatter? He is one who, without any colour of right, enters on an unoccupied house or land, intending to stay there as long as he can. He may seek to justify or excuse his conduct. He may say he was homeless and that this house or land was standing empty, doing nothing. But this plea is of no avail in Law.
—Lord Denning MR[33]

So what were the legal changes at this time, and how have UK squatters' rights changed over time? And what were the effects of the legal movements on the squatters of the 1970s? During the 1970s, the legal landscape was very different to now.[34] In order to deter eviction without a court order, squatters first relied on the Forcible Entry Act (1381), this act being repealed by the Criminal Law Act in 1977 and the offence of 'violent entry' requiring a person on the premises replaced that of entry alone.[35] Section 6 of the Criminal Law Act 1977 was thus printed out and pinned to the doors of squats. According to barrister David Watkinson, until the end of the 1970s, there was no duty on local housing authorities to secure accommodation for the homeless until the Housing (Homeless Persons) Act 1977. There was no security of tenure for local authority tenants until 1980 (Housing Act 1980), nor of tenure for tenants in the private furnished property sector until the Rent Act 1974. These legal movements were a reaction to the direct housing actions that had been going on politically and socially on the ground, and the London Squatters Campaign (among others), taking the housing shortage into their own hands. Also, a continuing homelessness and the existence of substantial areas of empty property as characteristic of the era, played a role. The housing crisis and changes in the law were further propelled by the delayed compulsory purchase schemes that had been ambitiously started in the 1960s; alongside landlord profiteering (the forcing out of established tenants in order to sell); and the housing boom of the early 1970s.

The legal moves forged changes in the process and length of time with regard to possession orders being altered in 1971. It was held that the court could not grant a possession order against persons whose names were unknown, allowing for possession if 'reasonable steps' on behalf of the landowner had been taken to recover the names.[36] In 1975, in *Burston Finance v. Wilkins*, a High Court judge decided that even if names were unknown, if squatters knew of the proceedings, then they were impelled to come to court no matter what, and whether or not 'reasonable steps' to consider their names had been taken, was irrelevant.[37] Again, in 1975, Lord Denning: 'Irregularities no longer nullify the proceedings. People who defy the law cannot be allowed to avoid it by putting up technical objections.'[38] By 1977, however, possession orders were shortened once again and the 'reasonable steps' requirement entirely removed.[39] On top of this, possession orders against squatters were made to take effect immediately, as of *McPhail v. Persons Unknown*, with the courts having no power to suspend a court order once it had been made and without the landowner's express agreement.[40] The Criminal Law Act 1977 made it easier to evict squatters (criminal law), whereby a squatter who resisted a request to leave on behalf of a 'displaced residential occupier' (DRO)[41] or a 'protected intending occupier' (PIO)[42] could be arrested and removed without a court order. Resisting a court bailiff was also moved to 'obstruction,' but squatting as an act still remained a civil and not a criminal offence.[43] This is essentially the same as what has been reproduced with LASPOA with regards to the clarification of squatting as criminal trespass in a building categorised as someone's home.

So what had been the response to the proposed changes to the law by squatters themselves early in the 1970s? In 1972, the Law Commission, the body responsible for suggesting reforms to the law in England and Wales, requested it be looked into whether the act of squatting could be moved over from a civil wrong to a criminal offence, looking back into the law of forcible entry (laws of 1381 and 1623) that could be made effective in a contemporary context. The Lord Chancellor, the most prominent legal figure in government, responded with a working paper in July 1974 'Working Paper No. 54: Criminal Law Offences of Entering and Remaining on Property,' considering reforms to the law and a new law of criminal trespass. When the Criminal Trespass law was first considered by both the government and the Law Commission, there was widespread discontent and worry on behalf of squatters in London, as this law was first planned to illegalise squatting outright. At an All London Squatters (ALS) meeting in 1974, it was decided there was a need to respond to these proposed changes, and the Campaign Against a Criminal Trespass Law (CACTL) was born.[44] Because the proposed changes posed a serious threat to other campaigns (and this is reminiscent of the situation in the UK in 2010–2012), the CACTL attracted a great deal of support from workers and students who were occupying their places of work and study. As something that has been seen as a link to the push for a change in the law forty years later, CACTL argued that the real purpose of the legislation was not to wipe out squatting but to stop protest occupations.[45]

CACTL grouped together with workers, whereby they proposed the changes to the laws to be an attack on workers, thus focusing the campaign specifically with a strong body of support. By stating the proposed changes to the legislation to be aimed at shutting down factory occupations, CACTL managed to have a great deal of success. CACTL backed occupations and direct actions with commentary and lobbying at more institutional levels. With their following of workerist interests, they took opportunities to canvass about the changes to the law during rallies at trade union branches, student unions, and trades councils.[46] At the time, there was mass unrest, workers for instance being involved in over two hundred factory occupations between 1971 and 1975.[47] According to Platt, by 1976, CACTL had the backing of thirty-six trades councils, eighty-five trade union branches, and fifty-one student unions.[48]

By the time the response and support for keeping squatters' rights had had its effect on the Law Commission's proposals in 1976, it was a very much watered-down version of their original intent to criminalise the law. There were five new offences created, the most importance of which was the squatting of embassies, houses where the owner was clearly an occupant, etc., which was criminalised (which is explained in the form of DROs, IPOs, etc.). But all in all, CACTL, a group of squatters using a combination of the will to understand and work with legal knowledge, combined with political support, stopped the criminalisation of squatting.[49] Despite the fact that squatting had not been made illegal, there were those who—due to the visibility of CACTL and their presence in demonstrations and occupations as well as the unclear nature of the Criminal Law Act 1977—were not sure whether squatting remained legal. Therefore, in 1978, the ASS launched a campaign, Squatting Is Still Legal, to reassure squatters that squatting was still a civil and not a criminal offence and encourage them to get back in occupation and directly taking houses.[50]

It was also as a result of big actions, such as that at Redbridge in February 1969, that changes were achieved on the ground. According to Steve Platt:

> The most important struggle though was in Redbridge, East London, an area close to the homes of several of the London Squatters Campaign members. Redbridge Council was planning a major central area redevelopment scheme for Ilford. The scheme had not been officially approved and would not be started for several years and yet the Council was deliberately leaving a large number of sound houses empty to rot. Attempts to persuade it to use these houses for short-term lets had failed and some houses were planned to be left empty for ten years. On February 8, four houses were occupied, families installed and barricades erected.[51]

Redbridge and other occupations paved the way for a certain degree of protection through the process of the courts, a level of time and security within which squatting was not protected previously at the level of sit-ins. Indeed, according to Platt, 'the London Squatters Campaign's adroit legal defence established precedents which benefitted squatters for many years and many people involved in Ilford went on to promote squatting in other areas.'[52]

Organised squatting declined more as a result of concessions than repression and the reason for such legalisation was the cost involved in police and state repression. During 1977, five thousand squats in London were legalised. These are 'licensed squatters,' whereby their organised resistance was co-opted through permission from the local authorities or private owners to remain. This is what Pruijt has described as a 'repressive-integration-cooptation' model of relations between states and urban social movements.[53] This state intervention and spread of licensed squats propelled certain groups of squatters to continue in the fight for unlicensed squats, as the philosophy and self-management propelling the squatting movement was seen to be contradicted by the strategy of licensing. Yet, paradoxically, there was also the fighting for the protection of squatters' rights at the same time. With regards to licensing, 'Each victory won by squatters, however small, increased the impetus towards further unlicensed squatting, particularly since licensing arrangements involved the use of only a very small proportion of empty dwellings.'[54] The manner in which this morphed and altered the history of the ASS will be discussed in the coming section, however, it is enough to mention now that there was a general amnesty following the passing of the 1977 legislation, led by the Greater London Council (GLC).

At the same time as the changes in the law were taking place, the GLC realised there were 1,850 squats in their council, which meant that they were left with the choice of either evicting 7,000 squatters or granting amnesty. They decided to offer tenancies to every squatter living in GLC dwellings on October 25, 1977, as long as they registered within a month. If they did not register, then 'all measures which the law allows' were to be used against future squatters and those who chose not to take up their tenancies. This was a direct election campaign decision, on behalf of the then Conservative administration of the GLC. According to Platt, '[The GLC] adopted imaginative and flexible policies at [that] stage merely to facilitate implementing totally rigid and reactionary policies at a later date.'[55]

What was the political background at the time during these changes? The politics, as has just been demonstrated with the amnesty, comes combined with the legislative changes, and despite the Law Commission being an independent body, its choice of legal changes still showing what issues were being put on the reform table by the governments during the 1970s, and indeed onwards until now. Of course housing issues and squatting were and always will be politically divisive concerns, and it can be seen from the use of negative media campaigns such as those in the 1970s (which are being relayed again today) how strongly there are those against squatting and its movements and participants. Typically, the 1970s are known for their era of punk, which is automatically connected to the squatting movement through their freeing of space and anti-authoritarian practices. Yet who were the governments during this decade? The government throughout the majority of the Law Commission recommendations was a Labour administration, which traditionally would have been thought to have been in line with supporting the causes of squatting. The political impetus against squatting could have been seen to be quelled through licensing, but this again has also been seen as a tactic of concession as opposed to acceptance. Whether these characteristics of law and politics alter over the next few decades is another consideration.

THE LEGAL MOVEMENT OF 1980: ADVISORY SERVICE FOR SQUATTERS (ASS)

In response to the need for legal advice, both the Advisory Service for Squatters and Release developed considerable expertise in helping squatters to fight cases and through their advice many court cases were won and many squatters successfully resisted attempts by police to con them out of their homes.
—Squatting: The Real Story[56]

As has already been explained, the legal manoeuvres during the 1970s were the most prevalent with regards to the development of squatting law. An extended version of the law of 'adverse possession' is that, according to the Limitation Act 1980, if the squatters apply for the possession of the property after a period of twelve years, the property can rightly become their own, unless the owner objects prior to the twelfth year. In order to get a snapshot of how the law was being operated on the ground, observing the actions of the ASS, a voluntary legal advice service for the homeless and specifically squatters, is useful. They are indicative of the reactions and actions of squatters and other groups in light of any form of legal activism, and legal movement overall.

In the late 1960s, the FSAS was founded in London, to help defend the rights of squatters. The idea of the FSAS was to represent squatter communities from different areas in London, and to aid the re-homing of families. At the beginning, it proved difficult to find representatives from the communities alone, and therefore sympathisers were also invited to join.[57] In *McPhail v. Persons Unknown*, the Court of Appeal reinforced that a landowner could re-enter a squatted property and use reasonable force to evict those occupying the property. As a reaction to the ruling, which placed all power in the hands of the possessor of the property (rather than the occupants), the All London Squatters (ALS) was founded, with the cause of defending the interest of unlicensed squatters. There were activists fighting for squatters' rights at the FSAS, but a new wave of advocates found that the FSAS did not do enough to protect unlicensed squatters' rights.[58] In fact, the role of licensing created a division within the FSAS, and paved way for the ALS, who were open to more direct action, and squats that were both unlicensed and licensed. The divisions within the squatting movement became obvious during the Centre Point occupation in January 1974. Centre Point is a large office block on Tottenham Court Road in London, by and large unoccupied during the 1970s. Given its location, the occupation was spectacular. The demonstration however lasted only a few days, not nearly as long as some from the ALS would have liked. The ALS preferred much more direct action, while the occupation was organised by the FSAS, which clearly showed the divisions.

The tensions eventually ended in the complete change in make-up of the organisation. By July 1975, the organisation was divided by autonomists and anarchists who wished for a more decentralised organisation, and those of the Trotskyist squatters who did not. Since then it has regrouped and reformed and is now known as the voluntary group previously mentioned, the ASS.[59] The ASS supports both licensed and unlicensed squatting, and still gives legal and general advice on squatting. They are currently working on a fourteenth edition of their *Squatters' Handbook*, given the 2012 changes in law.

In 1980, the government was dealing with the effects of the laws that had taken place during the 1970s, in order to tighten up the laws on squatting. The ASS acted in their advisory capacity, and arguably exemplified a very professional and legalistic understanding of adverse possession, court procedures and in-depth knowledge to offer those they helped, and sometimes, represented, in various squatting cases (which is still the case today). Even the existence of the ASS at all suggests an acknowledgement of the necessity to be knowledgeable

Squatters Handbook

11th Edition   £1

The *Squatters Handbook* produced by the Advisory Service for Squatters. Courtesy of Interference Archive.

in the law in order for squatting to continue, and therefore could be seen as a manifestation of a 'legal activism.' The same can be said for the CACTL and the effects that campaign had on the resultant rescuing of squatters' rights from criminalisation through the watering down of the Criminal Law Act 1977.

Despite the changes in the law, squatting was on the increase again in 1980 in London, and across the UK.[60] This can be seen as a result of the increasing cost of living and difficulties finding housing, coupled with the effects of the recession of the 1970s. The ASS was at the time, as it is today, overwhelmed with the provision of advice on squatting law, and yet then there was less organised squatting and more squatting as isolated occupations, perhaps than we see today.[61] In 1980, a collection of essays on squatting was published as the now seminal, *Squatting: The Real Story*, which looked back on the actions and reactions that had taken place since 1968. In the book, one member of the ASS stated that the changes in the law made very little difference to the existence of squatting, and this is something that resounds today as the laws on squatting have been altered once again.[62] The ASS was dealing with instances in law that spoke of 'non-existent' situations, whereby the law was altered due to a prevalence of fear and miscommunication, as again is the case today as a result of negative media coverage.[63] Since the original writing of this piece, Deanna Dadusc and E.T.C. Dee have written commendable work,[64] in addition to Mary Manjikian's exceptional analysis of squatting through a securitisation framework,[65] both of which have spoken of the way in which the media fuel, if not create, a negative story of squatting, with the squatter resultantly stigmatised as the 'other.' Next to the ASS, there were also other legal movements in operation during 1980, such as Release and the prison movement, who also sought an understanding of law in order to affect resistance. The year 1980 can be seen as a year in which the effects of the direct action of the previous years, in synchrony with the legal movements in the courts and parliament, were felt, but had reached a plateau.

What does this lack of coincidence between the structures of squatting movements, and the remit of law, speak to in regard to the supposed mirror that was introduced earlier in this piece, and the existence or otherwise of legal movements and legal activism? The role of legal movements and any reflection on the ground will be understood at greater length with the introduction of the Land Registration Act 2002, concerning the legal remit of rights available to squatters within terms of the law of adverse possession, and what these changes say about the placement of squatting within (or outside) law.

LEGAL MOVEMENTS IN 2011–2012

Since the 1970s and 1980, and in the lead up to 2012, there has been an encroaching shift towards the removal of squatters' rights from English law. The Criminal Justice Act of 1994 made some substantial changes to the law relating to squatting, bringing in interim possession orders on behalf of the owner and giving squatters a considerably reduced amount of time to remain and thus a re-duced version of squatters' rights. The then home secretary and mind behind the act, Michael Howard, said, 'There can be no excuse for seizing someone else's property for however short a time,' and thus measures in the Criminal Justice Bill were then designed to deal a great deterrence to squatters.[66] Towards the end of the 1980s, the Law Commission was once again put to consider reforms in land law, that affect the remit of squatters' rights directly, and indeed the scope of the changes tabled were seen once again to limit any security and pro-tection of the courts that squatters had from the 1970s. The Land Registration Act 2002 fundamentally altered the law of adverse possession, whereby after ten years of physical possession, a squatter has to apply to the 'Land Registry' to have their title recognised as owner. In a move that did not happen previ-ously, the original owner of the property is then notified by the Registry upon receiving the claim from the adverse possessor, and the owner can then defeat the application, simply by raising an objection. Sections 96 to 98 and Schedule 6 give the 'paper owner' the right to be notified that adverse possession is occurring, and as a result, recover possession.[67] This ultimately means that the occurrence of a squatter adversely possessing the title to a land they have been occupying for years, will become a thing of the past.

In May 2011, the Ministry of Justice announced the launch of its con-sultation on the criminalisation of squatting. Their plans were set out in a num-ber of proposals:

Option 1—Create a new offence of squatting in buildings;

Option 2—Amend section 7 of the Criminal Law Act 1977 to extend the offence to other types of premises;

Option 3—Repeal or amend the offence in section 6 of the Criminal Law Act 1977;

Option 4—Leave the criminal law unchanged but work with the enforcement authorities to improve enforcement of existing offences;

Option 5—Do nothing: continue with existing sanctions and enforcement activity.[68]

Since publishing the feedback gathered from the consultation, the Justice Secretary Kenneth Clarke fast-tracked the criminalisation of squatting by amending clause 26 (now clause 144) of the Legal Aid, Sentencing and Punishment of Offenders Act (LASPOA) to criminalise squatting in residen-tial buildings. Under the plans, anyone found squatting in a residential building was to face a year in jail, a £5,000 fine, or both. The government's amendment was passed by 283 votes to 13, a majority of 270. Despite this, an overwhelming 96 percent of those who responded to the consultation process had stated they did not wish to see any changes in the laws regarding squatting.

If there is any mirror at all, then there is clearly a repetition of the nega-tive positioning of squatting and squatters that was seen during the 1970s, which propelled the changes to the law and the enactment of the Criminal Law Act 1977. However, in this instance, there is indeed a right-wing government in place, and there was the same during the 2002 and 1994 changes. What Manjikian has concisely recognised is that no matter what leaning of politics a government may be, the grip of neoliberal fears for national security and the protection of tradi-tion, is quite clearly demonstrated in the indiscriminately draconian manner in which squatting has been treated by governments either left or right.[69]

2011 LEGAL MOVEMENT: SQUASH

Squatters' Action for Secure Homes, or SQUASH, was originally formed out of a network of squatters named Squattastic, started in London in December 2010 to counter government and media condemnation of squatting and squatters. They are made up of squatters, activists, researchers, charity workers, lawyers, and academics, and have a Legal and Research Group that during the consul-tation period worked specifically on keeping abreast of the proposed changes to the law. In November 2011, they tabled some urgent recommendations in the form of an amendment to the proposed government changes to the (then) clause 26 of the Legal Aid bill. Labour MP John McDonnell worked with SQUASH to get their recommendations through parliamentary processes and put forward the amendment to clause 26, which called for there to be no of-fence if a building has been empty for six months or more.[70]

SQUASH represents a clear awareness of the necessity of a legal un-derstanding and knowledge, when dealing specifically with squatting, and one that replicates the causes of the FSAS and the resultant ASS, but does this say anything about the law they are reacting to? Only that the only response from law-makers is the slow encroachment on squatters' rights, and the cyclical re-turn to the issue in times of economic difficulty, such as that which was seen during the 1970s and since 2008.

When comparing the success of the CACTL and SQUASH, there is a different approach when it comes to their affiliations. CACTL had the workers' movement upon which to latch their campaigns, whereas SQUASH had the option to involve themselves with a number of related causes, but per-haps did not maximise their connections enough. Within the time over which squatting has been pressed to be made illegal, yet again, there were national protests in the form of student occupations during 2010–2011, as well as the summer 2011 riots in the UK, finishing off the year with Occupy, the biggest global protest movement since the 1960s and 1970s, aside from the Global Justice Movement. Although there were links made with the students on be-half of SQUASH, having considered how CACTL utilised their connections with the workers and also therefore, gaining support from the workers, the anti-criminalisation movement of late could be said to have not made the best of the support they could have gathered through the students, the summer of resistance, and the Occupy movement. Despite this, SQUASH worked meticulously with MPs and the Lords to try and put forward the legal argument for not changing the law.

At the same time as all of these events were happening, expressing a summer of discontent, the illegalisation of squatting came as a clear legal reaction during times of repression by those in the seat of authority. It highlights the primeval role of the occupation of space and the constant conflict between the right to protest, to have a home, to occupy public space, as opposed to the rights of those who are the proprietors of the estates involved. The force of private property prevailed, as it often does.

LEGAL ACTIVISM

If squatters are going to frustrate the law by treading a path through its technicalities, they must tread very carefully indeed.
—Ron Bailey[71]

In Ron Bailey's account of the squatting movement in London from its birth in 1968, the squatters had to make sure that they were not breaking the law, for the security of the families that were involved. He states early on in his book *The Squatters*: 'It was important for us to avoid breaking the law in order to involve homeless families in the campaign. After all, we thought that if we could say to families that squatting was only civil trespass and not an offence for which they could be prosecuted, then we were far more likely to be able to involve them in squatting activities.'[72] In fact, there was one instance during the Redbridge occupation in 1974 where the squatters used the law in their favour, using a form of trickery against the police whereby they complied with a possession order in light of eviction, by moving a family out of a building. In their place, and within the time that the bailiffs were round to exact eviction, another family was moved in, and there was not a great deal the police could do. All the actions were completely within the law, knowing the law and the limits of what the law could do in response.[73]

The ASS handbook states the relevant law, and how to comply with the law in order to secure and occupy a building correctly.[74] There are also 'Practical Squatters Evenings' that are put on in various spaces around London. By acknowledging the legality of squatting, by being aware and having knowledge of the state system, squatters have acknowledged a loophole in the law. At the same time as finding this loophole, squatters have displayed an admiration for the law and a way of using this to determine a legal activism. This again is all seen in a slightly different light now that squatting is nearly entirely criminalised, and questions whether this admiration for the law will remain and whether squatting will always take place illegally anyway.

At the same time, the role of the courts has sometimes been sympathetic towards squatters, showing an admiration in turn. In a recent case brought against Camden Council on the basis of freedom of information to publicise the number of potential homes currently lying empty across the country, Judge Fiona Henderson stated, 'The public interest lies in putting empty properties back into use,' and argued that publication of the list would 'bring buildings back into use sooner and the housing needs of additional people would be met.'[75] This has also been argued by legal academic Robin Hickey, whereby the common law is seen to nigh on always uphold the rights of the squatter.[76]

To show a further ambiguity in the relations between squatting law and those it objectifies, the *McPhail v. Persons Unknown* case of the 1970s created the ASS as we know it today. There was the debate between the FSAS and ALS that displayed disagreements over licensing and the legitimation of squatting, and thus the role of law in squatting overall, depending on the division within the squatting community. There were also those who were unsure of the legality of squatting, putting off many potential squatters. This again shows how squatting being legal did make a difference to a number of those who considered squatting.

CONCLUSION

Squatters have always had a close relationship with the law. Many squatters have regarded the law as a source of protection, but the law has only fulfilled this role sporadically and to a diminishing extent. However, were it not for certain 'squatters' rights,' squatting would undoubtedly not have established itself as it has done. The adroit use of the law by squatters has frequently delayed evictions and provided time for organisation and negotiation.
—Squatting: The Real Story[77]

So can there be said to be an interaction in the form of legal movement between the law on squatting and the actions of squatters on the ground? And does the direction of the politics in the background make any difference at all? There is certainly at least one cyclical motion, in that squatters learn the law in response to the threat of draconian changes, but it seems as though the law does not learn from the squatters and the causes they represent. And this one-sidedness is of course embedded in a global system of property transfer and appropriation, which beclouds both politics of the right and the left. The drive to curb any alternative and self-managed use of space, through the death of squatting laws, could be seen as a manifestation of market-driven economic structures and the indiscriminate changes in law despite the political persuasion of national governments. Whether this matters to squatting movements has been highlighted through the argued legal activism of ASS and SQUASH, who acknowledge law and use it as a tool against the illegalisation of squatting itself. The role of law and the legality of squatting have been highlighted as a positive illustration of the general perception of property rights within a society overall. If the intersection between law and squatting suggests any form of reflection, it may well be deeply placed within the actors and participants of social movements as a whole.

Social movements have been recognised for their potential to reorder order, and this is what the ASS and SQUASH show through their proposed legal activism and their reflection on the legal and political processes occurring from above. To be part of a squatting movement is to be part of 'a network of small groups submerged in everyday life which require a personal involvement in experiencing and practicing cultural innovation.'[78] It also comes forth from a desire to take hold of law itself, to be autonomous, create law, to self-legislate, which is characteristic of the drive of the ASS and SQUASH.

As in any other movement, there is always the role of violence, and none is more forceful and powerful than that wielded by the state through the use of law. Keeping in line with this book's assessment of the extent to which violence is an element within the construct of the movements concerned, the legal changes have violent impacts felt by the squatters on the ground. Any squatter will understand the violent force of property rights, just by entering a building and surveying the destruction of the interior of a building. Part of the deterrent that landlords and councils use to stop squatters entering is to destroy any means of basic amenities that those looking for an emptied space may wish to use. This includes 'gutting,' the smashing up of all the plumbing, and the destruction of staircases, rendering floors other than the ground floor inaccessible. Land ownership, according to Anders Corr's summary of the anarchist-tinged literature on property, 'exists when an individual has the violent forces necessary to evict or subdue the inhabitants of a given piece of land and claims "ownership."'[79] He also highlights how this is a process that has taken place again and again, along different strata, within different areas of the world, and at alternate times and spaces, claiming that such a replication, 'will remain that way inasmuch as the system and ideology of spatial property is the salient inter-human relation to land.'[80] The squatting movement in England and Wales, and specifically that of London, which has been discussed here in relation to national law changes, is merely a microcosmic example that explains the same age-old processes of law and resistance across the globe.

According to the legal philosopher Jeremy Bentham, 'Property and law are born together, and die together. Before laws were made there was no property; take away laws, and property ceases.'[81] The role of law and violence, and the force of property rights, saturates all accounts of squatting. Critical legal geographer Nicholas Blomley propounds: 'Space gets produced, invoked, pulverized, marked, and differentiated through practical and discursive forms of legal violence. And property's violence is itself instantiated and legitimized, yet also complicated and contradicted in and through such spaces.'[82] Despite this, and whether or not squatting is legal or illegal, space will still be produced and reused by those who squat, whether illegal or otherwise. In England, Wales, Germany, Italy, and the Netherlands, squatting still takes place, despite the fact that the laws have criminalised the movement. This is even more so prescient in the case of the Netherlands, which up until 2010 was renowned for its regime of squatters' rights.

This analysis of squatting in relation to law illustrates the ambiguous and fluctuating relation between the two, and how squatting movements and legal movements may alternate in the future. Perhaps it has also provided an interesting insight into how one can utilise law in order to counter law. It is clear that there is a one-way conversation between the activists promoting squatting on the ground, their arguable incorporation of legal activism, and the decisions of governments of all creeds over the years that have been discussed. This is perhaps more a characteristic of the market-oriented drive that infiltrates the remit of property (and thus the need for homes and the use and occupation of space) and the indiscriminate disregard for party politics and the effects on property law. In order to break the cyclical motion of the tentatively proposed presence of both legal movements on the ground and within law-making institutions, it is hoped that by going beyond national law and making use of European Court of Human Rights decisions on adverse possession (despite the fact they are nearly always in favour of the proprietor), the development of the right to housing could create a viable obstacle to the encroachment of anti-squatting laws. In view of the fact that displacing someone from a building that had obvious signs of being their home without the permission of the legal owner has been illegal since the Criminal Law Act 1977, the necessity for a duplicate law just goes to demonstrate the accelerated deification and reification of individual property rights, over the social utility and sharing of resources held within the philosophy and practice of squatting. This recent shift in media-aggravated legislative change is a definitive move further in favour of the landowner as opposed to those who have no land, and those who support the redistribution of land.

What will be of interest will be exactly what effect the clause 144 of LASPOA will have on the prohibition of squatting. As the All Lambeth Squatters said in 1974, 'Remember—trying to stop squatting is like stamping on a greasy golfball.'

FURTHER READING

Not a great deal of resources exist on squatting in the UK, at least not within academia. You can go to any infoshop or squatted space, however, and be sure to find a wide-ranging and very vibrant collection of independent literature and alternative publications on squatting. This comes under the bracket of anarchist and autonomist literature as a whole, and guides to achieving a 'DIY' culture. There are a number of key publications that relate specifically to the UK scene and London. The ultimate guide to squatting in the UK and specifically London up until 1980 is *Squatting: The Real Story* (London: Bay Leaf Books, 1980), edited by Nick Wates and Christian Wolmar. It manages to collage together a great number of contributions as well as an array of primary source newspaper cuttings and images. A second famous and comprehensive account of the squatting movement in the UK is *The Squatters* (London: Penguin, 1973) written by Ron Bailey, who was a leading figure and lawyer of the second wave of squatting (1968–1980). This study, however, focuses on the late 1960s. Colin Ward's study *Cotters and Squatters: Housing's Hidden History* (Nottingham: Five leaves, 2002) goes even further back in time and focuses specifically on the post–World War II period in England and the first wave of UK direct housing activism back in the 1940s and 1950s.

Since the writing of this piece, a number of books have been written on squatting, such as those by the Squatting Europe Collective (SQEK), *Squatting in Europe: Radical Spaces, Urban Struggles* (Brooklyn: Autonomedia, 2013), as well as a more theoretically engaged monograph by Mary Manjikian, *The Securitisation of Property Squatting in Europe* (London: Routledge, 2013), to name but a few.

Important sources on the legal movements revolving around squatting are: A.M. Prichard, *Modern Legal Studies: Squatting* (London: Sweet and Maxwell, 1981); and the *Squatters' Handbook* published by the Advisory Service for Squatters. The first is written from a blackletter legal perspective, and although undoubtedly out of date now, it does give an interesting insight into the development of the law relating to squatting in its various guises throughout the past few centuries in England and Wales. Both the SQUASH Campaign and the ASS have excellent websites that have a vast amount of resources and information on squatting, particularly more contemporary debates with regard to the criminalisation of squatting in England and Wales.

Paul Chatterton and his Autonomous Geographies collective in Leeds have written a great number of publications on the social centre scene, not just necessarily that of the squatting kind. A notable contribution of his is 'Autonomy, the Struggle for Survival and the Self-Management of the Commons,' *Antipode* 42 (2010): 897–908.

More on the social centre movement and the supposed (or non-existent) rift between social centres that are squatted and those that are rented or owned, are two texts: Rogue Element, 'You Can't Rent Your Way out of a Social Relationship,' *Green Anarchist* no. 73–74 (2004) and Text Nothing, All and Nothing: For Radical Suicide, 'Towards Some Notes and Confusion on "You Can't Rent Your Way out of a Social Relationship,"' available through http://www.56a.org.uk/rent.html.

Reading the replies on both texts on http://www.indymedia.org.uk/en/regions/manchester/2004/08/296049.html was of great influence to the direction of my research and is a useful indication of the divisive role of squatting within the UK social centre scene.

Eight

SQUATTING IN THE EAST:
THE ROZBRAT SQUAT IN POLAND, 1994–2012

Grzegorz Piotrowski

INTRODUCTION: A BRIEF HISTORY OF THE ROZBRAT SQUAT

IN POLISH, *rozbrat* means 'to make peace and get detached from [usually an enemy].' It is also the name of the oldest and biggest squatted social centre in Central and Eastern Europe. The following text is an attempt to present its history and, in doing so, the challenges that the squatter movement faces in Poland and in Central and Eastern Europe.

Established in the autumn of 1994, on the grounds of an abandoned paint factory near the city centre of Poznań, in the western part of Poland, it has become one of the central hubs for the city's (and Poland's) alternative culture. It is not the only squatted social centre in Poland, as there were and are also squats in Gdańsk, Toruń, Wrocław, Warsaw, Gliwice, and Białystok. There were other squats in Poznań, although they were short-lived and focused solely on providing housing. Rozbrat seems to be the most influential and most typical of them all. Rozbrat was started by three people who, in the early 1990s, had just returned from a trip around Europe and were eager to find a location for collective living in their hometown. Luckily for them, the buildings of the old paint factory—although abandoned—were in good condition. They included the former offices of the company that produced not only paint but also other chemicals. Thus, in October 1994, a squat named Rozbrat was established.

Being illegal from the beginning (in Poland, squatting is generally a felony, especially when one has to break into the building to occupy it) its inhabitants faced some fines. Trespassing, however, is not prosecuted heavily in Poland, which made life for the approximately twenty squatters bearable. After a while, the authorities got used to them and tolerated their occupation of the factory. Rozbrat is a perfect place for squatting because of its unclear legal status, as the owners' whereabouts are unknown and they have not made a claim to the site. In other cases, where the owners are known and active or the buildings are owned by the municipality, eviction is rather quick.

Squeezed between recreational gardens, an old print house, a car dealer, and few residential estates, Rozbrat is well known in Poland for its political involvement and cultural activities. In the beginning, the squat only served as a place to live. Gradually, however, it began to change into a more open, counter-cultural place. While the first concerts, in 1995, were open only to people with invitations, they gradually evolved into open events.[1] Soon, hundreds of concerts were organised at Rozbrat, together with discussions, public lectures, film screenings, theatre plays, exhibitions, and parties.

Today, Rozbrat hosts a number of initiatives and is a home base for several different groups. There is a bike shop that specialises in single-speed bicycles and whose crew is connected with the Critical Mass group in Poznań.[2] There is a silk-screen print shop, an anarchist library and archive (since 1997), as well as an infoshop. The Food Not Bombs group prepares meals on the squat premises, and the site hosts both a chapter of the Polish Anarchist Federation and of the Inicjatywa Pracownicza (Workers' Initiative: a radical, syndicalist trade union). There is also a small feminist group and a publishing house called Bractwo Trojka (Trojka Brotherhood: the name comes from Russian and means either a three-horse carriage or a small chapter of an underground organisation. The latter meaning comes from late nineteenth-century revolutionaries). The samba group (previously named Rhythms of Resistance after a similar group in London, now called Breaking (Ear)drums, Pękające Bębenki, in a play of words) has its rehearsals here and there are even yoga classes.

In 2001, another room was adapted for the Kulawy Muł initiative (Lame Mule, after a phrase in a nineteenth-century Polish poem), which or-ganises recitals, poetry evenings, lectures, and discos. The back of Lame Mule is transformed into the Gallery, open for independent artists. In order to better manage the complex and involve different projects more politically, a group called Rozbrat Collective began taking care of daily management tasks, build-ing repairs, and grounds maintenance. The Rozbrat Collective also decides who can live in the squatted buildings. Under-aged people are excluded by default and residents who cause trouble have been requested to leave.

BECOMING POLITICAL: THE LATE 1990S

Most people associate Rozbrat with its political activities rather than with its function of providing shelter to its residents. Because Rozbrat was founded by anarchists, anarchism still dominates the collective and has become more visible and vibrant over time. As Rozbrat's popularity grew, 'freedom meetings' were organised, along with occasional consultation hours for people attempting to

Previous page spread: Punk concert at Rozbrat. Photo: Unknown.

avoid the military draft. In 1997, the Anarchist Federation settled at Rozbrat. Before, they were meeting at a bar called Tryby in the centre of the city. After that, the more active participants have gathered in the Rozbrat Collective.

Originally, Rozbrat activists organised meetings called Biesiady Wolnościowe (Libertarian Feasts), which served as a forum for both solving Rozbrat's internal problems and organizing public activities. Although the core of the organisers were anarchists, people with a wide range of other ideologies also attended. The direct successor of these meetings was the Anarchist Federation (AF), which created the Anarchist Library in 1997 and the Anarchist Club in 2000 (where the AF still holds its weekly meetings). The AF emerged out of a split within the activist scene—which rallied around issues such as ecology and the compulsory military service—between anarchist-oriented activists and less politically focused people. At a certain point, Rozbrat hosted two meetings a week, with the anarchist one being more exclusive. A few months later, the Libertarian Feasts disappeared. Soon after, the punk rock concerts were complemented by more political public events and the squat became the centre of an eruption of social activism.

In the wake of the alterglobalisation movement, the late 1990s saw a steep increase of social activism worldwide and Poland was no exception. The first demonstrations in Poland appeared like a set of chaotic responses to specific problems, without any structural campaigning. A large number of different issues emerged, from boycotting Chinese products and protesting against Nazi rallies to raising environmental awareness. Few campaigns from this period had an important role in creating today's activism in Poznań and in Poland. One of these was the struggle over St. Anne's Mountain in 1998. The conflict erupted when the authorities decided to build a highway that would cut through a nature reserve located at St. Anne's Mountain in southwest Poland. From the start, this decision faced serious criticisms from environmental organisations, social activists, and the public opinion. The conflict came to a head when a group of activists, among them many from Rozbrat, organised a protest camp in the village of Ligota in May and early June 1998. The eviction of the camp on June 8 resulted in serious clashes with the police and security personnel hired by the construction company. It was one of the first campaigns outside the city centre of Poznań in which Rozbrat activists participated, organizing solidarity events as well.

Another important campaign consisted of demonstrations against the war in Chechnya. The first was organised in 1999 under the banner of the Anarchist Federation. Soon, the Komitet Wolny Kaukaz (Free Caucasus Committee, KWK) was established and consisted not only of anarchists but also of members of the right-wing group Naszość, whose main agenda was to stage anti-Russian protests. This cooperation sparked many heated debates, also within the anarchist community. On February 23, 2003, the Poznań Chapter of the Free Caucasus Committee organised a protest in front of the Russian consulate in Poznań.[3] The group commemorated the deportation of the Chechen population by the Stalinist regime fifty-six years earlier. Several demonstrators managed to enter the premises, where they destroyed a Russian flag and wrote slogans on the wall with red paint. This caused a diplomatic scandal, and Russian media dubbed the event a 'rogue action.' This established the reputation of Rozbrat as a political group.

At the end of the 1990s, new tactics were introduced, inspired by similar actions in other countries, mainly in Western Europe. During the actions at St. Anna's Mountain, for example, activists climbed trees and chained themselves to tripods to block roads and construction sites. They also filled barrels with concrete with a tube in the middle through which two protesters could handcuff themselves together. This made it nearly impossible to either uncuff them or to remove them. Such barrels can be seen also today at Rozbrat, where they are kept in case of eviction.

These action repertoires were diffused among others during anti-border camps, which were organised by the German-based network Kein Mensch Ist Illegal (No One Is Illegal—Żaden Człowiek Nie Jest Nielegalny in Polish). The three biggest camps were organised in the summer of 1999 close to Zgorzelec/Goerlitz, near the Polish-German-Czech border; in 2000 in Ustrzyki, at the Polish-Slovak-Ukrainian border; and in 2001 in Krynki, at the Polish-Belarusian border, close to Lithuania. These camps hosted a few hundred activists each, and their programs consisted of discussions about the state of the movement, politics, and ideology, as well as training workshops in new tactics. Demonstrations were organised which usually lasted for several days. After the camp in Ustrzyki, conflicts arose among the Rozbrat activists, which led to the formation of a splinter group named Grupa Anarchistyczna Solidarność (Anarchist Solidarity Group, GAS). The differences were however not so big that the GAS activists could not hold their meetings at Rozbrat. GAS began publishing its own zines as well.[4] After several months, the group ceased to exist and some of its members went back to their previous activism.

At the same time, a new wave of activism set in under the banner of alterglobalism at the end of the 1990s. For Polish activists, including those from Rozbrat, the counter-summit in Prague in September 2000 against the summit of the IMF and the World Bank was a turning point. Not only did the counter-summit offer the chance to participate in a large international protest event, the protests and widespread media coverage also attracted many new people. The media hype continued until approximately 2004, with much attention for the anti-war campaigns organised by the broad Poznań Anti-War Coalition (Poznańska Koalicja Antywojenna, PKA), which staged numerous protests against the wars in Iraq and Afghanistan. The counter-summit in April 2004 in Warsaw against the European Economic Forum, however, showed that the alterglobalist wave was fading away, and gradually the activists from Rozbrat began to lose their interest in framing their claims in this way.

SHIFTING TOWARDS LOCAL ISSUES: THE 2000S

Around the year 2000, two important developments took place within the Rozbrat community. First, activists were faced with a wave of fines, court cases, and sentences that targeted almost every form of action from unannounced demonstrations to street happenings and many other forms of protest. Because of the anarchists' critical attitude towards cooperation with the authorities and legal forms of protests, they were subsequently involved in one court case after another.

Secondly, after long-drawn discussions, the group decided to concentrate its energies on long-lasting campaigns rather than short-term and ad hoc actions. These campaigns usually focused on local issues. First, the group attempted to build up a regional coalition of radical groups and activists by organizing regular festivals called Abramowszczyzna (named after Edward Abramowski, a Polish anarchist, political theorist, philosopher, and founder of the Polish cooperatives movement), which lasted up to four days and mobilised anarchists and activists from all over Poland to discuss political and theoretical issues.

At the same time, Poznań witnessed the rise of a number of local conflicts, which anarchist groups decided to amplify and use to bring their own agenda. One revolved around the plan to build an exclusive golf course on the location of a public park and recreational area in Smochowice, a suburb of Poznań. Another concerned the expansion of a military air base in Krzesiny, another suburban area. Anarchists and squatters joined these protests, bringing their knowledge about organising campaigns and demonstrations. A broad citizens' coalition was established called Porozumienie Społeczne Poznań—Miasto Dla Ludzi (Social Coalition Poznań—A City for the People). This initiative, however, was short-lived. Nevertheless, local issues and campaigns began to dominate activists' agenda and networks established by this cooperation on local issues became of great importance in later years.

Another important event was the establishment of a syndicalist trade union that started as the Inicjatywa Pracownicza FA (Workers' Initiative [of the] Anarchist Federation, IPFA). Shortly after, the organisation became more open and was transformed into the Inicjatywa Pracownicza (Workers' Initiative, IP). It was mostly organised by people connected to Rozbrat and was part of the strategy of reaching out to other social groups outside the activist scene. The turning point was the connection the squatters established with workers of the Hipolit Cegielski factory (HCP), not only one of the biggest employers in Poznań, but one with great symbolic value. It was the workers of the Cegielski factory who started the first revolt against the Communist regime in Poland in 1956 that led to the 'thaw' in the relations between the regime and the populace.

Following page spread: A group from Workers' Initiative at a protest that accompanied the UN Climate Change Conference in Poznań, December 2008. Photo: Grzegorz Piotrowski.

Soon after these events, in which fifty-seven people lost their lives, the first secretary of the Communist Party was replaced and the party withdrew from the
strict Stalinist line. Censorship regulations were loosened and the authorities
opened up for more dialogue with the people. This resulted in more freedom of
speech, the release of a number of political prisoners—some of whom were imprisoned for their involvement in anti-Communist organisations during World
War II—and an improvement of the relations with the Catholic Church. (The
cardinal of Poland, Stefan Wyszyński, was released from house arrest.)

The cooperation between the squatters and workers meant that the new
political agenda was taking root, and it influenced changes in political style.
Grassroots work, such as handing out flyers in front of factories, organizing
meetings, helping the workers with organizing strikes, assisting those who were
fired from their working places, and providing legal aid became prominent.
Since 2012, the activists from Rozbrat have also been involved with the housing and tenants' movement in Poznań. As in other cities, many houses that were
taken away from their owners and used by the local municipalities and communal housing are being re-privatised. Combined with a large demand on the
housing market, this caused a demand for rapid renovation and reselling, often
involving illegal methods. According to housing laws, the current tenants must
be given a three-year notice, but companies have been established that specialise
in the 'cleaning' of such houses, with workers cutting off electricity and water
pipes and using other means to get rid of the people living there. Activists from
Rozbrat—through an association established for this purpose, Wielkopolskie
Stowarzyszenie Lokatorów (Tenants Association of Wielkopolska)—have
started a movement against this trend, offering their help in organizing public protests, initiating a broad support and media campaigns, and using this
situation to attack the local authorities for the deficiencies of their policies on
communal and social housing. They have also attacked several banks that were
involved in financing investments in the re-privatised houses. The presence of
the squatters not only radicalised the tenants' movement, the squatters' knowledge of the use of media also brought about a great deal of attention.

As a result of eighteen years of continuous activities and actions,
Rozbrat is nowadays seen as a counter-example for the neoliberal policies of
local authorities. When, in 2009, there was a threat that the grounds on which
Rozbrat is located would be auctioned, a massive campaign was launched that
peaked with two demonstrations in March and May 2009. The demonstrations mobilised numbers of participants rarely seen in Poland. As the authors
of the Rozbrat website claimed: 'The original idea of Rozbrat was to set up a
commune composed of people who did not approve of a world that is based on
"a rat race." From there, it has evolved and developed: the place itself changed,
different people got involved in the organisation. The goal has broadened from
providing shelter to hosting cultural, social and political work.'[5]

CHALLENGES TO THE SQUAT: 2009–2010

Most of the challenges to Rozbrat as a social centre have been linked to its security. In the first few years of its existence, the biggest one was the risk of neo-Nazi attacks. One of the first campaigns organised by the squatters was to release an activist nicknamed Kudo from detention after he got into a fight with skinheads. The campaign was meant to support him and to put pressure on the court. Neo-Nazis also attacked Rozbrat. Early one morning in February 1996, a group of skinheads raided and thrashed the squat, seriously wounding a young woman in the process. The authorities caught and tried the attackers, who were subsequently sent to prison. After a short period of intense fighting between squatters and neo-Nazis in the mid-1990s, the neo-Nazi scene in Poznań declined. Recently, however, it seems to be re-emerging under the banners of autonomous nationalists. Since then, the struggle has become more symbolic and limited to vandalizing each other's graffiti with very sporadic direct confrontations.

The other challenge to the existence of Rozbrat has been the complicated question of the ownership of the land and the buildings the squat occupies. Two businessmen bought the old paint factory, soon after the transformation of 1989. They used it as collateral to secure loans from a small cooperative bank from Pruszków. However, the business partners disappeared and after a few years, the interest charged became bigger than the loan itself. This allowed the bank to take ownership of the property and begin the process of auctioning it. The reaction of the activists was twofold, they used legal procedures to block the auction while at the same time trying to discourage potential buyers by showing the activists' dedication.

The Rozbrat squatters organised two large demonstrations on March 20 and May 9, 2010, to mobilise supporters, raise public awareness, and encourage the local authorities to take action. The demonstrations mobilised 1,500 and 900 people respectively, thus making them the biggest demonstrations in Poznań in recent years. In comparison, the United Nations Climate Change Conference (COP14), which was held in Poznań in December 2008, led to a demonstration, which attracted around 1,000 protesters, half of whom came from abroad. This demonstration called for more action to prevent climate change.[6] The anti-war demonstrations of 2003 and after have mobilised no more than 300 activists. From that perspective, defending Rozbrat proved a powerful framework to mobilise different sections of local society. Most participants, however, were high school kids and university students. Poznań, with its population of 700,000 people, hosts around 130,000 university students. As some of these people had been involved in the alterglobalist movement, they used their experience and tactics in the campaign for the defence of Rozbrat.

The activists from Rozbrat seem to adapt protest and action repertoires from other social movements. Often, travelling activists connected to Rozbrat or visiting activists coming over for a lecture or a meeting transmitted new ideas and tactics. Previously mentioned tactics such as tree climbing, chaining oneself to tripods, and the use of concrete-filled barrels were tactics transported from England. These were also used in the defence of Rozbrat. When the squat was threatened with eviction for the first time in the late 1990s, activists introduced many of these tactics.

Culture jamming tactics, such as copying and parodying the symbols, slogans, and publicity styles of large firms and governments, were also copied from the alterglobalist movement—in particular from groups such as the Yes Men and Adbusters—and used for the struggle to defend Rozbrat. In 2009, for example, the city government introduced a new PR strategy, revolving around the slogan 'Poznań—miasto know-how' (Poznań—the city of know-how). Many groups and individuals criticised the use of an English term in the official slogan. In response, activists launched their own campaign called 'Miasto to nie firma' (The city is not a company). They used a similar logo and lettering as the official campaign, thus ridiculing the city's slogan and efforts. The slogan caught on and is now used in public debates and by journalists.

Additionally, during the already mentioned COP14 conference, a fake website was created with a graphic layout very similar to that of the official site but with the suffix of .org instead of the official .gov.[7] The text on the fake site criticised the leaders of countries and local authorities for not implementing environmentally friendly politics, for not caring enough about environmental protection, and for raising the prices of public transportation rather than creating an affordable system. The website was advertised on illegally hung banners in the city centre and made to appear as one of the first results of a Google search on 'COP14,' 'climate change conference Poznań,' or related terms. A few days later, an official statement from the summit organisers was released, explaining the difference between the websites. The false communication strategy continued with press releases and interviews.

During the second demonstration in defence of the squatted social centre in May 2010, activists used the same tactic as the Yes Men, who on July 4, 2009, printed a fake edition of the *New York Times*, in which they announced the end of the war in Iraq and other political decisions the activists were campaigning for.[8] In a similar vein, the activists from Poznań made a newspaper that looked almost exactly like one of the leading Polish newspapers, the *Gazeta Wyborcza*. Using similar fonts and layout, they criticised the policies of the municipality, explained the situation of Rozbrat, and presented its history. It was distributed during one of the demonstrations in defence of the squat.

Even though many threats to Rozbrat come from the outside, some of the challenges for Rozbrat and its community are internal. Mostly, they derive from the tensions between the residents of the squat and the activists who are not living there. Discussions between the two groups are mostly focused on two issues: the question of the openness of the place and the balancing between the 'subcultural ghetto' model (where the squat mainly serves a counter-cultural function for a specific group) and the 'social centre' model (which is more focused on politics and on mobilizing broad coalitions of people). The first issue leads to tensions between the residents, who feel that there are too many activities in the squat, preventing a 'normal' everyday life, while the activists not living at Rozbrat find that the squatters are not getting involved as much as they should. The second issue leads to tensions between the more political activists who wish reach out to new people, which requires downplaying the subcultural image, while other find that the needs of the already existing constituency should not be neglected.

These conflicts seem irreconcilable, and at some point a group of squatters decided to create their own place, intended solely for living. Magadan, as it was called, was evicted a few months after opening without public protests accompanying it, a sequence that was repeated for the next squatting attempts. These internal conflicts resulted in the changing of the structure of squatters over the years, who nowadays are much more involved in numerous activities held at Rozbrat. In late 2012, an anarchist bookstore/café named Zemsta was opened in the city centre of Poznań by some of the activists from Rozbrat. Zemsta's name was chosen via survey; it means 'revenge' and refers to a classic play by Aleksander Fredro, as Zemsta is located on Fredro Street. Zemsta not only sells books and journals but also hosts various cultural events from lectures to exhibitions, etc. Because it is centrally located and has close personal connections to Rozbrat while being less associated with anarchism, counter-culture, and squatting, this new place might take over the cultural activities of Rozbrat. Rozbrat, which now hosts only internal meetings and debates and music concerts, is at risk of becoming a subcultural ghetto.

ACTIVIST PROFILES

Squatting and social activism are usually the domain of young people and Rozbrat is no exception. Activists who joined the group in the early period of the late 1990s, however, still form the core of the group and dominate it ideologically. With new generations of activists coming and going, there is no visible threat to the anarchist orientation of the place. Aside from endless debates and discussions, the main campaigns generally seem to go unchallenged, as does the group's general societal stance, expressed in the slogan painted on the squat's wall: 'The world would be a better place if you would love your neighbour instead of loving your state.'

Most people active in Rozbrat are high school and university students, with the majority of the latter studying social and earth sciences (geography, geology, environmental conservation). Upon graduating from university, many become less active when faced with the problems of everyday life, but maintain contacts with others by attending parties and cultural events. Accordingly, they should be regarded more as part of the 'scene' of social activists, rather than as regular activists.

The scene as a theoretical concept deserves a few words of explanation. A scene is 'characterized by a local infrastructure of bars, collectives, alternative venues, squats, living projects, and media groups.'[9] It provides a space between the movement and its target audience and allows the core members of a social movement to meet and recruit new members for a cause. In times when a movement is in a 'submerged phase'—a term suggested by Italian sociologist Alberto Melucci to describe a social movement or a group in the times between peaks of activities or campaigns[10]—it provides a backbone for the movement. The size and vibrancy of the scene could be observed during the campaign for the defence of Rozbrat in 2010. These demonstrations were much bigger than those organised for more political reasons. Equally, the petitions—mainly addressed to the local authorities—were much more popular than others. Finally, the group received support from groups that usually distance themselves from the squatters. These included academics, theatre actors, other social groups usually in conflict with Rozbrat, and even one right-wing group (Naszość, whose members were part of the Free Caucasus Committee earlier).

Although the group claims to avoid hierarchy and relies upon consensus-based decision-making, it is possible to distinguish a few different circles of activists. First, there are the core activists, with a lot of experience (of either living in a squatted place or being politically active). They seem to set the tone of the debates and play a key role in the decision-making process. This leading role is not stated explicitly, of course, but rather springs forth from their charisma and skills in socio-techniques.[11] The other group of members are the much younger, mostly high school kids and students in their early years at the university, attracted by the counter-cultural and even revolutionary charm of the place. Among this group, the fluctuation is much higher and the transfer from this group to the other is a difficult one, to some extent because of the strong ties among the 'old' activists are also reinforced by their networks of friendship. If they do not manage to get through to the first group, the younger people stop visiting the place (at least regularly), usually at the time of having their first job or finishing the university. Members of this last group are involved with the scene (and are occasionally seen as only 'consumers of alternative culture' by other activists), and also include former activists who for one reason or another are no longer involved in more explicitly political projects.

ROZBRAT AND THE OUTSIDE WORLD

RELATIONSHIP WITH AUTHORITIES

One of the continuous lines of conflict is between the community of Rozbrat and the local authorities. Poznań is a rather conservative city, ruled for the last few decades by neoliberal-oriented politicians. Local politicians are usually less politicised than the national government and more focused on economic than ideological issues. They are often not associated with the leading political parties and the mayor of Poznań, Ryszard Grobelny, is a good example of this. Initially, he represented the Platforma Obywatelska (Civic Platform, PO), a liberal party that currently forms the government. Later, he ran as an independent candidate supported by the PO, and even later he ran as an independent candidate opposing the PO. He has also been a member of two other local parties. He is, however, rather stable and regarded as a centre-rightist in his policies. The right-wing members of the city council were often annoyed by the actions of the Rozbrat activists (such as graffiti, posters, and some campaigns), but never declared an open war against the centre.

Surprisingly, the self-organised community has rather friendly relations with the local police. The district where Rozbrat is located is a rather quiet, bourgeois residential area. Most of the political actions take place in the city centre of Poznań and are handled by other police precincts. As one of the officers told the press, local police avoid the squatted centre and are generally happy that the buildings have not become a meeting place for homeless people or drug users. The city's chief of police, on the other hand, has a rather different opinion on the squatters. Recently, he declared a war on graffiti in Poznań, using activists' tags as one of the examples. A number of court trials have also been filed by police against the activists and generally lost: the anarchists were found not guilty in all but one of the cases in the last fourteen years.[12]

Although many campaigns attack the local authorities of Poznań and criticise their policies and actions, recently they have also asked the city to support the alternative culture at Rozbrat. This request was in high contrast with the pride activists put in their independence and often stressed in their flyers and pamphlets. These claims intensified, however, after the threat of eviction became more real. In 2009, the bank claiming the site initiated a procedure to auction the lots. Appraisers visited the site twice in order to estimate its value. In 2011, activists asked to be allowed to move to a municipality-owned printing house located nearby (the printer bankrupted and stopped paying the rent). They proposed not to pay rent and in exchange renovate the building, pay for its maintenance, and organise non-commercial activities at the location. At the time of writing, the exact details of the arrangement and the contract were not known, especially after the family of the previous owners of the land raised their claims and the whole idea was put on hold.

The people from Rozbrat are heavily involved in the city's political affairs. Judging by their actions and activities in the public sphere, it seems that the activists have decided to be a constant—and critical—voice in the debates about the development of the town. This can be observed, for example, in the group's publications, most of which criticise the policies of the municipality. In public debate, the squatters receive a lot of support from academics, artists, and

others, as a big number of the squatters' arguments can be reduced to one general demand: to make Poznań more 'liveable.' Because of this, the most criticised areas of local policy are social housing, development plans, public transportation and cultural policies. In line with this, they have also initiated a campaign against gentrification.

The authorities' idea of the city's growth seems to be limited to providing good business opportunities. Social housing is in crisis. The biggest controversy in this area occurred around the building of barracks made of shipping containers intended to be adapted into living spaces for 'difficult inhabitants' as a punishment for repeatedly avoiding rent payments, destroying their previous social housing, causing public disturbance, and being a burden for their neighbours. The squatters argued that this policy would create a social ghetto and cause even more problems and they announced that they will use 'any means necessary' to block the construction of the houses. This received public support especially after journalists found out that the lists of people to be moved included the elderly and ill.

RELATIONS WITH OTHER GROUPS

Through the years, the activists of Rozbrat have gained the reputation of a confrontational group that provokes tensions both within and outside of the movement.

Most of these are either of a personal nature—which is difficult to avoid with such a small movement and activist scene as in Poznań—or can stem from Rozbrat's anarchist roots. Many centre on concepts of hierarchy and leadership which activists from Rozbrat find objectionable. As an example, Critical Mass, which started as a grassroots movement (as anywhere else in the world), at some point developed into a registered association in Poland. This is a common way in Poland to legalise social activities; such associations need to be registered at court and their internal regulations cannot be against Polish laws. Registering helps gain access to public information, can allow representation in legal cases, and is required when applying for grants. This, however, caused critical reactions from the bicycle-friendly part of the activists who wanted to keep the grassroots character of the movement. A similar conflict caused by emerging or existing hierarchies could be observed during the Climate Change Conference in December 2008, when anarchists and squatters boycotted the organizing committee—although they participated in the final demonstration as a separate bloc—and ignored the assemblies held by NGO members, because they objected to formal organisations. Only four activists attended even the NGO meeting organised at Rozbrat, although meetings are otherwise populated by around seventy activists from all over the world.

Left: Mural by Mariusz Waras/M-City. Photo: Grzegorz Piotrowski.

THE ROLE OF ALTERNATIVE CULTURE AND LIFESTYLE
Recently, a heated debate unfolded among activists about the meaning of counter-culture for activism and squatting in particular. This was sparked by some complaints of the anti-austerity Anger Days organisers in Warsaw, which was attended by around one hundred people. Seven times more attended a farewell concert of a hardcore band Apatia (Apathy, no pun intended) which occurred at the same time. These numbers sparked heated online debates, from which it seems that more people are interested in 'consuming' the alternative culture the squat offers than in getting involved in political activism. This situation should not come as a surprise, especially when one traces the development of social activism in Poland since the 1980s where political activism was linked to counter-culture and subculture for many years. The rebirth of Polish anarchism, for instance, happened simultaneously with the development of the punk-rock scene. This so-called 'cultural anarchism' is frequently characterised as 'antipolitical, critical towards revolution and revolutionary violence, left anti-theology and being anti-communist.'[13]

In the years that followed, most of the leftist social movements—regardless what this means in a post-socialist country like Poland—were closely connected to subcultures. Although this is a strong frame for mobilizing newcomers, it is also a source of criticisms and conflicts as the activists who are leaning towards a stronger engagement with political activism occasionally see the subcultural scene as a distraction. They believe these people should devote their time to 'something more constructive' than consumption of alternative culture. At the same time, the subcultural connection can also make other actors of the political and social scene hesitant to seek cooperation or even simply to visit a place. This was true for the workers from Cegielski, who later joined the Inicjatywa Pracownicza trade union. For them, it was obvious that in order to come to Rozbrat, one had to be a fan of punk rock music or a social activist.

Some, however, seek this image purposefully: for them, Rozbrat is just another stop on the pub-crawl itinerary, as squats have become an important spot on many cities' cultural maps and are listed in cultural sections of newspapers and magazines. Often, the style of squats—rugged, recycled furniture from dumpsters, DIY posters on the walls, graffiti, and a sense of chaos and disorganisation—is copied by more commercial venues. Such places can be found in cities all around Central and Eastern Europe, (most famously in Berlin) and some of the 'hottest' places in Warsaw (Jadłodajnia Filozoficzna, Pewex, Aurora); Prague (Cross Club, Meet Factory); or Budapest (Szimpla, Siraly, Jelen, Instant) look like squats. Although these are not political places, they are places where: (1) activists meet from time to time; (2) open and politically moderate events take place (like lectures or exhibitions); and (3) a potential space for recruiting new activists is created, as they may be attracted by the 'underground charm' of the places. The commercialisation of such a charm is also the result of the movement's media strategies and its success in framing its actions and communicating with the public.

IS ROZBRAT SPECIAL?

One inevitable question remains: is Rozbrat a special place in Central and Eastern Europe, or does it represent one or more general tendencies in the area? That it has remained in place and active for eighteen years already puts it in a special position, of course, not only in the region but also in the history of squatting in general. Many of the issues faced by Rozbrat activists, however, are common in other places as well.

First, the connections with subcultures and alternative lifestyles dominate the arena of social activism. Second, the issue of international diffusion of activist repertoires can be seen within the alterglobalist movement in general and in the squatting movement in particular. With the exception of Hungary, where a local punk band managed to occupy some buildings in 1986 and 1987 for a short period of time as part of the initiative Mindent Akarunk (We All Want It), squatting has almost no tradition in Central and Eastern Europe prior to 1989. Not only did the idea of squatting come largely from abroad, so did the tactics and ideas associated with it. The resulting lack of references to local cultures and histories has a twofold consequence. On one hand, the whole concept is less popular and attractive to local activists, though this has less to do with it coming from abroad and more with seeming culturally 'new' and too 'alien.' On the other, Polish squatters—as well as squatters from other Central and Eastern European countries—seem to identify themselves more with other squatters, in and outside of the country itself, than with other groups of local activists and seem to benefit from such transnational ties and solidarity actions. In Poznań, one could observe graffiti and banners against the evictions of the Ungdomshuset in Copenhagen and the Köpi in Berlin or Milada in Prague. Activists from Poznań also took part in the demonstration defending Köpi.

Rozbrat, and other squats in Central and Eastern Europe, see less development of alternative lifestyles and activism than their counterparts elsewhere. The number of protesters who came to the defence of Rozbrat is striking for Poland, but should not be regarded as a measure of the strength of the scene. A lot of activists, usually connected to squatting, came to Poznań for the occasion, but some local people also came to express their dissatisfaction with the cultural and social policies of the local authorities.

In Poznań, as in and other places in Central Europe, this support ended as soon as more direct action was required. The Ladronka squat in Prague was evicted soon after riots that broke out during the summit of the International Monetary Fund and the World Bank in 2000. One building of the Milada squat, also in Prague, was torn down in the early 2000s, but

another was evicted much later, because it was not on any official map. The campaigns to save them were unsuccessful. Strikingly, no further squatting attempts were made by the evicted groups. The Centrum squat in Budapest was similarly evicted after a week of functioning and the number of activists was insufficient to block the eviction or to generate enough support to occupy another location.

Along with others, social scientists Darcy Leach and Sebastian Haunss list ten crucial points for the definition of a scene, including that scenes are more likely to develop where conditions are conducive to squatting or where rents are low enough to support non-commercial initiatives; and that scenes are more likely to develop in more advanced welfare states, which are more conducive to full-time political engagement, and where social regulation facilitates independent, socially based fundraising methods.[14]

None of these points seem to be fulfilled in Central and Eastern Europe. After decades of state-owned property, the new regimes made the inviolability of private property an indisputable rule. Therefore, occupation of property, both private and state-owned, even when it is abandoned, is generally not accepted by the local authorities and has only little support among the majority of the population. This not only triggers harsh reactions from the authorities, such as the brutal eviction of the Centrum squat, but also demobilises potential supporters and discourages potential allies who might be less willing to participate in illegal activities.

CONCLUSIONS

Squatting in the former communist bloc is a very different phenomenon than its counterparts in Western Europe or in the United States. Here, the whole process began in the mid-1990s, was limited to anarchist and punk subcultures, and has virtually no support from a broader scene of social movements due to the different development of the latter. Many social activists of the communist time moved to the NGO sector after 1989, leaving the activist movement with a generational gap. This lack of stable movement social structures has had two consequences for the squatters. First, the group of potential squatters and supporters is rather limited in comparison to places like Italy, which as around 120 squatted social centres to Poland's handful. In the case of a threat to a squatted social centre, there are not enough people to support it. On the other hand, there is also a smaller demand for such spaces as squatted social centres because many political groups function as NGOs or other kinds of foundations and associations that can rent an office or get one from the local authorities. For this reason, people who decide to occupy abandoned properties are in the minority (albeit a very dedicated one) even within the activist scene.

For squatters, the space provided by a squat is not just a requirement but

Left: Author at the anti-fascist blockade in Warsaw on November 11, 2011. Photo: Grzegorz Piotrowski.

also a meaningful part of their identity. Any initiative that might compromise its ideological purity is therefore regarded as a potential threat—a common tendency in subcultures in which dress codes, music taste, and diet are seen as the core foundations of identity. In this paradigm, a 'true' environmentalist is almost always a vegetarian, just as a true punk rocker will not listen to pop music and a skinhead will not wear brightly coloured sport outfits or shoes. This subcultural way of thinking contributes to the relatively inward-looking character of squatted social centres in Central and Eastern Europe, as groups that run these are less likely to cooperate with other groups, to become a part of a broader coalition, or to engage in negotiations with the local authorities and any of their projects. When the primary goal of the centre is the support of the movement itself and the group that forms the space, its function as a space for interactions between the movement and the public can become of secondary importance. The resulting movement can be seen as a movement for its own sake: there is little cooperation with outsiders; attempts to open the space to more moderate people are met with harsh criticism; and no alternatives to the anarcho-punk organisational practices and ideological guidelines are permitted. At the same time, squats are highly likely to support another squats or social centres, such as Köpi in Berlin, Ungdomshuset in Copenhagen or local struggles in Wrocław and Białystok. There is even a football tournament organised annually for teams connected to squatted centres.

The generational gap mentioned above also contributes to the lack of historical, local traditions leaving the movement without roots. Many activists from the 1980s have left the scene and those who occupied the buildings that are now Rozbrat belonged to the first generation of activists politicised after the communist times.

The early 1990s were not only a time of rapid political transformations but also a time of a radical shift to the right. Even the social democratic party of Poland, a direct successor to the communist party that won the elections in 1993 and subsequently formed the government, was conservative in its values, agreeing to a very restrictive anti-abortion law and the criminalisation of drug possession. The ideological climate in post-communist Poland (as well as in the rest of the region) does not help the squatter movement. One of the consequences of the post-communist transition is the shift toward understanding property rights in a purely (neo)liberal way. Hence, every property occupation—even if the property is abandoned—gains little or no popular support. On the contrary, such groups located outside of the mainstream discourse can be regarded as nearly criminal and dismissed from serious debate or discussion. Groups such as squatters are also often connected with the left side of the political spectrum, which is still an issue in the public discourse because of the communist past.

However, in the last year the anarchist involvement in housing and tenants movements, in campaigns against privatisation (of public services and communal housing) and gentrification, have changed the public's view on squatting in Poland. Positive media coverage of the squatter movement could be observed in the beginning of 2013, when the Elba squat in Warsaw was evicted. It was followed by a large demonstration. On top of that, squatters' support for tenants of privatised rental houses has changed not only public opinion but also the attitudes of many local authorities towards the movement. As a result, squatting is perceived in less ideological terms, even though it retains its anti-capitalist edge. As squatters are slowly becoming a stable part of the landscape of Polish cities, it seems that Poles are getting used to squatting.

FURTHER READING

There is only a small amount of literature on squatting in Poland, both in Polish and English. Apart from this article, the author has published one other English text, a working paper for the International Centre for Research and Analysis: 'Squatted Social Centers in Central and Eastern Europe.' It is available through http://icra.pl/index.php/badania/seriapublikacjinaukowych/item/75-piotrowski-squatted-social-centers-in-central-and-eastern-europe.

Two Polish texts also exist. The first is based on a PhD thesis and contains reflections on civic engagement and civil society drawn from empirical research among feminists, environmentalists, and squatters: Piotr Żuk, *Społeczeństwo w działaniu: ekolodzy, feministki, skłotersi* (Warsaw: Wydawnictwo Naukowe Scholar, 2001). The second is a chapter in a book on the DIY music scene in Poland: Kamil Siemaszko, 'DIY—autonomiczna strefa muzyczna,' in Waldemar Kuligowski and Adam Pomieciński, *Oblicza buntu: praktyki i teorie sprzeciwu w kulturze współczesnej* (Poznań: Wydawnictwo Poznańskie, 2012).

There are also two films on the Poznań squatters, in Polish. Both can be found on YouTube. The first, a documentary, *Władza Precz!*, was produced by Polish TV but never aired. The second, *Rozbrat. Epizod 1*, is more activist-oriented.

Nine
SQUATTING AND AUTONOMOUS ACTION IN VIENNA, 1976–2012
Robert Foltin

THE SPONTIS AND THE 'ARENA' IN THE 1970S

THE 1968 REVOLT AND THE SPONTIS

Vienna saw less activism in 1968 than other cities around the world. Nevertheless, new political currents ranging from Maoism to second-wave feminism became active. In the following period, the politicizing of so-called *Randgruppen* (fringe groups), for example criminalised youths, gained some importance.

While left-wing activism in the first half of the 1970s had been dominated by neo-Leninist groups (Trotskyist and Maoist), the second half of the decade saw the rise of a variety of movements: subcultural and political communities and communes proposed changing everyday life, gays and lesbians organised for the first time politically, and the feminist movement reached its first peak.

Next to this, a new political current emerged: the so-called *Spontis* who sought to distance themselves from the dogmatic groups, mostly neo-Leninist ones. The Spontis also tried to change their own way of life as a first step towards changing the world. They lived communally, experimented with drugs, and were involved in political activities in an attempt to overcome the boundary between private life and politics.

Some of the Spontis considered themselves anarchists, while others looked to the development of the autonomous movement in Italy, which reached its climax in 1977. The movement in Italy ranged from the more theoretically oriented *Autonomia* groups—many translations of their texts appeared in German—to the *Indiani metropolitani*, who rejected all forms of organisation and insisted on spontaneity and humour.

The Spontis can be seen as the forerunners of the autonomous and squatter activists of the 1980s, as they participated not only in feminist, gay and lesbian, and ecology movements but were also involved in the first squatting activities. In the summer of 1975, for example, the Amerlinghaus was squatted, and became a political centre, which it has remained to this day. In 1976, the Arena followed.[1]

FIRST EXPERIENCES WITH SQUATTING: THE ARENA

Traditionally, the founding of the so-called Arena in the squatted Auslandsschlachthof (import and export slaughterhouse) in the summer of 1976 is seen as the closest Austria has come to the global events of 1968.[2] The first Arena was an enormous area of a dozen buildings that were used for different projects, comparable in size and design to Christiania in Copenhagen.

Up to now, it has remained the largest and most important squat in the history of Vienna. The participants included activists from traditional left-wing groups, anarchists, and many other cultural and social groups. Tens of thousands used the project, at least as visitors, and many recognised the Arena as an emancipatory project. At the end of the summer of 1976, pressure from the administration of Vienna, combined with internal conflicts, caused the participants to leave the site voluntarily.

In the second half of the 1970s, as in Germany, the Austrian movement against nuclear power plants reached its peak.[3] Through demonstrations and peaceful actions, the activists succeeded in forcing the authorities to hold a

This page spread: Four issues of *Arena Stadtzeitung*, 1979.

Previous page spread: Kultur- und Kommunikationszentrum Gassergasse, 1982. Photo: omo - archiv der ghetto company.

referendum on the plan to build Austria's first atomic power plant in the village of Zwentendorf. The referendum put an end to nuclear power in Austria and the campaign illustrated that it was not necessary to be militant to be victorious.

THE RISE OF THE AUTONOMOUS MOVEMENT IN THE 1980S

THE AUTONOMEN AND THE BURGGARTEN MOVEMENT

At the end of the 1970s, the Autonomen entered the stage of radical politics. They had their origins in the above-mentioned new left social movements, especially the Spontis. Some of the activists dubbed themselves *undogmatische Linke* (non-dogmatic left), others kept to the term Spontis.

The autonomous scene was rooted in the so-called youth movement that emerged between 1979 and 1981. During these years, radical youths clashed with the police in cities throughout Europe and the riots went hand-in-hand with a wave of occupations and squatter actions. In 1981, hundreds of houses were squatted in Berlin and other cities in Germany. From there, the movement spread to other cities such as Copenhagen. Amsterdam, too, had a strong squatter movement.

On a cultural level, these youth movements—as well as the autonomous scene that grew out of them—were heavily influenced by punk music. In Vienna, the first punk bands began to perform in the late 1970s. However, the real break-

through as a cultural movement happened later with the establishment of band practice rooms and with the first concerts in the GAGA-building in 1981.

In Vienna, the youth movement from which the Autonomen sprang started to make itself heard in the spring of 1979.[4] At this time, the Burggarten, a park in the centre of Vienna, became a sort of meeting place for hippies. Because it was forbidden to walk on the grass they were expelled regularly. It became a weekly ritual to thus provoke the authorities and play a cat-and-mouse game with the police.

At the same time, during assemblies in the Amerlinghaus, activists started to demand a self-managed social and cultural centre. Also at this time, the oppositional ÖVP (Austrian People's Party) hired the Viennese Phorushalle to organise a so-called *Ideenmarkt* (market of ideas), which they advertised as an 'alternative' event for youth.

In order to push their demand for an alternative centre, the event centre was occupied on the last day of the Ideenmarkt in October 1979 by the so-called Burggarten movement. After the eviction of the squatters on the next day, the police chased some hundred demonstrators through the city. Although some more actions were organised, such as a march on the town hall, the Burggarten movement did not succeed in acquiring a self-managed centre for culture and communication. However, the Burggarten and other parks were subsequently opened to the people.

BETWEEN SQUATTING AND LEASING

An anonymous group of activists, inspired by the many squatting actions in other countries, started to plan an action for Sunday, March 1, 1981.[5] There were no official announcements distributed for a rally, but a great number of graffiti slogans and leaflets called for a demonstration in the centre of the city.

The demonstration was meant to support a planned squat action in the first district which had already been prepared by a group of activists. Even so, the occupation failed because of a police intervention. Several hundreds to maybe even a thousand people gathered in the centre of the posh and stylish first district. When a scuffle happened and a couple of windows were smashed, the police arrested nearly a hundred demonstrators.

The incident, but above all the possibility that the conflict could escalate into riots, alarmed the city administration of Vienna. It feared that the unrest in other European cities would spread to Austria.[6] In May 1981, there were two further attempts to squat houses, but the authorities responded within hours and evicted the squatters. After this, however, the city accelerated negotiations with groups on the leasing of unused spaces.

To prevent squatting, flats and buildings that belonged to the community of Vienna were given to collectives and groups. The rooms were handed over with so-called *Prekariumsverträgen* (precarious contracts). No rent had to be paid, only the running costs. However, the contract could be repealed at any time. Nevertheless, some alternative and autonomous structures that still exist have their origins in such projects. An example of this is the Rosa-Lila-Villa, the first house in Vienna for lesbians and gays.

Also, the TGM (Technologisches Gewerbemuseum, 'Technical Craft Museum') was handed over to a collective and turned into the WuK House (an abbreviation of the words for workshops and culture). Other buildings which thus came into the hands of activists and collectives were the WÖK (Wiener öffentliche Küchen, 'Viennese Public Kitchens') in the Gassergasse. There was also a group of prominent Austrian musicians who agitated for a Rock House, which was eventually realised in 1983.[7]

Not all of these alternative centres were closely linked to the new youth movement. The WuK, for example, kept its distance from more radical communities such as punks and anarchists. When some punks tried to enter the WuK in order to live there and to use it as a meeting place (after their eviction out of the Gassergasse and the Aegidigasse, see below), they were thrown out. The Arena was transferred to a different place, the much smaller Inlandschlachthof (a former slaughterhouse), and legalised.

The new collectives and alternative centres had a significant influence on the cultural climate of the 1980s. Encouraged by the new social movements and the succeeding projects, and also by the emergence of new commercial pubs and places for musical and other cultural events, both culture and nightlife became much more diverse in Vienna.

THE SHORT HISTORY OF GAGA

In March 1981, the keys for the WÖK were handed over to the respective activists and became the Kultur- und Kommunikationszentrum Gassergasse ('centre for culture and communication Gassergasse,' GAGA). The GAGA was used by a variety of different groups, most of them actively political.[8] There was the so-called *Drucker* collective (the printers), an anarchist collective, the 'Movement March 1st' group, named after the events in March 1981, and INHALE (Initiative Hanf Legal, 'initiative for legalising hemp/marijuana'). The building also housed a number of projects, such as an alternative school and children's shop, a workshop for cars and one for bicycles, a carpentry shop, a released prisoner care project, and a housing council (a coordination group for collectives which looked for a place to live and work, by squatting or through negotiations), among others. The building also offered rooms to artists, musicians (not only punks), and photographers.

The collaboration did not work well. There were many conflicts between the more radical groups—for example, the anarchists and the Movement March 1st—and the others. Communication was hampered because participation in regular assemblies diminished rapidly.

Problems also arose with people living in the neighbourhood because of alleged orgies and illegal drug usage at GAGA. There were problems with the police, who raided the centre from time to time, mostly because of noise disturbances, and because some minor altercations occurred after parties.

In January 1983, police found a kilo of marijuana in a washing machine in the GAGA complex. Subsequently, the organisation INHALE was banned and the city administration froze the subsidies for the necessary running costs of GAGA. An open-air protest was announced for June 26, 1983, but clashes with neighbours escalated. Supported by right-wing extremists, they started to throw stones at the GAGA-participants. In the end, police stormed the GAGA and arrested everyone inside. Two days later, a solidarity demonstration in the inner city was repressed before it could start, and was again followed by a number of arrests. Following these disappointing experiences, the solidarity movement faded away during the summer of 1983. Nevertheless, a number of activists, who had been active in the GAGA, continued their political activism as the Autonomen.

THE PROFILE OF THE AUTONOMOUS MOVEMENT

In the first half of the 1980s, several groups in Vienna started calling themselves *autonom* (autonomous). Most did not have a clear concept of what the term meant, although there were some discussions on texts from the Italian movement and the German magazine *Autonomie–Neue Folge* (Autonomy–New Series). The autonomous movement was an anti-theoretical movement most similar to the Spontis of the 1970s. At best, they could be characterised as a subculture, comparable to the notion of 'Area' which was used to describe the respective movements of the 1970s in Italy (the Italian *Autonomia* movement had mainly been an informal network of groups, collectives and projects, rather than a centralised organisation).

Some of the autonomous activists preferred to be called anarchists, others saw themselves as anti-imperialists, but many of them felt only a cultural proximity to a kind of lifestyle which mixed the appearance of the punk scene with social and political activism. The activists often lived in communities and frequented social centres. The anti-imperialists in the movement showed sympathy with the armed struggle of the RAF (Rote Armee Fraktion, or Red Army Faction), others criticised this tendency for their authoritarian behaviour and the elitism of the armed groups ('The armed struggle is the only true form of struggle'). Regardless, it was very important for the Autonomen to express their solidarity with the RAF, because they were faced with heavy repression.

Most of the Autonomen, however, preferred street fights (although the 'violence' during these confrontations was often exaggerated by the media) and the militant actions of groups such as the RZ (*Revolutionäre Zellen*, 'revolutionary cells'), which refrained from lethal actions and did not behave in an elitist manner as the RAF did. These groups were relatively attractive because their actions complemented aboveground political campaigns and could be easily adopted by other groups.

The autonomous scene produced some short-lived journals. In the second half of the 1980s, these publications multiplied. Some were devoted to specific topics, such as squatting or anti-imperialism, others promoted more general political discussions. The *TATblatt*, which was first released in 1988, was relatively successful for several years keeping the public informed about activities of the autonomous scene and emerging social movements.

The Autonomen were sometimes described as the militant wing of the so-called 'new social movements' because of their dedication to direct, and sometimes militant, actions. The new social movements had developed in the wake of the 1968 revolt and differed from the classic workers' movement because they focused on activism in the 'reproduction sphere'—for example, housing, anti-racism, feminism, environment—and they generally preferred informal and horizontal organizing and involved many young people.

THE AUTONOMOUS AND OTHER SOCIAL MOVEMENTS

In the first half of the 1980s the emerging Autonomen became involved in the peace movement against atomic weapons, which was big at the time, often attracting more than a hundred thousand protesters. An 'autonomous and internationalist bloc' was organised within the peace movement, which demonstrated its strength by forming a 'black bloc' during demonstrations.

Autonomous activists also supported the occupation of a marsh area near the village of Hainburg, close to Vienna, in order to prevent the construction of a new electric power plant, which would have destroyed the local natural environment.[9] In December 1984, several thousand activists set up a camp there and for two weeks lived in tents and holes in the ground. The autonomous activists built barricades out of timber to block the road for machines and labourers who were hired to clear the land for construction. This led to conflicts with more moderate activists, who initially tried to stop them. Soon, however, the barricades proved effective, and they became important instruments for all activists. Dozens more were built, even by people who first argued against them. The autonomous activists were thus able to radicalise other campaigns.

In the end, the police brutally evicted the campaigners, and this was shown on television. The images motivated tens of thousands to demonstrate in Vienna and other cities against police brutality, and also against the proposed power plant. The government decided to give up the construction.

THE STRUGGLE FOR SELF-MANAGED BUILDINGS

From time to time there were efforts to occupy houses, but none of these attempts succeeded. The police remained in control. Because of this, in December 1985 a different strategy was used: a house in the Turnergasse (fifteenth district), which the city administration had already bought for young people, was squatted. Again, the squatters were evicted within a few hours, but half a year later, the house was finally given over to a group that had continued negotiations.

In the middle of the 1980s, one area became of central importance for the autonomous scene: the building complex Aegidigasse together with the adjacent Spalowskygasse.[10] In 1981, the latter had been handed over to an artistic group with connections to the political scene. And in the autumn of 1983, several flats in the neighbouring Aegidigasse were given to activists from the demolished GAGA. At the same time however, most of the apartments in the Aegidigasse were left empty; the last tenants were leaving during the first half of 1984. In the period that followed, apartment after apartment was squatted. The Aegidigasse became a 'silent' squat, ignored by the authorities.

When it became public that the Aegidigasse housed many squatters, the centre had become too important to evict them immediately. An infoshop was opened and more and more activities were organised, such as political discussions, meetings, and cultural events from exhibitions to concerts. Evicting the complex was rendered even more difficult, because some of the apartments were rented out legally to activists.

In the summer of 1986 the last existing contracts were repealed, and the squatters feared an eviction. However, for the time being the city administration decided to leave the squat alone. Because the Aegidigasse had become a well-known social centre, the political costs were considered too high. Also the fact that there were no plans for the buildings played a role.

Two years later, the procedure for acquiring spaces changed. In the summer of 1988, a group of residents of the Spalowskygasse complied with the city's orders to leave the building and accepted a substitute residence on the outskirts of Vienna. However, when the police wanted to check the emptied flats, they found that activists had barricaded the entrance. In the confrontation that followed, the squatters proved so strong that the police were forced to withdraw.

Negotiations between the police and the occupants failed. After this, the police deployed water cannons, which used water mixed with teargas, and the squatters were forced to retreat to Aegidigasse. The following morning, the barricaded door was broken down with a bulldozer and the Aegidigasse complex was searched. The nonviolent activists were severely beaten and nearly sixty people were arrested and held in custody for two weeks. Both houses were demolished immediately afterwards.

In the following months, activists organised several campaigns and started negotiations to acquire a substitute building for the several dozen activists of the Aegidi-Spalo (Aegidigasse and Spalowskygasse). Most of the actions were symbolic, such as camping on the site where the buildings had once stood, but there were also real occupations. The activists did not succeed.

MILITANT ACTION: THE OPERNBALL

The struggle for the Aegidi-Spalo was not the only event in which the autonomous activists acted militantly; during the second half of the 1980s, militancy became more common. The demonstrations against the annual Opernball became especially infamous. The ball was the most important event of the year for the Viennese opera house and also served as a meeting place of the rich and powerful from Austria and abroad.[11]

In 1987, it was announced that the minister-president of Bavaria, Franz Josef Strauss, would be the guest of honour. Strauss, a populist Christian democrat, was controversial for his right-wing views, but most of all for his support for the construction of a nuclear waste reprocessing plant in the Bavarian village of Wackersdorf. In the spring of 1986, after the accident at Chernobyl, the outrage over the intended construction soared, both in Bavaria and in neighbouring Austria.

Militant actions and autonomous activists played a prominent role within the protest movement against the reprocessing plant. Thus, the Autonomen were supported by moderate protesters and local inhabitants when they tried, during demonstrations, to tear down the fences around the construction site and when they clashed with police. Many Austrian protesters and activists participated in these militant clashes, and these protests were linked to a general denunciation of nuclear power and nuclear arms.

To protest against the visit of Strauss, the recently founded Green Party announced a rally in front of the opera house. The demonstration was planned as a peaceful protest, but when some fireworks and bottles were thrown against the opera house, the police began to clear the street in front of it. This provoked a massive riot, and smaller clashes between the police and activists throughout the evening. The incident had a great influence on the autonomous movement, and in the media, the Autonomen were recognised as an independent force for the first time.

Since 1987, militant demonstrations against the Opernball have become a tradition of sorts. In the following years, the public profile of the Autonomen rose, but the Opernball-demonstrations also started to attract apolitical, mostly male youths, who had no ties to the political scene. Rather, the annual clashes developed into a form of proletarian protest against the visibly rich. The most spectacular incidents linked to the Opernball demonstrations involved pushing a Mercedes into the police lines in 1989 and the looting of a supermarket in 1990. In 1991, the Opernball was cancelled because of the Gulf War against Iraq. A demonstration at a different location far away from the opera house attracted only a few hundred participants and was heavily guarded by the police. After this, the demonstration lost much of its appeal to the wider public. In recent years, protests against the Opernball have provoked a large police presence, although only a small number of demonstrators have shown up.

AFTER THE COLD WAR: THE 1990S

THE FALL OF THE BERLIN WALL AND NEW CAMPAIGNS
The final decade of the millennium started with the implosion of the Soviet

Union and the fall of the Berlin Wall. Did the crumbling of the East European regimes which had called themselves 'communist' influence the radical scene in a negative way? It does not appear so. Rather, the fall of the so-called Iron Curtain was followed by a flourishing of new social movements in Austria and Vienna.[12]

The Autonomen were caught up in the process as well and were involved in a number of campaigns. During the first half of the 1990s, a number of construction sites were occupied, mainly involving environmentally problematic projects like new motorways or drilling sites for oil. Anti-militarism also gained renewed importance: there had been campaigns to abolish the *Bundesheer* (the national army) and actions against the annual parade of the Austrian army in the 1970s; in the 1990s, the number of conscientious objectors to the military draft who also refused the alternative service increased.

As mentioned above, the autonomous magazine *TATblatt* played a major role in the communication between different initiatives, gaining influence far beyond the anarchists and Autonomen.

Most campaigns organised or supported by autonomous activists involved direct actions such as demonstrations, occupations, spray painting, blockades, and acts of vandalism. These were rarely violent but were often semi-illegal, transgressing the norms and rules of mainstream society.

In the same period, a new social centre was squatted and established: the Ernst-Kirchweger-Haus (EKH).[13] The centre was named after a communist activist who was killed by a right-wing extremist during an anti-fascist demonstration in March 1965. The building was in fact owned by the Kommunistische Partei Österreichs (Communist Party of Austria, KPÖ), but the party leadership felt uneasy about calling in the police. This was also due to internal conflicts about the political direction of the party, mainly on the question as to which social movements should be supported. In the end, the KPÖ agreed to lease parts of the building. Soon, the EKH became the most important social centre in Vienna and was run mainly by people who saw themselves as autonomous activists.

POLITICAL REORIENTATION

Even though the autonomous movement did not seem to be negatively affected by the fall of communism, the new geo-political situation and resulting global conflicts did lead to discussions and divisions within the movement. The U.S.-led Gulf War against Iraq in 1991 and the bloody civil wars in former Yugoslavia from 1992 onwards, in particular, led to conflicts as parts of the former radical left began to support imperialist wars and withdrew from emancipatory anti-militarism, either because of the violation of human rights in the Balkans or by the threat of an attack on Israel.

These debates also caused splits within the autonomous scene in Vienna. Here, the debates revolved not only around the conflicts in the Middle East and the Balkans, but also around the situation in the global South, which according to many was not taken into account enough. In the course of these debates, the criticism of autonomous politics in the 1980s grew. The 1980s autonomous movement was considered to have been far too naive in its support of anti-colonial and anti-imperialist movements, ignoring, for example, anti-democratic, sexist, and anti-Semitic tendencies within its ranks.

As a consequence, many tried to avoid the term *autonom* in the 1990s. Sometimes, the scene of the 1990s and post-1990s has been called *postautonom*, although mostly by outsiders. In the new millennium, many activists who see themselves as belonging to the autonomous movement favour the term 'communism,' while others prefer to describe themselves as anarchists. Because of these developments, I shall refer to the autonomous scene rather than use the term 'Autonomen.'

GROWING IMPORTANCE OF ANTI-FASCISM

In the 1990s, anti-fascism and anti-racism became the most important issues on the scene as the Austrian government further restricted the entry of non-Western immigrants and refugees and introduced a series of new laws against migrants.[14] Outside of government, the racist and anti-Semitic FPÖ (Freedom Party) also made a breakthrough under the leadership of the charismatic Jörg Haider.

Several demonstrations were organised against the FPÖ, most prominently the *Lichtermeer* (sea of lights) manifestation in 1993, in which several hundreds of thousands participated. While this was an impressive turnout, the demands of the rally were so moderate that even the ruling elites, responsible for many of the new laws, could participate. The SPÖ (social democrats) at this time flirted with anti-racist sentiments by advertising that they produced laws instead of hate speech. Unfortunately, these laws were themselves racist. The social democrats introduced the concept of accommodating asylum seekers in 'safe third countries,' that is, outside of Austria, and making their stay dependent on the availability of proper housing conditions. If these could not be provided for, the possibility of deportation was expressly left open.

More radical positions were marginalised. The autonomous scene was one of the few places were elementary human rights were defended, such as speaking out against the compulsory identification of migrants, and anti-racist activism has remained one of the main issues of the autonomous movement up to the present day.

In 1999, members of the self-proclaimed African community in Vienna started to organise independently against police violence. Their protests began with demonstrations against the frequent deaths of people of colour in police custody. The case of Marcus Omofuma, a Nigerian asylum seeker suffocated by the police during his deportation flight, led to massive demonstrations on May 1. Even in the media and more moderate groups, the concept of state-organised racism was openly discussed.

The protests were soon crushed by the police.[15] On May 27, police raided dozens of houses and flats of 'suspected drug dealers,' maintaining that the alleged 'drug dealers' had organised anti-racist demonstrations. About one hundred people, most of them people of colour, were arrested during what was referred to as Operation Spring. In the following years, many of them were convicted with heavy sentences on little evidence.[16] Since then, very few people of colour have dared to show up at demonstrations and political actions.

In the course of these events, even moderate left groups such as the Green Party were afraid to get involved and be linked as friends with alleged drug dealers. In the following years, the autonomous scene was one of the few left groups that remained committed to the traditional interpretation of anti-racism. The 1990s, however, saw the rise not only of Jörg Haider and his FPÖ but also of right-wing terrorist groups. Letter bombs were sent to anti-racist activists and politicians and four Roma were killed by a roadside bomb in February 2005. These incidents led to growing pressure on the FPÖ, who upheld contacts with right-wing extremists. The party, however, tried to blame the left for keeping up contacts with terrorist groups.

This happened after the death of two left-wing activists in the village of Ebergassing. They were found dead in April 1995, killed by a bomb which they had attached to an electricity pylon.[17] The vandalizing of pylons had been a very common form of protest against nuclear energy in Germany in the 1980s. In the following weeks, the FPÖ revealed that the social democratic minister of interior Caspar Einem previously donated small sums to the *TATblatt*, and accused the social democrats of being part of a 'network of left terrorists,' which also included radical activists and the *TATblatt*. The accusation led to a government crisis and as a consequence of the fallout, many liberal groups distanced themselves from the autonomous scene and the *TATblatt*.

Ironically, the circulation of the magazine rose steeply because of all the media attention. The print run reached a new height. At the same time, the autonomous scene remained important within many campaigns, as for example against the parades of the right-wing *Burschenschaften* (student fraternities). Still, this could not conceal the fact that the autonomous scene in Vienna stayed isolated and marginalised.

THE ANTI-GLOBALISATION MOVEMENT AT THE TURN OF THE MILLENNIUM

RENEWED PROTESTS AGAINST THE FPÖ

The FPÖ's entry to the national government in 2000, the first time for such an extreme right-wing party in Austria, incited a broad protest movement.[18] The protests started on February 1 with a dozen participants and rapidly grew to thousands. On February 4, the new government was inaugurated. On its way to the ceremony, the new government was forced to detour through a tunnel, because thousands of demonstrators had gathered above and threw vegetables at police lines.

From then onwards, daily demonstrations took place in the city. Within the new movement, civil disobedience played an important role and the protest movement could be characterised as nonviolent but militant. When, for example, the police tried to block a demonstration, the participants changed direction to avoid a confrontation. The authorities were challenged, but not physically attacked.

On February 19, several hundred thousand people gathered on the Heldenplatz to protest against the right-wing ministers in the government. After that rally, the daily demonstrations became weekly as tens of thousands demonstrated every Thursday for two years, with the number of participants decreasing to a few hundred. The *TATblatt* produced a daily overview of all the actions dubbed the *Widerstandschronologie* (chronology of resistance). The divide between the autonomous scene and other activists was, to a large extent, overcome.

In 2000 and 2001 there was a short revival of the Opernball demonstrations, which again ended in clashes with the police, although they were smaller than in the 1980s. After two years of government, the FPÖ split and new elections were held. The FPÖ lost votes, but the right-wing government continued, because the Christian democrats (ÖVP) had won much of the lost FPÖ-votes. The right-wing government was replaced only in 2007 by a coalition of social democrats and Christian democrats.

FROM THE ANTI-GLOBALISATION MOVEMENT TO 9/11

The FPÖ-protests coincided with the emergence of the anti-globalisation movement—also referred to as the 'movement of movements.' The demonstrations against the World Bank in Seattle in November 1999 marked the start of this new movement, which reached its climax during the protests against the G8 summit in Genoa in July 2001.

Many Austrian activists went to Genoa to protest, and more than a dozen members of a theatre collective (the *Volxtheaterkarawane*) were jailed for several weeks under the charge of being part of the 'black bloc.' An impressive solidarity campaign was organised for the members of the Volxtheaterkarawane, and many of the activities were organised by the same groups that had previously agitated against the right-wing government. The broad group of activists ranged from artists and cultural activists to people from the autonomous scene. After a few weeks, the members of the Volxtheaterkarawane were released and, years later, the accusations were dropped.

The terrorist attacks of September 11 caused the anti-globalisation movement to implode, but this dip lasted only briefly. Two years later, tens of thousands of protesters—many of them secondary school students—demonstrated against the upcoming third Gulf War. Big parts of the autonomous scene kept a certain distance from these protests. The debates that had broken out in the early 1990s—on war, intervention, and solidarity with 'anti-imperialist' regimes and movements—were intensified by the terrorist attacks. The autonomous scene seemed to lose importance during this period.

RENEWED STRUGGLE FOR AUTONOMOUS SPACES

In the autumn of 2004, residents and users of the EKH learned from the newspapers that the KPÖ had sold the building.[19] Soon after this, it became clear that the new owner was a former right-wing extremist. A solidarity movement formed to ward off a threatening eviction. In 2005, after months of uncertainty, a construction company with connections to the Viennese municipal administration bought the building and, after years of negotiations, signed a rent contract with the residents and users of the EKH in 2008.

Other projects were in danger as well. Most prominent among these was the self-managed bar and meeting place TÜWI. The rooms were owned by the university, which wanted to reorganise and cancel the contracts. The *Frauencafé* (women's café) also lacked participants. But a few years later, most initiatives were saved: The Frauencafé gained new activists and the uncertainty about TÜWI vanished after the *unibrennt* (university burning) movement to acquire new rooms. New projects, such as the *Idee direkte Aktion* (idea direct action, I:da); the *Schenke*, which has a *Kostnixladen* (no cost shop); the *Theorieladen* (theory shop); and an anarchist library. Some that were situated in the EKH (like *das qu[e]er*) changed places, but structures continue to exist there.

Most of these projects continue to survive without any financial subsidies from government institutions, although most of them have regular rent contracts, because the authorities do not tolerate the existence of illegal squats. This is a policy that the autonomous scene has up to now, not been able to undermine. Another way of alternative living in the form of so-called *Wagenplätze* (trailer parks) was introduced in 2007 as an attempt to live an alternative way of life transcending the traditional four walls.

New squatter movements emerged as well; the *Freiraum* collective (Free Space collective) unsuccessfully campaigned for a social centre at the new university campus and organised four occupations, three of them in the same building, adjacent to the famous Narrenturm, built in the eighteenth century to confine the mentally ill.[20]

The *Pankahyttn*-initiative (*Punker Hütte*, 'cabin for punks') more successfully squatted a great number of buildings in 2006 and 2007 (many of them symbolic and for a limited time) until they were eventually offered a house by the city government. The terms of use, however, are remarkable: on an unofficial level, the project is self-managed; officially, however, it is classified by the government as a social project run by social workers. The punks are not seen as political activists or artistic youths, but as troubled youths requiring help. Even though the punks emphasise their desire for autonomy, realised in the daily running of the project, they are officially deemed dependent youngsters in need of help.

THE INTERNATIONAL SQUATTING DAYS AND AFTER

In April 2008, one year after the eviction of the famous *Ungdomhuset* in Copenhagen, 'the international squatting days' were organised. In Austria, this campaign was relatively successful.[21] Houses and buildings were occupied in Innsbruck, Salzburg, Linz, and Graz. In Vienna, as well as other activities, a house in Spitalgasse was occupied with the aim of forming a 'queer-feminist centre.' The following day, the house was evicted with the spectacular support of a helicopter.

The following years saw several unsuccessful attempts at squatting and keeping houses, such as the squatting of a house in Triesterstrasse in October 2009. The activists were able to hold on to the building for ten days, and establish a promising project space for different groups. The project received many positive reports in the media, but the activists were evicted nevertheless. This sequence of events was repeated in July 2010, when a house in Eichenstrasse was squatted and kept for at least a week, before it was evicted. Of the many attempts to occupy houses in these years, these were the most spectacular.

Other actions and campaigns to secure urban spaces for public use have also taken place, such as the prevention of the construction of an underground car park by the occupation of the Bacherpark in the winter of 2006, and the occupation of the Augartenspitz, a part of a park, which had to make way for a proposed new concert house. Even though occupations were unsuccessful, they did influence the new student movement, which erupted a few days after the Triesterstrasse had been repossessed.

RECENT DEVELOPMENTS

PROTESTS AGAINST THE EXTREME RIGHT

In recent years, anti-fascist activism has again gained importance for autonomous activists. For example, people mobilised against the so-called *Ulrichsbergtreffen* (Ulrichsberg meeting) in Carinthia, one of the most important meetings for SS veterans and their admirers. The protesters were successful, and in 2009 the Austrian military stopped supporting this right-wing event.[22] A second regular meeting against which anti-fascist activists mobilised was the WKR Ball (*Wiener Korporations Ring*, 'Viennese ring of [student] fraternities'), which is a very important event for right-wing extremists from all over Europe and was situated in the imperial environment of the Hofburg Palace. This campaign was accompanied by militant demonstrations.[23] Anti-fascist activists organised demonstrations and events such as an action near the WKR-Ball in January 2008. At around midnight, the party people formed a demonstration and headed for the ball, where some scuffles and minor clashes ensued. Similar incidents occurred a year later.

These actions however, also incited responses from the authorities. In 2010, several hundred anti-fascists were surrounded ('kettled') by the police

Following page spread: Pankahyttn, May 2008. Photo: Pankahyttn.

KEINE GESETZE

ERRATEN·
MOKRATEN

A1
CONTAINER

www.a1container.at

02.05.2008

even before they were able to start their demonstration, which had been forbidden by the city government. Most of the demonstrators were sentenced because of their participation in an illegal demonstration.

To avoid such a scenario in January 2011, there was no single meeting place, but instead at least three protest marches, involving a few dozen to some hundred participants, who moved informally through the city. Several activists were arrested, but the main result was that the police blocked whole districts in the inner city for public and private transport. By 2012, the situation had changed. Because the right-wing WKR-Ball had been scheduled for January 27, the day also marking the liberation of Auschwitz, outrage spread to a broader public and more than ten thousand participated in demonstrations and thousands tried to block access streets in the inner city. The Hofburg cancelled the WKR-Ball in 2013. In spite of the renaming of the event Akademikerball (academics' ball), protests continued. On January 24, 2014, thousands formed a blockade, despite impressive police measures including a space ban for large parts of the first district and a ban on wearing hooded sweaters in the whole inner city. Clashes with the police ensued and one person was arrested and as of June 2014 is still in jail.

REPRESSION AND SHORT-LIVED MOVEMENTS

In recent years, repression against political activists has increased. In May 2008, ten animal rights activists were arrested and held in custody for several months because they were accused of having run a criminal organisation.[24] Many of the convicted did not have any connection to the autonomous scene.

The trial started in March 2010 and ended in May 2011, with all accusations dropped. This success was made possible by engaged activists, as their investigations exposed an undercover agent whose testimony in fact proved the accused innocent.

A few months later, in the summer of 2010, several people were again arrested in a different situation. They were accused of having executed an arson attack: a dustbin in front of an unemployment office had been set on fire. In addition to this, they were accused of forming a criminal organisation. They were held in custody for a number of weeks. In October 2012, all four of the accused were acquitted.

Since 2009, a number of short-lived movements have emerged, such as teachers' and students' protests against longer school days and better working conditions. Anti-racist activism has continued. In April 2010, for example, a few students were rescued from deportation by their schoolmates and supported in their efforts to hide from the police. To try to prevent another deportation, a police car was blocked by activists for several hours on the *Gürtel*, a major traffic artery of the city. Unfortunately, this attempt was unsuccessful. However, the most important protest arose in autumn 2009, when the massive student movement, *unibrennt*, emerged.

UNIBRENNT AND UNIVERSITY ACTIVISM

Austria has a long history of student movements that break out, dominate the public discourse, and fade away without any visible result. In the years 1987 and 1996, there were protests against financial cuts that were part of more general austerity measures, and in 2000, students protested against the implementation of tuition fees. Tens of thousands of students were mobilised, but in the end capitulated.[25]

The protests of 2009 seemed to follow the same procedure, but with some significant differences. Because the movement erupted at a point when no single reform at hand that had to be resisted, students voiced different, sometimes contradictory, demands that ranged from small improvements such as longer opening times for libraries to more general educational demands such as more funding of universities and fewer restrictions for students. There were also more general demands such as a guaranteed basic income for all.

When the Akademie der Bildenden Künste (Academy of Fine Arts) decided to implement the so-called Bologna process measures, aimed at making study credits comparable in all states of the EU, students decided to occupy the central hall of their university on October 20.[26] After a demonstration two days later, the Audimax, the biggest lecture hall in Vienna was occupied as well.

In the hours that followed, a large number of students joined the occupants and the movement spread to nearly all universities in Austria in the following days. Everywhere, university students occupied lecture halls and stayed during the night. Hundreds of newly formed working groups blossomed. The activists tried to organise themselves in a horizontal way: there were no fixed spokespersons; there was a rotation of representatives; people stuck to short, understandable statements; and people agreed to have equal gender representation. There were quarrels in the beginning on gay/lesbian and feminist positions, but in the end, at most of the occupied places pro-feminist statements and resolutions were passed.

Though only a few left-wing and autonomous activists were present in the large mass of activists and occupants, they influenced the activities via direct intervention as well as more generally via resonance as the occupation of buildings and urban spaces was inspired by the actions of squatter movements. The critique of representation and experiments with self-organisation also had their origins in anarchist and autonomous projects.

The student occupations reverberated internationally, a new experience for Austrian activists. In the months that followed, many universities in Germany and some in other European cities were occupied. At the same time, the unibrennt campaign cannot be viewed separately from international movements, from the massive student rebellions in countries like Great Britain in 2010 and Chile in 2011, and in the Arab Spring, all of which triggered new revolutionary hopes across the globe.

Following page spread: Occupation of the Pallas Athena statue in front of the parliament during one of the daily demonstrations after the inauguration of the ÖVP–FPÖ government, February 2000. Photo: ACC/RAW.

After a few months, normalcy began to once again dominate and it was relatively easy for the university administration to evict the last squatters out of the Audimax before Christmas 2009. But a new generation of activists had emerged through the occupations which now broadened its scope of action.

In June 2011, a coalition of different groups of activists squatted a complex of buildings called the Lobmeyrhof for nearly a week before they were evicted. In October 2011, a large building (the Epizentrum [epicentre]) in the gentrified seventh district was occupied for more than three weeks. Both actions mobilised new activists and gained much sympathy in the neighbourhood and beyond. The relatively brutal crackdown of a solidarity demonstration with the repossession of the Epizentrum on November 8 provoked the occupation of a new squat in the same neighbourhood two days later.

The present movements are inspired by already existing squatter movements and practices on the one hand, and a new wave of activism, inspired by international developments on the other. The new activists see themselves in line with the radical-democratic ideas of Spain's *indignados* in 2011. But there are also new strands of discussion about insurrectionary theories (inspired by the book *The Coming Insurrection* and the riots in Greece) among newly politicised activists.

Time will tell if and how the anarchist and autonomous scene will merge with the new movements and, thus, be able to contribute to the struggle against austerity politics and capitalism in general. What the two currents at least share is the fact that both struggle for 'real' democracy, which means much more than participation by the ballot.

FURTHER READING

Before the turn of the millennium, only a few studies were published on 1968 and some of the spectacular actions and campaigns that followed. These include the struggles against the proposed power plant in Zwentendorf and the power plant in Hainburg. Furthermore, some articles about squatting in the early 1980s were published in cultural anthologies. Later, books followed which focused on the cultural climate in the 1980s.

For these publications, see: Olaf Bockhorn et al., eds., *Kulturjahrbuch 2. Wiener Beiträge zu Kulturwissenschaft und Kulturpolitik* (Vienna: Verlag für Gesellschaftskritik, 1983); Hubert Ehalt et al., eds., *Geschichtswerkstatt, Stadtteilarbeit, Aktionsforschung. Perspektiven emanzipatorischer Bildungs- und Kulturarbeit* (Vienna: Verlag für Gesellschaftskritik, 1984); Peter Lachnit et al., *Wien wirklich. Ein Stadtführer durch den Alltag und seine Geschichte* (Vienna: Verlag für Gesellschaftskritik, 1983); Max Fürth et al., *Schwarzes Café: . . . das andere Wien 1981–2001. Wir haben keine Chance aber wir nutzen sie* (Vienna: Triton, 2001) and Martin Drexler et al., *Idealzone Wien: Die schnellen Jahre* (Vienna: Falter, 1998).

Even so, there were no texts on the autonomous scene and its actions before my book on social movements in Austria was published: Robert Foltin, *Und wir bewegen uns doch. Soziale Bewegungen in Österreich* (Vienna: Edition Grundrisse, 2004). This study is written from an autonomous (post-operaist) viewpoint and focuses on social movements during the period 1968–2000. It covers, among other things, squatter actions at the beginning of the 1980s, the emergence of the Autonomen, their most important actions during the second half of the 1980s, and their development afterwards.

Andreas Suttner's study *'Beton brennt.' Hausbesetzer und Selbstverwaltung im Berlin, Wien und Zürich der 80er* (Münster: Lit Verlag, 2011) deals with squatting in the same period, and focuses on the Kultur-und Kommunikationszentrum Gassergasse.

In autumn 2010, the Pankahyttn squat organised an exhibition called *Punk in Wien.* It was not only about punk culture but also about squatting, riots, and many other autonomous events. Unfortunately, the archive which grew out of this event will only become accessible at a later stage.

Perhaps inspired by the exhibition in the Pankahyttn, but most of all because the organisers received material and pictures dealing with the Arena, the Wien Museum organised an exposition in April 2012 called *Besetzt! Kampf um Freiräume seit den 1970ern* (Occupied! Struggle for free spaces since the 1970s). Although it focused on the occupation of the Arena, the accompanying catalogue—with the same title, published by Czernin publishing house—also contains information about squatting and subsequent autonomous actions.

Some material on more recent developments already exists as well. The sequel to my first book focuses on the newly emerging movements from the turn of the millennium until 2011: Robert Foltin, *Und wir bewegen uns noch. Zur jüngeren Geschichte sozialer Bewegungen in Österreich* (Vienna: Mandelbaum, 2011). An additional new project aims to document historical and contemporary squatter actions and autonomous 'Freiräume' (free spaces): http://www.besetzungsarchiv.org.

All the above-mentioned literature is in German; one text in English about the struggle for urban space in Vienna does exist: Julia Edthofer's 'This Is What Radical Democracy Looks Like! Reclaiming Urban Space in Vienna' in *Everyday Life in the Segmented City*, edited by Camilla Perrone et al. (Bingley: Emerald Group Publishing, 2011), 95–119.

ABOUT THE EDITORS

Leendert van Hoogenhuijze studied history at Leiden University and was co-editor of the Dutch socialist annual *Kritiek*. His most recent publications include contributions to *Kritiek* and the book *Linke Philosophie Heute. Eine Einführung zu Judith Butler, Antonio Negri und Slavoj Zizek* (Stuttgart: Schmetterling, 2012), which he co-edited with Bart van der Steen and Jasper Lukkezen. He currently lives and works in Reading, United Kingdom.

Ask Katzeff studied at Copenhagen University, where he specialised in the politics and practice of the alterglobalisation movement. He is co-editor of the journals *Arbejderhistorie* and *Øjeblikket* and wrote his doctoral dissertation at Copenhagen University, focusing on the interaction between urban development and squatting in Europe from the 1970s onwards.

Bart van der Steen studied history at Leiden University and wrote his doctoral dissertation at the European University Institute in Florence, where he studied the squatter and autonomous movements in Amsterdam and Hamburg during the 1980s. His dissertation is titled *Between Street Fight and Stadtguerrilla: The Autonomous Movement in Amsterdam and Hamburg during the 1980s*.

His fields of specialisation include the history of revolutionary socialism, labour movements, and autonomous movements. His most recent publications include *Wij gingen onze eigen weg. Herinneringen van revolutionaire socialisten in Nederland, 1930–1950* (Delft: Eburon, 2011), *Linke Philosophie Heute*, and *Een banier waar geen smet op rust. Een geschiedenis van het trotskisme in Nederland, 1938–heden* (Soesterberg: Aspekt, 2014).

ABOUT THE AUTHORS

PREFACE

A longtime activist for peace and justice, George Katsiaficas has written books on the global uprising of 1968 and European social movements, in which he developed the concept of the eros effect to explain the sudden emergence of globally synchronized insurgencies. Together with Kathleen Cleaver, he co-edited *Liberation, Imagination and the Black Panther Party*. His latest work is *Asia's Unknown Uprisings*, an analysis of the Asian wave of uprisings in the 1980s and 1990s that overthrew eight dictatorships in nine places. He is based in Gwangju, South Korea, and the Wentworth Institute of Technology in Boston. His website is http://www.eroseffect.com.

FOREWORD

Geronimo joined a citizen's committee against nuclear power plants at the end of the 1970s. In the beginning of the 1980s he was trained as a car mechanic and became member of the trade union IG Metall. Since the mid-1980s he lives in West Berlin, experienced the May 1 riots of 1987 there and joined the 1987 campaign against the IMF and World Bank summit in Berlin. In 1990 he fell in love with the woman of his dreams during a squat action in Neukölln (Berlin). After the fall of the Berlin Wall, he was active in campaigns against the Gulf War and pogroms against migrants and refugees in Hoyerswerda and Rostock. During the 1990s he joined the No-Olympia campaign, co-organized an Autonomie-conference and anti-racist border camps. Since the turn of the millennium, he has protested against the remembrance of the Wehrmacht by *Gebirgsjäger* (light infantry mountain troops) of the Bundeswehr in Bavaria and against labor market reforms by the central government.

AMSTERDAM

Nazima Kadir is an anthropologist based in London. She has a PhD in anthropology from Yale University and a BA in English literature and education from Swarthmore College. As part of her doctoral dissertation work, she lived and worked in a squatters' community in Amsterdam for three and a half years. Her research was developed into a cooperative sitcom, *Our Autonomous Life*, broadcast on Dutch television in the spring of 2012. In addition to academic ethnographic research and teaching, she has worked as a human rights advocate at the UN, an investigator of police misconduct for the City of New York, a union organiser of teaching assistants at Yale University and for hotel workers in Los Angeles, and most recently as a commercial researcher. As a scholar of social movements, she refuses to participate in the exploitative labour machinery of the academic world.

GREECE

Gregor Kritidis was born in 1971 and studied political science, sociology, and social psychology at the University of Hannover and Athens. He received his PhD from Hannover University in 2007. He has been working in adult education for several years and since 2000 is the editor of the internet magazine www.sopos.org. His most recent publications include: 'Irgendwann nehmen die Tränen Rache. Zur Renaissance des Anarchismus in Griechenland' in *Das Argument* 289 (2010), 826–38; and 'Die Demokratie in Griechenland zwischen Ende und Wiedergeburt,' in *Krisen Proteste. Beiträge aus Sozial.Geschichte Online*, edited by Peter Birke and Max Henninger (Berlin: Assoziation A, 2012).

BARCELONA

Claudio Cattaneo is research associate at the Institute of Environmental Science and Technology, Universitat Autónoma de Barcelona. He wrote his doctoral dissertation on the ecological economics of urban squatters in Barcelona. He is an active member of Research and Degrowth and is currently involved in the Can Masdeu, a rural-urban squat established in 2001 on the hills of Collserola, Barcelona. Recent publications include Squatting Europe Kollective, Claudio Cattaneo and Miguel Martínez, eds., *The Squatters' Movement in Europe: Everyday Commons and Autonomy as Alternatives to Capitalism* (London: Pluto Press, 2014) and 'The Money-Free Autonomy of Spanish Squatters' in *Life without Money*, edited by Anitra Nelson and Frans Timmerman (London: Pluto Press, 2011).

Enrique Tudela has a master's degree in contemporary history from the Universitat de Barcelona. He has written about the workers' movement and wildcat strikes during the last period of Franco's dictatorship and internal migration within the Spanish state in the 1940s, after the Civil War. Currently, he is completing his PhD at the Universitat de Barcelona and is involved in the Barcelona squat, Can Masdeu. He is the author of *Nuestro pan. La huelga del 70* (Granada: Editorial Comares, 2010) and has contributed to *Luchas autónomas en los años 70* (Madrid: Traficantes de Sueños, 2008), coordinated by Fundación Espai en Blanc.

BERLIN

Alex Vasudevan is a lecturer in cultural and historical geography at the University of Nottingham. His research focuses on radical politics in Germany and the wider geographies of neoliberal globalisation. He has published widely in *Antipode, Cultural Geographies, Environment Planning A and D, Geoforum,* and *Social and Cultural Geography.* He is currently working on a book that explores the historical and political geographies of the squatter movement in Berlin.

BRIGHTON

The numbers of the Bash Street Kids are legion, and they are not some grumpy middle-aged bloke grumbling about how everything was better in the Eighties. The Needle Collective has squatted in the UK, the Czech Republic, and the Netherlands. Currently they live, work, and play in Brighton.

COPENHAGEN

Flemming Mikkelsen, senior research fellow, is affiliated with the Department of Sociology, University of Copenhagen. His research has explored issues of social history, historical sociology, political sociology, ethnic relations, and social movements. Currently he works on an international project titled Popular Contention and Democracy in the Nordic Countries, 1700–2010. Recent publications include *Transnational identitet under forandring* [*Changing Transnational Identities: Social, Religious and Political Mobilization of Immigrants in Denmark, 1965–2010*] (Copenhagen: Museum Tusculanums Forlag, 2011); and 'Class and Social Movements in Scandinavia since 1945' in *Moving the Social: Journal of Social History and the History of Social Movements* 48 (2012).

René Karpantschof is a former activist in the Copenhagen squatter and autonomous movement. He holds a PhD in sociology and an MA in history from the University of Copenhagen, where he is a lecturer at the Department of Sociology. His publications focus on social movements and contentious politics in Denmark from the eighteenth century onwards, including squatter-related titles such as 'Kopenhagen, Jagtvej 69. Ein Jugendzentrum zwischen Besetzungen, Politik und Polizei (1981–2007)' in *Besetze deine Stadt!—bz din by! Häuserkämpfe und Stadtentwicklung in Kopenhagen,* Peter Birke and Chris Holmsted Larsen, eds. (Berlin: Assoziation A, 2007), 53–78; and 'Bargaining and Barricades: The Political Struggle over the Freetown Christiania 1971–2011' in *Space for Urban Alternatives? Christiania 1971–2011,* Håkan Thörn, Cathrin Wasshede, and Tomas Nilson, eds. (Stockholm: Gidlunds Förlag, 2011), 38–67.

LONDON

Lucy Finchett-Maddock is Lecturer in Law at the School of Law, Politics and Sociology, University of Sussex. She completed her PhD at Birkbeck College School of Law (University of London) with a study on squatted social centres and how these spaces and communities create their own form of 'social centre' law. She is the author of the forthcoming book *Protest, Property and the Commons: Performances of Law and Resistance*.

POZNAŃ

Grzegorz Piotrowski graduated from Adam Mickiewicz University and received his PhD from the European University Institute in 2011. Currently, he works at the Södertörn University in Sweden researching the anarchist movement. His latest publications include: 'Between the Dissidents and the Regime: Young People by the End of the 1980s in Central and Eastern Europe' in *Debatte: Journal of Contemporary Central and Eastern Europe* 18, no. 2 (2010): 145–62; and 'Jarocin: A Free Enclave behind the Iron Curtain' in *East Central Europe* 38, no. 2–3 (2011): 291–306.

VIENNA

Robert Foltin was born in 1957, grew up in Salzburg, and has been living in Vienna since the 1970s. In both cities, he was involved in anarchist and autonomous scenes ('To change life and to change the world'). Currently, he is a member of the editorial board of *grundrisse.zeitschrift für linke theorie und debatte*. He has published studies on autonomous theory and its relation to queer and feminist discussions, and two books on social movements in Austria. He is author of *Und wir bewegen uns noch* (Vienna: Mandelbaum, 2011); *Die Körper der Multitude* (Stuttgart: Schmetterling, 2010); *Und wir bewegen uns doch* (Vienna: Edition Grundrisse, 2000); and with M. Birkner coauthor of *(Post-)Operaismus. Von der Arbeiterautonomie zur Multitude* (Stuttgart: Schmetterling, 2006).

NOTES

PREFACE
1   Bart van der Steen, *Between Street Fight and Stadtguerrilla: The Autonomous Movement in Amsterdam and Hamburg during the 1980s* (PhD thesis, 2012), 36.

FOREWORD
1   The term used by the communist rulers to account for the 'differences' between communist reality and the socialist utopia.
2   Karl-Werner Brand et al., *Aufbruch in eine andere Gesellschaft. Neue soziale Bewegungen in der Bundesrepublik* (Frankfurt: Campus, 1986), 202–3.
3   Michael Haller, ed., *Aussteigen oder rebellieren. Jugendliche gegen Staat und Gesellschaft* (Reinbek bei Hamburg: Rowohlt, 1981).
4   *Häuserkampf I: Wir wollen alles. Der Beginn einer Bewegung* (Hamburg: Laika, 2012).
5   The nowadays uncommon term 'Tartuffe' refers to a seventeenth-century comedy by Molière in which he caricatured the intrigues and swindles of Catholic obscurantists at the court and subjects them to a, for his time, revolutionary criticism. Naturally, the societal role of women at that time was in no way similar to that after the bourgeois revolution.
6   *Handbuch für Hausbesetzer*, http://raz.blogsport.de/images/hfhb_01.pdf, 2002.
7   Polizeischutzamt Hamburg, *Hausräumung Eckhofstrasse, 23 Mai 1973*, http://www.youtube.com/watch?v=146v6DRIelM.
8   'Hausbesetzung in Freiburg,' deutsche Indymedia, February 15, 2007, http://de.indymedia.org/2007/02/168494.shtml.
9   Amantine, *Gender und Häuserkampf* (Münster: Unrast, 2011).
10   Ibid., 158.

INTRODUCTION
1   We would like to thank Detlef Siegfried and Jasper van der Steen for their valuable comments to earlier versions of this text.
2   David Harvey, *Rebel Cities: From the Right to the City to the Urban Revolution* (London: Verso, 2012); Paul Mason, *Why It's Kicking Off Everywhere* (London: Verso, 2012); Wolf Wetzel, ed., *Aufstand in den Städten: Krise, Proteste, Strategien* (Münster: Unrast, 2012).
3   The Occupy movement started with an appeal from the journal *Adbusters* to occupy Wall Street peacefully. In an email to its subscribers in June 2011, it wrote 'America needs its own Tahrir.' For Occupy: Noam Chomsky, *Occupy* (New York: Zuccotti Park Press, 2012); Carla Blumenkrantz et al., eds., *Occupy! Scenes from Occupied America* (London: Verso, 2012); Alessio Lunghi and Seth Wheeler, eds., *Occupy Everything: Reflections on Why It's Kicking Off Everywhere* (London: Minor Compositions, 2012). For solidarity

of Egyptian protesters with Madison, see Medea Benjamin, 'From Cairo to Madison: Hope and Solidarity Are Alive,' *Huffington Post*, http://www.huffingtonpost.com/medea-benjamin/from-cairo-to-madison-hop_b_826143.html. The article shows a photo from a Tahrir square protester holding a sign stating 'Egypt supports Wisconsin workers.'

4　　For the riots in the banlieues, see: Kollektiv Rage, eds., *Banlieues: Die Zeit der Forderungen ist vorbei* (Berlin: Assoziation A, 2008); and Laurent Mucchielli, 'Urbane Aufstände im heutigen Frankreich,' *Sozial.Geschichte Online* 2 (2010): 64–115, http://duepublico.uni-duisburg-essen.de/servlets/DerivateServlet/Derivate-24050/05_mucchielli_frankreich. pdf. See also: Slavoj Žižek, 'Some Politically Incorrect Reflections on Urban Violence in Paris and New Orleans and Related Matters,' in *Urban Politics Now/Reflect #06*, ed. BAVO (Rotterdam: NAi Publishers, 2007). For the uprising in Athens, see: A.G. Schwarz et al., *We Are an Image from the Future: The Greek Revolt of December 2008* (Oakland: AK Press, 2010); and Dimitris Dalakoglou and Antonis Vradis, eds., *Revolt and Crisis in Greece: Between a Present Yet to Pass and a Future Still to Come* (Oakland: AK Press, 2011). Three interesting publications on London are: Aufheben, 'Intakes: Communities, Commodities and Class in the August 2011 Riots,' *Aufheben* 20 (2011): 1–17, http://libcom.org/files/Intakes%20-%20Communities,%20commodities%20and%20class%20-%20Aufheben. pdf; Moritz Altenreid, *Aufstände, Rassismus und die Krise des Kapitalismus: England in Ausnahmezustand* (Münster: Edition Assemblage, 2012); and *Wenn die Toten erwachen: Die Riots in England* (Hamburg: Laika, 2011). For the 15M movement, see Neil Hughes, '"Young People Took to the Streets and All of a Sudden All of the Political Parties Got Old": The 15M Movement in Spain,' *Social Movement Studies* 10 (2011): 407–13.

5　　David Harvey, 'The Right to the City,' *New Left Review* 53 (2008): 23–40; On the Copenhagen Youth House: *Besetze deine Stadt!—bz din by! Häuserkämpfe und Stadtentwicklung in Kopenhagen*, Peter Birke and Chris Holmsted Larsen, eds. (Berlin: Assoziation A, 2007), http://www.assoziation-a.de/dokumente/Besetze_deine_Stadt. pdf; and René Karpantschof and Martin Lindblom, *Kampen om ungdomshuset: Studier i et oprør* (Copenhagen: Frydenlund, 2009); on the Gängeviertel: Gängeviertel e.V., *Mehr als ein Viertel: Ansichten und Absichten aus dem Hamburger Gängeviertel* (Berlin: Assoziation A, 2012); Eckhard Freiwald, *Hamburgs Gängeviertel* (Erfurt: Sutton, 2011); and Peter Birke, 'Herrscht hier Banko? Die aktuellen Proteste gegen das Unternehmen Hamburg,' *Sozial.Geschichte* 3 (2010): 148–91, http://duepublico.uni-duisburg-essen.de/servlets/DerivateServlet/Derivate-24619/10_Birke_Banko.pdf.

6　　In this respect, it is remarkable that both Germany and the Netherlands seem so far to have been untouched by the urban social conflicts unfolding in surrounding countries. In 1980, they were rather at the heart of it. For the urban revolts in Europe around 1980, see Helmut Willems, *Jugendunruhen und Protestbewegungen: Eine Studie zur Dynamik innergesellschaftlicher Konflikte in vier europäischen Ländern* (Opladen: Leske + Budrich, 1997). For contemporary observations on these protests, see: Günther Amendt, 'Leichte Krawallerie,' *Konkret* 8 (August 1980): 17–21; Reto Hänny, *Zürich Anfang September* (Frankfurt am Main: Suhrkamp, 1980); Gerard Anderiesen, 'Tanks in the Streets: The Growing Conflict over Housing in Amsterdam,' *International Journal of Urban and Regional Research* 5 (1980): 83–95; Henk Hofland, *De stadsoorlog: Amsterdam '80* (Alphen aan den Rijn: Sijthof, 1981); Michael Haller, ed., *Aussteigen oder rebellieren: Jugendliche gegen Staat und Gesellschaft* (Hamburg: Spiegel-Verlag, 1981); *Der Spiegel* 52 (December 1980), http://www.spiegel.de/spiegel/print/index-1980-52.html. See also: Isabel Wolf, *Hausbesetzungen in der Bundesrepublik: Eine Presseanalyse der Jahre 1980/1982* (PhD thesis, 2006).

7　　Freia Anders, 'Wohnraum, Freiraum, Widerstand. Die Formierung der Autonomen in den Konflikten um Hausbesetzungen Anfang der achtziger Jahre,' in *Das Alternative Milieu: Antibürgerlicher Lebensstil und linke Politik in der Bundesrepublik Deutschland und Europa, 1968–1983*, eds. Detlef Siegfried and Sven Reichardt, (Berlin: Wallstein, 2010): 473–98.

8　　Jan Willem van der Raad, *Kraken in Amsterdam* (Amsterdam: Roelof Keller Stichting,

1982); A.G. Grauwacke, *Autonome in Bewegung: Aus den ersten 23 Jahre* (Berlin: Assoziation A, 2003).

9   The radical author George Katsiaficas makes this link clear in his momentous study *The Subversion of Politics: European Autonomous Movements and the Decolonization of Everyday Life* (Oakland: AK Press, 2006), http://www.eroseffect.com/books/subversion.html. Geronimo also discusses the link between the Italian Autonomia movement of the 1970s and the autonomous movement of the 1980s: Geronimo, *Fire and Flames: A History of the German Autonomist Movement* (Oakland: PM Press, 2012).

10   See for example the following studies in the Netherlands: Wetenschappelijke Raad voor Regeringsbeleid, *Democratie en geweld: Probleemanalyse naar aanleiding van de gebeurtenissen in Amsterdam op 30 april 1980* (The Hague: Staatsuitgeverij, 1980), http://www.wrr.nl/fileadmin/nl/publicaties/PDF-Rapporten/Democratie_en_geweld.pdf; Otto Adang, *Hooligans, Autonomen, Agenten: Geweld en politie-optreden in relsituaties* (Alphen aan de Rijn: Samsom, 1998); and Frank van Gemert et al., *Kraken in Amsterdam anno 2009* (Amsterdam: VU, 2009), http://www.rechten.vu.nl/nl/Images/kraken%20anno%202009_tcm22-155474.pdf. For Germany, see for example: Deutscher Bundestag, *Bericht der Enquete-Kommission 'Jugendprotest im demokratischen Staat'* (Bonn: Hegener, 1983); Bundesminister für Jugend, Familie und Gesundheit, 'Zur Alternativen Kultur in der Bundesrepublik Deutschland,' *Aus Politik und Zeitgeschichte* no. 39 (1981): 3–15; and Marlene Bock et al., *Zwischen Resignation und Gewalt: Jugendprotest in den achtziger Jahren* (Opladen: Leske + Budrich, 1989). More recent publications from Germany are: Bundesamt für Verfassungsschutz, *Gewaltbereite Autonome: Ziele, Strukturen, Aktionen* (Bonn: Bundesamt für Verfassungsschutz, 1994); Bundesamt für Verfassungsschutz, *Militante Autonome: Charakteristika, Strukturen, Aktionsfelder* (Cologne: Bundesamt für Verfassungsschutz, 1999).

11   For the Netherlands, see for example: Ton Dijst, *De bloem der natie in Amsterdam. Kraken, subcultuur en het probleem van de openbare orde* (Leiden: COMT, 1986); and Dick de Ruyter, *Een baksteen als bewustzijn. De geweldskultuur van de kraakbeweging* (Den Bosch: Marge, 1986). For Germany, see: Haide Manns and Wolf-Sören Treusch, ' "Hau Weg die Scheiße." Autonomer Widerstand in der Bundesrepublik,' *Vorgänge* 26, no. 1 (1987): 65–74; and Sebastian Haunss, *Identität in Bewegung. Identität in Bewegung: Prozesse kollektiver Identität bei den Autonomen und der Schwulenbewegung* (Wiesbaden: VS Verlag, 2004), http://shaunss.files.wordpress.com/2011/10/haunss-2004-identitaet-in-bewegung.pdf.

12   Examples are Katsiaficas, *The Subversion of Politics*; Geronimo, *Fire and Flames*; and Adilkno, *Cracking the Movement: Squatting Beyond the Media* (New York: Autonomedia, 1994), http://thing.desk.nl/bilwet/Cracking/contents.html; Nick Anning et al., *Squatting: The Real Story* (London: Bay Leaf Books, 1980).

13   For Amsterdam: Eric Duivenvoorden, *Een voet tussen de deur: Geschiedenis van de Nederlandse kraakbeweging, 1964–1999* (Amsterdam: Arbeiderspers, 2000); Lynn Owens, *Cracking under Pressure: Narrating the Decline of the Amsterdam Squatters' Movement* (Amsterdam: Amsterdam University Press, 2009); and Justus Uitermark, 'Framing Urban Injustices: The Case of the Amsterdam Squatter Movement,' *Space and Polity* 8 (2004): 227–44. For Copenhagen: Flemming Mikkelsen and René Karpantschof, 'Youth as a Political Movement: Development of the Squatters' and Autonomous Movement in Copenhagen, 1981–95,' *International Journal of Urban and Regional Research* 25 (2001): 593–608; and Håkan Thörn et al., eds., *Space for Urban Alternatives? Christiania, 1971–2011* (Vilnius: Gidlunds, 2011), http://gupea.ub.gu.se/bitstream/2077/26558/3/gupea_2077_26558_3.pdf. For Zurich, see also: Heinz Nigg, *Wir wollen alles, und zwar subito! Die achtziger Jugendunruhen in der Schweiz und ihr Folgen* (Zurich: Limat, 2001). See also: http://www.av-produktionen.ch/80/home.html; Hans Peter Kriesi, *Die Zürcher Bewegung: Bilder, Interaktionen, Zusammenhänge* (Frankfurt am Main: Campus, 1984); and Andreas Suttner, *Beton brennt: Hausbesetzer und Selbstverwaltung in Berlin, Wien und Zürich der 80er* (Vienna: Lit, 2011). For Berlin, see: Geronimo, *Fire and Flames*; and Grauwacke, *Autonome in Bewegung*. Representative of this tendency are the studies by

Duivenvoorden and Grauwacke. Although both claim in their title to cover the history of the movement in the whole of the Netherlands and Germany respectively, they in fact focus on Amsterdam and Berlin.

14 Katsiaficas, *The Subversion of Politics*. Katsiaficas also pays attention to the roots of the movement of the 1980s, by providing an account of autonomous politics in Italy in the 1960s and 1970s. However, 1980s Italy is not discussed. Another strong overview of (the history of) squatting in Europe is provided by: Hans Pruijt, 'The Logic of Urban Squatting,' *International Journal of Urban and Regional Research* 37 (2012): 19–45.

15 This argument will be discussed in more detail in this volume. See also Hans Peter Kriesi et al., *New Social Movements in Western Europe: A Comparative Analysis* (Minneapolis: University of Minnesota Press, 1995); and Gøsta Esping-Andersen, *The Three Worlds of Welfare Capitalism* (Cambridge: Polity Press, 1990). For an interesting review of this argument, see: Wim van Noort, 'Herfsttij van de ecologische politiek. Opkomst, bloei en verval van groene partijen' in *Kritiek. Jaarboek voor socialistische discussie en analyse* (Amsterdam: Aksant, 2008): 98–116.

16 See, along with Anning et al., *Squatting: The Real Story*; and Ron Bayley, *The Squatters* (Middlesex: Penguin, 1973), which focuses mainly on the 1960s, also Kesia Reeve's dissertation on the UK squatter's movement: *The Squatters Movement in London, 1968–1980*.

17 Birgit Kraatz, 'Der Traum vom Paradies. Über die Stadtindianer und Autonomia in Italien' in *Aussteigen oder rebellieren*, Haller, ed., 35–47; Peter Birkner and Robert Foltin, 'Toni Negri. Postoperaismus als Theorie in Bewegung' in *Linke Philosophie Heute. Eine Einführung zu Judith Butler, Antonio Negri und Slavoj Žižek*, Bart van der Steen et al., eds., (Stuttgart: Schmetterling, 2012), 52–92, 69; Antonio Negri et al., *Books for Burning: Between Civil War and Democracy in 1970s Italy* (London: Verso, 2005).

18 Kriesi, *New Social Movements in Western Europe*; Jan Willem Duivendak, *The Power of Politics: New Social Movements in an Old Polity. France 1965–1989* (PhD thesis, 1992); Ruud Koopmans, *Democracy from Below: New Social Movements and the Political System in West Germany* (Boulder: Westview Press, 1995); Marco Guigni, *Entre stratégie et opportunité: Les nouveaux mouvements sociaux en Suisse* (PhD thesis, 1992); Jan Willem Duivendak et al., *Tussen verbeelding en macht: 25 jaar nieuwe sociale bewegingen in Nederland* (Amsterdam: Sua, 1992).

In recent times, more data sets have been generated, which can be downloaded. A database on European Protest and Coercion Data can be found on: http://www.nsd.uib.no/macrodataguide/set.html?id=52&sub=1. This database offers 'valid interval data' on protest and coercion in twenty-eight European countries from 1980 through 1995. Next to this, there is a data set on protest events in Germany: PRODAT Dokumentation und Analyse von Protestereignissen in der Bundesrepublik and can be found on: http://www.wzb.eu/de/forschung/beendete-forschungsprogramme/zivilgesellschaft-und-politische-mobilisierung/projekte/prodat-dokument. This database collects information on protests in Germany from 1950 to 2002. See also Dieter Rucht and Roland Roth, 'Soziale Bewegungen und Protest. Eine theoretische und empirische Bilanz,' in *Die sozialen Bewegungen in Deutschland seit 1945. Ein Handbuch*, Dieter Rucht and Roland Roth eds. (Frankfurt am Main: Campus, 2008), 635–68.

19 New social movements pick up issues not directly linked to the world of labor such as housing, environmental issues, and gender relations, and often consist of people not falling under the classic definition of industrial laborers. Introductions to new social movement history and theory are: Donatella Della Porta and Mario Diani, *Social Movements: An Introduction* (Malden: Blackwell, 2006); and Sidney Tarrow, *Power in Movement: Social Movements, Collective Action and Politics* (Cambridge: Cambridge University Press, 1994).

20 This argument complements the work of Gøsta Esping-Anderson, who identifies three different welfare systems in the Western world: liberal, corporatist, and social democratic. The second and third are mainly situated in Central and Northwestern Europe. Esping-Andersen, *The Three Worlds of Welfare Capitalism*.

21 Angelika Ebbinghaus, 'Was bleibt vom Operaismus' in *Kontroversen über den Zustand der Welt: Weltmarkt, Arbeitsformen, Hegemoniezyklen*, eds. Marcel van der Linden and Christoph Lieber (Hamburg: VSA, 2007), 45–62.

22 Next to Katsiaficas, *Subversion of Politics*, see also Donatella Della Porta, *Social Movements, Political Violence and the State: A Comparative Analysis of Italy and Germany* (Cambridge: Cambridge University Press, 1995); and Sidney Tarrow, *Democracy and Disorder: Protest and Politics in Italy, 1965–1975* (Oxford: Clarendon Press, 1989).

23 See his chapter in this volume, 233–53.

24 Pierpaulo Mudu, 'Resisting and Challenging Neoliberalism: The Development of Italian Social Centres,' *Antipode* 36 (2004), 917–41; Consortio Aaster et al., *Centro sociali: Geografie del desiderio. Dati, statistiche, progetti, mappe, divenire* (Milan: Shake, 1996), http://www.inventati.org/apm/archivio/P5/09/02/Centri_sociali_Geografie_del_desiderio_1996.pdf; Mavi Maggio, 'Urban Movements in Italy: The Struggle for Sociality and Communication,' in *Possible Urban Worlds: Urban Strategies at the End of the 20th Century*, ed. Richard Wolff (Basel: Birkhaüser, 1998), 232–37; Vincenzo Ruggiero, 'New Social Movements and the 'Centri Sociali' in Milan,' *Sociological Review* 48, no. 3 (2000): 167–85.

25 *What's This Place? Stories from Radical Social Centres in the UK and Ireland* (Leeds, 2008), http://socialcentrestories.wordpress.com; Stuart Hodkinson and Paul Chatterton, 'Autonomy in the City? Reflections on the Social Centres Movement in the UK,' *City* 10 (2006): 305–15.

26 For East Berlin, see: Susan Arnd et al., *Berlin Mainzer Strasse: 'Wohnen ist wichtiger als das Gesetz'* (Berlin: BasisDruck, 1992). For Leipzig: BetsetzerInnenkongress, *Reader zum Bundesweiten Besetzerinnenkongress vom 12–14 Mai in Leipzig* (Leipzig: Conne Island, 1995); Dieter Rink, 'Der Traum ist aus? Hausbesetzer in Leipzig-Connewitz in den 90er Jahren,' Dieter Roth and Roland Rucht, eds., *Jugendkulturen, Politik und Protest: Vom Widerstand zum Kommerz?* (Opladen: Leske + Budrich, 2000): 119–40; 'Leipzig schwarz-rot—Ein Ruckblick auf 20 Jahre autonome Linke in Leipzig,' http://www.anarchismus.at/die-autonomen/6118-20-jahre-autonome-linke-in-leipzig; Conne Island, ed., *20 yrs: Noch lange nicht Geschichte* (Berlin: Verbrecher Verlag, 2011). For Metelkova, see: Maja Breznik, 'The Role of Culture in the Strategies of "City Regeneration,"' Nada Švob-Ðokiæ, *Cultural Transitions in Southeastern Europe* (Institute for international relations: Zagreb, 2007), 81–94, http://culturelink.org/publics/joint/cultid08/Svob-Djokic_Creative_City.pdf#page=89.

27 See the chapter of Nazima Kadir in this volume, 21–61, and the film *It Was Our City* (dir. Joost Seelen, 1997).

28 For Amsterdam, see: Politieke vleugel van de kraakbeweging, *Parels voor de zwijnen: Het verval en het verraad binnen de actie-beweging in Nederland* (Amsterdam, 1987). For Germany, see: Fels, *Die Heinz Schenk Debatte: Texte zur Kritik an den Autonomen. Organisierungsdebatte. Gründung der Gruppe 'Für eine linke Strömung'* (Berlin: Fels, 2011), http://fels.nadir.org/multi_files/fels/heinz-schenk-debatte_0.pdf; 'Ich sag' wie es ist' in *Interim* no. 26 (1988): 1–37.

29 Geronimo, *Glut und Asche: Reflexionen zur Politik der autonomen Bewegung* (Münster: Unrast, 1997).

30 The factors influencing the rise and development of squatter movements is discussed later in this introduction.

31 Relatively new studies such as Owens, *Cracking under Pressure*, and Uitermark, 'Framing Urban Injustices,' keep on focusing on the 1980s and are uncritical of the established grand narrative, even though they attempt to also incorporate the more recent history of the movement.

32 For the barricades in the Vondelstraat, see Anderiesen, 'Tanks in the Streets.' For the Ryesgade, see the contribution on Copenhagen in this volume, 179–205, and the film *BZAT – Ni dage bag barrikaderne* (1986), http://www.youtube.com/watch?v=bZZmwKJz5JM. For the Hamburg Barrikadentage, see the film *Irgendwie, Irgendwo, Irgendwann* (1986–

1987), http://www.youtube.com/watch?v=eBD1eBEKcmc, (fragment). For the Mainzer Strasse: Arnd, *Berlin Mainzer Strasse*.

33   See, for example, Katsiaficas's foreword to the 2006 edition of his *Subversion of Politics*, in which he writes on the autonomous movement: 'The surge of movement actions . . . has decidedly subsided. . . . Scattered building occupations occur; squatted bars and collective centers remain open . . . Autonome tactics . . . remain a practical contribution to the question of organization. . . . Yet are the representative assemblies and collectives of the Autonomen sufficiently powerful organizational forms for today? Clearly the answer is no.' Ten years earlier, in 1995, the social scientist Ruud Koopmans predicted that the autonomous movement in Germany would probably not disappear, but had become politically insignificant. See: Koopmans, *Democracy from Below*, 210–14. That same year, the left liberal newspaper *Tageszeitung* commented on an autonomous conference with the question, 'Wie lange wird es die Autonomen noch geben?' ('How long will the autonomen go on?') (*Tageszeitung*, April 18, 1995).

34   Johannes Agnoli, *1968 und die Folgen* (Freiburg: Ça Ira, 1998); Axel Schildt and Detlef Siegfried, eds., *Between Marx and Coca-Cola: Youth Cultures in Changing European Societies, 1960–1980* (Oxford: Berghahn, 2006).

35   According to a broadcast of the Westdeutschen Rundfunk, hhttp://www1.wdr.de/themen/archiv/stichtag/stichtag_uebersicht100.html. See also: Häuserrat Frankfurt, *Wohnungskampf in Frankfurt* (Munich: Trikont, 1974); Serhat Karakayali, 'Lotta Continua in Frankfurt, Türken-Terror in Köln. Migrantische Kämpfe in der Geschichte der Bundesrepublik,' in *Vorwärts und viel vergessen: Beiträge zur Geschichte und Geschichtsschreibung neuer sozialer Bewegungen*, eds. Bernd Hüttner et al. (Bremen: AG SPAK, 2005), also available on the website of *grundrisse.zeitschrift für linke theorie und debatte*: http://www.grundrisse.net/grundrisse14/14serhat_karakayali.htm.

36   Duivenvoorden, *Een voet tussen de deur*.

37   The descriptions of squatters, journalists, and researchers of the early 1980s movement seem to prove this point. See: Stefan Aust and Sabine Rosenblatt, *Hausbesetzer: Wofür sie kämpfen, wie sie leben und wie sie leben wollen* (Hamburg: Hoffmann und Campe, 1981, http://anarch.an.ohost.de/schriften/Aust,%20Stefan%20&%20Rosenbladt,%20Sabine%20-%20Hausbesetzer.pdf; Bock, *Zwischen Resignation und Gewalt*; Annegriet Wietsma et al., *Als je leven je lief is. Vraaggesprekken met krakers en kraaksters* (Amsterdam: Lont, 1982).

38   Gisela Notz, 'Die autonomen Frauenbewegungen der Siebziger Jahre. Entstehungsgeschichte, Organisationsformen, politische Konzepte,' *Archiv für Sozialgeschichte* 44 (2004): 123–48.

39   This for example plays an important role in the argument of Virginie Mamadouh in *De stad in eigen hand: Provo's, kabouters en krakers als stedelijke sociale beweging* (Amsterdam: Sua, 1992).

40   The song appeared on their album *Alle gegen Alle* (1983). In German, the lyrics are: 'Immer kritisch und politisch / Marx und Lenin auf dem Nachttisch / Doch ihr habt was gegen Rabatz / Und macht den Bullen gerne Platz . . . Und werden wir mal aggressiv / Seid ihr auf einmal konservativ.'

41   See for the posters and visual history of the German autonomous movement: HKS 13, ed., *hoch die kampf dem: 20 Jahre Plakate autonomer Bewegungen* (Berlin: Assoziation A, 1999); HKS 13, ed., *vorwärts bis zum nieder mit: 30 Jahre Plakate unkontrollierter Bewegungen* (Berlin: Assoziation A, 2001). For an extensive overview of German autonomous posters and flyers, see: http://plakat.nadir.org. For a similar overview of Dutch posters, see Henk Hofland et al., *Een teken aan de wand: Album van de Nederlandse samenleving* (Amsterdam: Bert Bakker, 1983); Eric Duivenvoorden, *Met emmer en kwast: Veertig jaar Nederlandse actieaffiches, 1965–2005* (Amsterdam: Fort van Sjakoo, 2005); and http://www.iisg.nl/staatsarchief/affiches/index.php.

42   For the relation between punk and hardcore and the autonomous movement, see Gerrit Hoekman, *Pogo, Punk und Politik* (Münster: Unrast, 2011); and Gabriel Kuhn, *Sober*

Living for the Revolution: Hardcore Punk, Straight Edge and Radical Politics (Oakland: PM Press, 2010). For the relation between techno and the 1990s party scene and radical politics, see: Tim Malyon, 'Tossed in the Fire and They Never Got Burned: The Exodus Collective' in *DIY Culture: Party and Protest in Nineties Britain*, ed. George McKay (London: Verso, 1998), 187–207; and Torsun Burkhardt and Daniel Kulla, *Raven wegen Deutschland. Ein Doku-Roman* (Mainz: Ventil, 2011).

43   See the chapter on Brighton in this volume, 152–77.

44   There are to our knowledge no detailed studies yet on the history of (attitudes towards) drug consumption within the autonomous movement. For more general overviews, see: Stephen Snelders, 'LSD en XTC in de westerse maatschappij,' *Groniek* no.138 (1997), 61–71; Klaus Weinhauer, *Freedom of Choice? Drug Consumption in Berlin and London (1960s–1980s)* (Houndsmill: Palgrave, 2013); and Klaus Weinhauer, 'Drug Consumption in London and Western Berlin during the 1960/70s. Local and Transnational Perspectives,' *Social History of Alcohol and Drugs: An Interdisciplinary Journal* 20 (2006): 187–224.

45   For the influence of feminism and queer politics on the movement in Germany, see Amantine, *Gender und Häuserkampf* (Münster: Unrast, 2011). These discussions also affect the self-representation of the movement. For Germany, the social scientist Jan Schwarzmeier comments: 'From the end of the 1980s . . . [the movement] distances itself from all too martial images on printworks. Thus, instead of disguised and armed persons with cocky attitudes, the rebellious child is ever more often used for autonomous posters since the 1988 anti-IWF-campaign. . . . It comes across "not threatening, but creative and playful" and undermines the gendered position of militancy as a masculine behavior.' Jan Schwarzmeier, *Die Autonomen. Zwischen Subkultur und sozialer Bewegung* (PhD thesis, 1999), 197, note 2.

46   Amantine, *Gender und Häuserkampf*.

47   See the foreword to Adilkno, *Cracking the Movement* by Mik Ezdanitoff. See also: Uto Poigner, 'Das Schöne und das Häßliche: Kosmetik, Feminismus und Punk,' in *Das Alternative Milieu*, eds. Siegfried and Reichardt, 222–43.

48   See for example the history of the Göttingen Autonome Antifa (M), who consciously used a militant pose without engaging in militant confrontation: Bernd Langer, *Operation 1653: Stay Rude, Stay Rebel* (Berlin: Plättners, 2004), 206–13; and Schwarzmeier, *Die Autonomen*, 159–70.

49   Some however have explained the lack of political demands by the fact that in both settings racism played an important role. They could thus be compared to the 1965 Watts riots, which played an important role for the civil rights movement. However, because the traditional demands of civil rights movements—equal opportunities, integration, and participation—have in present-day Europe been incorporated by the neoliberal government discourse, social movements are literally left speechless. See, Kollektiv Rage, *Banlieues*, and Altenreid, *Aufstände, Rassismus und die Krise des Kapitalismus*; and Felix Klopotek, 'Klasse ohne Plan,' *Konkret* no. 8 (August 2012): 54–55.

50   Historian David Starkey in BBC *Newsnight*, December 8, 2011, http://www.bbc.co.uk/news/uk-14513517.

51   Sagris, *We Are an Image from the Future*, 370; and Gabriel Kuhn, *Soccer vs. the State: Tackling Football and Radical Politics* (Oakland: PM Press, 2011).

52   Nigg, *Wir wollen alles, und zwar subito!*.

53   Jerry Goossens and Jeroen Vedder, *Het gejuich was massaal: Punk in Nederland, 1976–1983* (Amsterdam: Mets, 1996), 80–81.

54   See for example: Hoekman, *Pogo, Punk und Politik*; Kuhn, *Sober Living for the Revolution*; Malyon, 'Tossed in the Fire and They Never Got Burned'; Burkhardt and Kulla, *Raven wegen Deutschland*; and Kuhn, *Soccer vs. the State*.

55   See *Der Spiegel* 51 (1980).

56   For a detailed chronology of the Berlin squatters' movement and the influence of the state's response, see: Grauwacke, *Autonome in Bewegung*, 36–85.

57   See for this development and the role of capital and neoliberalism: Neil Smith, *The New*

Urban Frontier: Gentrification and the Revanchist City (London: Routledge, 1996); Neil Smith, Uneven Development: Nature, Capital and the Production of Space (New York: Blackwell, 1984); and David Harvey, A Brief History of Neoliberalism (Oxford: Oxford University Press, 2005).

58   Hans Pruijt, 'The Impact of Citizens' Protest on City Planning in Amsterdam,' in Cultural Heritage and the Future of the Historic Inner city of Amsterdam, eds. Léon Deben et al. (Amsterdam: Amsterdam University Press, 2004), 228–44.

59   Harald Bodenschatz et al., Schluß mit der Zerstörung? Stadterneuerung und städtische Opposition in West-Berlin, Amsterdam und London (Giessen: Anabas, 1983); and Andrej Holm and Armin Kuhn, 'Squatting and Urban Renewal: The Interaction of Squatter Movements and Strategies of Urban Restructuring in Berlin,' International Journal of Urban Research 35 (2011): 644–58.

60   Bart van der Steen, 'Eerst de krakers, dan de cocktailbars,' De Groene Amsterdammer, July 1, 2010, http://www.groene.nl/2010/1/eerst-de-krakers-dan-de-cocktailbars.

61   Christian Werthschulte, 'Das Autonome Zentrum in Köln wird doch nicht geräumt,' Jungle World 14 (April 7, 2011), http://jungle-world.com/artikel/2011/14/42951.html.

62   In this context, the work of Andrej Holm is of particular interest. See: Wir bleiben alle! Gentrifizierung, Städtische Konflikte um Aufwertung und Verdrängung (Münster: Unrast, 2010); Stadterneuerung in der Berliner Republik. Modernisierung in Berlin-Prenzlauer Berg (Opladen: Leske + Budrich, 2002); Holm and Kuhn, 'Squatting and Urban Renewal,' and 'Gut gemeint statt gut gemacht,' Jungle World 33 (August 16, 2012), http://jungle-world.com/artikel/2012/33/46043.html; and his blog: http://gentrificationblog.wordpress.com.

AMSTERDAM

1   I would like to thank the following people for their support and feedback during the writing of this text: Bart van der Steen, whose patience, support, and analytically incisive comments went far beyond the call of duty of any editor; Martin Hertzberg, whose invaluable critique served to challenge my thinking and were integrated into the text; and Elise van Nederveen Meerkerk, whose strategic feedback helped me to unlock a structural puzzle while writing.

2   Lynn Owens, Kraaking under Pressure: The Decline of the Amsterdam Squatters' Movement (PhD thesis, 2004), 49.

3   Eric Duivenvoorden, Een voet tussen de deur: Geschiedenis van de kraakbeweging (1964–1999) (Amsterdam: Arbeiderspers, 2000), 52.

4   Paulus Tesser, Rapportage Minderheden 1995: Concentratie en Segregatie (The Hague: Sociaal-Cultureel Planbureau, 1995), 56.

5   Virginie Mamadouh, De Stad in eigen hand: Provo's, kabouters en krakers als stedelijke sociale beweging (Amsterdam: Sua, 1992).

6   Maria van Diepen and Ankie de Bruijn-Muller, 'Kraakakties in Gliphoeve. Sociale chaos als voorwaarde voor kapitalistiese ontwikkeling,' Zone no. 2 (1977): 27–44.

7   Personal conversation with Martin Hertzberg, SPOK, May 23, 2012.

8   Francesco Alberoni, Movement and Institution (New York: Columbia University Press, 1984).

ATHENS

1   'Occupation without Reason, Just to Make the Experience,' Kathimerini, October 19, 2008.

2   Fotopoulos, a philosopher and economist who emigrated to London in 1966 and became an activist in the students' movement there, and is editor of the International Journal of Inclusive Democracy, which promotes the tradition of libertarian socialism.

3   Maria Margaronis, 'Greek Anti-fascist Protesters "Tortured by Police" after Golden Dawn Clash,' Guardian, October 9, 2012, http://www.guardian.co.uk/world/2012/oct/09/greek-antifascist-protesters-torture-police.

4   See http://www.viome.org.

BARCELONA

1   Federació de Asociacions de Veins de Barcelona (FAVB), *La veu del carrer* 118 (May 2011), 8.

2   For a review of this experience, see: http://www.autonomiaobrera.net.

3   Felipe Pasajes, 'Arquelogía de la autonomía obrera en Barcelona, 1964–1973,' Espai en Blanc et al., *Luchas Autónomas en los años setenta* (Madrid: Traficantes de Sueños, 2008), 73–113.

4   Teo Maldo, 'Barcelona en la *glocalitzció*,' in *Barcelona marca registrada: Un model per desarmar* by Unió Temporal de Escribes (Barcelona: Virus, 2004), 13–26; and Francisco Martí and Eduardo Moreno, *Barcelona: A donde vas?* (Barcelona: Dirosa editorial, 1974).

5   Enrique Leyva, Ivan Miró and Xavier Urbano, *De la protesta al contrapoder: Nous protagonistes socials en la Barcelona metropolitana* (Barcelona: Virus, 2007), 41.

6   Xavier Cañadas Gascón, *El Caso Scala: Terrorismo de Estado y algo más* (Barcelona: Virus, 2008).

7   Joan Zambrana, *La alternativa libertaria (Catalunya 1976–1979)* (Barcelona: Edicions Fet a má-CEDALL, 2000). See also: http://www.cedall.org/Documentacio/Castella/cedall203130300.htm.

8   Xavier Pérez, coordinator, *Una illusió compartida: Ateneu Popular 9 Barris 25 anys* (Lleida: Pagés editors, 2004).

9   Pablo César Carmona-Pasqual, 'Autonomía y contracultura. Trabajo revuelta y vida cotidiana en la transición,' Espai en Blanc, *Luchas Autónomas*, 203–31.

10   This definition is among others used by George Katsiaficas in *The Subversion of Politics: European Autonomous Social Movements and the Decolonization of Everyday Life* (Oakland: AK Press, 2006). See also: http://eroseffect.com/books/subversion.html.

11   Joni D., *Que pagui Pujol! Una crónica punk de la Barcelona dels '80* (Barcelona: La Ciutat Invisible, 2010). Due to the lack of literature on this period, we have made frequent references to this primary source.

12   Ramón Fernandez-Duran, *El movimiento alternativo en la R.F.A.: El caso de Berlin* (Madrid: Autonomous Edition, 1985).

13   D., *Que pagui Pujol!*.

14   Interview with Joni D., in *Rojo y negro* 248 (2011).

15   D., *Que pagui Pujol!*.

16   Movimiento Objeción de Conciencia, *En legítima desobediencia: Tres décadas de objeción, insumisión y anti-militarismo* (Madrid: Traficantes de Sueños, 2002).

17   D., *Que pagui Pujol!*.

18   Juan-Ramón Capella, 'Samaranch: la transición,' *Mientras Tanto* 5 (2010).

19   H. Pedraforca, 'Barcelona: marca registrada I banderí del ciudadanisme,' in *Barcelona marca registrada: Un model per desarmar* by Unió Temporal de Escribes (Barcelona: Virus, 2004), 83–87.

20   Literatura Gris (firm), *Las huelgas estudiantiles de 1986–1987 en España y Francia* (Madrid: Traficantes de Sueños/Colectivo Maldeojo, 2001).

21   VV.AA., *Os Cangaceiros: España en el corazón* (Logroño: Pepitas de Calabaza, 2005).

22   D., *Que pagui Pujol!*, 106.

23   Ibid.

24   Albert Martinez, interview on August 14, 2011.

25   See: http://usrpa.squat.net/.

26   Antoni Batista, *Okupes, la mobilització sorprenent* (Barcelona: Plaza & Janes, 2002).

27   Albert Martinez, interview on August 14, 2011.

28   'Coordinadora Feminista Autónoma: una experiencia d'autoorganització entre dones,' *Mujeres Preokupando* 8 (2009).

29   José Manuel Naredo, 'La burbuja inmobiliario-financiera en la coyuntura económica reciente, (1985–1995),' *Aula Magna* (1996). See also: http://www.elpais.com/articulo/cataluna/Barcelona/Nace/plataforma/vecinal/afectados/planes/urbanisticos/Barcelona/elpepiautcat/20020607elpcat_15/Tes.

30   J.M.V. Peña, *El Forat* (2004).

31   For another case of successful civil resistance see for instance: http://canricart.info.

32   Taller VIU. *El cielo está enladrillado* (Barcelona: Edicions Bellaterra, 2006). See also: http://sindominio.net/violenciaurbanistica/?q=node/5.

33   Claudio Cattaneo, *The Ecological Economics of Urban Squatters in Barcelona* (PhD thesis, 2008).

34   Daniel Lopez Garcia et al., *Con la comida no se juega* (Madrid: Traficantes de sueños, 2003).

35   Claudio Cattaneo and Marc Gavaldá, 'The Experience of Rurban Squats in Collserola, Barcelona: What Kind of Degrowth?' *Journal of Cleaner Production* 18 (2010): 581–89.

36   Autoria Colectiva, *Los pies en la tierra* (Barcelona: Virus, 2006). See also: http://www.reclaimthefields.org.

37   See: http://www.collserola.org/index_Plataforma_Solana.html; and http://www.favb.cat/node/381.

38   See: http://alespenespunyalades.blogspot.com.

39   Locals had been protesting against the plan for fourteen years. They had performed numerous legal and direct actions, culminating in a blockade against the bulldozers for three consecutive days in 2008. During this blockade, more than sixty people were arrested. Currently, the works have been suspended because the project developer went bankrupt during the real estate crash, but repression still follows with a few people facing high penalty charges. See: http://www.moviments.net/noalplacaufec.

40   Silvia López Gil, *Nuevos feminismos: Sentidos comunes en la dispersion. Una historia de trayectorias y rupturas en el Estado español* (Madrid: Traficantes de sueños, 2011), 96–97.

41   See: http://mambo.pimienta.org.

42   See: http://www.canpiella.cat.

43   See: http://www.huertosurbanosbarcelona.wordpress.com.

44   See: http://nacional.cup.cat/; and http://www.youtube.com/watch?v=gDQoRM2oc6M.

45   See: http://www.lavanguardia.com/politica/20111016/54231611683/el-15-m-ocupa-un-edificio-de-barcelona-para-alojar-a-desahuciados.html; and http://www.publico.es/espana/402080/edificio-15-o-el-simbolo-contra-los-desahucios.

BERLIN

1   Susan Arndt et al., eds., *Berlin Mainzer Strasse: Wohnen ist wichtiger als das Gesetz* (Berlin: Basisdruck, 1992). A longer version of this essay has previously been published as Alex Vasudevan, 'Dramaturgies of Dissent: The Spatial Politics of Squatting in Berlin, 1968–,' *Social and Cultural Geography* 12, no. 3 (2011): 283–303, and is reprinted by permission of the publisher.

2   Dougal Sheridan, 'The Space of Subculture in the City: Getting Specific about Berlin's Indeterminate Territories,' *Field Journal* 1 (2007): 102.

3   Mathias Heyden, 'Evolving Participatory Design: A Report from Berlin, Reaching Beyond,' *Field Journal* 2 (2008): 34.

4   Belinda Davis, 'New Leftists and West Germany: Fascism, Violence, and the Public Sphere, 1967–1974,' in *Coping with the Nazi Past: West German Debates on Nazism and Generational Conflict, 1955–1975*, eds. Philipp Gassert and Alan Steinweis (New York: Berghahn, 2006), 210–37; Belinda Davis, 'The City as Theater of Protest: West Berlin and West Germany,' in *The Spaces of the Modern City: Imaginaries, Politics, and Everyday Life*, eds. Gyan Prakash and Kevin Krause (Princeton: Princeton University Press, 2008), 247–74; Jeremy Varon, *Bringing the War Home: The Weather Underground, the Red Army Faction, and Revolutionary Violence in the Sixties and Seventies* (Berkeley: University of California Press, 2004); and Sabine von Dirke, *'All Power to the Imagination': The West German Counterculture from the Student Movement to the Greens* (Lincoln: University of Nebraska Press, 1997).

5   Jenny Pickerill and Paul Chatterton, 'Notes towards Autonomous Geographies: Creation, Resistance and Self-Management as Survival Tactics,' *Progress in Human Geography* 30 (2006): 743.

6   Though see: Ruud Koopmans, *Democracy from Below: New Social Movements and the Political System in West Germany* (Oxford: Westview Press, 1995); and Roger Karapin, *Protest Politics in Germany: Movements on the Left and Right Since the 1960s* (University Park: PSU Press, 2007).

7   Tim Ingold, *Perceptions of the Environment: Essays on Livelihood, Dwelling, and Skill* (London: Routledge, 2000).

8   Lauren Berlant, *The Female Complaint: The Unfinished Business of Sentimentality in American Culture* (Durham, NC: Duke University Press, 2008).

9   Nicholas Blomley, *Unsettling the City: Urban Land and the Politics of Property* (London: Routledge, 2009); Andrej Holm, *Die Restrukturierung des Raumes: Stadterneuerung der 90er Jahre in Ostberlin* (Bielefeld: Transcript, 2006); Kurt Iveson, *Publics and the City* (Oxford: Blackwell, 2007); Don Mitchell, *The Right to the City: Social Justice and the Fight for Public Space* (New York: Guilford Press, 2003); Neil Smith, *The New Urban Frontier: Gentrification and the Revanchist City* (New York: Routledge, 1996); and Lynn Staehli and Don Mitchell, *The People's Property: Power, Politics, and the Public* (London: Routledge, 2007).

10   David Harvey, 'The Right to the City,' *New Left Review* 53 (2008): 25.

11   Derek Gregory, 'Introduction: Troubling geographies,' in *David Harvey: A Critical Reader*, eds. Noel Castree and Derek Gregory (Oxford: Blackwell, 2006), 10.

12   Vinai Gidwani, 'Limits to Capital: Questions of Provenance and Politics,' *Antipode* 36 (2004): 527–42; David Harvey, *The New Imperialism* (Oxford: Oxford University Press, 2003); Alexander Vasudevan et al., 'Spaces of Enclosure,' *Geoforum* 39 (2008): 141–46.

13   Ayona Datta, 'Architecture of Low-Income Widow Housing: "Spatial Opportunities" in Madipur, West Delhi,' *Cultural Geographies* 15 (2008): 233.

14   Pickerill and Chatterton, 'Notes towards Autonomous Geographies.'

15   Davis, 'The City as Theatre of Protest.'

16   Ibid., 247.

17   Kreuzberg Museum, Squatting File.

18   Ingrid Gilcher-Holtey et al., eds., *Politisches Theater nach 1968. Regie, Dramatik und Organisation* (Frankfurt am Main: Campus, 2006); Dorothea Kraus, *Theater-Protest: Zur Politisierung von Strasse und Bühne in den 1960er Jahren* (Frankfurt am Main: Campus, 2007).

19   Davis, 'The City as Theatre of Protest,' 264.

20   Andrei Markovits and Philip Gorski, *The German Left: Red, Green and Beyond* (Oxford: Oxford University Press, 1993).

21   Félix Guattari, 'Subjectivities: for Better and for Worse,' in *The Guattari Reader*, ed. Gary Genosko (Oxford: Blackwell Publishers, 1996), 196.

22   Kunst & KulturCentrum Kreuzberg, *Dokumentation* (Berlin: KuKuCK, 1984), 13.

23   Félix Guattari, *La Révolution moléculaire* (Fontenay-sous-Bois: Encres/Recherches, 1977). For Guattari, 'molecular revolution' describes a process of *micro-political* transformation that operates below the level of perception and through which a body's capacity to act and be acted upon is transformed.

24   Gavin Brown, 'Mutinous Eruptions: Autonomous Spaces of Radical Queer Activism,' *Environment and Planning* 29 (2007): 2696.

25   Bernd Laurisch, *Kein Abriß unter dieser Nummer* (Giessen: Anabas, 1981); Mathias Heyden and Ines Schaber, 'Here Is the Rose, Here Is the Dance!,' in *Who Says Concrete Doesn't Burn, Have You Tried? West Berlin Film in the '80s*, Sefanie Strasthaus and Florian Wüst eds. (Berlin: b_books, 2008), 132–48.

26   Heyden and Schaber, 'Here Is the Rose, Here Is the Dance!,' 140.

27   Sheridan, 'The Space of Subculture in the City,' 101; Blomley, *Unsettling the City*, 79.

28   Kreuzberg Museum, Squatting File.

29   James Holston, *Insurgent Citizenship: Disjunctions of Democracy and Modernity in Brazil* (Princeton: Princeton University Press, 2008).

30   Heyden and Schaber, 'Here Is the Rose, Here Is the Dance!'

31   Werner Hegemann, *Das steinerne Berlin. Gesichte der größten Mietskasernenstadt der Welt* (Braunschweig: Vieweg, 1979 [1930]).

32   Claus Bernet, 'The "Hobrecht Plan" and Berlin's Urban Structure,' *Urban History* 31 (2004): 400–419; Brian Ladd, *Urban Planning and Civic Order in Germany, 1860–1914* (Cambridge: Harvard University Press, 1990); and Klaus Strohmeyer, *James Hobrecht und die Modernisierung der Stadt* (Berlin: Wissenschafts-Verlag, 2000).

33   Ladd, *Urban Planning and Civic Order in Germany*, 81.

34   Jonas Geist and Klaus Kürvers, *Das Berliner Mietshaus* [3 vols.] (Munich: Prestel, 1980–1989); Bernet, 'The "Hobrecht Plan" and Berlin's Urban Structure.'

35   Bernet, 'The "Hobrecht Plan" and Berlin's Urban Structure,' 413.

36   AbdouMaliq Simone, *For the City yet to Come: Changing African Life in Four Cities* (Durham: Duke University Press, 2004), 9.

37   David Harvey, *The Urban Experience* (Baltimore: Johns Hopkins University Press, 1989), 83.

38   Brian Ladd, *The Ghosts of Berlin* (Chicago: University of Chicago Press, 1997), 102.

39   Sheridan, 'The Space of Subculture in the City.'

40   Ibid., 117, 115.

41   Simone, *For the City yet to Come*, 12.

42   Shannon Jackson, *Lines of Activity: Performance, Historiography, Hull-House Domesticity* (Ann Arbor: University of Michigan Press, 2000), 17.

43   Petra Bosse and Veronika Zimmer, eds., *Ökologische Maßnahmen in Frauenstadtteilzentrums: Schokoladenfabrik in Berlin-Kreuzberg* (Berlin: Stern, 1988), 10.

44   Regenbogenfabrik Block 109 e.V, *Festschrift zum 25. Jubiläum der Regenbogenfabrik* (Berlin: Kreuzberg Museum, 2006), 26.

45   Research for this paper draws on an ongoing project which combines archival work and semi-structured interviews with dozens of former participants in the Berlin squatting scene. Interviews were conducted between February 2008 and July 2009. For the sake of consistency, I have altered the names of all interviewees.

46   Quoted in: Davis, 'The City as Theater of Protest,' 269.

47   Regenbogenfabrik, *Festschrift zum 25. Jubiläum*, 5.

48   Karl Marx, *Grundrisse* (London: Penguin, 2005), 611.

49   Henri Lefebvre, 'Right to the City,' in *Henri Lefebvre: Writing on Cities*, eds. Eleonore Kofman and Elizabeth Lebas (Oxford: Blackwell, 1996), 158.

50   Joachim Fahrun, 'Hausbesetzung als Kunstaktion inszeniert,' *Berliner Morgenpost*, June 22, 1992.

51   Stillkam 5 ½ e.V., *Konzept für ein Haus zum gemeinsamen Wohnen und Arbeiten* (unpublished MS)

52   Ibid.; Heyden, 'Evolving Participatory Design,' 35.

53   Quoted in: Caroline Tisdall, *Art into Society: Society into Art* (London: ICA, 1974), 48.

54   Gereon Asmuth, 'The Making of K77,' *Die Tageszeitung*, June 21, 2002.

55   Heyden, 'Evolving Participatory Design,' 35.

56   Asmuth, 'The Making of K77.'

57   M. Heyden, *Die Freiraumgestaltung der K 77* (unpublished, MS).

58   Heyden, 'Evolving Participatory Design,' 35–36.

59   Ibid., 36–37.

60   Pierre Bourdieu, *Outline of a Theory of Practice* (Cambridge: Cambridge University Press, 1977).

61   Heyden, 'Evolving Participatory Design,' 37.

62   Matthias Bernt and Andrej Holm, 'Is It or Is It Not? The Conceptualisation of Gentrification and Displacement and Its Political Implications in the Case of Prenzlauer Berg,' *City* 13 (2009): 312–24; Holm, *Die Restrukturierung des Raumes*.

63   Heyden, 'Evolving Participatory Design,' 37.

64   Jesko Fezer and Mathias Heyden, eds., *Hier entsteht: Strategien partizipative Architektur und räumlicher Aneignung* (Berlin: b_books, 2004); Florian Haydn and Robert Temel, eds., *Temporäre Räume: Konzepte zur Stadtnutzung* (Bern: Birkhauser, 2006).

65 Harvey, 'The Right to the City,' 23.
66 Michael Hardt and Antonio Negri, *Commonwealth* (Cambridge: The Belknap Press, 2009).

BRIGHTON

1 R. Bailey, *The Squatters* (London: Penguin, 1973).
2 *Brighton and Hove Gazette*, June 25, 1969.
3 The following article has the action listed as performed by Angry Brigade, http://libcom.org/history/angry-brigade-documents-chronology. Whether this is true, we do not know.
4 *Brighton Voice* 25 (July 1975).
5 Nick Anning et al., *Squatting: The Real Story* (London: Bay Leaf Books, 1980).
6 *Brighton Voice* 44 (February 1978).
7 The Bash Street Kids, http://www.uncarved.org/music/apunk/nostalgia.html.
8 *Brighton in the Nineties: A Community Guide* (1990).
9 For more details, see Danny Burns, *Poll Tax Rebellion* (San Francisco: AK Press, 1992).
10 *Kill or Chill* 4 (1995).
11 'Autonomous Spaces,' *Do or Die* 8 (1999).
12 *Sporzine*, no. 1.
13 *Sporzine*, no. 3.
14 For example, see the two contrary articles under 'Space Invaders,' *Do or Die* 10 (2003).
15 *Rough Music* 9 (April 2006).
16 *Argus*, June 3, 2008.

COPENHAGEN

1 Besides secondary sources and various publications, the cornerstone of our empirical research is based on two databases. The first covers the life course of one of the most vivid, and, some would say, violent youth movements after World War II, that is, the second-generation squatter movement that lasted from approximately 1982 until 1994. Data on confrontational actions were gathered from the squatter movement's own publications and from leading daily newspapers. The dataset consists of 522 contentious actions, and allows for a deeper investigation of particular aspects of protest as well as forms of action, issues and claims, actors, organizations, strategies, and ideology. As a supplement to the action dataset we have used data on the 'permanent' occupied buildings 1981–1994. It was there that most of the squatters lived, met with others and recruited new members, and it was within those physical surroundings that they built up the organizational basis of the movement. To cover the latest revival of the squatter movement—that is the third generation of squatters—we have compiled information on 280 contentious gatherings 2006–2007, especially related to the strife about the Youth House.
2 Doug McAdam, Sidney Tarrow, Charles Tilly, *Dynamics of Contention* (Cambridge: Cambridge University Press, 2001); Roger Karapin, *Protest Politics in Germany: Movements on the Left and Right since the 1960s* (University Park: Pennsylvania State University Press, 2007).
3 William Sewell Jr., 'Space in Contentious Politics,' in *Silence and Voice in the Study of Contentious Politics*, Ronald Aminzade et al., eds. (Cambridge: Cambridge University Press, 2001), 55–56.
4 Michael Lipsky, ed., *Law and Order: Police Encounters* (New York: Aldine, 1970), 1.
5 Doug McAdam and Dieter Rucht, 'The Cross-National Diffusion of Movement Ideas,' *Annals of the American Academy of Political and Social Science* 528 (1993): 56–74; and Flemming Mikkelsen, 'Contention and Social Movements in an International and Transnational Perspective: Denmark 1914–1995,' *Journal of Historical Sociology* 12 (1999): 128–57.
6 Ruud Koopmans, *Democracy from Below: New Social Movements and the Political System in West Germany* (Boulder: Westview Press, 1995); and Helmut Willems, *Jugendunruhen und Protestbewegungen* (Opladen: Laske+Budrich, 1997).

7   Rene Karpantschof, *Nynazismen og dens modstandere i Danmark* (Esbjerg: Sydjysk Universitetsforlag, 1999).
8   René Karpantschof and Flemming Mikkelsen, 'Rise and Fall of the Racist Right-Wing Movement in Denmark, 1982–2006' (paper presented at the 13th Nordic Migration Conference, AMID, Aalborg University, revised version 2009).
9   The widespread sympathy for the Youth House activists is shown by a series of opinion polls on the Youth House issue 2006–2008. For further explanation see Karpantschof, 'Ungdomshusoprøret 2006–2008.'
10   René Karpantschof, 'Bargaining and Barricades: The Political Struggle over the Freetown Christiania 1971–2011,' in *Space for Urban Alternatives? Christiania 1971–2011*, ed. Håkan Thörn et al. (Stockholm: Gidlunds Förlag, 2011), 38–67.
11   On violence, politics, and police in Denmark after World War II see René Karpantschof and Flemming Mikkelsen, 'Vold, politik og demokrati i Danmark efter 2. Verdenskrig,' *Arbejderhistorie* 1 (2008): 56–94.
12   Sidney Tarrow, *The New Transnational Activism* (Cambridge UK: Cambridge University Press, 2005).
13   Jack Goldstone, 'Introduction: Bridging Institutionalized and Noninstitutionalized Politics,' in *States, Parties, and Social Movements*, Jack Goldstone ed. (Cambridge, UK: Cambridge University Press, 2003), 1–24.
14   Crawford Macpherson, *The Life and Times of Liberal Democracy* (Oxford: Oxford University Press, 1977); and Jean Grugel, *Democratization: A Critical Introduction* (New York: Palgrave, 2002).

LONDON
1   *The Theory and Practice of Autonomy* (Cambridge, UK: Cambridge University Press, 1988), 13.
2   Quoted in Nick Wates and Christian Wolmar, eds., *Squatting: The Real Story* (London: Bay Leaf Books, 1980), 47.
3   See LBC Lambeth v. Persons Unknown (2009).
4   See: http://thelibraryhouse.wordpress.com.
5   The mirror thesis is summarised by Steven Vago: 'Every legal system stands in close relationship to the ideas, aims and purposes of society. Law *reflects* the intellectual, social, economic, and political climate of its time.' See: Brian Tamanaha, *A General Jurisprudence of Law and Society* (Oxford: Oxford University Press, 2001), 2.
6   Carl Schmitt, *Constitutional Theory* (Durham, NC: Duke University Press, 2008).
7   Ibid.
8   The 1925 Land Registration Act and the 2002 Land Registration Act.
9   The Torrens system is one that seeks to see all estates and titles in land, on one register, and thus showing a hopefully exact reflection of the dividing up of land ownership at one given time.
10   Gary Minda, *Postmodern Legal Movements: Law and Jurisprudence at Century's End* (New York: New York University Press, 1995), 1.
11   Ibid., 247.
12   Ibid., 253.
13   Paul Bignell and Lettice Franklin, 'Young, Urban Professional Seeks Home: Vacant Premises Will Do,' *The Independent*, August 22, 2010.
14   Anders Corr, *No Trespassing: Squatting, Rent Strikes, and Land Struggles Worldwide* (Cambridge, Mass.: South End Press, 1999), 25–26.
15   Wates and Wolmar, *Squatting: The Real Story*, 101.
16   Dworkin, *The Theory and Practice of Autonomy*, 13.
17   Ron Bailey, *The Squatters* (Penguin: London, 1973), 21.
18   Dworkin, *The Theory and Practice of Autonomy*, 13.
19   Bailey, *The Squatters*, 21.
20   Dworkin, *The Theory and Practice of Autonomy*, 13.

21   Ibid., 20.

22   Ibid., 24.

23   Wates and Wolmar, *Squatting: The Real Story*, 14.

24   Ibid.

25   Dworkin, *The Theory and Practice of Autonomy*, 31.

26   Wates and Wolmar, *Squatting: The Real Story*, 15.

27   In response to this, the birth of the movement that is seen today came about in conjunc-
      tion with public awareness of the homeless situation through the TV series *Cathy Come
      Home* concerning a young homeless girl, the establishment of the charity Shelter, and also
      election promises on housing.

28   Bailey, *The Squatters*, 31–32.

29   The London Autonomists organised the social space, the Wapping Autonomy Centre
      (1981–1982).

30   See 'housing cuts = homelessness,' http://evictionresistance.squat.net/2012/08.

31   Bignell and Franklin, 'Young, Urban Professional Seeks Home.'

32   Ibid.

33   Lord Denning MR, in McPhail v Persons, Names Unknown [1973] Ch. 447 (AC (Civ
      Div)) Ch 447.

34   David Watkinson, 'Squatters Rights since 1977 and the Effect of the European
      Convention on Housing Law,' 'Law on Trial,' 'Housing Evening,' Lectures at Birkbeck
      College, University of London, July 2, 2010.

35   See: McPhail v. Persons, Names Unknown.

36   See Wykeham Terrace, Brighton Re 1969 [1971] Ch. 204 Ch. Div. Ch 204.

37   See Burston Finance v. Wilkins [1975] 240 E.G. 375.

38   See Warwick University v. De Graaf 1975 1 WLR 1135 (AC (Civ Div)).

39   Watkinson, 'Squatters Rights since 1977.'

40   Ibid.

41   An occupant who had been displaced by squatters entering their property.

42   An occupant who was about to move in before the squatters arrived.

43   In general, see Watkinson, 'Squatters Rights since 1977.'

44   Stephen Platt, 'A Whole New Ball Game: Winning Concessions and Learning to Live
      with the New Law,' in Wates and Wolmar, *Squatting: The Real Story*, 82–103.

45   In 1976, CACTL received support from thirty-six trades councils, eighty-five trade
      union branches, fifty-one student unions and many other organisations. See Platt, 'A
      Whole New Ball Game.'

46   Aufheben collective, 'Kill or Chill: An Analysis of the Opposition to the Criminal Justice
      Bill' in *Aufheben* 4 (1995), http://libcom.org/library/kill-chill-aufheben-4.

47   Ibid.

48   Platt, 'A Whole New Ball Game.'

49   Ibid.

50   Ibid.

51   Wates and Wolmar, *Squatting: The Real Story*, 18.

52   Ibid., 15.

53   Hans Pruijt, 'Is the Institutionalization of Urban Movements Inevitable? A Comparison
      of the Opportunities for Sustained Squatting in New York City and Amsterdam,'
      International Journal of Urban and Regional Research 27 (2003): 133–57.

54   Wates and Wolmar, *Squatting: The Real Story*, 33.

55   Platt, 'A Whole New Ball Game.'

56   Wates and Wolmar, *Squatting: The Real Story*, 162.

57   Bailey, *The Squatters*, 178.

58   Advisory Service for Squatters (ASS), http://www.squatter.org.uk.

59   According to Platt: 'It was against this background that some squatters attempted in
      1977, yet again, to form a more coordinated organisation to counter the opposition they
      were now facing. A squatters' conference emerged in July 1977 from the long series of

follow-up meetings that were held in the months after the conference. Membership was open to all squatters, ex-squatters and licensees for a cost of 25p and 10p per month, and the Squatters Charter, a statement of the Union's aims combined with a code of behaviour for squatters, was adopted as the Union's policy.' See Platt, 'A Whole New Ball Game.'

60   Wates and Wolmar, *Squatting: The Real Story*, 162.

61   Ibid.

62   Member, ASS, 2011.

63   Ibid.

64   See Deanna Dadusc and E.T.C. Dee, 'The Criminalisation of Squatting: Discourses, Moral Panics and Resistances in the Netherlands, England and Wales,' 'Vulnerable Demons' Workshop, Durham Law School, March 2013.

65   See Mary Manjikian, *Securitisation of Property Squatting in Europe* (London: Routledge, 2013).

66   Sections 75 and 76 are with regard to 'Interim Possession Orders' ('IPO'), the new fast-track way of evicting squatters. Once all of the correct proceedings have been followed and the courts have granted the IPO, the squatters concerned have twenty-four hours in which to leave the premises, after the order has been served. See: http://www.urban75.org/legal/cja.html.

67   The Act does not cover unregistered land (Section 96 (1)).

68   Options 1, 2, and 3 have the greatest impact on the legal, social, and political regime of squatting. Option 1 wishes to create the crime of 'intentional trespass,' whereby there is no reliance on the sanctity of court before a squatter can be forcibly removed. With regards to Option 2, Section 7 of the Criminal Law Act 1977, currently states that it is an offence for a person, who is on a residential premises as a trespasser, to refuse to leave when required to do so by a DRO or a PIO of the property. Option 2 would use this section, and extend this so that it also applies to squatters who refuse to leave other types of property, such as those of a commercial nature: 'Commercial property owners would therefore have a similar level of protection to displaced residential occupiers and protected intending occupiers.' Option 3 deals directly with squatters' rights and Section 6 of the Criminal Law Act 1977. Section 6 makes it an offence for a person, without lawful authority, to use or threaten violence to enter a property where someone inside is opposed to their entry. Currently only DROs or PIOs can legally remove someone from a residential building, however, the wish is to extend this to other categories of property owners. Option 3 threatens the safety and security of the homeless and destitute, and would give further police powers in relation to arbitrating occupations. See: Ministry of Justice, (2011), 'Options for Dealing with Squatters,' CP 12/2011, 15, found at https://consult.justice.gov.uk./digital-communications/dealing-with-squatters.

69   See Manjikian, *Securitisation of Property Squatting in Europe*, 8–11.

70   SQUASH and McDonnell's amendment balanced the issues that were raised through the consultation process, while at the same time maintain the regime of squatters' rights, suggesting: that the law only covers residential property left empty for less than six months; that the offence is not applicable in cases where the person is a care leaver or who has in the previous year been registered homeless/at risk; and that the offence will not be retrospectively applied. Both McDonnell and SQUASH highlighted that, on average, between 650,000 and 700,000 residential properties have stood empty over the last five years. Most are private properties, and 300,000 have been empty for more than six months. Again, the amendment was defeated by 300 votes to 23.

71   Bailey, *The Squatters*, 131.

72   Ibid., 34.

73   Ibid., 68–69.

74   See http://www.squatter.org.uk/.

75   SQUASH, information found at: http://www.squashcampaign.org/2011/09/squatting-campaigners-hail-judge%E2%80%99s-ruling-on-empty-homes/.

76 See Robin Hickey, 'Constructions of the "Squatter" in Property Law,' 'Vulnerable Demons' Workshop, Durham Law School, March 2013.
77 Wates and Wolmar, *Squatting: The Real Story*, 162.
78 Alberto Melucci, *Nomads of the Present: Social Movements and the Needs of Contemporary Society* (Philadelphia: Temple University Press, 1989).
79 Corr, *No Trespassing*, 12–15.
80 Ibid.
81 J. Bentham in Nicholas Blomley, 'Law, Property, and the Spaces of Violence: The Frontier, the Survey, and the Grid,' *Annals of the Association of American Geographers* 93 (2003): 124.
82 Blomley, 'Law, Property, and the Spaces of Violence,' 135.

POZNAŃ

1 The first concert was of the legendary Scottish punk band Oi Polloi that had its gig in Poznań canceled by the organiser. But after an invitation, they came to Rozbrat and played for the people staying there.
2 The Critical Mass started in 1992 in the United States as regular gathering of cyclists, who wanted not only to ride their bicycles together but also to stress the bike-unfriendly nature of many city centres. The initiative has spread all over the world. Generally, Critical Mass groups cycle together every last Friday of the month, during afternoon rush hours and in large numbers.
3 http://www.rozbrat.org/archiwalia-wolny-kaukaz.
4 Zines are unofficial movement publications. The term comes from the art underground in the United States and soon became very popular among activists in Central and Eastern Europe. Most of the zines are political, but some of them focus on art or other subjects. All are made according to DIY (do it yourself) principles.
5 http://www.rozbrat.org/rozbrat.
6 While Rozbrat was used as a place for meetings concerning this campaign, Rozbrat activists were little involved.
7 The activists' website is no longer accessible.
8 See http://theyesmen.org/hijinks/newyorktimes.
9 Darcy K. Leach and Sebastian Haunss, 'Scenes and Social Movements,' in *Culture, Social Movements and Protest*, Hank Johnston, ed. (Farnham: Ashgate, 2009), 262.
10 Alberto Melucci, 'Social Movements and the Democratization of Everyday Life,' *Civil Society and the State: New European Perspectives*, John Keane ed. (London: Verso, 1989).
11 This situation was already analysed and criticised as early as 1972 by Jo Freeman in the pamphlet *Tyranny of Structurelessness*, http://www.jofreeman.com/joreen/tyranny.htm.
12 Piotr Żytnicki, 'Gry Uliczne,' Gazeta Wyborcza.pl, http://wyborcza.pl/1,87648,12627466,Gry_uliczne.html, accessed April 10, 2013.
13 Jarosław Urbański, 'Anarchizm—kryzys i transformacja,' [Anarchism—Crisis and Transformation] *Przegląd Anarchistyczny* 9 (2009): 100. The left anti-theology refers to leftist dogmas and ideas that are similar to religious ones, but are anti-religious by default.
14 Leach and Haunss, 'Scenes and Social Movements,' 270.

VIENNA

1 The Amerlinghaus lies in the seventh district. In 1978 it became a political centre, subsidised by the community of Vienna. It has remained an important centre but it is threatened by financial problems. It has depended upon fixed subsidies that over decades have been eroded by inflation..
2 Robert Foltin, *Und wir bewegen uns doch: Soziale Bewegungen in Österreich* (Vienna: Edition Grundrisse, 2004), 116.
3 Foltin, *Und wir bewegen uns doch*, 110.
4 Andreas Suttner, *'Beton brennt': Hausbesetzer und Selbstverwaltung im Berlin, Wien und Zürich der 80er* (Münster: Lit Verlag, 2011), 236; Foltin, *Und wir bewegen uns doch*, 129.
5 Foltin, *Und wir bewegen uns doch*, 130.

6   Regarding the reactions of institutions and politicians, see Suttner, *Beton brennt*, 242.
7   Ibid., 273.
8   Dieter Schrage, 'Wie ein unterirdischer Strom der Rebellion,' edited by Olaf Bockhorn et al., *Kulturjahrbuch 2: Wiener Beiträge zu Kulturwissenschaft und Kulturpolitik* (Vienna: Verlag für Gesellschaftkritik, 1983), 68; Foltin, *Und wir bewegen uns doch*, 132. For a detailed description, see Suttner, *Beton brennt*, 475.
9   Foltin, *Und wir bewegen uns doch*, 140.
10   Ibid., 176.
11   Ibid., 174.
12   Ibid., 183.
13   Ibid., 180.
14   Ibid., 222.
15   Ibid., 239.
16   This was documented in the film *Operation Spring*, produced by Angelika Schuster and Tristan Sindelgruber, which was released in 2005. The film shows the incredible racism of the Austrian jurisdiction.
17   For some years, the police and the media were looking for a so-called third man, but eventually it became clear that the two who died were the only ones involved in the attempt to damage the pylon.
18   Foltin, *Und wir bewegen uns doch*, 250.
19   Robert Foltin, *Und wir bewegen uns noch. Zur jüngeren Geschichte sozialer Bewegungen in Österreich* (Vienna: Mandelbaum, 2011), 125.
20   Foltin, *Und wir bewegen uns noch*, 135.
21   Ibid., 142.
22   Arbeitskreis gegen den kärntner Konsens, eds., *Friede, Freude, deutscher Eintopf: Rechte Mythen, NS-Verharmlosung und antifaschistischer Protest* (Vienna: Mandelbaum, 2011).
23   Foltin, *Und wir bewegen uns noch*, 157.
24   Christof Mackinger and Birgit Pack, Birgit, eds., *§278a. Gemeint sind wir alle. Der Prozess gegen die Tierbefreiungs-Bewegung und seine Hintergründe* (Vienna: Mandelbaum, 2011).
25   Foltin, *Und wir bewegen uns doch*, 164, 231, 235.
26   Ibid., 190.

INDEX

'Passim' (literally 'scattered') indicates intermittent discussion of a topic over a cluster of pages. Page numbers in *italic* refer to illustrations.

Kan Pasqual, 108, 117–18
Kan Titella, Barcelona, 109
Kapaw, Copenhagen, 189, 192
Karamanlis, Konstantinos, 67, 70, 80
Kasa de la Muntanya, Barcelona, 104, 105, 114, 127
Kastanienallee 77 (K77), East Berlin, 17, 142, 143, *144–46*, *148*, 149, 150
Katsiaficas, George, 5, 288n33
Kein Mensch Ist Illegal, 236
kitchens, 56, 149, 166, 194, 259. *See also* soup kitchens
KKE Interior, 64, 66, 70, 75, 80
knokploegen (hired thugs), 28, 35, 36, 37, 44
Komitet Wolny Kaukaz (KWK), 235
Kommunistische Partei Österreichs (KPÖ), 264
Kommunistiko Komma Ellados (KKE), 64–66 passim, 70–82 passim, 90, 91. *See also* Communist Youth of Greece (KNE)
Koopmans, Ruud, 288n33
Köpi, Berlin, 249, 252
Korneya. *See* Ateneu de Korneya, Barcelona
Koskotas, Giorgos, 77
Kouneva, Kostantina, 86
kraakbonzen (squatter bosses), 36
'kraaker' (word), 3
Kraakpandendienst, 27
kraakspreekuren, 28, 36, 41, 43–44, 53, 56, 57
Kreuzberg, Berlin, 18, 131, 135–43 passim
Kriesi, Hans Peter, 6
KuKuCk (Kunst & KulturCentrum Kreuzberg), 139
Kultur- und Kommunikationszentrum Gassergasse (GAGA), 258, 259–60, 262

L

labour unions. *See* unions
Ladd, Brian, 140, 141
Ladronka, Prague, 249
La Hamsa, Barcelona, 107, 114, 127
La Makabra, Barcelona, 114
landlord profiteering, 217

Land Registration Act 2002, 223, 224
La Pedrera, Barcelona, 114
LASPOA. *See* Legal Aid, Sentencing and Punishment of Offenders Act (UK)
law and laws, 15; Denmark, 189; Greece, 78; Netherlands, 27, 40, 58; Poland, 240; Spain, 105, 113; United Kingdom, 154, 160–63 passim, 168, 175; West Germany, 136, 139. *See also* criminalisation of squatting; Legal Aid, Sentencing and Punishment of Offenders Act (UK); trespass law
Law Commission (UK), 217–18, 220, 224
lawsuits, 40, 114
Leach, Darcy, 251
leasing, rent-free. *See* rent-free leasing
Legal Aid, Sentencing and Punishment of Offenders Act (UK), 175, 209, 213, 214, 217, 224, 229
legalisation of squats, 16–17, 45, 117, 135, 139, 180–81, 219
Lelas Karagiannis, Athens. *See* Villa Lelas Karagiannis, Athens
Leninism, 11, 64, 66, 67, 182, 204, 255
lesbians and gays, 12, 109, 122, 153, 255–56, 259, 273
Les Naus, Barcelona, 105, 108
libraries, 97, 119, 167, 234, 235, 268, 273; torching of, 83
Library House, London, 207
Limitation Acts (UK), 216, 220–21
Lipsky, Michael, 181
Ljubljana, 7
lobbyists and lobbying, 15, 27, 37, 45, 58, 82, 138, 214, 218
El Lokal, Barcelona, 103, 108
London, 11, 14, 155, 176, 206–31 passim
London Action Resource Centre, 167
London Squatters Campaign, 155, 213, 214, 217, 219
Lucas, Caroline, 171, 175
Lucky Luyk, Amsterdam, 29, 35–36
Lund, Sweden, 192

FIRE AND FLAMES
A HISTORY OF THE GERMAN AUTONOMIST MOVEMENT

GERONIMO, WITH AN INTRODUCTION BY GEORGE KATSIAFICAS AND AFTERWORD BY GABRIEL KUHN

ISBN: 978-1-60486-097-9
$19.95, 208 pages, 6x9"

Fire and Flames was the first comprehensive study of the German autonomous movement ever published. Released in 1990, it reached its fifth edition by 1997, with the legendary German *Konkret* journal concluding that "the movement had produced its own classic." The author, writing under the pseudonym of Geronimo, has been an autonomous activist since the movement burst onto the scene in 1980-81. In this book, he traces its origins in the Italian Autonomia project and the German social movements of the 1970s, before describing the battles for squats, "free spaces," and alternative forms of living that defined the first decade of the autonomous movement. Tactics of the "Autonome" were militant, including the construction of barricades or throwing molotov cocktails at the police. Because of their outfit (heavy black clothing, ski masks, helmets), the Autonome were dubbed the "black bloc" by the German media, and their tactics have been successfully adopted and employed at anti-capitalist protests worldwide.

Fire and Flames is no detached academic study, but a passionate, hands-on, and engaging account of the beginnings of one of Europe's most intriguing protest movements of the last thirty years. An introduction by George Katsiaficas, author of *The Subversion of Politics*, and an afterword by Gabriel Kuhn, a long-time autonomous activist and author, add historical context and an update on the current state of the Autonomen.

Praise:

"The target audience is not the academic middle-class with passive sympathies for rioting, nor the all-knowing critical critics, but the activists of a young generation."
—Edition I.D. Archiv

"Some years ago, an experienced autonomous activist from Berlin sat down, talked to friends and comrades about the development of the scene, and, with *Fire and Flames*, wrote the best book about the movement that we have."
—Düsseldorfer Stadtzeitung für Politik und Kultur

TURNING MONEY INTO REBELLION
THE UNLIKELY STORY OF DENMARK'S REVOLUTIONARY BANK ROBBERS

EDITED BY GABRIEL KUHN

ISBN: 978-1-60486-316-1
$19.95, 224 pages, 6x9"

Blekingegade is a quiet Copenhagen street. It is also where, in May 1989, the police discovered an apartment that had served Denmark's most notorious twentieth-century bank robbers as a hideaway for years. The Blekingegade Group members belonged to a communist organization and lived modest lives in the Danish capital. Over a period of almost two decades, they sent millions of dollars acquired in spectacular heists to Third World liberation movements, in particular the Popular Front for the Liberation of Palestine (PFLP). In May 1991, seven of them were convicted and went to prison.

The story of the Blekingegade Group is one of the most puzzling and captivating chapters from the European anti-imperialist milieu of the 1970s and '80s. *Turning Money into Rebellion: The Unlikely Story of Denmark's Revolutionary Bank Robbers* is the first-ever account of the story in English, covering a fascinating journey from anti-war demonstrations in the late 1960s via travels to Middle Eastern capitals and African refugee camps to the group's fateful last robbery that earned them a record haul and left a police officer dead.

The book includes historical documents, illustrations, and an exclusive interview with Torkil Lauesen and Jan Weimann, two of the group's longest-standing members. It is a compelling tale of turning radical theory into action and concerns analysis and strategy as much as morality and political practice. Perhaps most importantly, it revolves around the cardinal question of revolutionary politics: What to do, and how to do it?

Praise:
"This book is a fascinating and bracing account of how a group of communists in Denmark sought to aid the peoples of the Third World in their struggles against imperialism and the dire poverty that comes with it. The book contains many valuable lessons as to the practicalities of effective international solidarity, but just as importantly, it is a testament to the intellectual courage of the Blekingegade Group."
—Zak Cope, author of *Dimensions of Prejudice: Towards a Political Economy of Bigotry*

PM Press was founded at the end of 2007 by a small collection of folks with decades of publishing, media, and organizing experience. PM Press co-conspirators have published and distributed hundreds of books, pamphlets, CDs, and DVDs. Members of PM have founded enduring book fairs, spearheaded victorious tenant organizing campaigns, and worked closely with bookstores, academic conferences, and even rock bands to deliver political and challenging ideas to all walks of life. We're old enough to know what we're doing and young enough to know what's at stake.

We seek to create radical and stimulating fiction and non-fiction books, pamphlets, T-shirts, visual and audio materials to entertain, educate, and inspire you. We aim to distribute these through every available channel with every available technology—whether that means you are seeing anarchist classics at our bookfair stalls; reading our latest vegan cookbook at the café; downloading geeky fiction e-books; or digging new music and timely videos from our website.

PM Press is always on the lookout for talented and skilled volunteers, artists, activists and writers to work with. If you have a great idea for a project or can contribute in some way, please get in touch.

In the seven years since its founding—and on a mere shoestring—PM Press has risen to the formidable challenge of publishing and distributing knowledge and entertainment for the struggles ahead. With over 250 releases to date, we have published an impressive and stimulating array of literature, art, music, politics, and culture. Using every available medium, we've succeeded in connecting those hungry for ideas and information to those putting them into practice.

Friends of PM allows you to directly help impact, amplify, and revitalize the discourse and actions of radical writers, filmmakers, and artists. It provides us with a stable foundation from which we can build upon our early successes and provides a much-needed subsidy for the materials that can't necessarily pay their own way. You can help make that happen—and receive every new title automatically delivered to your door once a month—by joining as a Friend of PM Press. And, we'll throw in a free T-shirt when you sign up.

Here are your options:
• $30 a month: Get all books and pamphlets plus 50% discount on all webstore purchases
• $40 a month: Get all PM Press releases (including CDs and DVDs) plus 50% discount on all webstore purchases
• $100 a month: Superstar—Everything plus PM merchandise, free downloads, and 50% discount on all webstore purchases

For those who can't afford $30 or more a month, we're introducing Sustainer Rates at $15, $10 and $5. Sustainers get a free PM Press t-shirt and a 50% discount on all purchases from our website.

Your Visa or Mastercard will be billed once a month, until you tell us to stop. Or until our efforts succeed in bringing the revolution around. Or the financial meltdown of Capital makes plastic redundant. Whichever comes first.

PM PRESS PO Box 23912 Oakland CA 94623 www.pmpress.org